3rd Workshop on Computational Approaches to Linguistic Code-Switching 2018

Held at ACL 2018

Melbourne, Australia
19 July 2018

ISBN: 978-1-5108-6719-2

ACL 2018

Computational Approaches to Linguistic Code-Switching

Proceedings of the Third Workshop

July 19, 2018
Melbourne, Australia

Workshop Sponsor:

amazon

Introduction

Code-switching (CS) is the phenomenon by which multilingual speakers switch back and forth between their common languages in written or spoken communication. CS is pervasive in informal text communications such as news groups, tweets, blogs, and other social media of multilingual communities. Such genres are increasingly being studied as rich sources of social, commercial and political information. Apart from the informal genre challenge associated with such data within a single language processing scenario, the CS phenomenon adds another significant layer of complexity to the processing of the data. Efficiently and robustly processing CS data presents a new frontier for our NLP algorithms on all levels. The goal of this workshop is to bring together researchers interested in exploring these new frontiers, discussing state of the art research in CS, and identifying the next steps in this fascinating research area.

The workshop program includes exciting papers discussing new approaches for CS data and the development of linguistic resources needed to process and study CS. We received a total of 16 regular workshop submissions of which we accepted 11 for publication, five of them as workshop talks and six as posters.

Another component of the workshop is the First Shared Task on Named Entity Recognition (NER) of CS Data. The shared task focused on social media and included two language pairs: Modern Standard Arabic-Dialectal Arabic and English-Spanish. We had a total of 9 participants from which we received 8 submissions on English-Spanish and 6 submissions on Modern Standard Arabic-Dialectal Arabic. We received papers from all these submissions. All shared task systems will be presented during the workshop poster session and two of them will also present a talk. We would like to thank all authors who submitted their contributions to this workshop and all shared task participants for taking on the challenge of NER in code-switched data. We also thank the program committee members for their help in providing meaningful reviews. Lastly, we thank the ACL 2018 organizers for the opportunity to put together this workshop and Amazon for their generous sponsorship.

See you all in Melbourne, Australia at ACL 2018!

Workshop co-chairs,
Gustavo Aguilar
Fahad AlGhamdi
Victor Soto
Thamar Solorio
Mona Diab
Julia Hirschberg

Workshop Co-Chairs:

Gustavo Aguilar, University of Houston
Fahad AlGhamdi, George Washington University
Victor Soto, Columbia University
Thamar Solorio, University of Houston
Mona Diab, George Washington University
Julia Hirschberg, Columbia University

Shared Task Co-Chairs:

Gustavo Aguilar, University of Houston
Fahad AlGhamdi, George Washington University

Publications Chair:

Victor Soto, Columbia University

Program Committee:

Kalika Bali, Microsoft Research India
Elabbas Benmamoun, Duke University
Alan W. Black, Carnegie Mellon University
Agnes Bolonyia, NC State University
Barbara Bullock, University of Texas at Austin
Özlem Çetinoglu, Universität Stuttgart
Monojit Choudhury, Microsoft Research India
Suzanne Dikker, New York University
Björn Gambäck, Norwegian Universities of Science and Technology
Constantine Lignos, University of Southern California Information Sciences Institute
Mitchell P. Marcus, University of Pennsylvania
Cecilia Montes-Alcala, Georgia Institute of Technology
Raymond Mooney, University of Texas at Austin
Borja Navarro Colorado, Universidad de Alicante
Younes Samih, Heinrich Heine - Universität Düsseldorf
Yves Scherrer, University of Helsinki
Chilin Shih, University of Illinois at Urbana-Champaign
David Suendermann, Educational Testing Service
Jacqueline Toribio, University of Texas at Austin
David Vilares, Universidad de Coruña
Emre Yilmaz, CLS/CLST, Radboud University Nijmegen

Invited Speakers:

Pascale Fung, Hong Kong University of Science & Technology
Melinda Fricke, University of Pittsburgh

Table of Contents

Joint Part-of-Speech and Language ID Tagging for Code-Switched Data
Victor Soto and Julia Hirschberg 1

Phone Merging For Code-Switched Speech Recognition
Sunit Sivasankaran, Brij Mohan Lal Srivastava, Sunayana Sitaram, Kalika Bali and Monojit Choudhury 11

Improving Neural Network Performance by Injecting Background Knowledge: Detecting Code-switching and Borrowing in Algerian texts
Wafia Adouane, Jean-Philippe Bernardy and Simon Dobnik 20

Code-Mixed Question Answering Challenge: Crowd-sourcing Data and Techniques
Khyathi Chandu, Ekaterina Loginova, Vishal Gupta, Josef van Genabith, Günter Neuman, Manoj Chinnakotla, Eric Nyberg and Alan W. Black 29

Transliteration Better than Translation? Answering Code-mixed Questions over a Knowledge Base
Vishal Gupta, Manoj Chinnakotla and Manish Shrivastava 39

Language Identification and Analysis of Code-Switched Social Media Text
Deepthi Mave, Suraj Maharjan and Thamar Solorio 51

Code-Switching Language Modeling using Syntax-Aware Multi-Task Learning
Genta Indra Winata, Andrea Madotto, Chien-Sheng Wu and Pascale Fung 62

Predicting the presence of a Matrix Language in code-switching
Barbara Bullock, Wally Guzman, Jacqueline Serigos, Vivek Sharath and Almeida Jacqueline Toribio 68

Automatic Detection of Code-switching Style from Acoustics
SaiKrishna Rallabandi, Sunayana Sitaram and Alan W. Black 76

Accommodation of Conversational Code-Choice
Anshul Bawa, Monojit Choudhury and Kalika Bali 82

Language Informed Modeling of Code-Switched Text
Khyathi Chandu, Thomas Manzini, Sumeet Singh and Alan W. Black 92

GHHT at CALCS 2018: Named Entity Recognition for Dialectal Arabic Using Neural Networks
Mohammed Attia, Younes Samih and Wolfgang Maier 98

Simple Features for Strong Performance on Named Entity Recognition in Code-Switched Twitter Data
Devanshu Jain, Maria Kustikova, Mayank Darbari, Rishabh Gupta and Stephen Mayhew 103

Bilingual Character Representation for Efficiently Addressing Out-of-Vocabulary Words in Code-Switching Named Entity Recognition
Genta Indra Winata, Chien-Sheng Wu, Andrea Madotto and Pascale Fung 110

Named Entity Recognition on Code-Switched Data Using Conditional Random Fields
Utpal Kumar Sikdar, Biswanath Barik and Björn Gambäck 115

The University of Texas System Submission for the Code-Switching Workshop Shared Task 2018
Florian Janke, Tongrui Li, Eric Rincón, Gualberto Guzmán, Barbara Bullock and Almeida Jacqueline Toribio 120

Tackling Code-Switched NER: Participation of CMU
Parvathy Geetha, Khyathi Chandu and Alan W. Black 126

Multilingual Named Entity Recognition on Spanish-English Code-switched Tweets using Support Vector Machines
Daniel Claeser, Samantha Kent and Dennis Felske 132

Named Entity Recognition on Code-Switched Data: Overview of the CALCS 2018 Shared Task
Gustavo Aguilar, Fahad AlGhamdi, Victor Soto, Mona Diab, Julia Hirschberg and Thamar Solorio
138

IIT (BHU) Submission for the ACL Shared Task on Named Entity Recognition on Code-switched Data
Shashwat Trivedi, Harsh Rangwani and Anil Kumar Singh 148

Code-Switched Named Entity Recognition with Embedding Attention
Changhan Wang, Kyunghyun Cho and Douwe Kiela 154

Workshop Program

Thursday, July 19, 2018

09:00–10:30   Session 1 Invited Talk and Oral Presentations

9:00–9:05   *Opening Remarks*
Thamar Solorio

9:05–9:50   *Invited Talk: Learning to Codeswitch*
Pascale Fung

9:50–10:10   *Joint Part-of-Speech and Language ID Tagging for Code-Switched Data*
Victor Soto and Julia Hirschberg

10:10–10:30   *Phone Merging For Code-Switched Speech Recognition*
Sunit Sivasankaran, Brij Mohan Lal Srivastava, Sunayana Sitaram, Kalika Bali and
Monojit Choudhury

10:30–11:00   Coffee Break

11:00–12:00   Session 2 Oral Presentations

11:00–11:20   *Improving Neural Network Performance by Injecting Background Knowledge: Detecting Code-switching and Borrowing in Algerian texts*
Wafia Adouane, Jean-Philippe Bernardy and Simon Dobnik

11:20–11:40   *Code-Mixed Question Answering Challenge: Crowd-sourcing Data and Techniques*
Khyathi Chandu, Ekaterina Loginova, Vishal Gupta, Josef van Genabith, Günter
Neuman, Manoj Chinnakotla, Eric Nyberg and Alan W. Black

11:40–12:00   *Transliteration Better than Translation? Answering Code-mixed Questions over a
Knowledge Base*
Vishal Gupta, Manoj Chinnakotla and Manish Shrivastava

12:00–13:30   **Lunch Break**

13:30–14:15   **Session 3 Invited Talk**

13:30–14:15   *Invited Talk: Variation in Codeswitched Language: a Psycholinguistic Approach to What, When, and Why*
Melinda Fricke

14:15–15:30   **Session 4 Poster Session**

Language Identification and Analysis of Code-Switched Social Media Text
Deepthi Mave, Suraj Maharjan and Thamar Solorio

Code-Switching Language Modeling using Syntax-Aware Multi-Task Learning
Genta Indra Winata, Andrea Madotto, Chien-Sheng Wu and Pascale Fung

Predicting the presence of a Matrix Language in code-switching
Barbara Bullock, Wally Guzman, Jacqueline Serigos, Vivek Sharath and Almeida Jacqueline Toribio

Automatic Detection of Code-switching Style from Acoustics
SaiKrishna Rallabandi, Sunayana Sitaram and Alan W. Black

Accommodation of Conversational Code-Choice
Anshul Bawa, Monojit Choudhury and Kalika Bali

Language Informed Modeling of Code-Switched Text
Khyathi Chandu, Thomas Manzini, Sumeet Singh and Alan W. Black

GHHT at CALCS 2018: Named Entity Recognition for Dialectal Arabic Using Neural Networks
Mohammed Attia, Younes Samih and Wolfgang Maier

Simple Features for Strong Performance on Named Entity Recognition in Code-Switched Twitter Data
Devanshu Jain, Maria Kustikova, Mayank Darbari, Rishabh Gupta and Stephen Mayhew

Bilingual Character Representation for Efficiently Addressing Out-of-Vocabulary Words in Code-Switching Named Entity Recognition
Genta Indra Winata, Chien-Sheng Wu, Andrea Madotto and Pascale Fung

Named Entity Recognition on Code-Switched Data Using Conditional Random Fields
Utpal Kumar Sikdar, Biswanath Barik and Björn Gambäck

The University of Texas System Submission for the Code-Switching Workshop Shared Task 2018
Florian Janke, Tongrui Li, Eric Rincón, Gualberto Guzmán, Barbara Bullock and Almeida Jacqueline Toribio

Tackling Code-Switched NER: Participation of CMU
Parvathy Geetha, Khyathi Chandu and Alan W. Black

Multilingual Named Entity Recognition on Spanish-English Code-switched Tweets using Support Vector Machines
Daniel Claeser, Samantha Kent and Dennis Felske

15:30–16:00   **Coffee Break**

16:00–17:00   **Session 5 Shared Task Talks**

16:00–16:10   *Named Entity Recognition on Code-Switched Data: Overview of the CALCS 2018 Shared Task*
Gustavo Aguilar, Fahad AlGhamdi, Victor Soto, Mona Diab, Julia Hirschberg and Thamar Solorio

16:10–16:30   *IIT (BHU) Submission for the ACL Shared Task on Named Entity Recognition on Code-switched Data*
Shashwat Trivedi, Harsh Rangwani and Anil Kumar Singh

16:30–16:50   *Code-Switched Named Entity Recognition with Embedding Attention*
Changhan Wang, Kyunghyun Cho and Douwe Kiela

16:50–17:00   *Closing Remarks*
Victor Soto

Joint Part-of-Speech and Language ID Tagging for Code-Switched Data

Victor Soto
Department of Computer Science
Columbia University
New York, NY 10027
vsoto@cs.columbia.edu

Julia Hirschberg
Department of Computer Science
Columbia University
New York, NY 10027
julia@cs.columbia.edu

Abstract

Code-switching is the fluent alternation between two or more languages in conversation between bilinguals. Large populations of speakers code-switch during communication, but little effort has been made to develop tools for code-switching, including part-of-speech taggers. In this paper, we propose an approach to POS tagging of code-switched English-Spanish data based on recurrent neural networks. We test our model on known monolingual benchmarks to demonstrate that our neural POS tagging model is on par with state-of-the-art methods. We next test our code-switched methods on the Miami Bangor corpus of English-Spanish conversation, focusing on two types of experiments: POS tagging alone, for which we achieve 96.34% accuracy, and joint part-of-speech and language ID tagging, which achieves similar POS tagging accuracy (96.39%) and very high language ID accuracy (98.78%). Finally, we show that our proposed models outperform other state-of-the-art code-switched taggers.

1 Introduction

Code-switching (CS) is the phenomenon by which multilingual speakers switch between languages in written or spoken communication. For example, a English-Spanish speaker might say "El teacher me dijo que Juanito is very good at math." CS can be observed in various linguistic levels: phonological, morphological, lexical, and syntactic and can be classified as *intra-sentential* (if the switch occurs within the boundaries of a sentence or utterance), or *inter-sentential* (if the switch occurs between two sentences or utterances). The impor-

tance of developing NLP technologies for CS data is immense. In the US alone there is an estimated population of 56.6 million Hispanic people (US Census Bureau, 2014), of which 40 million are native speakers (US Census Bureau, 2015). Most of these speakers routinely code-switch. However, very little research has been done to develop NLP approaches to CS language, due largely to the lack of sufficient corpora of high-quality annotated data to train on. Yet CS presents serious challenges to all language technologies, including part-of-speech (POS) tagging, parsing, language modeling, machine translation, and automatic speech recognition, since techniques developed on one language quickly break down when that language is mixed with another.

One of Artificial Intelligence's ultimate goals is to enable seamless natural language interactions between artificial agents and human users. In order to achieve that goal, it is imperative that users be able to communicate with artificial agents as they do with other humans. In addition to such real time interactions, CS language is also pervasive in social media (David, 2001; Danet and Herring, 2007; Cárdenas-Claros and Isharyanti, 2009). So, any system which attempts to communicate with these users or to mine their social media content needs to deal with CS language.

POS tagging is a key component of any Natural Language Understanding system and one of the first researchers employ to process data. As such, it is crucial that POS taggers be able to process CS content. Monolingual POS taggers stumble when processing CS sentences due to out-of-vocabulary words in one language, confusable words that exist in both language lexicons, and differences in the syntax of the two languages. For example, when running monolingual English and Spanish taggers on the CS English-Spanish shown in Figure 1, the English tagger erroneously tagged most Spanish

1

Proceedings of The Third Workshop on Computational Approaches to Code-Switching, pages 1–10
Melbourne, Australia, July 19, 2018. ©2018 Association for Computational Linguistics

Words:	Ella	lo	había	leído	when	she	was	in	third	grade
Translation:	*She*	*it*	*had*	*read*	-	-	-	-	-	-
Gold:	PRON	PRON	AUX	VERB	SCONJ	PRON	VERB	ADP	ADJ	NOUN
EN Tagger:	NOUN	ADV	NOUN	VERB	ADV	PRON	VERB	ADP	ADJ	NOUN
ES Tagger:	PRON	PRON	AUX	VERB	PROPN	PROPN	PROPN	ADP	X	PROPN
EN+ES Tagger:	PRON	PRON	AUX	VERB	ADV	PRON	VERB	ADV	ADJ	NOUN
CS Tagger:	PRON	PRON	AUX	VERB	SCONJ	PRON	VERB	ADP	ADJ	NOUN

Figure 1: Example of an English-Spanish code-switched sentence. The figure shows the original code-switched sentence, English translations of each token, gold POS tags and the tagging output of an English tagger, a Spanish tagger, a tagger trained on English and Spanish sentences, and a tagger trained on a corpus of code-switched sentences, in that order. Errors made by each tagger are underlined.

tokens, and similarly the Spanish tagger mistagged most English tokens. A tagger trained on monolingual English and Spanish sentences (EN+ES tagger) fared better, making only two mistakes: on the word "when", where the switch occurs (confusing the subordinating conjunction for an adverb), and the word "in" (which exists in both vocabularies). A tagger trained on CS instances of English-Spanish, however, was able to tag the whole sentence correctly.

In this paper, we present a comprehensive study of POS tagging for CS utterances that includes the following: a) use of a state-of-the-art bidirectional recurrent neural network b) use of a large CS English-Spanish corpus annotated with high-quality labels from the Universal POS tagset; c) extensive analyses of the performance of our taggers on monolingual and CS sentences; d) study of the performance of a tagger trained on the subset of the monolingual sentences of the CS corpus (in-genre baseline); e) examination of the effect of language identifiers both as feature inputs and for joint language identification and POS tagging; and f) comparison to state-of-the-art taggers for code-switching on the same corpus.

2 Related Work

A variety of tasks have been studied in CS data. For language identification (LID), Rosner and Farrugia (2007) proposed a word-level Hidden Markov Model and a character-level Markov Model to revert to when a word is out-of-vocabulary, and tested these on a corpus of Maltese-English sentences, achieving 95% accuracy. Working on a Bengali-Hindi-English dataset of Facebook posts, Barman et al. (2014) employed classifiers using n-gram and contextual features to obtain 95% accuracy.

In the first statistical approach to POS-tagging on CS data, Solorio and Liu (2008) collected the Spanglish corpus, a small set of 922 English-Spanish sentences. They proposed several heuristics to combine monolingual taggers with limited success, achieving 86% accuracy when choosing the output of a monolingual tagger based on the dictionary language ID of each token. However, an SVM trained on the output of the monolingual taggers performed better than their oracle, reaching 93.48% accuracy. On the same dataset, Rodrigues (2013) compared the performance of a POS-tagger trained on CS sentences with a dynamic model that switched between taggers based on gold language identifiers; they found the latter to work better (89.96% and 90.45% respectively). Note, however, that the monolingual taggers from (Solorio and Liu, 2008) were trained on other larger corpora, while all the models used in (Rodrigues, 2013) were trained on the Spanglish corpus.

Jamatia et al. (2015) used CS English-Hindi Facebook and Twitter posts to train and test POS taggers. They found a Conditional Random Field model to perform best (71.6% accuracy), and a combination of monolingual taggers similar to the one in (Solorio and Liu, 2008) achieved 72.0% accuracy. Again using Hindi-English Facebook posts, Vyas et al. (2014) ran Hindi and English monolingual taggers on monolingual chunks of each sentence. Sequiera et al. (2015) tested algorithms from (Solorio and Liu, 2008) and (Vyas et al., 2014) on the Facebook dataset from (Vyas et al., 2014) and the Facebook+Twitter dataset from (Jamatia et al., 2015), and found that (Solorio and Liu, 2008) yielded better results. Similarly, Barman et al. (2016) compared the methods proposed in (Solorio and Liu, 2008) and (Vyas et al., 2014) on a subset of 1,239 code-mixed Facebook posts from (Barman et al., 2014) and found that a modified version of (Solorio and Liu, 2008) performed best. They also experimented with performing joint POS and LID tagging using 2-level factorial Conditional Random Field and achieved statistically similar results.

AlGhamdi et al. (2016) tested seven different POS tagging strategies for CS data: four consisted of combinations of monolingual systems and the other three were integrated systems. They tested them on MSA-Egyptian Arabic and English-Spanish. The first three combined strategies consisted of running monolingual POS taggers and language ID taggers in different order and combining the outputs in a single multilingual prediction. The fourth approach involved training an SVM on the output of the monolingual taggers. The three integrated approaches trained a supervised model on a) the Miami Bangor corpus (which contains switched and monolingual utterances), b) the union of two monolingual corpora (Ancora-ES and Penn Treebank), c) the union of the three corpora. The monolingual approaches consistently underperformed compared to the other strategies. The SVM approach consistently outperformed the integrated approaches. However, this method was trained on both monolingual and multilingual resources – the Penn Treebank Data for the English model, and the Ancora-ES dataset for the Spanish model. In Section 6.4, we run experiments in similar conditions to the integrated approaches from (AlGhamdi et al., 2016), which we will compare to our work. The main contributions of this paper over this previous research on POS tagging for CS data, are the following: a) Our tagger is a bi-directional LSTM that achieves POS tagging accuracy comparable to state-of-the-art taggers on benchmark datasets like the Wall Street Journal corpus and the Universal Dependencies corpora. It is the first such model used to train code-switched POS taggers; b) Our model can simultaneously perform POS and LID tagging without loss of POS tagging accuracy; c) We run experiments on the Miami Bangor corpus of Spanish and English conversational speech. However, unlike (AlGhamdi et al., 2016) which used POS tags obtained from an automatic tagger and then mapped to a deprecated version of the Universal POS tagset, our experiments are run on newly crowd-sourced Universal POS tags (Soto and Hirschberg, 2017), which were obtained with high accuracy and inter-annotator agreement.

3 A Model for Neural POS Tagging

For our experiments we use a bi-directional LSTM network similar to the one proposed by Wang et al. (2015) with the following set of features: 1) word embeddings, 2) prefix and suffix embeddings of one, two and three characters, and 3) four boolean features that encode whether the word is all upper case, all lower case, formatted as a title, or contains any digits. In total, the input space consists of seven embeddings and four boolean features. For the embeddings, we compute word, prefix and suffix lexicons, excluding tokens that appear less than five times in the training set, and then assign a unique integer to each token. We also reserve two integers for the padding and out-of-lexicon symbols.

We present two architectures for POS tagging and one for joint POS and LID tagging. In the most basic architecture the word, prefix and suffix embeddings and the linear activation units are concatenated into a single layer. The second layer of the network is a bidirectional LSTM. Finally, the output layer is a softmax activation layer, whose i-th output unit at time t represents the probability of the word w_t being the part-of-speech POS_i. We refer to this model as Bi-LSTM POS Tagger for the rest of the article and in our tables. For the second model, given the multilingual nature of our experiments, we modify the input space of our Bi-LSTM tagger to make use of the language ID information in our corpus. We add six more boolean features to represent the language ID (one for each label) and add six linear activation units in the first hidden layer, which are then concatenated with the rest of linear activation units and word embeddings in the basic model. This model is referred to as Bi-LSTM POS tagger + LID features.

Finally, our third model simultaneously tags words with POS and LID labels. The architecture of this model follows the Bi-LSTM POS architecture very closely adding a second output layer with softmax activations for LID prediction. Note that the POS and LID output layers are independent and are connected by their weight matrices to the hidden layer, and both loss functions are given the same weight. This model is referred to as joint POS+LID tagger. We implemented our code using the library for deep learning Keras (Chollet, 2015), on a Tensorflow backend (Abadi et al., 2015).

Corpus	Split	# Sents	# Toks
WSJ	Train	38.2K	912.3K
	Dev.	5.5K	131.7K
	Test	5.5K	129.7K
UD-EN	Train	12.5K	204.6K
	Dev.	2K	25.1K
	Test	2K	25.1K
UD-ES	Train	14.2K	403.9K
	Dev.	1.6K	43.5K
	Test	274	8.4K
Miami Bangor	Full	42.9K	333.1K
	Train	38.7K	300.3K
	Test	4.2K	32.8K
	Train Inter-CS	36.0K	267.3K
	Test Intra-CS	285	3.6K

Table 1: Datasets used for our experiments.

Split	Full	Train	Test	CS
EN	53.48	53.41	54.14	38.98
ES	27.78	27.86	27.04	46.12
PUNCT	15.71	15.76	15.55	12.26
AMBIG	2.27	2.25	2.49	2.06
MIXED	0.01	0.01	0.00	0.01
OTHER	0.76	0.76	0.79	0.60

Table 2: Language composition (%) of the MB corpus.

4 Datasets

Throughout our experiments we use three corpora for different purposes. The Wall Street Journal (WSJ) corpus is used to demonstrate that our proposed Bi-LSTM POS tagger is on par with current state-of-the-art English POS taggers. The Universal Dependencies (UD) corpus is used to train baseline monolingual POS taggers in English and Spanish that we can use to test on our CS data since both employ the Universal POS tagset (Petrov et al., 2012). The Miami Bangor corpus, which contains instances of inter- and intra-sentential CS utterances in English and Spanish, is used for training and testing CS models and comparing these to monolingual models. Table 1 shows the number of sentences/utterances and tokens in each dataset split. For the MB corpus, Inter-CS refers to the subset of monolingual sentences and Intra-CS refers to the subset of CS sentences.

4.1 Wall Street Journal Corpus

The WSJ corpus (Marcus et al., 1999) is a monolingual English news corpus comprised of 49208 sentences and over 1.1 million tokens. It is tagged with the Treebank tagset (Santorini, 1990; Marcus et al., 1993), which has a total of 45 tags. We use the standard training, development and test splits from (Collins, 2002) which span sections 0-18 19-21 and 22-24 respectively.

4.2 Universal Dependency Corpora

Universal Dependencies (UD) is a project to develop cross-linguistically consistent treebank annotations for many languages. The English UD corpus (Silveira et al., 2014) is built from the English Web Treebank (Bies et al., 2012). The corpus contains data from web media sources, including web logs, newsgroups, emails, reviews and Yahoo! answers. The trees were automatically converted into Stanford Dependencies and then hand-corrected to Universal Dependencies. The corpus contains 16,622 sentences and over 254K tokens. The Spanish UD corpus (McDonald et al., 2013) is built from the content head version of the Universal Dependency Treebank v2.0, to which several token-level morphology features were added. It is comprised of news blog data and has a total of 16,013 sentences and over 455k tokens.

4.3 Miami Bangor Corpus

The Miami Bangor (MB) corpus is a conversational speech corpus recorded from bilingual English-Spanish speakers living in Miami, FL. It includes 56 conversations recorded from 84 speakers. The corpus consists of 242,475 words (333,069 including punctuation tokens) and 35 hours of recorded conversation. The language markers in the corpus were manually annotated. Table 2 shows the language composition of the corpus. The dominant language in this corpus is English (53.48% of the tokens), followed by Spanish (27.78%). The ambiguous label includes words that are difficult to tag as either English or Spanish due to lack of context (e.g. "no"). Since, in the original corpus, punctuation tokens were labeled as ambiguous, we created an additional punctuation tag for our experiments. The mixed category contains tokens that are formed by morphemes and roots from both languages (e.g. "ripear") and the category 'Other' untranscribed tokens. However, the composition of the subset of CS sentences is different: Spanish becomes the dominant language, comprising 46.12% of the tokens compared to 38.98% of the English tokens.

The utterances in the original MB corpus were transcribed in the CHAT transcription and coding format (MacWhinney, 2000), which allows annotators to divide full utterances in chunks to repre-

	Full	Train	Test	CS
#Switches(K)	4.2	3.8	0.4	4.2
Avg.#swts/utt	0.098	0.098	0.095	1.41
Swt.words(%)	1.26	1.27	1.22	11.00
Swt.utts(#)	2980	2695	285	2980
Swt.utts(%)	6.94	6.96	6.79	100
0 swt.(%)	93.06	93.04	93.21	0.00
1 swt.(%)	4.79	4.78	4.83	69.03
2 swt.(%)	1.71	1.73	1.55	24.62
Max#Swt.	8	8	7	8

Table 3: CS in the Miami Bangor Corpus. The top subtable shows the number of switches, the average number of switches per utterances, the amount of switched words (word after which a switch occurs), and the amount of switched utterances in each partition. The bottom subtable shows the percentage of utterances that contain n switches.

sent citations and other speech discourse phenomena. However, working on full utterances is more suitable in the context of POS tagging. Therefore, following the guidelines in (MacWhinney, 2009), we used the utterance linkers and utterance terminators to reconstruct full utterances when possible. After this, the corpus had a total of 16013 sentences and 333K tokens.

The original MB corpus was automatically glossed and tagged with POS tags using the Bangor Autoglosser (Donnelly and Deuchar, 2011a,b). The autoglosser finds the gloss for each token in the corpus and assigns the tag or group of tags most common for that word in the annotated language. However, here we use the Universal POS tags obtained by (Soto and Hirschberg, 2017). These tags were collected using crowdsourcing tasks and automatic labeling, with high annotation accuracy and label recall. We split the MB corpus into training and test. For the test split we randomly drew 4,200 utterances. The training split is used for 4-fold cross-validation. Table 3 shows the degree of multilingualism in the MB corpus and the two splits. In the full dataset, about 6.94% of the utterances contain intra-sentential switches. Note that full dataset and its train and test splits (columns 2 to 4) have very similar degrees of multilingualism according to the reported measures, whereas the subset of intra-sentential CS sentences (column 5) has a much higher rate of switched tokens (11%, from 1.26%) and average number of switches per sentence (1.41, from 0.098). More than 93% of CS utterances contain one or two switches; some contain up to eight switches. For example, the following sentence contains five switches (marked with '|'): *"... y en | summer | y en | fall | tengo que hacer | one class."*

5 Methodology

For the experiments involving the Bangor corpus, we perform 4-fold cross-validation (CV) on the training corpus to run grid search and obtain the best learning rate and decay learning rate parameter values. For the experiments on WSJ and UD, we use the official development set. The performance of the best parameter values is reported as "Dev" accuracy. We then train a model using the best parameter values on the full train set and obtain predictions for the test set (reported as "Test"). When pertinent we also report results on the subset of intra-sentential CS utterances of the test set (reported as "Intra-CS Test").

During CV, each model is trained for a maximum number of 75 epochs using batches of 128 examples. We use early stopping to halt training when the development POS accuracy has not improved for the last three epochs, and keep only the best performing model. However, when training the final model, we stop training after the number of epochs that the best model trained for during CV. The loss function used is categorical cross-entropy and we use ADAM (Kingma and Ba, 2015) with its default β_1, β_2 and ϵ parameter values as the stochastic optimization method.

The word embeddings (Bengio et al., 2003) we use are trained with the rest of the network during training following the Keras implementation (Gal and Ghahramani, 2016). The size of the embedding layers is 128 for the word embeddings and 4, 8 and 16 for the prefix and suffix embeddings of length 1, 2 and 3 respectively. The Bi-LSTM hidden layer has 200 units for each direction.

Finally, we run McNemar's test (McNemar, 1947) to show significant statistical difference between pairs of classifiers when the accuracy of the classifiers is similar, and report statistical significance for p-values smaller than 0.05.

6 Experiments & Results

In this section, we present our experiments using the three Bi-LSTM models introduced in Section 3 and the datasets from Section 4. Our goal is a) to show that the basic Bi-LSTM POS tagger performs very well against known POS tagging benchmarks; b) to obtain baseline performances for monolingual taggers when tested on CS data;

and c) to train and test the proposed models on CS data and analyze their performance when trained on different proportions of monolingual and CS data.

6.1 WSJ results

We begin by evaluating the performance of the Bi-LSTM POS tagger on the benchmark WSJ corpus to show that it is on par with current state-of-the-art English POS taggers. We train taggers on three incremental feature sets to measure how much each feature adds. Using only word embeddings we achieve 95.14% accuracy on the test set; adding word features increases accuracy to 95.84%; and adding the prefix and suffix embeddings further increases accuracy by up to 97.10%. This demonstrates that our tagger is on par with current state-of-the-art systems which report 97.78% (Ling et al., 2015), 97.45% (Andor et al., 2016), 97.35% (Huang et al., 2012), 97.34% (Moore, 2014) and 97.33% (Shen et al., 2007) accuracy on their standard test set. Systems most similar to our Bi-LSTM tagger with basic features reported 97.20% in (Collobert et al., 2011) and 97.26% (Wang et al., 2015).

6.2 Universal tagset baseline

In the second set of experiments we train baseline monolingual Spanish and English taggers on the UD corpora: one monolingual Spanish and one monolingual English tagger, and one tagger trained on both corpora. The goal of these experiments is to obtain taggers trained on the Universal tagset that we can use to obtain a baseline performance of monolingual taggers on the CS Bangor corpus. The results are shown in Table 4. The accuracy of the baseline UD taggers is slightly worse than the WSJ taggers, probably due to the smaller size of the UD datasets. The accuracy of the taggers on their own test sets is 94.78% and 95.02% for English and Spanish respectively. In comparison, Stanford's neural dependency parser (Dozat et al., 2017) reports accuracy values of 95.11% and 96.59% respectively.

In order to approximate how a monolingual tagger trained on established datasets performs on a conversational CS dataset, we test the baseline UD taggers on the MB test set and observe a dramatic drop in accuracy, due perhaps to the difference in genre (web blog data vs. transcribed conversation) and the bilingual nature of the Miami corpus. Note that, when training on both EN and ES UD, the

Training	UD		MB	
	Dev	Test	Test	CS Test
UD EN	94.53	94.78	69.97	56.20
UD ES	96.20	95.02	45.13	55.32
UD EN&ES	94.88	94.25	88.17	87.18

Table 4: Bi-LSTM POS tagging accuracy (%) on the Universal Dependency corpora. The left subtable shows the accuracy on the UD dev and test sets. The right subtables shows the accuracy on the MB test set and on the subset of CS utterances.

Training	Task	Dev	Test	CS Test
MB	Tagger	96.27	96.34	96.10
	Tagger+LID	96.35	96.49	**96.44**
	Joint Tagger	96.30	96.39	95.97
MB + UD	Tagger	96.34	96.47	95.99
	Tagger+LID	**96.40**	**96.63**	**96.44**
	Joint Tagger	96.39	96.61	96.35
MB Inter-CS	Tagger	96.24	96.03	95.27
	Tagger+LID	96.26	96.16	95.55
	Joint Tagger	96.25	96.11	95.22

Table 5: POS tagging accuracy (%) on the MB corpus. Underlined font indicates best result in test set by each training setting across different tagging models. Bold results indicate best overall result in that test set.

Bi-LSTM taggers reach 88.17% accuracy, from only 69.97 and 45.13% by the monolingual taggers. When looking at the multilingual subset of sentences from the test set (CS Test in Table 4), we observe that the English model decreases in accuracy further, whereas the Spanish tagger has better performance. This is due to the CS sentences having more Spanish than English.

6.3 Miami Bangor results

In the third set of experiments we train the three proposed models (Bi-LSTM tagger, Bi-LSTM tagger with LID features and joint POS and LID tagger) on: a) the full MB corpus, b) the joint MB and UD ES&EN corpora, and c) instances of inter-sentential CS utterances from the MB corpus. The LID features were obtained from the MB corpus language tags. POS and LID accuracy results are shown in Table 5 and Table 6 respectively.

When training on the full MB corpus (top subtable from table 5), the POS tagger achieves 96.34% accuracy, a significant improvement from the 88.17% of the UD EN&ES. The improvement holds up on the subset of CS utterances, achieving 96.10% accuracy. Adding the LID features improves performance by 0.15 and 0.34 absolute percentage points. In both cases these differences are statistically significant ($p = 0.03$). Furthermore, when running joint POS and LID tagging, we see that tagging accuracy decreases slightly with respect to the POS tagger with LID features. This result reaffirms the contribution of the LID features. The difference in performance between the joint tagger and the basic tagger is slightly higher but not statistically significant ($p \sim 0.5$), showing that joint decoding does not harm overall performance. The best POS tagging accuracy is always achieved by the Bi-LSTM tagger with LID features on both Test and CS Test; however, the joint Tagger is very close at no more than 0.1 percentage points on Test. When adding the UD corpora during training (middle subtable from Table 5) we see some improvements for the three models (0.13, 0.14 and 0.22 absolute percentage points respectively), and once again the difference in performance between the basic tagger and the tagger with LID features is statistically significant ($p < 0.05$).

We performed statistical tests to measure how different the models trained on MB are from the models trained on MB+UD and found that the addition of more monolingual data only makes a difference for the joint tagger ($p < 0.01$) when looking at the performance on the Test set. On the CS test set, these models achieve about the same performance in POS tagging with a slight decrease for the basic tagger (-0.11 points, not significant) and a slight increase in accuracy for the joint tagger (0.38 percentage points, again not significant). Thus, it is clear that our model is able to learn from a few CS examples – even when many more monolingual sentences, from a different genre, are added to the train set.

Finally, we trained models on the subset of monolingual English and Spanish sentences from the MB training set to measure how a model trained on the same genre would be able to generalize on unseen intra-sentential CS sentences (bottom subtable from Table 5, marked as Inter-CS). This model would be closer to an in-genre inter-sentential CS tagger, tested on intra-sentential CS. Compared to the models trained on UD EN&ES, this model performs much better: 96.03% compared to 88.17% on the MB test set. This is mainly due to the fact that the UD corpus is *not* conversational speech. When comparing this result to the taggers trained on the full MB corpus, it can be seen that these new models achieved the lowest test accuracy across all models, probably due to

Training	Dev	Test	CS Test
MB	98.82	98.78	98.01
MB + UD EN&ES	98.60	98.49	97.93
MB Inter-CS Subset	98.53	97.99	90.25

Table 6: LID tagging accuracy by the Bi-LSTM joint POS+LID Tagger on the MB corpus.

the lack of bilingual examples in their training set. The difference in performance is more pronounced on the subset of CS utterances. Again, we ran statistical tests to compare these three new taggers to the taggers trained on the full MB corpus, and we found that their differences were statistically significant in the three cases ($p < 0.001$).

With respect to the LID accuracy of the joint Tagger, the best model is the one trained on the MB corpus, followed very closely by the model trained on MB and UD data. In both cases, the test set accuracy is above 98.49%. The accuracy on the CS test subset is sightly lower at 98.01% and 97.93%. The monolingual Bangor tagger sees a decrease in test accuracy (97.99%) and a bigger drop, down to 90.25%, on the CS subset. All the differences in performance between every pair of the three LID taggers are statistically significant ($p < 10^{-5}$).

6.4 Comparison to Previous Work

We compare the performance of our models to the Integrated and Combined models proposed in (AlGhamdi et al., 2016). In that paper, POS tagging results are reported on the MB corpus, but using a preliminary mapping to the first iteration of the Universal tagset (12 tags, as opposed to the current 17); furthermore, the train and test splits were different. Therefore, we decided to replicate their experiments using our data configuration and compare them to our own classifiers. With respect to their "Integrated" models, INT3:AllMonoData+CSD is comparable to our POS Tagger trained on the full MB set and UD EN&ES (ours at 96.47% compared to 92.33%); INT2:AllMono is comparable to our POS Tagger trained on UD EN&ES (ours at 88.17% compared to 84.47%) and INT1:CSD is comparable to our POS Tagger trained on Bangor (ours at 96.34% versus 92.71%). For their "Combined" models, COMB4:MonoLT-SVM trained two monolingual taggers on the UD-EN and UD-ES corpora and then a SVM on top from the output of the taggers on the MB corpus. We do not perform system

	EN	ES	EN&ES	Bangor
OOV	40.9	32.7	10.7	7.9
SAcc.	2.5	4.2	21.8	60.7
WAcc.	56.2	55.3	87.2	96.1
CSFAcc.	10.9	12.6	57.5	84.2
CSFWAcc.	12.6	16.1	63.3	86.7
AvgMinDistCSF	4.0	5.4	3.9	3.5
%ErrorsInCSF	26.9	24.3	32.5	36.9

Table 7: Out-of-vocabulary (OOV) rate, sentence (Sacc) and word accuracy (Wacc) at the sentence level, fragment (CSFAcc) and word accuracy (CSFWacc) at the fragment level, average minimum distance from tagging error to CSF (AvgMinDistCSF), and percentage of errors that occur within a CSF (%ErrorsInCSF).

combination in this paper, but in terms of data, this model would be most similar to our POS tagger trained on Miami and EN&ES UD, in which we reached 96.47% compared to their 92.20%. Furthermore, we note that our joint POS+LID tagger also has better POS accuracy than its counterparts Integrated systems from (AlGhamdi et al., 2016) in addition to performing LID tagging.

7   Error Analysis

In this section we aim to analyze the performance of the POS taggers on the CS sentences of the Bangor test set and more specifically, on the CS fragments (CSF) of those test sentences. We define a CSF as the minimum contiguous span of words where a CS occurs. Most often a CSF will be two words long, spanning a Spanish token and an English one or vice versa, but it is also possible for fragments to be longer than that, given that a Mixed or Ambiguous token could occur within a fragment. The average CSF length in the Bangor test set is 2.16. We compare the performance of the UD-EN, UD-ES, UD-EN&ES and the Bangor-trained taggers on the Bangor CS Test set to understand the difference in errors made by monolingual and CS taggers. Table 7 shows the following measures: OOV rate, POS tagging accuracy at the sentence and word level, POS tagging accuracy in CS fragments at the fragment and word level, the average distance from a POS tagging error to the nearest CSF (AvgMinDistCSF) and the percentage of POS tagging errors that occur within the boundaries of a CS utterance (%ErrorsInCSF). All measures are computed on the CS subset of test sentences of the Bangor corpus using the basic POS taggers trained on UD-EN, UD-ES, UD EN&ES

and the Bangor corpus. In the table, we see that the multilingual models have much lower OOV rates, which translates into much higher sentence-level and word-level POS tagging accuracy. The CS Bangor-trained model fares much better than the UD EN&ES model in terms of word-level accuracy (96.1 versus 87.2%), especially when looking at the sentence-level accuracy (60.7 versus 21.8%), because the Bangor model is able to deal with code-switches. When looking at the tagging accuracy on the CS utterances the relative gains at the word level are even larger. This demonstrates that training on CS sentences is an important factor to achieving high-performing POS tagging accuracy.

It can also be seen from the table that, as the models achieve CS tagging accuracy, tagging errors are still concentrated near or within CSFs – for the UD EN&ES and Bangor models, AvgMinDistCSF and %ErrorsInCS decrease as the CSF-level accuracies increase. This shows that even as the models improve at tagging CS fragments, CS fragments still remain the most challenging aspect of the task.

8   Conclusions

In this paper, we have presented a neural model for POS tagging and language identification on CS data. The neural network is a state-of-the-art bidirectional LSTM with prefix, suffix and word embeddings and four boolean features. We used the Miami Bangor corpus to train and test models and showed that: a) monolingual taggers trained on benchmark training sets perform poorly on the test set of the CS corpus, b) our CS models achieve high POS accuracy when trained and tested on CS sentences, c) expanding the feature set to include language ID as input features yielded the best performing models, d) a joint POS and language ID tagger performs comparably to the POS tagger and its LID accuracy is higher than 98%, and e) a model trained on instances of in-genre inter-sentential CS performs much better than the monolingual baselines, but yielded worse test results than the model trained on instances of inter-sentential and intra-sentential code-switching. Furthermore, we compared to our results to the previous state-of-the-art POS tagger for this corpus and showed that our classifiers outperform them in every configuration.

References

Martín Abadi, Ashish Agarwal, Paul Barham, Eugene Brevdo, Zhifeng Chen, Craig Citro, Greg S. Corrado, Andy Davis, Jeffrey Dean, Matthieu Devin, Sanjay Ghemawat, Ian Goodfellow, Andrew Harp, Geoffrey Irving, Michael Isard, Yangqing Jia, Rafal Jozefowicz, Lukasz Kaiser, Manjunath Kudlur, Josh Levenberg, Dan Mané, Rajat Monga, Sherry Moore, Derek Murray, Chris Olah, Mike Schuster, Jonathon Shlens, Benoit Steiner, Ilya Sutskever, Kunal Talwar, Paul Tucker, Vincent Vanhoucke, Vijay Vasudevan, Fernanda Viégas, Oriol Vinyals, Pete Warden, Martin Wattenberg, Martin Wicke, Yuan Yu, and Xiaoqiang Zheng. 2015. TensorFlow: Large-scale machine learning on heterogeneous systems. Software available from tensorflow.org.

Fahad AlGhamdi, Giovanni Molina, Mona Diab, Thamar Solorio, Abdelati Hawwari, Victor Soto, and Julia Hirschberg. 2016. Part of speech tagging for code switched data. In *Proc. of the Second Workshop on Computational Approaches to Code Switching*, pages 98–107.

Daniel Andor, Chris Alberti, David Weiss, Aliaksei Severyn, Alessandro Presta, Kuzman Ganchev, Slav Petrov, and Michael Collins. 2016. Globally normalized transition-based neural networks. *arXiv preprint arXiv:1603.06042*.

Utsab Barman, Amitava Das, Joachim Wagner, and Jennifer Foster. 2014. Code mixing: A challenge for language identification in the language of social media. In *Proc. of The First Workshop on Computational Approaches to Code Switching*, pages 13–23.

Utsab Barman, Joachim Wagner, and Jennifer Foster. 2016. Part-of-speech tagging of code-mixed social media content: Pipeline, stacking and joint modelling. In *Proc. of The Second Workshop on Computational Approaches to Code Switching*, pages 42–51.

Yoshua Bengio, Réjean Ducharme, Pascal Vincent, and Christian Jauvin. 2003. A neural probabilistic language model. *Journal of machine learning research*, 3(Feb):1137–1155.

Ann Bies, Justin Mott, Colin Warner, and Seth Kulick. 2012. English web treebank LDC2012T13. https://catalog.ldc.upenn.edu/LDC2012T13.

Mónica Stella Cárdenas-Claros and Neny Isharyanti. 2009. Code-switching and code-mixing in Internet chatting: between 'yes', 'ya', and 'si' – a case study. *The JALT CALL Journal*, 5(3):67–78.

François Chollet. 2015. Keras. https://github.com/fchollet/keras.

Michael Collins. 2002. Discriminative training methods for hidden markov models: Theory and experiments with perceptron algorithms. In *Proceedings of the ACL-02 conference on Empirical methods in natural language processing-Volume 10*, pages 1–8. Association for Computational Linguistics.

Ronan Collobert, Jason Weston, Léon Bottou, Michael Karlen, Koray Kavukcuoglu, and Pavel Kuksa. 2011. Natural language processing (almost) from scratch. *Journal of Machine Learning Research*, 12(Aug):2493–2537.

Brenda Danet and Susan C Herring. 2007. *The multilingual Internet: Language, culture, and communication online*. Oxford University Press on Demand.

Crystal David. 2001. *Language and the Internet*. Cambridge, CUP.

Kevin Donnelly and Margaret Deuchar. 2011a. The Bangor Autoglosser: a multilingual tagger for conversational text. *ITA11, Wrexham, Wales*.

Kevin Donnelly and Margaret Deuchar. 2011b. Using constraint grammar in the Bangor Autoglosser to disambiguate multilingual spoken text. In *Constraint Grammar Applications: Proceedings of the NODALIDA 2011 Workshop, Riga, Latvia*, pages 17–25.

Timothy Dozat, Peng Qi, and Christopher D. Manning. 2017. Stanfords graph-based neural dependency parser at the CoNLL 2017 shared task. In *Proc. of the CoNLL 2017 Shared Task: Multilingual Parsing from Raw Text to Universal Dependencies*, pages 20–30.

Yarin Gal and Zoubin Ghahramani. 2016. A theoretically grounded application of dropout in recurrent neural networks. In *Advances in Neural Information Processing Systems*, pages 1019–1027.

Liang Huang, Suphan Fayong, and Yang Guo. 2012. Structured perceptron with inexact search. In *Proceedings of the 2012 Conference of the North American Chapter of the Association for Computational Linguistics: Human Language Technologies*, pages 142–151. Association for Computational Linguistics.

Anupam Jamatia, Björn Gambäck, and Amitava Das. 2015. Part-of-speech tagging for code-mixed English-Hindi Twitter and Facebook chat messages. In *Proc. of Recent Advances in Natural Language Processing*, pages 239–248.

Diederik P Kingma and Jimmy Lei Ba. 2015. ADAM: A method for stochastic optimization. In *Proceedings of the Third International Conference on Learning Representations (ICLR)*.

Wang Ling, Tiago Luís, Luís Marujo, Ramón Fernandez Astudillo, Silvio Amir, Chris Dyer, Alan W Black, and Isabel Trancoso. 2015. Finding function in form: Compositional character models for open vocabulary word representation. *arXiv preprint arXiv:1508.02096*.

Brian MacWhinney. 2000. *The CHILDES project: Tools for analyzing talk.*, 3rd edition. Lawrence Erlbaum Associates, Inc.

Brian MacWhinney. 2009. The CHILDES project part 1: The chat transcription format. *Department of Psychology*.

Mitchell P Marcus, Mary Ann Marcinkiewicz, and Beatrice Santorini. 1993. Building a large annotated corpus of English: The Penn Treebank. *Computational linguistics*, 19(2):313–330.

Mitchell P Marcus, Beatrice Santorini, Mary Ann Marcinkiewicz, and Ann Taylor. 1999. Treebank-3 LDC99T42. `https://catalog.ldc.upenn.edu/ldc99t42`.

Ryan T McDonald, Joakim Nivre, Yvonne Quirmbach-Brundage, Yoav Goldberg, Dipanjan Das, Kuzman Ganchev, Keith B Hall, Slav Petrov, Hao Zhang, Oscar Täckström, et al. 2013. Universal dependency annotation for multilingual parsing. In *ACL (2)*, pages 92–97.

Quinn McNemar. 1947. Note on the sampling error of the difference between correlated proportions or percentages. *Psychometrika*, 12(2):153–157.

Robert Moore. 2014. Fast high-accuracy part-of-speech tagging by independent classifiers. In *COLING*, pages 1165–1176.

Slav Petrov, Dipanjan Das, and Ryan McDonald. 2012. A universal part-of-speech tagset. In *Proceedings of the Eight International Conference on Language Resources and Evaluation (LREC'12)*, Istanbul, Turkey. European Language Resources Association (ELRA).

Paul Rodrigues. 2013. Part of speech tagging bilingual speech transcripts with intrasentential model switching. In *AAAI Spring Symposium*, pages 56–63.

Mike Rosner and Paulseph-John Farrugia. 2007. A tagging algorithm for mixed language identification in a noisy domain. In *Proc. of INTERSPEECH*, pages 190–193.

Beatrice Santorini. 1990. *Part-of-speech tagging guidelines for the Penn Treebank Project (3rd revision)*, 3 edition. LDC, UPenn. 2nd Printing.

Royal Sequiera, Monojit Choudhury, and Kalika Bali. 2015. POS tagging of Hindi-English code mixed text from social media: Some machine learning experiments. In *Proc. of ICON*.

Libin Shen, Giorgio Satta, and Aravind Joshi. 2007. Guided learning for bidirectional sequence classification. In *ACL*, volume 7, pages 760–767.

Natalia Silveira, Timothy Dozat, Marie-Catherine de Marneffe, Samuel Bowman, Miriam Connor, John Bauer, and Christopher D. Manning. 2014. A gold standard dependency corpus for English. In *Proceedings of the Ninth International Conference on Language Resources and Evaluation (LREC-2014)*.

Thamar Solorio and Yang Liu. 2008. Part-of-speech tagging for English-Spanish code-switched text. In *Proc. of EMNLP*, pages 1051–1060.

Victor Soto and Julia Hirschberg. 2017. Crowdsourcing universal part-of-speech tags for code-switching. *Interspeech*.

US Census Bureau. 2014. Annual estimates of the resident population by sex, age, race, and Hispanic origin for the United States: April 1, 2010 to July 1, 2014. `https://factfinder.census.gov/bkmk/table/1.0/en/PEP/2014/PEPASR6H?slice=hisp~hisp!year~est72014`.

US Census Bureau. 2015. American community survey 1-year estimates: S1601 - language spoken at home. `https://factfinder.census.gov/bkmk/table/1.0/en/ACS/15_1YR/S1601`.

Yogarshi Vyas, Spandana Gella, and Jatin Sharma. 2014. POS tagging of English-Hindi code-mixed social media content. In *Proc. of EMNLP*, pages 974–979.

Peilu Wang, Yao Qian, Frank K Soong, Lei He, and Hai Zhao. 2015. A unified tagging solution: Bidirectional LSTM recurrent neural network with word embedding. *arXiv preprint arXiv:1511.00215*.

Phone Merging for Code-switched Speech Recognition

Sunit Sivasankaran *
Université de Lorraine, CNRS,
Inria, LORIA,
F-54000 Nancy, France
sunit.sivasankaran@inria.fr

**Brij Mohan Lal Srivastava, Sunayana Sitaram,
Kalika Bali, Monojit Choudhury**
Microsoft Research - Bangalore, India
{ v-bmlals,susitara,kalikab,
monojitc}@microsoft.com

Abstract

Speakers in multilingual communities often switch between or mix multiple languages in the same conversation. Automatic Speech Recognition (ASR) of code-switched speech faces many challenges including the influence of phones of different languages on each other. This paper shows evidence that phone sharing between languages improves the Acoustic Model performance for Hindi-English code-switched speech. We compare *baseline* system built with separate phones for Hindi and English with systems where the phones were manually merged based on linguistic knowledge. Encouraged by the improved ASR performance after manually merging the phones, we further investigate multiple data-driven methods to identify phones to be merged across the languages. We show detailed analysis of automatic phone merging in this language pair and the impact it has on individual phone accuracies and WER. Though the best performance gain of 1.2% WER was observed with manually merged phones, we show experimentally that the manual phone merge is not optimal.

1 Introduction

Multilingual speakers tend to alternate between several languages within a conversation. This phenomenon is referred to as code-switching (CS). Automatic Speech Recognition for CS speech is challenging. Code-switched speech recognition present challenges in acoustic, language and pronunciation modeling of speech. Acoustic Mod-

els (AMs) need to model phones in a mixed language setting, where co-articulation effects from one language may influence the other. Moreover, language models needs to be capable of predicting code-switch points between the two languages. The vocabulary size may be double of what is present in monolingual systems. Accents and native language influence may pose challenges to pronunciation models. Another major challenge in building code-switched ASR is the lack of data for different language-pairs. To curb the issue of contextual data availability per phone, we study the effect of manual merging and two automatic merging over the performance of Hindi-English code-switched speech recognition system.

In systems with a small amount of data for training the AMs, phones that are similar to each other in the two languages being mixed can be merged, leading to more data for each phone. This may be especially useful in the case of related languages, or when a strong native language accent is expected to influence pronunciations in the other language. We experiment with phone merging in AMs of Hindi-English code-switched conversational speech, and show that we can get improvements on Word Error Rate (WER) by merging certain phones.

One technique to merge phones in the two languages being mixed is to use a common phoneset such as the International Phonetic Alphabet (IPA), or knowledge from a bilingual speaker to decide which phones can be merged (*manualmerge*). However, this may not always find the optimal merges, particularly if the phoneset we are starting with is not the appropriate representation for the dialect present in the speech. Another technique is to automatically find candidate merges by taking into account phone errors made by the ASR system in presence of a **monolingual context** (*data-driven*). Thirdly, we can create lex-

---

* This work was done while interning at Microsoft Research-India

Proceedings of The Third Workshop on Computational Approaches to Code-Switching, pages 11–19
Melbourne, Australia, July 19, 2018. ©2018 Association for Computational Linguistics

icons with all possible pronunciation variants covering all candidate phones and allow the decoder to choose the correct pronunciation variant during decoding (*probabilistic*). We implement and discuss these techniques for phone merging in Hindi-English code-switched speech recognition.

The paper is organized as follows. Section 2 relates this work to prior work in code-switched speech recognition. Section 3 describes the Hindi-English speech data that we used. We describe our proposed techniques and experiments with phone merging in Section 4 and conclude the paper in Section 5.

2   Relation to Prior Work

Code-switched speech recognition has been studied in the context of acoustic, language and pronunciation modeling. The Language Identification (LID) based approach is to identify the language boundaries and subsequently use an appropriate monolingual ASR system to recognize monolingual fragments (Chan et al., 2004) or run multiple recognizers in parallel with an LID system (Ahmed and Tan, 2012; Weiner, 2012). Another approach is to train an AM on bilingual data (Lyu et al., 2006; Vu et al., 2012) or to use one of the monolingual AMs (Bhuvanagirir and Kopparapu, 2012) or to pool the existing monolingual AMs by sharing phones belonging to both languages. Yeh et al. (Yeh and Lee, 2015) tackle the problem of code-switching in which a speaker speaks mainly in one language, leading to an imbalance in the amount of data available in the two languages, with cross-lingual data sharing approaches. (Pandey et al., 2017) also propose studies to adapt matrix language (monolingual Hindi) resource to build better code-mixed acoustic model in case of read speech.

Yilmaz et al. (Yılmaz et al., 2016) describe two DNN architectures for recognizing Frisian-Dutch code-switched speech. They use language dependent phones in which each phone is tagged with the language and modeled separately. They also use language independent phones by modeling them jointly and merging them on the basis of the associated IPA symbol. In their experiments, they find that the language dependent approach performs better. (Lyudovyk and Pylypenko, 2014) describe an approach for code-switched speech recognition of closely related languages, namely, Ukrainian and Russian by creating a bilingual pro-nunciation lexicon.

(Chan et al., 2009) describe a two pass approach for Cantonese-English mixed speech recognition, in which they develop a cross-lingual phonetic AM, with the phone set designed based on linguistic knowledge. (Yu et al., 2004) present three approaches for bilingual phone modeling for Mandarin-English speech, namely combining phone inventories, use IPA mappings to construct a bilingual phone set and clustering phones with hierarchical clustering by using the Bhattacharyya distance and the acoustic likelihood. The third approach outperforms the IPA-based mapping and is comparable to the combination of the phone inventories.

A closely related area of research is the Multi-Lingual speech recognition (Toshniwal et al., 2018; Schultz and Waibel, 1997, 2001; Lin et al., 2009; Vu et al., 2014). Though the problems in multi-lingual ASR and ASR for code-switched data seem similar such as; large phonetic space due to the incorporation of the phones of both languages, code-switched ASR has its own set of challenges. For example, even with a large corpus, getting enough data at code-switched points for both the Acoustic Model and the Language Models is very challenging.

3   Data

The dataset used in this work contains conversational speech recordings spoken in code-switched Hindi and English. Hindi-English bilinguals were given a topic and asked to have a conversation about the topic with another bilingual. They were not explicitly asked to code-switch during recording, but around 40% of the data contains at least one English word in an utterance. The conversations were transcribed by bilingual transcribers. Hindi words were transcribed in the native Hindi script Devanagari, and English words in Roman script. There was no distinction made between borrowed words and code-switching, which led to some inconsistencies in transcription. Each conversation was broken down into utterances ranging from very short one word utterances to long sentences.

A summary of the Hindi-English code switched dataset used in our experiments is shown in Table 1. The code-switching statistics mentioned are particular to this dataset and is subject to change depending on the speaker. However, the phone

Data	Utts	# of Spkrs	Hrs	Total Words	En (%)	Unique Words	En (%)
Train	41276	429	46	560893	16.6	18900	40.23
Test	5193	53	5.6	69177	16.5	6000	41.01
Dev	4689	53	5.7	68995	16.05	6051	40.04

Table 1: Hindi-English code switched data

merging experiments described in this paper is still relevant due to the performance gains of the acoustic model.

4 Phone merging

In this section, we first describe the baseline ASR system built by combining the Hindi and English phonesets, followed by experiments conducted on phone merging and the resulting impact on Word Error Rate (WER). All experiments were carried out using Kaldi (Povey et al., 2011) and the phone merging techniques are implemented in Python.

4.1 Baseline ASR System

The CMU Pronunciation dictionary (Weide, 1998) containing 39 phones was used as the lexicon for all the English words in the data. This is not the most appropriate choice given that all the speakers in the data speak Indian English, however, due to the lack of a publicly available large Indian English lexicon, we used CMUdict. To generate the lexicon for the Hindi words, we used the Festvox Indic front end (Parlikar et al.), which does basic grapheme to phone conversion for Hindi, including schwa deletion and contextual nasalization. The Hindi phoneset consisted of 50 phones after removing some very low frequency phones.

We used Feature-space maximum likelihood linear regression (fMLLR) (Gales, 1998) to train a context-dependent GMM-HMM acoustic model and a trigram Language Model (LM) built on the transcripts during decoding. With this system, we obtained a baseline Word Error Rate (WER) of 40.36%.

We evaluated the accuracies at phone level by comparing the transition arcs that correspond to phones in the decoded lattices with the alignments obtained from the GMM-HMM model as ground truth. Figure 1 shows a scatter plot of the phone accuracy with respect to the log of the data available per phone in the test dataset. Evidently, we observe higher accuracies for phones with larger

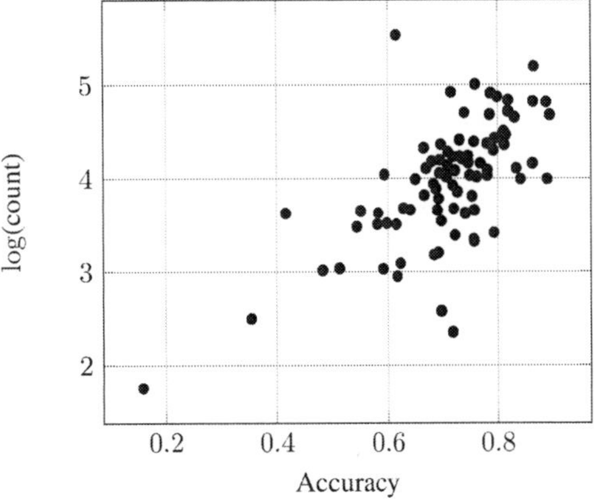

Figure 1: Scatter plot of log of data count per phone with respect to the phone accuracy on the test set.

count with a few exceptions such as, /nN_HP/, /zh/ and /dR_HP/.

4.2 Manually merging similar sounding phones

To increase the data availability per phone, we merged similar sounds in both languages even if they are not exactly the same linguistically (in terms of their articulation). The mapping between Hindi phones and CMUdict phones in the Festvox Indic frontend, built for enabling a Hindi TTS system to pronounce English words (Sitaram and Black, 2016), was used for this purpose. All the merged phones (a total of 31) were prefixed with "-HP-M".

To analyze the impact of merging, we started by merging a pair of phones - the English phone *eh* (example "*academic* ae k ah d *eh* m ih k") with a similar sounding Hindi phone *E-HP* (example in Roman script: "*kehana* k-HP *E-HP* hv-HP nB-HP Aa-HP"). This resulted in 38 English phones, 49 Hindi phones and 1 merged phone resulting in 88 unique phones. We obtained a WER of 40.21 using a GMM-HMM acoustic model, which

13

is a negligible improvement over the system with no merging. The bar plot in Figure 2 shows the change in the accuracies for each phones with respect to the baseline. We notice an improvement of 4.18% and 4.5% in the accuracy of the '*eh*' and '*E-HP*' phones respectively. Similar performance was obtained while merging the English phone *n* with the Hindi phone *nB-HP*. In both cases, a decrease in accuracies for a few phones were observed.

Then, we merged all the 31 pairs of similar sounding English and Hindi phones. We refer to this system as the "all merged" system, for which we obtained a WER of 39.7%. There was a noticeable improvement in the accuracies of about 75% of the phones as shown in Figure 3 . We observed a decrease in accuracies for phones which do not have similar sounding equivalents to merge, such as the Hindi phones 'sr-HP' and 'nN-HP' and the English phone 'ng'. Large improvements in the phone accuracies, amounting to around 50%, were observed in merged phones such as 'ow-HP' (merged with the English phone 'ao') and 'tr-HP' (merged with the English phone 't'). Conspicuously, the highest improvements were for phones with low count prior to merging.

4.3 Measuring phone accuracy changes

To evaluate the performance of these systems in terms of phone accuracy, we computed the weighted average of change in accuracies. The weights correspond to the data available per phone. We measure Weighted Average of Phoneme Improvement (henceforth referred to as $WAPI$) as:

$$WAPI = \frac{\sum_i w_i \times \Delta acc_i}{\sum_i w_i},$$

where w_i and Δacc_i represent the data available per phone and change in phone accuracy with respect to the baseline respectively. A summary of the $WAPI$ score for different acoustic models is shown in Table 2. The "all merged" system gives the highest WAPI score of 2.45%, whereas merging 'eh' with 'E-HP' and 'n' with 'nB-HP' results in a WAPI score of 0.31 and 0.47 respectively. Interestingly merging both 'eh' with 'E-HP' and 'n' with 'nB-HP' results in WAPI score of 0.49 which is higher compared to individually merging these phones.

From the above experiments we infer that merging phones result in more data for data-starved

Phones Merged	WAPI
All	2.45
eh with E-HP	0.31
n with nB-HP	0.47
eh with E-HP & n with nB-HP	0.49
P_{30}	-0.59
P_{70}	1.63

Table 2: Weighted average of phone improvement (WAPI) scores for different phone merging.

phones which in turn improves the phone accuracies.

4.4 Improved Acoustic Models

We also performed the same experiments using two Deep Neural Network (DNN) based acoustic models. The first model was built using 5 hidden layers with p-norm (Zhang et al., 2014) as the non-linearity. The input dimension of each hidden layer was 5000 and output dimension was 500. We used 40 dimensional MFCC along with 4 splicing frames on each side, appended with 100 dimensional i-vectors (Dehak et al., 2011) as input features. We also built a time-delay neural network (TDNN) (Peddinti et al., 2015) with 6 hidden layers and ReLU as the non linearity.

Merging	GMM	p-norm DNN	TDNN
No merge	40.36	32.81	29.15
All merge	39.70	31.89	28.78
DDPM	52.95	45.99	42.16
DDPM $(\alpha_c(p))$	41.07	34.69	31.52
DDPM (α_c)	40.75	34.48	31.28
P_{30}	41.21	33.40	29.84
P_{70}	40.92	34.30	28.94

Table 3: Word Error Rates of all systems. DDPM stands for Data Driven Phone Merge. It has 3 variants as mentioned in section 4.5

Table 3 summarizes the WER for the different systems. The all-merge model with p-norm DNN had a WER of 31.89% (with confidence interval of 0.34%). This is 2.8% lower than the baseline DNN model with no merging. The TDNN network outperformed both the GMM and p-norm based DNN AMs. The relative WER improvement of 1.29% using TDNN with merging is statistically significant compared to TDNN model without merging.

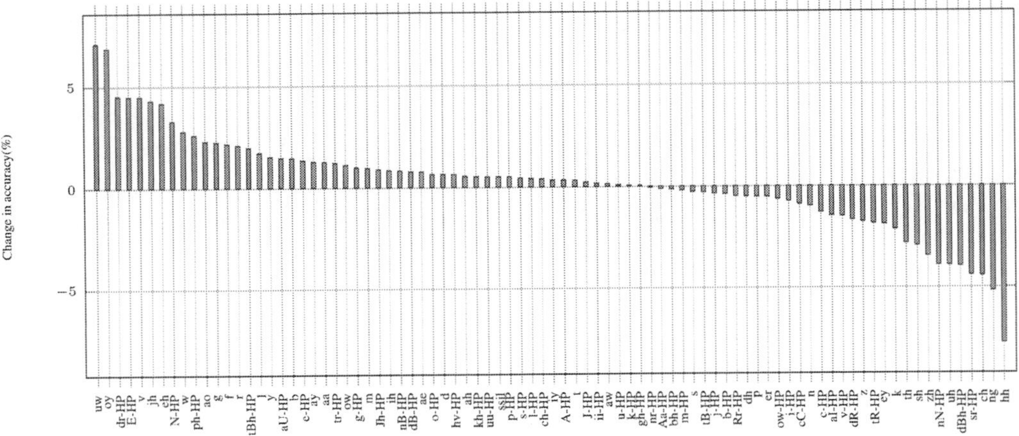

Figure 2: Accuracy changes (%) in the phone accuracies when eh (En) phone is merged with E-HP (Hi) phone

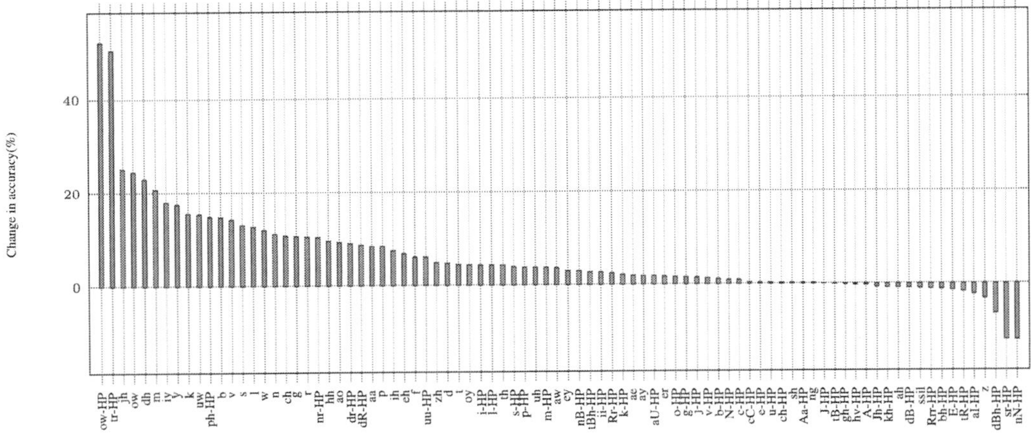

Figure 3: Change in phone accuracies after merging all similar sounding Hindi and English phones.

Motivated by this improved ASR performance, we investigate approaches to merge phones using data driven methods. We hypothesize that the data driven methods will provide us with clues on the acoustic similarity between phones to be merged.

4.5 Data-driven phone merging (DDPM)

The potential phone pairs to merge can be identified based on the errors made by the decoder, with respect to the alignments. A TDNN acoustic model trained using the unmerged (89 phones) phoneset was used to decode the utterances from the dev dataset, with a low LM weight of 1 so as to minimize the influence of LM. Phoneme sequences are then derived by parsing the best path through the decoded lattice. The same acoustic model is also used to align the dev data and obtain the corresponding true phone sequences and their durations. We choose pairs of aligned and decoded utterances with a strict threshold of 80% or more overlap in duration. Using the alignments, we identify English phones which were wrongly decoded as Hindi phones. We call them cross-language swaps. Frequent swapping between English-Hindi phone pair, indicates the need for the pair to be merged.

Using this approach we observe several merges that were present in the manual merge. For instance, (e_HP, ey), (A_HP, ah), (ii_HP, iy), (m_HP, m), (b_HP, b), (ph_HP, f). Errors such as, (Aa_HP, l), (u_HP, ah), (j_HP, ey), (g_HP, l), were also noticed. WER of 52.95, 45.99 and 42.16 were obtained using GMM, DNN and TDNN models respectively, after merging the phones identified by

15

the data-driven method. The decrease in performance can be attributed to the wrong phone swaps.

4.5.1 Inducing context sensitivity through reliability coefficients

Spurious phone swaps degrade the performance of the ASR substantially. This can be reduced by taking into account the phone context. We associate a notion of *context reliability* with each context c, which is defined as the proportion of correct *within-language* phone predictions by the decoder out of all the instances of a context c. We compute this reliability as a coefficient (α_c) for left, right and both contexts in two different ways. α_c can be computed with respect to a specific center phone ($\alpha_c(p)$) as:

$$\alpha_c(p) = \frac{\text{correct instances of } p \text{ with } c}{\text{total instances of } p \text{ with } c} \quad (1)$$
$$= P(x = p|c)$$

An alternate method referred to as global context reliability coefficient, is to compute the context reliability coefficient for every context irrespective of the center phone p. This is obtained by computing the ratio of the counts of the correct instances for any arbitrary phone in presence of context c to the total instances of context c:

$$\alpha_c = \frac{\text{correct instances of context c}}{\text{total instances of context c}} \quad (2)$$

The computed α_c are applied as weights while combining the probability of *cross-language* swaps conditioned on the context c.

Our goal is to compute the conditional probability of the decoded phone(x_d) given the alignment phone (x_a), which is $P(x_d|x_a)$. The phone ($\hat{x}_d$) with the highest probability will be chosen as the potential merge for x_a (eq. 3).

$$\hat{x}_d = \arg\max_{x_d} P(x_d|x_a) \quad (3)$$

The context information is incorporated by computing the conditional probability specific to a context as $P(x_d|x_a, c)$ and then marginalizing over all possible c to obtain the swap probability $P(x_d|x_a)$ (eq. 4).

$$P(x_d|x_a) = \sum_c P(x_d|x_a, c)P(c|x_a)$$
$$\approx \sum_c P(x_d|x_a, c)P(x_a|c)P(c) \quad (4)$$
$$\approx \sum_c P(x_d|x_a, c)\alpha_c P(c)$$

$P(c)$ is the prior probability for each context c which is computed using the dev dataset. We assign a neutral reliability (α_0) score of 0.01 and prior $P(c)$ of 0.01 to all the unseen contexts. The min and max values of α_c are 0.0 and 1.0 respectively.

Figure 4 shows cross-language phone confusion matrices for the two context-sensitive data driven phone merging approaches. We observe that phone-specific coefficients are able to capture only the most prominent merges while global coefficients produce merges that highly correlate with the manual merge. This might be due to the division of context information across phones which reduces the context sensitivity. This clearly suggests that some contexts help in producing better predictions than others, regardless of the reference phone. Although many of the swaps predicted using DDPM closely resemble the manual merges, the manual merge method outperformed global-DDPM by approx. 3% absolute as seen in Table 3. The distribution of α_c values show that the left and the right context exhibit high confidence scores, whereas low confidence scores were observed when both the context were considered. Hence, we will benefit by removing the spurious low-confidence contexts while merging.

Figure 5 presents the swap likelihood of the predicted phone-pairs in decreasing order. We observe that phone pairs that have the highest swap likelihoods include nasals, close vowels and stops. It is interesting that the data driven method identified new phone merges such as (ae, Aa_HP) and (aa, ow_HP) compared to manual merged phones. We believe that incorporating these new phone merges into the manually merged phone set will improve the ASR performance. Further experiments need to be conducted to verify this claim.

4.6 Probabilistic merging

Next, we propose a method to allow the acoustic model to select appropriate phones during decoding. We trained an acoustic model using the merged phones while also retaining the Hindi and English phones. For example, the phone set for the new AM contained the English phone 'eh', the Hindi phone 'E-HP' as well as the merged phone 'E-HP-M'. The intuition behind this approach is to let the decoder choose between multiple pronunciation variants in the lexicon so as to determine the pronunciation used by a speaker who code-

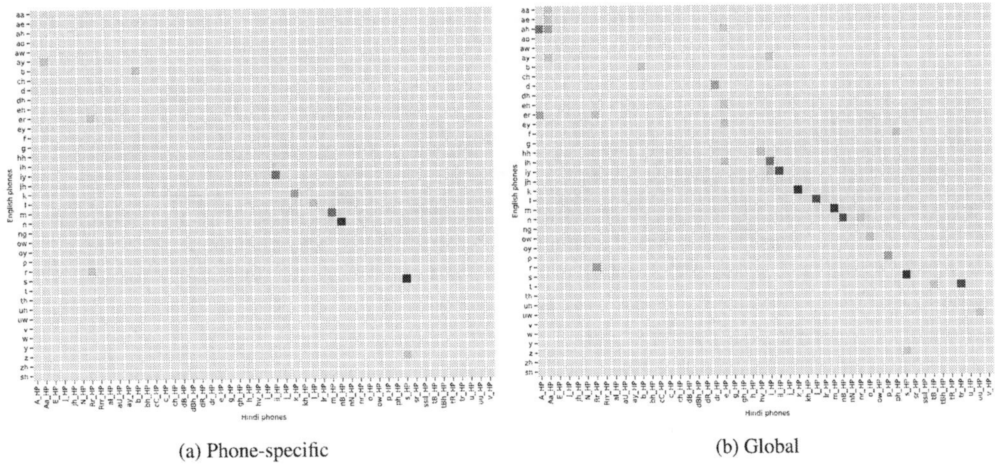

(a) Phone-specific   (b) Global

Figure 4: Cross-language phone confusion matrices using phone-specific ($\alpha_c(p)$) and global (α_c) context reliability coefficients

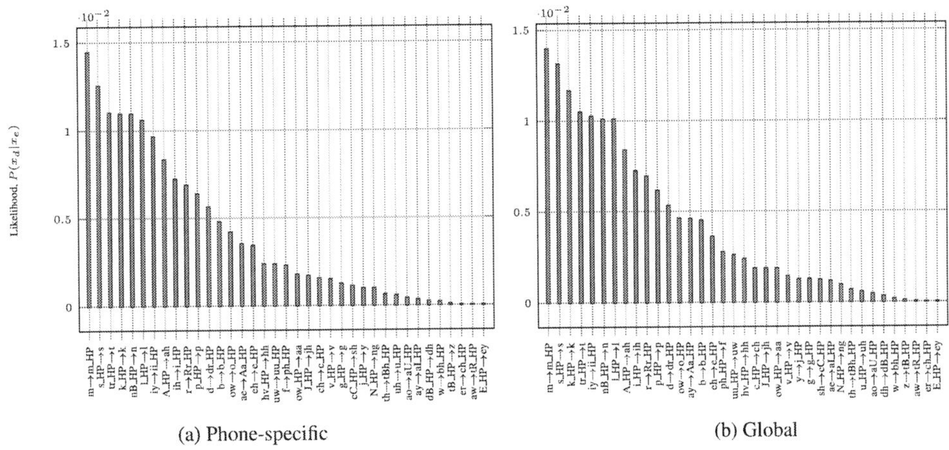

(a) Phone-specific   (b) Global

Figure 5: Swap-pair likelihood for phone-specific ($\alpha_c(p)$) and global (α_c) context reliability coefficients.

switched. This approach has been shown to work well in speech synthesis for pronunciation modeling of homographs (Sitaram et al., 2015). Table 4 compares the number of unique Hindi, English and merged phones for the different systems mentioned.

During training, we modified the lexicon so as to retain part of the data for the unmerged phones and assigned the rest to the merged phones. We assigned 30% and 70% of the data to merged phones which we refer to as P_{30} and P_{70}. During decoding, we created a different lexicon allowing all possible pronunciation variants. We obtained WERs of 41.21% and 40.92% using the HMM-GMM based AM for P_{30} and P_{70} models respectively which are lower than the baseline. WAPI

	En	Hi	Merged	Total
Baseline	39	50	0	89
All merge	8	19	31	58
DDPM	9	20	30	59
DDPM ($\alpha_c(p)$)	20	25	14	59
DDPM (α_c)	21	24	14	59
Probabilistic Merging	39	50	31	120

Table 4: Number of phones before and after merging

17

score of 1.63 for P_{70} model was higher compared to -0.59 of P_{30} model but lower compared to the all merge model. Table 4 shows the number of English, Hindi and merged phones for each technique.

The WER is a function of number of insertion, deletion and substitution errors as well as the correct token numbers. Figure 6 shows the relative percentage change in the insertion, deletion and substitution values of the " all merge", P_{30} and P_{70} model compared to the baseline system using TDNN as AM. The best system should have the lowest insertion, deletion and substitution errors and highest correct tokens. The "all merge" model, which has the best WER scores, has higher insertion and substitution errors but performs better on deletion errors and recognition of correct tokens. We can infer that certain phone merges are causing higher insertion and substitution errors and should be avoided, thus concluding that the manually merged phones are sub-optimal.

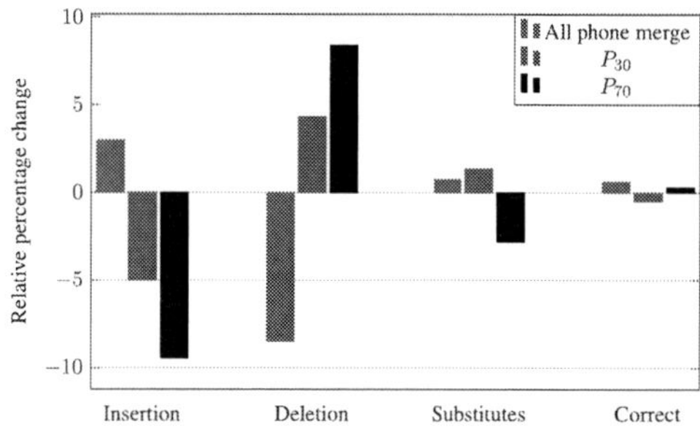

Figure 6: Percentage change in insertion, deletion, substitution and correct token recognition numbers compared to the baseline system with TDNN as AM. The best system should have the lowest of insertion, substitution and deletion numbers and the highest of correct token numbers. The number of word tokens in baseline system for insertion, deletion, substitution and correct tokens are 3342, 5735, 11089 and 49011 respectively.

5   Conclusion

In this work, we compare phone merging techniques in context of code-mixed Hindi-English speech with a baseline system built using a union of both phone sets. We first merge similar sounding phones across both languages manually in order to reduce the phone set size and increase the data availability per phone. We observe a 3% relative improvement in the WER values compared

to the baseline using a p-norm based DNN model along with a significant improvement in phone accuracies. We then propose data-driven approaches to merge phones automatically. To correct the errors made by data-driven method, we weight the cross-language swaps using reliable within-language contexts. These methods gave newer phone merge recommendations which can be useful to improve the ASR performance. We further propose probabilistic methods where in the decoder is provided with both the merged as well as the unmerged phones which reduced the insertion errors compared to the manually merged system. these techniques came close to, but did not improve upon the manually merged ASR system. Error analysis of manual merging indicates that it is not optimal and there is a need for better data-driven techniques to automatically merge phones for code-switched ASR.

6   Acknowledgments

We thank the anonymous reviewers for carefully reading our manuscript and offering valuable suggestions.

References

Basem HA Ahmed and Tien-Ping Tan. 2012. Automatic speech recognition of code switching speech using 1-best rescoring. In *Asian Language Processing (IALP), 2012 International Conference on*, pages 137–140. IEEE.

Kiran Bhuvanagirir and Sunil Kumar Kopparapu. 2012. Mixed language speech recognition without explicit identification of language. *American Journal of Signal Processing*, 2(5):92–97.

Joyce YC Chan, Houwei Cao, PC Ching, and Tan Lee. 2009. Automatic recognition of cantonese-english code-mixing speech. *Computational Linguistics and Chinese Language Processing*, 14(3):281–304.

Joyce YC Chan, PC Ching, Tan Lee, and Helen M Meng. 2004. Detection of language boundary in code-switching utterances by bi-phone probabilities. In *Chinese Spoken Language Processing, 2004 International Symposium on*, pages 293–296. IEEE.

Najim Dehak, Patrick J Kenny, Réda Dehak, Pierre Dumouchel, and Pierre Ouellet. 2011. Front-end factor analysis for speaker verification. *IEEE Transactions on Audio, Speech, and Language Processing*, 19(4):788–798.

Mark JF Gales. 1998. Maximum likelihood linear transformations for hmm-based speech recognition. *Computer speech & language*, 12(2):75–98.

Hui Lin, Li Deng, Dong Yu, Yi-fan Gong, Alex Acero, and Chin-Hui Lee. 2009. A study on multilingual acoustic modeling for large vocabulary asr. In *Acoustics, Speech and Signal Processing, 2009. ICASSP 2009. IEEE International Conference on*, pages 4333–4336. IEEE.

Dau-Cheng Lyu, Ren-Yuan Lyu, Yuang-chin Chiang, and Chun-Nan Hsu. 2006. Speech recognition on code-switching among the chinese dialects. In *2006 IEEE International Conference on Acoustics Speech and Signal Processing Proceedings*, volume 1, pages I–I. IEEE.

Tetyana Lyudovyk and Valeriy Pylypenko. 2014. Code-switching speech recognition for closely related languages. *Proc. SLTU*, pages 188–193.

Ayushi Pandey, Brij Mohan Lai Srivastava, and Suryakanth V Gangashetty. 2017. Adapting monolingual resources for code-mixed hindi-english speech recognition. In *Asian Language Processing (IALP), 2017 International Conference on*, pages 218–221. IEEE.

Alok Parlikar, Sunayana Sitaram, Andrew Wilkinson, and Alan W Black. The festvox indic frontend for grapheme to phoneme conversion. In *WILDRE: Workshop on Indian Langauge Data, Resources and Evaluation, 2016*.

Vijayaditya Peddinti, Daniel Povey, and Sanjeev Khudanpur. 2015. A time delay neural network architecture for efficient modeling of long temporal contexts. In *Sixteenth Annual Conference of the International Speech Communication Association*.

Daniel Povey, Arnab Ghoshal, Gilles Boulianne, Lukas Burget, Ondrej Glembek, Nagendra Goel, Mirko Hannemann, Petr Motlicek, Yanmin Qian, Petr Schwarz, et al. 2011. The kaldi speech recognition toolkit. In *IEEE 2011 workshop on automatic speech recognition and understanding*, EPFL-CONF-192584. IEEE Signal Processing Society.

Tanja Schultz and Alex Waibel. 1997. Fast bootstrapping of lvcsr systems with multilingual phoneme sets. In *Fifth European Conference on Speech Communication and Technology*.

Tanja Schultz and Alex Waibel. 2001. Language-independent and language-adaptive acoustic modeling for speech recognition. *Speech Communication*, 35(1-2):31–51.

Sunayana Sitaram and Alan W Black. 2016. Speech synthesis of code-mixed text. In *LREC*.

Sunayana Sitaram, Serena Jeblee, and Alan W Black. 2015. Using acoustics to improve pronunciation for synthesis of low resource languages. In *Sixteenth Annual Conference of the International Speech Communication Association*.

Shubham Toshniwal, Tara N Sainath, Ron J Weiss, Bo Li, Pedro Moreno, Eugene Weinstein, and Kanishka Rao. 2018. Multilingual speech recognition with a single end-to-end model. In *ICASSP*. IEEE.

Ngoc Thang Vu, David Imseng, Daniel Povey, Petr Motlicek, Tanja Schultz, and Hervé Bourlard. 2014. Multilingual deep neural network based acoustic modeling for rapid language adaptation. In *Acoustics, Speech and Signal Processing (ICASSP), 2014 IEEE International Conference on*, pages 7639–7643. IEEE.

Ngoc Thang Vu, Dau-Cheng Lyu, Jochen Weiner, Dominic Telaar, Tim Schlippe, Fabian Blaicher, Eng-Siong Chng, Tanja Schultz, and Haizhou Li. 2012. A first speech recognition system for mandarin-english code-switch conversational speech. In *2012 IEEE International Conference on Acoustics, Speech and Signal Processing (ICASSP)*, pages 4889–4892. IEEE.

Robert L Weide. 1998. The cmu pronouncing dictionary. *URL: http://www. speech. cs. cmu. edu/cgibin/cmudict*.

Jochen Weiner. 2012. *Integration of language identification into a recognition system for spoken conversations containing code-switches*. Ph.D. thesis, Language Technologies Institute.

Ching-Feng Yeh and Lin-Shan Lee. 2015. An improved framework for recognizing highly imbalanced bilingual code-switched lectures with cross-language acoustic modeling and frame-level language identification. *IEEE/ACM Transactions on Audio, Speech, and Language Processing*, 23(7):1144–1159.

Emre Yılmaz, Henk van den Heuvel, and David van Leeuwen. 2016. Investigating bilingual deep neural networks for automatic recognition of code-switching frisian speech. *Procedia Computer Science*, 81:159–166.

Shengmin Yu, Shitwu Zhang, and Bo Xu. 2004. Chinese-english bilingual phone modeling for cross-language speech recognition. In *Acoustics, Speech, and Signal Processing, 2004. Proceedings.(ICASSP'04). IEEE International Conference on*, volume 1, pages I–917. IEEE.

Xiaohui Zhang, Jan Trmal, Daniel Povey, and Sanjeev Khudanpur. 2014. Improving deep neural network acoustic models using generalized maxout networks. In *Acoustics, Speech and Signal Processing (ICASSP), 2014 IEEE International Conference on*, pages 215–219. IEEE.

Improving Neural Network Performance by Injecting Background Knowledge: Detecting Code-switching and Borrowing in Algerian texts

Wafia Adouane, Jean-Philippe Bernardy and Simon Dobnik
Department of Philosophy, Linguistics and Theory of Science (FLoV),
Centre for Linguistic Theory and Studies in Probability (CLASP), University of Gothenburg
`{wafia.adouane, jean-philippe.bernardy, simon.dobnik}@gu.se`

Abstract

We explore the effect of injecting background knowledge to different deep neural network (DNN) configurations in order to mitigate the problem of the scarcity of annotated data when applying these models on datasets of low-resourced languages. The background knowledge is encoded in the form of lexicons and pre-trained sub-word embeddings. The DNN models are evaluated on the task of detecting code-switching and borrowing points in non-standardised user-generated Algerian texts. Overall results show that DNNs benefit from adding background knowledge. However, the gain varies between models and categories. The proposed DNN architectures are generic and could be applied to other low-resourced languages.

1 Introduction

Recent success of DNNs in various natural language processing (NLP) tasks has attracted attention from the research community attempting to extend their application to new tasks. Nevertheless, the large amount of labelled data required to train DNNs limits their application to new tasks and new languages because it is hard to find large labelled corpora for these domains. The issue is even more severe for low-resourced languages.

Another serious problem with most current NLP approaches and systems is that they are trained on well-edited standardised monolingual corpora, such as the Wall Street Journal, Wikipedia, etc. This could be explained by the fact that for a long time NLP has been influenced by the dominant descriptive linguistic theories affected by the standard language ideology which assumes that natural languages are uniform and monolingual. However, standardisation is not universal (Milroy, 2001), meaning that not all languages are standardised. Therefore, lexical, structural and phonological variation is, for instance, the norm in natural language and not an exception, meaning that well-edited texts do not really reflect the natural usage of natural languages, but only represent formal languages.

The discrepancy between the assumed uniformity of language both in linguistic theory and NLP and their variable nature is accentuated by new technologies, such as social media platforms and messaging services. These new communication platforms have facilitated the proliferation of writing in non-standardised languages on the web, such as colloquial Arabic or what is commonly referred to as dialectal Arabic. This is because in interactive scenarios people usually use spoken-like (colloquial) language or, in multilingual societies where people have access to several linguistic codes at the same time, a mixture of languages/language varieties. Consequently, this new kind of written data has created a serious problem regarding the usability of the existing NLP tools and approaches as they fail to properly process it, even in the case of well-resourced languages.

The contribution of the paper is to explore how to mitigate the problems (i) of the scarcity of annotated data when using DNNs with low-resourced languages, and to what extent can we take advantage of the limited available resources, and (ii) to provide NLP approaches and tools that would be able to deal with non-standardised texts and language-mixing. In particular, for (i) we investigate what are the optimal ways of injecting available background knowledge to different configurations of DNNs in order to improve their performance. For (ii) we take the case of the language used in Algeria as it poses serious challenges for the available NLP approaches and tools.

Proceedings of The Third Workshop on Computational Approaches to Code-Switching, pages 20–28
Melbourne, Australia, July 19, 2018. ©2018 Association for Computational Linguistics

It is a low-resourced multilingual colloquial language. We chose the task of a word-level language identification which is a first step towards processing such texts. The task focuses on detecting code-switching and borrowing points in a text which represents the same utterance. Knowing what parts of text belong to what language variety allows to perform better qualitative and quantitative analysis of such texts with other tools.

The paper is organised as follows: in Section 2 we briefly describe the complex linguistic situation in Algeria as a result of a language contact. The section aims to explain the linguistic challenges of processing such texts and motivates our choices based on established sociolinguistic theories. In Section 3 we present our available linguistic resources and different DNN configurations. In Section 4 we describe our experimental setup and analyse the results. Finally, in Section 5 we compare our contribution to previous related work.

2 Linguistic Background

In North Africa in general, and in Algeria in particular, intense language contact between various related and unrelated languages has resulted in a complex linguistic situation where several languages are used in a single communicative event. A few cases of language contact have attracted the attention of the linguistic community while the monolingual norm dominates in linguistics. One kind of language contact situation has been described by Ferguson (1959) as *diglossia* which refers to a situation where two linguistic systems coexist in a functional distribution within the same speech community. In another kind of language contact situations, several languages coexist but not in a well-defined functional distribution. This situation is referred to as *bilingualism* (Sayahi, 2014) which could result from either informal contact between coexisting languages like Berber and Arabic, or from formal education where in addition to other language people learn French with varying degrees of competence.

Based on the Fishman's model (Fishman, 1967), North African Arabic, known as Maghrebi Arabic, is classified as a linguistic situation in the speech community characterised by diglossia with bilingualism. The intense language contact between related and unrelated languages has resulted mainly in two widespread linguistic phenomena: code-switching and borrowing. As de-

fined by Poplack and Meechan (1998), code-switching is (ideally) integration of material from one language to another without any phonological, morphological or syntactic integration, whereas borrowing is when material is integrated.

For computational purposes, we focus on *diglossic code-switching* (Sayahi, 2014), which happens between related languages such as switching between Arabic varieties, and *bilingual code-switching*, which happens between unrelated languages such as switching between one Arabic variety and other coexisting language such as Berber, French or English. Regarding borrowing, it is practically not possible to clearly distinguish whether a word in one Arabic variety is integrated into another variety or not because there are no lexicons for Arabic varieties, except for the standard one, and we also do not have access to acoustic representations of words. Based on this, we can practically focus only on *bilingual borrowing* rather than on *diglossic borrowing*.

(1)   a. ديري سربيتة صغيرا في طاسة تاع ما او دوبي فيها اسبيجيك وكمديلو يبها نوغمال هاك مداري ندير يريح تم تم

   b. Put a small towel in a cup of water and dissolve Aspegic in it and cover him with it, it is what I usually do. He will feel quickly better.

As illustration, (1) is a user-generated utterance which contains words in Modern Standard Arabic (صغيرا، في، فيها), note that the word صغيرا is misspelled and should be spelt like صغيرة, words in local Algerian Arabic (ديري، تاع، ما، او، دوبي، وكمديلو، يبها، هاك، مداري، ندير، يريح، تم تم), French words integrated in Arabic (سربيتة، طاسة), and a French word without integration (نوغمال).

3 Linguistic Resources and Models

3.1 Linguistic Resources

We use the dataset by (Adouane and Dobnik, 2017) where each word is tagged with a label identifying its category which could be a language/language variety, including local Arabic varieties (ALG), Modern Standard Arabic (MSA), French (FRC), Berber (BER), English (ENG), non-Arabic words integrated in local Arabic or what is referred to as borrowing (BOR), in addition to language independent categories such as named entities (NER), digits (DIG) and interjections (SND). To the best of our knowledge this is the only available labelled dataset for code-switching and borrowing for Algerian. As the labelled dataset is small, we also collected a larger unlabelled dataset from the same sources as the authors of the labelled dataset, and pre-processed them in the same way. Table 1 gives information about the datasets where texts refer to social media texts with an average length of 19 words, words refer to linguistic words excluding other tokens (digits, punctuation, emoticons), and types refer to unique words.

Dataset	#Texts	#Words	#Types
Labelled	10,590	213,792	57,054
Unlabelled	311,130	4,928,827	350,759

Table 1: Statistics about the datasets.

We also use the lexicons compiled by the authors of the labelled dataset, with further cleaning. The lexicons include lists of inflected words checked manually, one list per category. Words belonging to more than one category are not included. Table 2 gives more information about the sizes of the lexicons.

Category	ALG	MSA	FRC	BOR	NER	ENG	BER
#Types	42,788	94,167	3,206	3,509	1,945	165	21,789

Table 2: Statistics about the lexicons.

3.2 Models

We approach the task of detecting code-switching and borrowing points in text as a sequence tagging problem where the aim is to assign a tag to each word in the text depending on its context. We use two DNN architectures, namely Recurrent Neural Network (RNN) and Convolutional Neural Network (CNN) with different configurations summarised in Figure 1.

The first option is to use an RNN to map character embeddings to tags directly. Alternatively, we can use word embeddings. Word embedding

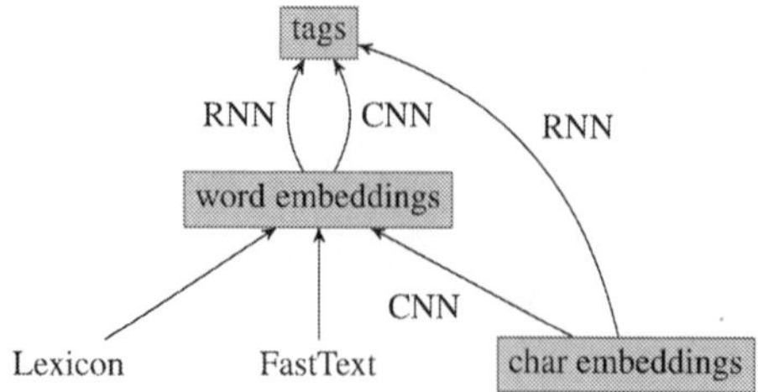

Figure 1: A summary of possible tagging models.

can be any combination of (a) fixed lexicon information (b) fasttext embeddings (c) a custom CNN built from character embeddings. The word embeddings can be mapped to tags using either an RNN or a CNN, or a simple dense layer with softmax activation.

Except for the pure Lexicon-based model, all other models have access to characters and thus to the internal structure of words (phoneme and morphemes), which we expect to be predictive of a particular variety. All models are trained end-to-end, except for the fasttext embeddings and the lexicon. We report only the configurations of models which give the best performance, with the fine-tuned parameters, namely the number of units for each RNN layer, dropout rate, the number of features and the filter size for each CNN layer. The parameters are fine-tuned on a separate development set containing 1,000 texts (13,771 tokens).

3.2.1 Character-level RNN

The character-level RNN is composed of two LSTM layers of 400 units each, with a dropout of 10%, followed by a dense layer with softmax activation. Due to the nature of RNNs, the network assigns one language variant per input symbol, and thus per character — but the task is to predict a tag for each word. To deal with this limitation, we consider only the tag associated with the last character of a word.

3.2.2 Word-level RNN

The word-level RNN is composed of a standard LSTM layer with 400 units with a dropout of 10%, followed by a dense layer.

3.2.3 Character-level CNN

The character-level CNN is composed of two convolution layers with 60 features with a filter size 5, with a relu activation and a dropout of 10%, followed by max pooling in the temporal dimension.

3.2.4 Word-level CNN

The word-level CNN is composed of two convolution layers with a filter size 3, with a relu activation and a dropout of 10%, followed by a dense layer with softmax activation. The first layer uses 100 features and the second 60 features.

3.2.5 Lexicon-based Model

In order to take advantage of the available lexicons, Table 2, we represent their words as one-hot encoding vector, which we refer to as lexicon embeddings. The lexicon-based model is composed of the lexicon embeddings followed by two convolution layers with a filter size 3, with a relu activation and a dropout of 10%, followed by a dense layer with softmax activation. The first layer uses 100 features and the second 60 features.

3.2.6 FastText-based Model

In order to take advantage of the unlabelled dataset, Table 1, containing a high level of misspellings and spelling variation, we assume that word embeddings that are based on sub-word information capture spelling variation and morphological information better than the embeddings that take word as a unit. For this purpose we use FastText library designed to train word embeddings where a word is represented as the sum of its sub-strings (Bojanowski et al., 2016). We created five fasttext embeddings trained on the unlabelled dataset with different parameters. We found that the optimal parameters are: word vector dimension of 300, and the range of the size of the sub-strings representing a word between 3 and 6 characters, with a context size of 5 words, trained on 20 epochs. The FastText-based model is composed of the fasttext embeddings followed by two convolution layers with filter size 3, with a relu activation and a dropout of 10%, followed by a dense layer with softmax activation. The first layer uses 100 features and the second 60 features.

4 Experimental Setup and Results

All models and configurations are evaluated under the same conditions using 10-fold cross-validation on the labelled dataset. As a baseline we take an existing system (Adouane and Dobnik, 2017), a classification-based system which uses a chain of additional back-off strategies which involve lexicons, linguistic rules, and finally the selection of the most frequent category. We refer to this system as the baseline.

First, we train the RNN and CNN models only on the labelled data (supervised learning) without any background knowledge. We also examine the effect of the FastText-based and the Lexicon-based models separately to quantify the contribution of each. Then we combine both models to optimise their performance. Second, in order to take advantage of all available linguistic resources, we add to each of the RNN and the CNN models background knowledge in the form of (i) lexicon embeddings; (ii) fasttext embeddings; (iii) a combination of both lexicon and fasttext embeddings; and (iv) bootstrap the unlabelled dataset with the baseline system and train the best performing DNN model on it to investigate whether bootstrapping improves its performance.

All results are reported as the average performance of the 10-fold cross-validation for each model at epoch 100 using the parameters mentioned earlier. For short, we use FastText to refer to the FastText-based model and fasttext to refer to the fasttext embeddings, Lexicon to refer to the Lexicon-based model and lexicon to refer to the lexicon embeddings.

4.1 Models without Background Knowledge

In Table 3 we report the average error rate of the experiments without background knowledge for only the best performing RNN, CNN, Lexicon, and FastText models.

	Model	ER (%)
1	Char-level RNN	13.38
2	Char-level CNN	**8.18**
3	FastText	16.46
4	Lexicon	20.62
5	FastText + Lexicon	9.21
6	Baseline	9.52

Table 3: Average error rate of the models without background knowledge.

Results show that the baseline (6) outperforms the Char-level RNN (1), FastText (3) and Lexicon (4) models. However, the baseline is outperformed by the Char-level CNN model (2) with 1.34% error reduction. Combining FastText and Lexicon in one model (5) performs much better than using each model separately, and slightly outperforms the baseline by 0.31% error reduction.

In Figure 2 we report the average performance

of each model per category, measured as precision, recall, f-score and loss. Notice that we do not report the loss for the baseline because of the way the system was designed. The results show that the baseline system performs better on the majority categories, ALG and MSA, with an average f-score of 91.91 and 90.44 respectively as well as on non-linguistic categories like DIG and SND with an average f-score of 97.17 and 93.88 respectively.

However, the baseline system performs less well on the minority categories, BER and FRC with an average f-score of 80.41 and 80.31 respectively, and performs even worse on NER and BOR with an average f-score of 72.55 and 64.70 respectively. It performs the worst on ENG with an average f-score of 49.45. Regarding the minority categories, precision is high on BER (94.51%), BOR (93.61%), FRC (92.97%) and lower on NER (88.20%) and ENG (71.41%). However the recall is low on all categories BER (72.76%), FRC (70.70%), NER (61.74%) and the lowest on BOR (49.44%), and ENG (39.37%).

The error analysis of the baseline system shows that the system is mostly confused between related language varieties like ALG-MSA as they share a lot of words, as well as between varieties that share lexically ambiguous words like FRC-ALG, BOR-ALG, FRC-BOR, NER-ALG, BER-ALG. Several words were neither seen in the training data nor were they covered by the available lexicons which, given that the unknown words are tagged as ALG, leads to confusions such as ENG-ALG, NER-ALG, BER-ALG, BOR-ALG, and FRC-ALG.

(2)   a. بويسك قالو غادي يقطعو لما سمانة لجاية راني شريت فاردو ما فيه ٢٠ قرعة سعيدة تاع ليتر ونص

     b. Since they said that they will cut water next week, I have bought a load of 20 bottles of Saida of 1.5 litre.

The MSA-NER confusion is mainly caused by the fact that many NERs are simply common nouns in MSA. For instance, سعيدة could be an adjective in the feminine form in MSA meaning *happy*, or a feminine proper name, or something else. In the context of example (2) it is NER as it refers to the name of a product. The word ما means *water* in ALG, but it is also used as a negation particle in MSA and frequently in ALG, a relative pronoun in MSA, and a noun meaning *mother* in ALG. Likewise قرعة means *bottle* in ALG, but it also means *contest* or *competition* in MSA.

The f-score and precision of the Char-level RNN model is lower from the baseline on all categories, and the recall is better on BOR 64.11% compared to only 49.44% on the baseline, and FRC 72.12% compared to 70.70% respectively. ENG, BER, NER, BOR and FRC are the hardest categories to identify with the following respective loss values: -9.56, -6.72, -3.89, -3.57, -2.80, and all categories are confused with ALG, the majority class.

The f-score of the Char-level CNN model is better on SND, MSA, FRC, DIG, BOR, ALG compared to the baseline, but it performs worse on NER, ENG, BER. This could be contributed by the worse recall on these categories which follows the same trend as the f-score. However, in terms of precision, the Char-level CNN model performs better on ALG, BER, ENG and SND and worse on the remaining categories, with the same kind of confusions as the baseline.

The f-score of the FastText model is low on all categories compared to the baseline. The same holds for recall and precision except on BER where the precision is better 96.18% compared to 94.51% on the baseline. The model produces the same kind of errors as the previous models, but which are most similar to the Char-level CNN model.

Compared to the baseline, the Lexicon model performs better in terms of the f-score on BOR (80.94 compared to 64.70), ENG (73.72 compared to 49.45), and FRC (83.60 compared to 80.30). However it performs significantly worse on BER (18.31 compared to 80.41). This is likely because of the limited coverage of the lexicons. The results also indicate the bias of the lexicons to those categories that are more difficult to distinguish automatically. On the other hand, in terms of the recall, the Lexicon model outperforms the baseline on all categories, except on ALG. In terms of the precision, it is only better on ALG and ENG. The model makes similar errors as the FastText model, only more frequently.

Combining FastText and Lexicon models has a positive effect as the f-score, recall and precision increase on all categories, mainly on BOR (f-score of 47.10 to 84.74), ENG (F-score of 32.05 to 70.59) and NER (f-score of 58.90 to 80.35). The

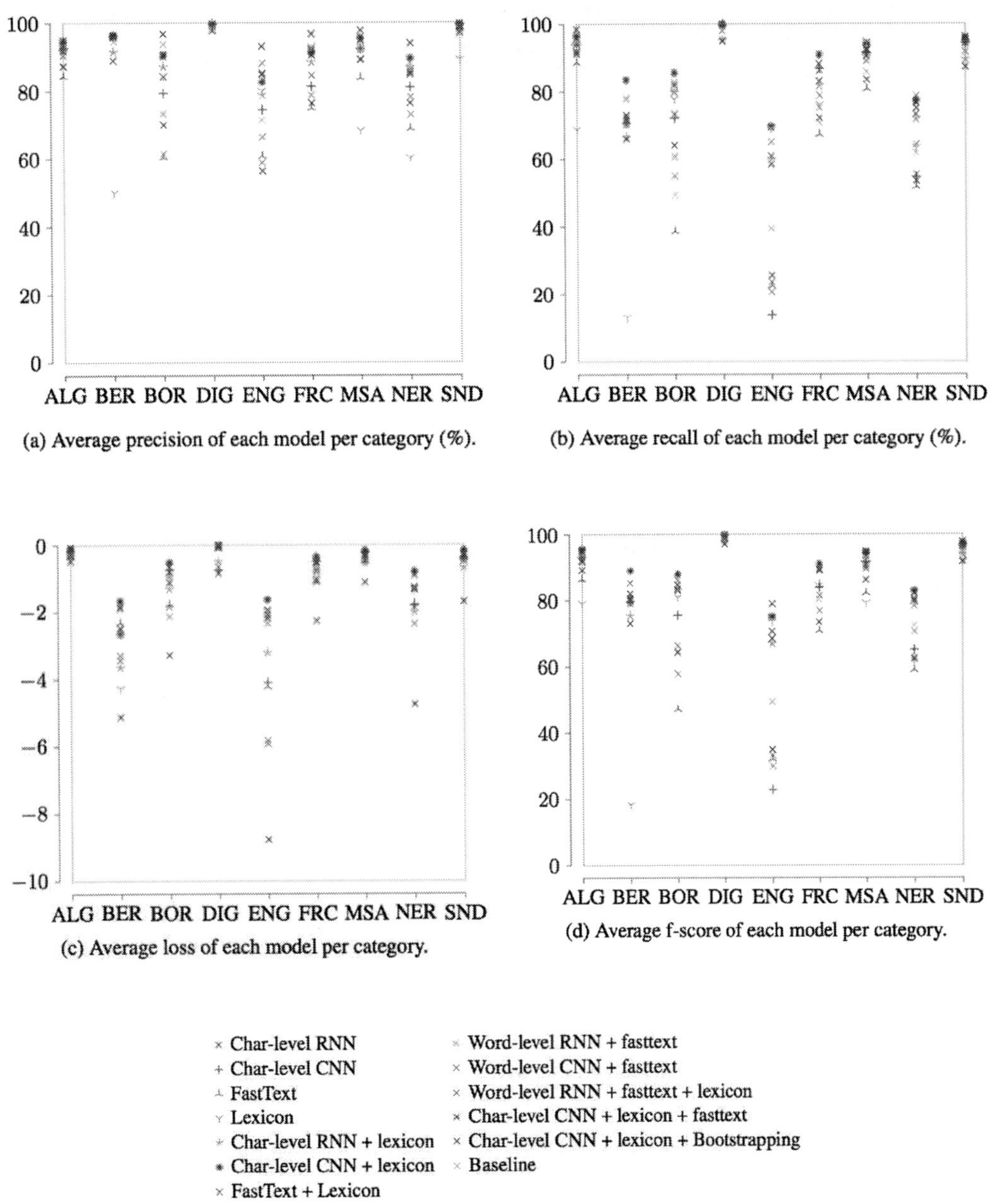

(a) Average precision of each model per category (%).

(b) Average recall of each model per category (%).

(c) Average loss of each model per category.

(d) Average f-score of each model per category.

Figure 2: Average performance of each model per category.

combined model makes the same errors as previous models but less frequently.

Overall, the results in this section show that a simple Char-level CNN model outperforms the more complicated baseline system which uses a back-off strategy and extra resources. However the Char-level CNN model performs worse on the minority classes, particularly on NER, ENG and BER. On the other hand, the other models perform better on the minority classes in terms of recall, but they perform worse on the remaining categories because of the limited coverage of the lexicons or because of lexical ambiguity. This means that the performance of these models is in complementary distribution. We will explore this observation in the following section.

4.2 Models with Background Knowledge

One possible improvement of the models in Section 4.1 is to inject information from the lexicons and the knowledge encoded in the fasttext to the DNN models. In Table 4 we report the average error rate of only the best performing experiments combining different models and resources.

	Model	ER (%)
1	Char-level RNN + lexicon	8.27
2	Word-level RNN + fasttext	8.20
3	Word-level RNN + fasttext + lexicon	**5,34**
4	Char-level CNN + lexicon	**5.18**
5	Word-level CNN + fasttext	9.75
6	Char-level CNN + lexicon + fasttext	6.23
7	Char-level CNN + lexicon + Bootstrapping	5.23
8	Baseline	9.52

Table 4: Average error rate of the models with background knowledge.

The results show that RNN models (with original error rate of 13.38% for Char-level RNN) benefit from both adding the lexicon (1) and the fasttext (2). The gain is even higher when combining both with the Word-level RNN (3). The CNN models behave differently when adding lexicon and fasttext. The Char-level CNN (4) performs best with the lexicon with 3% error reduction. The Word-level CNN (5) performs worse with fasttext compared to basic Char-level CNN introducing a 1.57% increase in the error rate (Table 3). Also the Char-level CNN (6) does not benefit from combining lexicon and fasttext. It appears that the latter introduces noise that CNN is sensitive to. Likewise, additional bootstrapped training data does not help the otherwise best performing Char-level

CNN + lexicon model (7). This may be also explained by the additional noise in the bootstrapped data.

Figure 2 indicates that adding lexicon information has a positive effect on the overall performance of the RNN models. The gain from the lexicons is noticeable on all categories where precision, recall and f-score increase, most importantly on BER, BOR, ENG, FRC and NER. The same kind of errors are present as with the previous models but fewer in number. For instance the number of errors between ALG-MSA drops from 1,077 to 724, and between FRC-ALG from 104 to 64.

Adding lexicon information to the Char-level CNN model boosts its overall performance over models not using lexicons. All the categories benefit from the lexicon information and their f-score, recall and precision increase, most importantly on the minority categories such as ENG, with the same errors but less frequent. However, adding fasttext does not improve the performance of the Word-level CNN model. Its average f-score decreases on all categories except on ENG where it increases from 22.76 to 29.91.

Compared with the Char-level CNN + lexicon model, adding fasttext to Char-level CNN does not have the same positive effect. The only significant gain is an increase in precision on ENG from 82.59% to 84.79%. Char-level CNN + fasttext + lexicon model performs better than the FastText + Lexicon model. It seems that fasttext does not help the CNN model.

On the other hand, adding fasttext to an RNN boosts its performance. The error rate drops to 13.38% (Char-level RNN) and 8.20% (Word-level RNN). While the precision of each category improves, the recall drops on both BOR and ENG categories, by 3.35% and 1.97% respectively. The f-score increases on all categories except on ENG where it drops by 1.76%.

Examining the effect of lexicon and fasttext on the RNN models, we find that the precision on the minority categories, chiefly BOR, ENG, FRC, NER is higher when adding lexicon (87.10%, 78.77%, 88.36%, and 86.77%) compared to when adding fasttext (73.26%, 66.37%, 84.45% and 78.07%), but the precision on BER is better when adding the fasttext (96.18% compared to 91.51%). The same trend is observed for recall where BER is the only category that benefits from fasttext compared to lexicon (70.65% compared to 66.47%). ENG is the category which is most negatively effected when adding fasttext with a drastic decrease of 36.45% (23.62% with fasttext and 60.07% with lexicon), followed by BOR with 18.98% decrease, and NER with 7.54% decrease. The f-scores have the same pattern as the recall.

A gain of adding lexicon to the Word-level RNN + fasttext model is observed on all categories. While precision increases on all categories, for example on ENG from 78.77% without the lexicon to 88.04% with the lexicon, it slightly decreases for NER from 86.77% to 85.97% and SND from 99.00% to 98.86%. The recall and f-score increase on all categories.

The gain from using the bootstrapped data is mainly reflected in an increase in precision on the minority categories such as ENG, BOR, FRC and NER (93.04%, 96.71%, 96.68% and 93.85% compared to 82.60%, 90.56%, 91.31% and 89.43% respectively without using the bootstrapped data). In terms of recall, the bootstrapped data only boosts ALG and SND categories. The f-scores of the model trained without the bootstrapped data are better on all categories. The insignificant effect of the bootstrapped data could be attributed to the additional noise introduced by the baseline system.

5   Related Work

The emerging digitised multilingual data that followed the introduction of new technologies and communication services has attracted attention of the NLP research community in terms of how to process such linguistic data that resulted from language contact between several related and unrelated languages, for example in detection of code-switching where mainly traditional sequence labelling methods are used for Bengali-English-Hindi (Barman et al., 2014a), Nepali-English (Barman et al., 2014b), Spanish-English and MSA-Egyptian Arabic (Diab et al., 2016), MSA-Moroccan Arabic (Samih and Maier, 2016), MSA-Algerian Arabic-Berber-French-English (Adouane and Dobnik, 2017), etc.

The work most closely related to ours is described in (Samih et al., 2016) who used a supervised LSTM-RNN model combined with Conditional Random Fields to detect switching points between related languages (MSA - Egyptian Arabic) trained on a small dataset from Twitter. However, the system was only evaluated on the major-

ity categories. Similarly, Kocmi and Bojar (2017) proposed a supervised bidirectional LSTM-RNN trained on artificially created multilingual edited texts. These does not fully reflect all the complexities of real linguistic use in a multilingual scenario.

Adouane et al. (2018) propose a character-level GRU-RNN on the same task as described here backed by the available unlabelled data. They report that their supervised RNN model performs the best on labels with more representative samples. Adding neural language model that was pre-trained on noisy unlabelled data does not help, but bootstrapping the unlabelled data with another system improves the performance of all their systems. In this work we use different DNN architectures (RNNs and CNNs), and we aim to examine the behaviour of each model when injecting background knowledge in the form of encoded information from the available lexicons and a pre-trained sub-word embeddings from unlabelled data. Our goal is to take advantage of the available NLP resources, with as little processing as possible to mitigate the problem of scarce annotated data.

6   Conclusion

We have presented DNN models for detecting code-switching and borrowing for an under-resourced language. We investigated how to improve these models by injecting background knowledge in the form of lexicons and/or pre-trained sub-word embeddings trained on an unlabelled corpus, thus taking advantage of the scarce NLP resources currently available. The results show that the models behave differently for each category of added knowledge. While adding information from the lexicons markedly improves the performance of all models, adding knowledge in the form of pre-trained sub-word embeddings improves the RNN model more than the CNN model. Bootstrapping does not bring a significant overall contribution to performance of our models which is surprising given the previous reports in the literature. However, it does boost precision of the minority categories. One future direction worth exploring is how to deal with the problem of misspellings and spelling variations to reduce the irregularities in non-standardised user-generated data as this appears to have a strong effect on the performance of RNN and CNN models.

Acknowledgement

The research reported in this paper was supported by a grant from the Swedish Research Council (VR project 2014-39) for the establishment of the Centre for Linguistic Theory and Studies in Probability (CLASP) at the University of Gothenburg.

References

Wafia Adouane and Simon Dobnik. 2017. *Identification of Languages in Algerian Arabic Multilingual Documents*. Association for Computational Linguistics.

Wafia Adouane, Simon Dobnik, Jean-Philippe Bernardy, and Nasredine Semmar. 2018. *A Comparison of Character Neural Language Model and Bootstrapping for Language Identification in Multilingual Noisy Texts*. In Proceedings of the Second Workshop on Subword and Character Level Models in NLP, New Orleans, Louisiana USA.

Utsab Barman, Amitava Das, Joachim Wagner, and Jennifer Foster. 2014a. Code-mixing: A challenge for Language Identification in the Language of Social Media. In *In Proceedings of the First Workshop on Computational Approaches to Code-Switching*.

Utsab Barman, Joachim Wagner, Grzegorz Chrupala, and Jennifer Foster. 2014b. Dcu-uvt: Word-Level Language Classification with Code-Mixed Data.

Piotr Bojanowski, Edouard Grave, Armand Joulin, and Tomas Mikolov. 2016. Enriching Word Vectors with Subword Information. *arXiv preprint arXiv:1607.04606*.

Mona Diab, Pascale Fung, Mahmoud Ghoneim, Julia Hirschberg, and Thamar Solorio. 2016. *Proceedings of the Second Workshop on Computational Approaches to Code Switching*. Association for Computational Linguistics, Austin, Texas.

Charles Albert Ferguson. 1959. Diglossia. *WORD, Routledge*, 15(2):325–340.

Joshua Aaron Fishman. 1967. Bilingualism with and without Diglossia; Diglossia with and without Bilingualism. *Journal of Social Issues*, 23:29 – 38.

Tom Kocmi and Ondřej Bojar. 2017. Lanidenn: Multilingual Language Identification on Text Stream. In *Proceedings of the 15th Conference of the European Chapter of the Association for Computational Linguistics: Volume 1, Long Papers*, pages 927–936. Association for Computational Linguistics.

James Milroy. 2001. Language Ideologies and the Consequence of Standardization. *Journal of Sociolinguistics*, 5:530 – 555.

Shana Poplack and Marjory Meechan. 1998. How Languages Fit Together in Codemixing. *The International Journal of Bilingualism*, 2(2):127–138.

Younes Samih, Suraj Maharjan, Mohammed Attia, Laura Kallmeyer, and Thamar Solorio. 2016. Multilingual Code-switching Identification via LSTM Recurrent Neural Networks. In *Proceedings of the Second Workshop on Computational Approaches to Code Switching*, pages 50–59.

Younes Samih and Wolfgang Maier. 2016. Detecting Code-Switching in Moroccan Arabic. In *Proceedings of SocialNLP @ IJCAI-2016*.

Lotfi Sayahi. 2014. *Diglossia and Language Contact: Language Variation and Change in North Africa*. Cambridge Approaches to Language Contact. Cambridge University Press.

Code-Mixed Question Answering Challenge: Crowd-sourcing Data and Techniques

*Khyathi Raghavi Chandu   °Ekaterina Loginova
△Vishal Gupta   °Josef van Genabith   °Günter Neuman
▽Manoj Chinnakotla   *Eric Nyberg   *Alan Black

*Language Technologies Institute, Carnegie Mellon University
°Deutsche Forschungszentrum für Künstliche Intelligenz, △IIIT Hyderabad, ▽Microsoft, USA
{kchandu, ehn, awb}@andrew.cmu.edu
{ekaterina.loginova, Josef.van_Genabith, neumann}@dfki.de
vishal.gupta@research.iiit.ac.in, manojc@microsoft.com

Abstract

Code-Mixing (CM) is the phenomenon of alternating between two or more languages which is prevalent in bi- and multi-lingual communities. Most NLP applications today are still designed with the assumption of a single interaction language and are most likely to break given a CM utterance with multiple languages mixed at a morphological, phrase or sentence level. For example, popular commercial search engines do not yet fully understand the intents expressed in CM queries. As a first step towards fostering research which supports CM in NLP applications, we systematically crowd-sourced and curated an evaluation dataset for factoid question answering in three CM languages - Hinglish (Hindi+English), Tenglish (Telugu+English) and Tamlish (Tamil+English) which belong to two language families. We share the details of our data collection process, techniques which were used to avoid inducing lexical bias amongst the crowd workers and other CM specific linguistic properties of the dataset. Our final dataset, which is available freely for research purposes, has 1,694 Hinglish, 2,848 Tamlish and 1,391 Tenglish factoid questions and their answers. We discuss the techniques used by the participants for the first edition of this ongoing challenge.

1 Introduction

Code-Mixing (CM) is formally defined as the embedding of linguistic units such as phrases, words, and morphemes of one language into an utterance of another language, which is commonly observed in multilingual communities ((Myers-Scotton, 1997), (Poplack, 1980), (Muysken, 2000)). Traditionally, some studies (Yow and Patrycia, 2011) have viewed the mixing of two independent codes as lack of fluency of the segment of population in either of the languages. However, an alternate perspective (Milroy and Muysken, 1995) argues that mixing of two traditionally isolated linguistic codes potentially creates a third legitimate code. Researchers (Crystal, 1997) have also presented several socio-cultural reasons and motivations for switching. There have been studies to depict the usage of particular language based on the emotional attachment and the sentiment of the person towards that topic (Rudra et al., 2016). In this paper, we adopt the perspective of descriptive linguistics and make an effort to describe this prevalent form of language as it occurs, without adopting a prescriptive approach.

Ubiquitous access to social media tools and platforms have also made CM the preferred choice for both formal and informal communication. In such settings, where the communication is either semi-formal or informal, researchers ((Bali et al., 2014), (Barman et al., 2014)) have observed a higher tendency for multilingual speakers to use CM. We studied a sample of conversation logs from a commercial chit-chat based conversational agent in the Indian market. The agent was trained to engage in informal chat conversations with the help of a database of Twitter conversations from the Indian market. Since India is a multilingual country with a large number of multilingual speakers, we notice that users often freely use each language individually or their CM versions while conversing with the agent. We notice that, in around 3% of overall conversations, users were found to be chatting with the agent in CM language such as *'hello, kya chal raha hai'* (Meaning: hello, what's up?). Interestingly, in cases where the response of the agent was in CM language such as *'sorry yaar'* (Meaning: sorry friend), users too

Proceedings of The Third Workshop on Computational Approaches to Code-Switching, pages 29–38
Melbourne, Australia, July 19, 2018. ©2018 Association for Computational Linguistics

responded back in CM language in 27% of those times. There have been other studies regarding the quantitative and qualitative aspects of code-switching on social media along similar lines (Hidayat, 2008). However, a large number of NLP applications, such as Question Answering (QA), Dialogue Systems, Summarization etc, still continue to be designed with the assumption of a single interaction language such as English (Brill et al., 2002), Hindi ((Kumar et al., 2005)), Chinese ((Yongkui et al., 2003), (Sun et al., 2008)). Such systems are most likely to break given a CM utterance which has multiple languages mixed at sentence, phrase or morphological level. Hence, it is highly imperative for researchers to focus on building more robust end-user NLP applications which can understand and process CM language.

Building a good evaluation dataset for Factoid QA in CM is wrought with challenges such as a) ensuring that the annotators are unbiased in anyway to artificially use CM b) recruiting a good team of native bi-lingual speakers as annotators c) maintaining a good quality and diversity of questions across intents, answer types and entities. In this paper, we describe our experience in dealing with the above challenges while creating the dataset. We used a crowd-sourcing platform for collecting data where the crowd workers were restricted to only native language (Hindi, Telugu and Tamil) speakers. We shared a detailed set of guidelines and instructions about the task with the crowd workers and also ran them through some basic quality checks before collection of actual data. Finally, we were able to collect around 1,694 Hinglish, 2,848 Tamlish and 1,391 Tenglish factoid questions along with their answers. We have organized a Code-Mixed Question Answering challenge based on this data for the first edition of this challenge. There are 7 teams that registered and took the data from us. In this paper, we discuss the preliminary techniques that 2 of these groups used. To summarize, the following are the main contributions of this paper:

• We curated an evaluation dataset for the task of Factoid QA in CM languages with more than 5000 QA pairs for Hinglish, Tamlish and Tenglish languages. We also make it freely available for research purposes.

• We share our experiences related to eliciting lexically unbiased CM questions by using images as anchor points.

• We present the techniques used in the first edition of the CM QA challenge.

2 Related Work

Early work in this domain include investigating CM phenomenon in a formal and computational framework (Joshi, 1982) and developing formalisms (Goyal et al., 2003), (Sinha and Thakur, 2005). Recent years have seen attention towards part of speech tagging for CM languages and gathering corpora ((Vyas et al., 2014), (Solorio and Liu, 2008), (Jamatia et al., 2015), (Soto and Hirschberg, 2017)) for it. Language identification in mixed language scenarios has also been studied recently ((Barman et al., 2014), (Chittaranjan et al., 2014)) and has also been aggressively addressed as a shared task at major conferences ((Solorio et al., 2014), (Sequiera et al., 2015)). Some of the other applications that were picked up in research in CM over the past few years include Named Entity Recognition (Zirikly and Diab, 2015), semantic parsing (Duong et al., 2017), dependency parsing (Partanen et al., 2018) and shallow parsing (Sharma et al., 2016). While the above work focusses on important language processing challenges in CM, we are more interested in end-user NLP applications which support CM such as Factoid QA in CM languages.

Eliciting a corpus of CM questions by paraphrasing an English question was used to perform question classification (Raghavi et al., 2015). While this method has the advantage of having a ground truth parallel text, the possibility of lexical bias from the English question while framing the code-mixed question exists. An extension to this work was proposed by building an end-to-end web based CM question answering system named WebShodh (Chandu et al., 2017). Efforts have been made to develop cross lingual QA systems that take questions in English and answer back in English but search for candidate answers in Hindi newspapers (Sekine and Grishman, 2003) along with other machine learning approaches (Nanda et al., 2016). There has been some work in the early 2000s to generate a dialog based QA system in Telugu to support Railway inquiries (Reddy and Bandyopadhyay, 2006). This kind of cross language QA system is being researched for European languages as well (Neumann and Sacaleanu, 2003). A dataset of 506 questions from messages from Facebook was proposed in the Bengali-English CM domain (Banerjee et al., 2016). Our dataset is over ten times larger than this data and takes into account the lexical variation brought in by collecting questions from images and code-mixed articles.

3 Dataset Collection

In order to study differences between lexical bias from entrainment and elicit lexically diverse questions, we employ two modes of data collection: eliciting code-mixed questions from a) images and b) code-mixed articles. The former are general questions and the latter are context specific questions (similar to machine reading). Techniques of collecting queries for a dialog system by presenting scenarios symbolically and diagrammatically was previously used (Black et al., 2011) in order to minimize supplying lexical and phrasal cues. For collection of Hinglish data, we used both these approaches whereas for collecting Tenglish and Tamlish data, we used only images. This is because for Hinglish, we could find informative blogging websites based on which it is easier to frame factoid code-mixed questions. However, to the best of our knowledge, during the time of our annotation, such fact based code-mixed content was still not available in Tenglish/Tamlish. It is also noted that it is less likely to get questions that have abstract answers (beyond the realm of physical entities) when they are collected based on images.

3.1 Challenges in Code-Mixed Factoid Questions Collection

We faced the following challenges during the data collection task.

1. How would we eliminate the bias towards using English in general scenarios while using a search engine etc.,? In other words, we need to encourage crowd workers to provide us with data that is neither biased to English monolingual questions due to preconceptions of the language preference while interacting with a computer, nor bias them to provide mixed language data if it does not feel natural to them.

2. How do we eliminate responses from people who are not native speakers? To mitigate this problem, we have given the instructions to each of these target languages in romanized code-mixed version of the corresponding languages mixed with English. This has the dual advantage of being understood only by those who have enough competence in the matrix language as well as easing them into code-mixing and making them comfortable with it.

3. How do we elicit factoid questions? This is a trivial issue. We had to explain what a factoid question is while providing sufficient examples of factoid and non-factoid questions.

4. How do we collect questions that are general enough that they could be answered without providing the context of the images (for image based questions)? The design of the task to collect questions based on images, in order to study the comparative lexical bias when a code-mixed article is given, has resulted in a lot of questions that are related to multi-modal reasoning. For example, Tenglish question *'image lo entha mandi unnaaru?'* (Meaning: How many people are there in the image?) requires a visual in order to answer. We removed such questions in the post processing after data collection.

We ensured a good mix of categories while selecting the target fulcrum entity images (example: guitar, bicycle), location (example: Eiffel Tower, Golden Gate Bridge), person (example: Roger Federer, Eminem), event (example: World War 2, Dandi March). Out of these, we manually selected 80 images from which factoid questions can be asked. To gather questions based on articles, we first scraped documents from *hinglishpedia.com*, randomly selected 80 articles from them and made sure that all of them were code-mixed. The crowd-workers are then requested to form factoid questions based on these articles such that the answers to the questions are present in the corresponding article.

3.2 Crowd-sourcing for Question & Answer Collection

We engaged with two streams of demographics while collecting the data: university students and crowd-workers. Each participant is allowed to provide us with only 20 questions to avoid idiolectic biases i.e, biases of each individual. In the first step, we performed the activity in a more controlled environment in university classrooms. The instructors of the classrooms were requested to give a brief presentation we made about what code-mixing is along with some example questions. This was performed to alleviate the bias against mixing while interacting with a machine. The students (with native languages among Hindi, Telugu and Tamil) were given clear explanations about factoid and non-factoid questions in order to elicit the right kind of questions for our task.

In the second phase, we migrated this setup to Amazon Mechanical Turk task, where crowd-workers were redirected to our interface[1] of mixed language instructions based on their native language. Each accepted Human Intelligence Test

---

[1] `https://docs.google.com/`
`document/d/1CTFTjmU6RKUwsNH1z0Sjl_`
`8EZt8dz1-VGF5VwPLIpy0/edit?usp=`
`sharing(toanonymize)`

Category of Questions	Num	Multilingual Index	Language Entropy	Integration Index	Avg Length
Hinglish image questions	1,419	0.72	0.61	0.25	7.50
Hinglish article questions	275	0.88	0.66	0.29	8.90
Tamlish questions	2,848	0.69	0.59	0.24	5.56
Tenglish questions	1,391	0.80	0.64	0.28	5.90

Table 1: *Data Statistics: The code-mixing metrics for Hinglish (Hindi+English), Tamlish (Tamil+English) and Tenglish (Telugu+English) questions*

(HIT) was compensated with \$2.50 on the Turk setup. We have got a lot more responses for Tamlish questions as compared to both Hinglish and Tenglish together as reflected in Table 1. In this scenario, although the turkers have not been formally explained about what code-mixing is apart from providing them with instructions and examples, most of the data we received included mixed language Romanized questions. While in the former scenario, the collected questions were explicitly moderated to remain within bilingual and multilingual environments, like in India, the latter scenario does not ensure this, as they do not have to be present in India. The extent of code-mixing and fluency of the questions may vary as compared to the questions collected from Indian classroom environment due to the difference in their socio-cultural environments. Though we have mentioned in the instructions to provide us with questions that sound natural to the participants, we acknowledge that it may not have been completely natural as they were explicitly requested to mix two languages. The third phase involves collecting answers to all the questions. Monolingual questions and image-based questions that contain referring expressions, such as *'in this figure'* were removed before collecting answers. To filter out noisy and random answers, the set-up includes a qualifying CM question for which we clearly knew the answer. When collecting answers, we only accept them from workers who correctly answer the qualifying question.

3.3 Curation and Post-processing

After data collection, we removed duplicate entries and also performed one step of human verification. This responsibility was divided into two phases. The first step was employing certain post processing steps in order to remove the questions that did not match the presented specifications and rejecting them. One major problem is the use of referring expressions and determiners corresponding to the images about which the questions were asked. In each of the three languages, we made a list of all possible spelling variants of referring expressions like *'image/picture mein'*

(Meaning: in the image), *'ye'* (Meaning: this), *'iss'* (Meaning: this) and separated the questions that contain these expressions. The same process was not done for questions collected based on code-mixed articles. This is because referring expressions corresponding to the given text do not hinder searching for an answer in the given snippet. Lexical level language identification is performed to remove the questions that do not have atleast one word from both the languages. These selected questions after filtering are then curated and gone through manually to add back the questions that made sense before rejecting the HITs. The next level of curation was performed during the answer collection phase. This was necessary because it was still possible to bypass these curation conditions. For example, there were some entries that seemed like English queries with an additional suffix belonging to the corresponding native language at the end of some of the words. For example, *'Whatil isil waterfalla borderil America and Canada?'* (Tamlish question for 'What is the waterfall in the border of America and Canada'). On the other hand there are queries that seemed to have been translated using an online translation tool into the matrix language and randomly inserting some English words in between. For example, *'Mein which Indian state did Mother Teresa kaam kiya?'* (Hinglish question). This example seems to be a lexical level translation of first, eighth and ninth words of the English question 'In which Indian state did Mother Teresa work (past-tense)?' into Hindi. 67.87% of the data collected from Turk was acceptable and passed our curation tests. Among the remaining, about 21% were rejected due to the use of referring expressions, 11% due to erroneous attempts by typing junk words. All the questions passed the curation tests for more than 90% of the accepted HITs and some of the questions were acceptable for the remaining 10%. This implies that the instructions provided for the task were sufficiently clear to elicit CM factoid questions. The above are the statistics for the data corresponding to the crowd sourced platform that might provide a baseline estimate for collecting useful data for this domain on such platforms.

Since the number of curators is much less (approximately 6 people) than the number of crowd-workers, we need to understand that the curation process is much more expensive in terms of manual effort. The above steps are taken to elicit quality data for our purposes. The tasks of collecting questions and answers were deliberately separated for two reasons. One is to ensure clarity of the task and make sure that the users are giving naturally code-mixed questions and asking them to provide answers in English within the same task might lead to unnecessary biases or confusion. The second reason is that when asked to provide questions and answers together, one might tend to ask the simplest questions to which answers are already known to them. This in turn might have reduced the variety of questions for the same anchor point. We have also collected feedback about each question whether it is a factoid and if additional multi-modal information is needed to answer it, during the answer collection phase.

4 Data Analysis

Recent studies have focused on empirical measurements of code-switching (Guzmán et al., 2017). The multilingual index(M-Index), Language Entropy and Integration index(I-index) measure the extent of mixing and switching frequency. Table 1 presents the statistics of out dataset along with these metrics for mixing. The average number of words per question is higher in Hinglish compared to Tamlish and Tenglish. The M-index for all the 3 language pairs are in comparable ranges while it is slightly less for Tamlish. The questions are provided along with the following information: (1) language information (2) question type annotated as 'context dependent' (for article based questions) and 'context independent' (for images based questions) and (3) corresponding article for article based questions.

4.1 Answer Type Distribution

In order to analyze the distribution of question types in our dataset, we sampled questions, from Tenglish and Hinglish, which contain either of the following two selected images - 'Taj Mahal' and 'Hiroshima'. We use the coarse and fine-grained type hierarchies proposed by (Li and Roth, 2006) for annotating the questions. For the first image: 'Taj Mahal', we had 91 Tenglish questions and 71 Hinglish questions. For Tenglish questions, the distribution of coarse level types were 34 PERSON, 8 ENTITY, 30 LOCATION and 19 NUMERIC. For Hinglish questions, the coarse-

type distribution was found to be 25 PERSON, 9 ENTITY, 22 LOCATION and 15 NUMERIC. An interesting observation we noticed was that - there were 23 Tenglish and 17 Hinglish variants of the question *'Who built Taj Mahal?'* and similarly there were 12 Tenglish and 8 Hinglish variants of the question *'In which city is Taj Mahal located?'*. A similar analysis for the other focus entity 'Hiroshima' gave us 21 Tenglish questions distributed as 7 NUMERIC, 9 LOCATION, 4 ENTITY, 1 PERSON type questions and 14 Hinglish questions distributed as 10 NUMERIC, 2 LOCATION, 1 ENTITY and 1 PERSON type questions. Among these we observed 4 and 8 variants in Tenglish and Hinglish respectively for the question *'In which year did attack on Hiroshima and Nagasaki take place?'*. These statistics reveal that, for the same image shown to them, participants issued questions resulting in a variety of answer types in the target code-mixed languages. Figure 1 shows the percentage distribution of the question types for 'Taj Mahal' and 'Hiroshima' across the three language pairs.

In order to gain better intuitions on the *'why and how'* of code-mixing, the collected questions are studied with respect to idiolectic language preferences, i.e the idiosyncrasies of mixing the languages and the extent of code-mixing across languages. To study the individual mixing biases in the data, *Multilingual Index* is calculated for each individual in each of the language pairs. Figure 2 shows histograms for idiolects of Hinglish, Tenglish and Tamlish. As can be observed from the figure, Hinglish and Tenglish has many crowd-workers towards the higher end of multilingual index whereas Tamlish has a rather smoother distribution except for the last range.

4.2 Lexical Bias in Article based Questions

The bias of copying the words was mitigated to an extent by the usage of images as anchor points to collect questions. However, studying the lexical bias when a code-mixed article is given acts as a proxy to study entrainment. The variant of expressing the questions from code-mixed articles serves two purposes. One is to study the differences in difficulty of down stream task of retrieving for question answering as compared to the image based questions. In this category of questions, the answer is present in the snippets that are given and the focus is primarily on retrieving the answers from within the given text. The second is to study the varying lexical biases to frame a question when code-mixed content is given versus when it is not. To study this empiri-

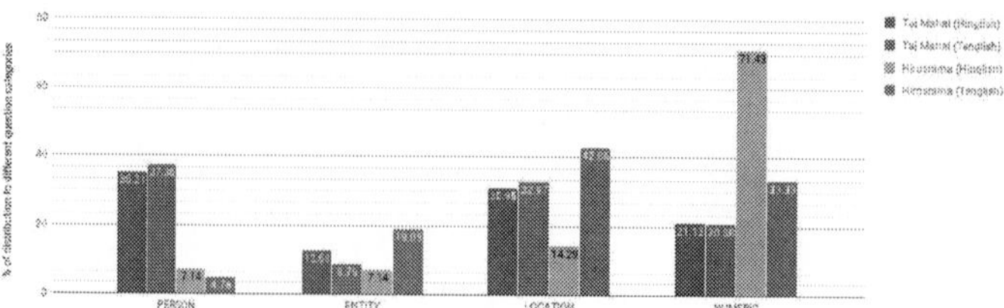

Figure 1: Distribution of question types in Hinglish and Tenglish for 2 topics: Taj Mahal and Hiroshima

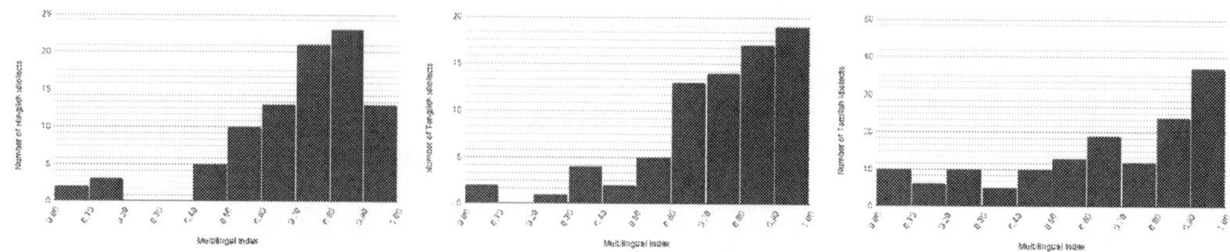

(a) Hinglish idiolectic mixing distribu-(b) Tenglish idiolectic mixing distribu-(c) Tamlish idiolectic mixing distribution
tion   tion

Figure 2: Histograms for Multilingual index for idiolects for Hinglish, Tenglish and Tamlish

cally, we calculated the percentage of intersection of words between question and articles. The average of overlapping words is 54.20%, while the minimum and maximum are 12.5% and 92.31% respectively. Similarly, the longest overlapping subsequences have a mean of 2.24 with a minimum of 1 word and a maximum of 16 words.

4.3 Mixing Phenomena observed in the Data

One of the interesting categories of mixing that is observed in the data is mixing gender information of the native and the mixed form of the word. For example, consider the question from the data, *'earth kab form hui thi?'* (English meaning: When was Earth formed?). A paraphrase of the same question is *'dharthi kab form hui thi?'*. In Hindi, the gender of the verb has to agree with the subject. While the gender of Earth is masculine (which should have agreed with *'hua'* and not *'hui'*), the gender of *dharthi* (which agrees with *'hui'*) is feminine as perceived by a native speaker. But as observed in the question, feminine form *'hui'* is used with 'Earth' which is mixed word from English. Sebba (2009) refers to this as one type of 'harmonization strategy' in language mixing and it is one that he says might be typical of highly literate bilinguals. We believe the naturalness of the data is highly dependent on the nativity of annotators. Throughout our process, we took as much care to ensure that we use native speakers of the language for our annotation. However, there were still a few exceptions. We

also tried avoiding completely random, spurious and noisy inputs by checking if they were simply permutations of the original input and their lexically translated words.

A known problem in dealing with code-mixed text is non-standardized Romanization of native language when mixed with English. Phonological perceptions of a syllable can be represented differently. For example, from the data a couple of the very frequent such variations are *'kon'* and *'kaun'* for 'who' in Hindi, and *'he'* and *'hai'* for 'is' in Hindi. For both these words, the latter variants are closer to the pronunciation of the Hindi words, but the other sounds are in colloquial usage frequently as well. Consider the question, *'Friends serial ke kitne seasons banaye ja chukein hain?'* (Meaning: How many seasons were made for Friends serial?). Using *'n'* in *'chukein'* indicates that the person literally transliterated the Hindi spelling into Roman spelling because colloquially the *'n'* sound is often omitted while speaking. A similar observation applies to the word *'kartein'* (Meaning: do). Similarly, 'pe' is a more colloquial usage of the word 'par' (Meaning: on). Though 'pe' is never used in standard written Hindi, the data collected has both variants of the words. Similar observations in Tenglish data include variations for *'cheyinchaadu'* and *'ceyincadu'* (both the words mean 'did'). This problem compounds in Tenglish since Telugu is an agglutinative lan-

34

guage. For example, in the variants *'chesthu un-aadu'* and *'chesthunnadu'* (meaning: have been doing (masculine form)), the two words can be written together as a single word or separately.

Some of the examples show forcible mixing since the instructions specifically mentioned to provide code-mixed questions. For example, *'Android ko Google ne kab buy kiya tha?'* (Meaning: 'When did Google buy Android?'). The word *'khareed'* which means 'buy' is a very common Hindi word and in such cases, the native word is used more naturally as opposed to the mixed word. 10 such examples were selected from Hinglish and shown to 5 native speakers of Hindi to annotate if they seem natural, unnatural or neutral. All these examples were marked as either unnatural (36%) or neutral (64%) and none of them were marked as natural. This shows that there is some pattern or notion of mixing words for native speakers.

In some other examples, we also observed what can be considered an opposite of forced mixing. For example, in question *'1994 mein premier kiya hua pramukh American comedy TV saathiyon ka naam kya hai?'* (Meaning: What is the name of the famous American comedy TV show Friends that was premiered in 1994?), words like *'pramukh'* (Meaning: famous) and *'saathiyon'* (Meaning: friends) are less common in common usage compared to their English mixing counterparts. Also, note that this is uncommon since the named entity 'Friends' is translated to the Hindi counterpart. Another known phenomenon is the mixing of languages at morphological level which was observed very commonly in the data. This poses a problem for word level modeling or formulation for addressing the down stream tasks such as our current case of question answering. For example, in the Tenglish question *'Eiffel Tower ni entha mandi architectlu design chesaru?'* (Meaning: How many architects designed Eiffel Tower?), the word *'architectlu'* (Meaning: architects) is mixed at morphological level by English word 'architect' and Telugu suffix *'lu'*, which is a plural marker.

5 CM QA Challenge: Techniques

The CM QA challenge was announced and broadcasted during the summer of 2017. The task is to provide a ranked list of relevant answers for given CM queries. The image based questions are annotated as 'general' and the article based questions are provided with the corresponding articles. While 7 teams have registered to take part in the challenge and have collected data from the organizers, a couple of teams have successfully completed participating in the challenge. In this section, we discuss the techniques used by two participating groups to address the first edition of this challenge.

As discussed in Section 3, there are 2 categories of questions; (1) general questions where there is no context, and (2) article based questions for which the answers are retrieved from a given context. To address the latter type, paragraphs from Wikipedia are leveraged as general context. One team (from Deutsche Forschungszentrum für Künstliche Intelligenz (DFKI)) addressed this by identifying the named entities in the CM query and look them up in the summaries of Wikipedia articles [2]. These summaries typically contain 5 sentences. The second team (from IIIT Hyderabad) trained a similarity model using DSSM (Huang et al., 2013) to retrieve and rank the answer bearing sentences from Wikipedia. Both the groups have worked along similar lines to address questions with general context.

The team from DFKI dealt with article based questions as well. At this stage, both the categories of questions contain query and information about relevant paragraph. A pre-trained Document Reader model DrQA proposed by Chen et al. (2017) on a popular machine reading QA dataset SQuAD (Rajpurkar et al., 2016) is used for this domain. This model answers open domain factoid questions using Wikipedia by not considering document retrieval. An open source implementation of this model[3] is used and our results are lower than we expected: average EM is 0.0691 and average F1 is 0.1001 on the training dataset. In the category of general questions (image based) where the relevant paragraph is not given, the predicted answer is similar in meaning to the ground truth but can be broader. For instance, when the Hinglish answering 'eminem ka profession kya hai?' (Meaning: What is Eminem's profession?), this system gives 'rapper, record producer, and actor', as compared to 'Rapper'. Though the system is correct, the answer gathered included only 'rapper' which most data collection techniques for QA face an issue. To train these models, Hindi embedding space is mapped into the English one. A standard approach in relation to Hindi was investigated by (Bhattacharya et al., 2016) involving finding a translation matrix (using linear regression) that minimizes the reconstruction error between target language embeddings and translated embeddings.

---

[2] `https://pypi.org/project/wikipedia`
[3] `https://github.com/facebookresearch/DrQA`

This idea is developed by using a neural network and a random forest regression to find translation matrix. By using Polyglot Hindi and English embeddings with Universal Word-Hindi Dictionary we achieve MSE score of 0.057.

6   Challenges observed in CM QA

Gathering more data: The training subset contains 1295 unique question-answer pairs, which poses a significant challenge to train complex models from scratch. As an alternative, a transfer learning technique can be used, using a model pre-trained on a large-scale open-domain factoid dataset, such as SQuAD. For instance, community question answering forums can be used, which naturally contains a lot of code-mixed language due to the extensive borrowing of technical terms. Such setup has two benefits: it eases the problem of collecting new data and alleviates the need to manually label it.

Spell Checking: Since the question-answer pairs are coming from an informal background, some of them are misspelt. Language identification is an overhead to deal with this using traditional spell checking techniques. An extensive use of dictionaries is the most obvious approach, but a more practical solution might be to use character-based methods and introduce artificial noise to make models more robust.

Romanization variability: It should also be noted that apart from spell checking, there is variability in romanization output. For example, the Hindi word 'jidhar'(Meaning: where) can either be written as 'jidhr'. As it is unclear which of the models of transliteration would a user prefer, a developer needs to keep all options open.

Poor translation from open source tools: In many cases, translation tools completely distort the meaning of the sentence. An illustrative example of this is: 'Sun ka colour kya hai?' (What is the colour of the Sun?) - 'What is the color of listening?' and so on. As one can see, an English collocation 'full name' is not preserved, but translated into 'Fullham'. In some cases it can be explained by the incorrect use of capitalization: 'niagara falls kaunse desh mein hai?' is translated into 'What is the name of the person who is suffering from diabetes?', but using capitalized 'N' gives correct translation. It is worth noting that incorrect query translation contributed to approximately 35% of errors.

Answer granularity: Moreover, while performing error analysis, we have found a few cases where a level of required granularity for an answer was unclear. A common type of error for the model was to output 'Champ de Mars in Paris, France' when asked 'Eiffel Tower kahan hai?' (Where is the Eiffel Tower?), while the ground truth answer was 'france'. Errors like that account for approximately 7% of all the wrong predictions in the development set. Such cases suggest that considerable attention must be paid during labeling of a corpus. One can either keep a list of acceptable answers or provide refined guidelines for both annotators and developers. In the latter, it might help to analyze human performance on the same dataset to understand what is the most common answer granularity level.

Cross-lingual embeddings: Finally, when working with neural models, we have to carefully approach the construction of embedding spaces. While in the current version we have worked only with English translations, a neater approach would be to directly use both languages. (Ruder, 2017) provides an extensive survey of the available approaches. Whereas more and more resources are emerging for Hindi, such as MUSE (Conneau et al., 2017), few researchers have addressed the task for Telugu and Tamil.

7   Conclusions

In this paper, as a first step towards fostering research in the area of Factoid QA in CM languages, we present our evaluation dataset consisting of more than 5000 crowd-sourced questions along with their answers in three CM languages - Hinglish, Tenglish and Tamlish. We received a lot more Tamlish questions on crowd sourced platform compared to the other two languages. We also shared our experiences while curating this evaluation dataset such as usage of images as anchor points to avoid lexical biasing towards CM. We have looked at the extent of lexical biasing of the words in article based questions. In future, we would also like to see if the participants are inverting the language for the words present in the articles. The dataset features a diverse range of answer types across all the CM languages. We also shared some interesting properties of this dataset related to lexical bias and other phenomenon related to code mixing. In future, we would like to explore techniques to generate synthetic CM data from large-scale datasets.We plan on continuing the data collection process to elicit more data. This paper also reports the first edition of the challenge and plan on continuing it in the coming years as well. We have made our dataset freely available for research purposes to encourage more research work and result in significant advances in the area of Factoid QA in CM languages.

References

Kalika Bali, Jatin Sharma, Monojit Choudhury, and Yogarshi Vyas. 2014. " i am borrowing ya mixing?" an analysis of english-hindi code mixing in facebook. In *Proceedings of the First Workshop on Computational Approaches to Code Switching*, pages 116–126.

Somnath Banerjee, Sudip Kumar Naskar, Paolo Rosso, and Sivaji Bandyopadhyay. 2016. The first cross-script code-mixed question answering corpus. In *MultiLingMine@ ECIR*, pages 56–65.

Utsab Barman, Amitava Das, Joachim Wagner, and Jennifer Foster. 2014. Code mixing: A challenge for language identification in the language of social media. In *Proceedings of the first workshop on computational approaches to code switching*, pages 13–23.

Paheli Bhattacharya, Pawan Goyal, and Sudeshna Sarkar. 2016. Using word embeddings for query translation for hindi to english cross language information retrieval. *Computación y Sistemas*, 20(3):435–447.

Alan W Black, Susanne Burger, Alistair Conkie, Helen Hastie, Simon Keizer, Oliver Lemon, Nicolas Merigaud, Gabriel Parent, Gabriel Schubiner, Blaise Thomson, et al. 2011. Spoken dialog challenge 2010: Comparison of live and control test results. In *Proceedings of the SIGDIAL 2011 Conference*, pages 2–7. ACL.

Eric Brill, Susan Dumais, and Michele Banko. 2002. An analysis of the askmsr question-answering system. In *Proceedings of the ACL-02 conference on Empirical methods in natural language processing-Volume 10*, pages 257–264. Association for Computational Linguistics.

Khyathi Raghavi Chandu, Manoj Chinnakotla, Alan W Black, and Manish Shrivastava. 2017. Webshodh: A code mixed factoid question answering system for web. In *International Conference of the Cross-Language Evaluation Forum for European Languages*, pages 104–111. Springer.

Danqi Chen, Adam Fisch, Jason Weston, and Antoine Bordes. 2017. Reading wikipedia to answer open-domain questions. *arXiv preprint arXiv:1704.00051*.

Gokul Chittaranjan, Yogarshi Vyas, Kalika Bali, and Monojit Choudhury. 2014. Word-level language identification using crf: Code-switching shared task report of msr india system. In *Proceedings of The First Workshop on Computational Approaches to Code Switching*, pages 73–79.

Alexis Conneau, Guillaume Lample, Marc'Aurelio Ranzato, Ludovic Denoyer, and Hervé Jégou. 2017. Word translation without parallel data. *arXiv preprint arXiv:1710.04087*.

David Crystal. 1997. *The Cambridge encyclopedia of language*, volume 1. Cambridge University Press Cambridge.

Long Duong, Hadi Afshar, Dominique Estival, Glen Pink, Philip Cohen, and Mark Johnson. 2017. Multilingual semantic parsing and code-switching. In *Proceedings of the 21st Conference on Computational Natural Language Learning (CoNLL 2017)*, pages 379–389.

P Goyal, Manav R Mital, A Mukerjee, Achla M Raina, D Sharma, P Shukla, and K Vikram. 2003. A bilingual parser for hindi, english and code-switching structures. In *10th Conference of The European Chapter*, page 15.

Gualberto Guzmán, Joseph Ricard, Jacqueline Serigos, Barbara E Bullock, and Almeida Jacqueline Toribio. 2017. Metrics for modeling code-switching across corpora. *Proc. Interspeech 2017*, pages 67–71.

Taofik Hidayat. 2008. An analysis of code switching used by facebookers.

Po-Sen Huang, Xiaodong He, Jianfeng Gao, Li Deng, Alex Acero, and Larry Heck. 2013. Learning deep structured semantic models for web search using clickthrough data. In *Proceedings of the 22nd ACM international conference on Conference on information & knowledge management*, pages 2333–2338. ACM.

Anupam Jamatia, Björn Gambäck, and Amitava Das. 2015. Part-of-speech tagging for code-mixed english-hindi twitter and facebook chat messages. In *Proceedings of the International Conference Recent Advances in Natural Language Processing*, pages 239–248.

Aravind K Joshi. 1982. Processing of sentences with intra-sentential code-switching. In *Proceedings of the 9th conference on Computational linguistics-Volume 1*, pages 145–150. Academia Praha.

Praveen Kumar, Shrikant Kashyap, Ankush Mittal, and Sumit Gupta. 2005. A hindi question answering system for e-learning documents. In *Intelligent Sensing and Information Processing, 2005. ICISIP 2005. Third International Conference on*, pages 80–85. IEEE.

Xin Li and Dan Roth. 2006. Learning question classifiers: the role of semantic information. *Natural Language Engineering*, 12(3):229–249.

Lesley Milroy and Pieter Muysken. 1995. *One speaker, two languages: Cross-disciplinary perspectives on code-switching*. Cambridge University Press.

Pieter Muysken. 2000. *Bilingual speech: A typology of code-mixing*, volume 11. Cambridge University Press.

Carol Myers-Scotton. 1997. *Duelling languages: Grammatical structure in codeswitching.* Oxford University Press.

Garima Nanda, Mohit Dua, and Krishma Singla. 2016. A hindi question answering system using machine learning approach. In *ICCTICT 2016*, pages 311–314. IEEE.

Günter Neumann and Bogdan Sacaleanu. 2003. A cross–language question/answering–system for german and english. In *Workshop of the Cross-Language Evaluation Forum for European Languages*, pages 559–571. Springer.

Niko Partanen, KyungTae Lim, Michael Rießler, and Thierry Poibeau. 2018. Dependency parsing of code-switching data with cross-lingual feature representations. In *Proceedings of the Fourth International Workshop on Computatinal Linguistics of Uralic Languages*, pages 1–17.

Shana Poplack. 1980. Sometimes ill start a sentence in spanish y termino en espanol: toward a typology of code-switching1. *Linguistics*, 18(7-8):581–618.

Khyathi Chandu Raghavi, Manoj Kumar Chinnakotla, and Manish Shrivastava. 2015. Answer ka type kya he?: Learning to classify questions in code-mixed language. In *Proceedings of WWW 2015*, pages 853–858. ACM.

Pranav Rajpurkar, Jian Zhang, Konstantin Lopyrev, and Percy Liang. 2016. Squad: 100,000+ questions for machine comprehension of text. In *Proceedings of the 2016 Conference on Empirical Methods in Natural Language Processing*, pages 2383–2392, Austin, Texas. Association for Computational Linguistics.

Rami Reddy Nandi Reddy and Sivaji Bandyopadhyay. 2006. Dialogue based question answering system in telugu. In *Proceedings of the Workshop on Multilingual Question Answering*, pages 53–60. Association for Computational Linguistics.

Sebastian Ruder. 2017. A survey of cross-lingual embedding models. *arXiv preprint arXiv:1706.04902.*

Koustav Rudra, Shruti Rijhwani, Rafiya Begum, Kalika Bali, Monojit Choudhury, and Niloy Ganguly. 2016. Understanding language preference for expression of opinion and sentiment: What do hindi-english speakers do on twitter? In *Proceedings of EMNLP 2016*, pages 1131–1141.

Mark Sebba. 2009. *On the notions of congruence and convergence in code-switching.* Cambridge University Press.

Satoshi Sekine and Ralph Grishman. 2003. Hindi-english cross-lingual question-answering system. *ACM Transactions on Asian Language Information Processing (TALIP)*, 2(3):181–192.

Royal Sequiera, Monojit Choudhury, Parth Gupta, Paolo Rosso, Shubham Kumar, Somnath Banerjee, Sudip Kumar Naskar, Sivaji Bandyopadhyay, Gokul Chittaranjan, Amitava Das, et al. 2015. Overview of fire-2015 shared task on mixed script information retrieval. In *FIRE Workshops*, volume 1587, pages 19–25.

Arnav Sharma, Sakshi Gupta, Raveesh Motlani, Piyush Bansal, Manish Srivastava, Radhika Mamidi, and Dipti M Sharma. 2016. Shallow parsing pipeline for hindi-english code-mixed social media text. *arXiv preprint arXiv:1604.03136.*

R Mahesh K Sinha and Anil Thakur. 2005. Machine translation of bi-lingual hindi-english (hinglish) text. *10th Machine Translation summit (MT Summit X), Phuket, Thailand*, pages 149–156.

Thamar Solorio, Elizabeth Blair, Suraj Maharjan, Steven Bethard, Mona Diab, Mahmoud Ghoneim, Abdelati Hawwari, Fahad AlGhamdi, Julia Hirschberg, Alison Chang, et al. 2014. Overview for the first shared task on language identification in code-switched data. In *Proceedings of the First Workshop on Computational Approaches to Code Switching*, pages 62–72.

Thamar Solorio and Yang Liu. 2008. Part-of-speech tagging for english-spanish code-switched text. In *Proceedings of the Conference on Empirical Methods in Natural Language Processing*, pages 1051–1060. Association for Computational Linguistics.

Victor Soto and Julia Hirschberg. 2017. Crowdsourcing universal part-of-speech tags for codeswitching. *arXiv preprint arXiv:1703.08537.*

Ang Sun, Minghu Jiang, Yifan He, Lin Chen, and Baozong Yuan. 2008. Chinese question answering based on syntax analysis and answer classification. *Acta Electronica Sinica*, 36(5):833–839.

Yogarshi Vyas, Spandana Gella, Jatin Sharma, Kalika Bali, and Monojit Choudhury. 2014. Pos tagging of english-hindi code-mixed social media content. In *Proceedings of the EMNLP 2014*, pages 974–979.

ZHANG Yongkui, ZHAO Zheqian, BAI Lijun, and CHEN Xinqing. 2003. Internet-based chinese question-answering system. *Computer Engineering*, 15:34.

W Quin Yow and Ferninda Patrycia. 2011. Challenging the linguistic incompetency hypothesis: Language competency predicts code-switching.

Ayah Zirikly and Mona Diab. 2015. Named entity recognition for arabic social media. In *Proceedings of the 1st Workshop on Vector Space Modeling for Natural Language Processing*, pages 176–185.

Transliteration Better than Translation? Answering Code-mixed Questions over a Knowledge Base

Vishal Gupta
IIIT Hyderabad, India
vishal.gupta@
research.iiit.ac.in

Manoj Chinnakotla
Microsoft, Bellevue, USA
manojc@
microsoft.com

Manish Shrivastava
IIIT Hyderabad, India
m.shrivastava@
iiit.ac.in

Abstract

Humans can learn multiple languages. If they know a fact in one language, they can answer a question in another language they understand. They can also answer Code-mix (CM) questions: questions which contain both languages. This ability is attributed to the unique learning ability of humans. Our task aims to study if machines can achieve this. We demonstrate how effectively a machine can answer CM questions. In this work, we adopt a two-step approach: candidate generation and candidate re-ranking to answer questions. We propose a Triplet-Siamese-Hybrid CNN (TSHCNN) to re-rank candidate answers. We show experiments on the SimpleQuestions dataset. Our network is trained only on English questions provided in this dataset and noisy Hindi translations of these questions and can answer English-Hindi CM questions effectively without the need of translation into English. Back-transliterated CM questions outperform their lexical and sentence level translated counterparts by 5% & 35% respectively, highlighting the efficacy of our approach in a resource-constrained setting.

1 Introduction

Question Answering (QA) has received significant attention in the Natural Language (NLP) community. There are many variations (open-domain, knowledge bases, reading comprehension) as well as datasets (Joshi et al., 2017; Hopkins et al., 2017; Rajpurkar et al., 2016; Bordes et al., 2015) for the question answering task. However, many approaches (Lukovnikov et al., 2017; Yin et al., 2016; Fader et al., 2014; Chen et al., 2017a; Hermann et al., 2015) attempted in QA so far have been focused on monolingual questions. This is true for both methods and techniques as well as resources.

Code-mixing (referred to as CM) refers to the phenomenon of "embedding of linguistic units such as phrases, words and morphemes of one language into an utterance of another language" (Myers-Scotton, 2002). People in multilingual societies commonly use code-mixed sentences in conversations (Grover et al., 2017), to search on the web (Wang and Komlodi, 2016) and to ask questions (Raghavi et al., 2017). However, current Question Answering (QA) systems do not support CM and are only designed to work with a single language. This limitation makes it unsuitable for multilingual users to naturally interact with the QA system, specifically in scenarios wherein they do not know the right word in the target language.

CM presents serious challenges for the language processing community (Çetinoğlu et al., 2016; Vyas et al., 2014), including parsing, Machine Translation (MT), automatic speech recognition (ASR), information retrieval (IR) and extraction (IE), and semantic processing. Even for problems such as language identification, or part of speech tagging, that are considered solved for monolingual languages, performance degrades when mixed-language is present. Lack of language resources such as annotated corpora, part-of-speech taggers and parsers poses a considerable challenge for automated processing and analysis of CM languages. This further amplifies the challenge for CM QA. This CM question answering task

Proceedings of The Third Workshop on Computational Approaches to Code-Switching, pages 39–50
Melbourne, Australia, July 19, 2018. ©2018 Association for Computational Linguistics

is challenging not just because of having multiple languages with different semantics but also because of the different word order of source language and CM, making it difficult to extract essential features from the input text.

We base our work on the premise that humans can answer CM questions easily provided they understand the languages used in the question. They require no additional training in the form of CM questions to comprehend a CM question. So, one way to tackle CM questions is to translate them into a single language and use monolingual QA systems (Lukovnikov et al., 2017; Yin et al., 2016; Fader et al., 2014). Machine Translation systems perform poorly on CM sentences. The only other viable option is lexical translation (word by word translation). Lexical translation requires language identification, which Bhat et al. (2018) show to be solved. We show that our model trained on both English and Hindi can perform better on CM question directly than its lexical translation. This removes the need to obtain a large bilingual mapping of words for lexical translation. Also, such a sizeable bilingual mapping may be hard to obtain for low-resource languages.

Knowledge Bases (KBs) like Freebase (Google, 2017) and DBpedia [1] contain a vast wealth of information. Information is structured in the form of tuples, i.e. a combination of subject, predicate and object (s, p, o) in these KBs. Such KBs contain information predominately in English, and low resource languages tend to lose out on having a rich information source.

We use bilingual embeddings to fill the gaps due to lack of resources. We also develop a K-Nearest Bilingual Embedding Transformation (KNBET) which exploits bilingual embeddings to outperform the performance of lexical translation.

We overcome challenges discussed above in our paper and develop a CM QA system over KB, named CMQA, using only monolingual data from individual languages. We demonstrate our system with Hinglish (Matrix language: Hindi, Embedded language: English) CM questions. Our evaluation shows promising results given that no CM data was used to train our model. This shows promise that we do not need CM data but can use monolingual data to train a CM QA system. Our results show that our system is much more useful as compared to translating a CM question.

Our contributions are as follows:

1. We show how we can answer CM questions given an English corpus, noisy Hindi supervision and imperfect bilingual embeddings.

2. We introduce a Triplet-Siamese-Hybrid Convolutional Neural Network (TSHCNN) that jointly learns to rank candidate answers.

3. We provide a test dataset of 250 Hindi-English CM questions to researchers. This dataset is mapped with Freebase tuples and English questions from the SimpleQuestions dataset.

To the best of our knowledge, we are the first to tackle the problem of End-to-End Code-Mixed Question Answering over Knowledge Bases in a resource-constrained setting. Earlier approaches for CM QA (Raghavi et al., 2017) require a bilingual dictionary to translate words to English and an existing Google like-search engine to get answers, which we do not require.

The rest of the paper is structured as follows: We survey related work in Section 2 and describe the task description in Section 3. We explain our system in Section 4. We describe experiments in Section 5 and provide a detailed analysis and discussion in Section 6 and conclude in Section 7.

2   Related Work

Question Answering and Knowledge Bases Question answering is a well studied problem over knowledge bases (KBs) (Lukovnikov et al., 2017; Yin et al., 2016; Fader et al., 2014) and in open domain (Chen et al., 2017a; Hermann et al., 2015). Learning to rank approaches have also been applied to QA successfully (Agarwal et al., 2012; Bordes et al., 2014). Many earlier works (Ture and Jojic, 2017; Yu et al., 2017; Yin et al., 2016) which tackle SimpleQuestions divide the task into two steps: mention detection and relation

---

[1] http://dbpedia.org/

prediction, whereas we jointly do both using our model. Lukovnikov et al. (2017) is more similar to our approach wherein they train a neural network in an end-to-end manner.

CodeMixing and CodeSwitching Code-mixing and code-switching has recently gathered much attention from researchers (Bhat et al., 2018; Rijhwani et al., 2017; Raghavi et al., 2015, 2017; Banerjee et al., 2016; Dey and Fung, 2014; Bhat et al., 2017). CM research is mostly confined towards developing parsers and other language pipeline primitives (Bhat et al., 2018, 2017). There has been some work in CM sentiment analysis (Joshi et al., 2016). Raghavi et al. (2015) demonstrate question type classification for CM questions and Raghavi et al. (2017) also demonstrate a CM factoid QA system that searches for the lexically translated CM question using Google Search on a small dataset of 100 CM questions. To the best of our knowledge, there has been no work on building an end-to-end CM QA system over a KB.

Bilingual Embeddings Recent work has shown that it is possible to obtain bilingual embeddings using only a minimal set of parallel lexicons (Smith et al., 2017; Artetxe et al., 2017; Ammar et al., 2016; Luong et al., 2015; P et al., 2014) or without any parallel lexicons (Zhang et al., 2017; Conneau et al., 2017). Our approach, can use these bilingual embeddings and supervised corpus for a resource-rich language, to enable CM applications for resource-poor languages.

Cross-lingual Question Answering Closely related is the problem of cross-lingual QA. There have been various approaches (Ahn et al., 2004; Lin and Kuo, 2010; Ren et al., 2010; Ture and Boschee, 2016) to cross-lingual QA. Some approaches (Lin and Kuo, 2010) rely on translating the entire question. Others (Ren et al., 2010), have also explored using lexical translations for this task. Recently, Ture et al. (Ture and Boschee, 2016) proposed models that combine different translation settings. There have been some efforts (Pouran Ben Veyseh, 2016; Hakimov et al., 2017; Chen et al., 2017b) to attempt cross-lingual question answering over knowledge bases.

3 Task Description

The SimpleQuestions task presented by Bordes et al. (2015) can be defined as follows. Let $\mathcal{K} = \{(s_i, p_i, o_i)\}$ be a knowledge base represented as a set of tuples, where s_i represents a subject entity, p_i a predicate (also referred as relation), and o_i an object entity. The task of SimpleQuestions is then: Given a question represented as a sentence, i.e. a sequence of words $q = \{w_1, ..., w_n\}$, find a tuple $\{\hat{s}, \hat{p}, \hat{o}\} \in \mathcal{K}$ such that $\hat{o}$ is the correct answer for question q. This task can be reformulated to finding the correct subject $\hat{s}$ and predicate $\hat{p}$ that question q refers to and which characterise the set of triples in $\mathcal{K}$ that contains the answer to q.

Consider the example, given question *"Which city in Canada did Ian Tyson originated from?"*, the Freebase subject entity **m.041ftf** representing the Canadian artist Ian Tyson and the relation **fb:music/artist/origin**, can answer it.

4 Our System: CMQA

In this section, we describe our system which consists of two components: (1) the Candidate Generation module for finding relevant candidates and (2) a Candidate Re-ranking model, for getting the top answer from the list of candidate answers.

4.1 Candidate Generation

Any freebase tuple (specifically, the object in a tuple is the answer to the question) can be an answer to our question. We use an efficient (non-deep learning) candidate retrieval system to narrow down our search space and focus on re-ranking only the most relevant candidates. Solr[2] is an open-source implementation of an inverted index search system. We use Solr to index all our freebase tuples (FB2M) and then query for the top-k relevant candidates given the question as a query. We use BM25 as the scoring metric to rank results. Since we index freebase tuples which are in English (translating the entire KB would require a very large amount of effort and we restrict ourselves to using only the provided English KB), any non-English word in the query does not contribute

---

[2]http://lucene.apache.org/solr/

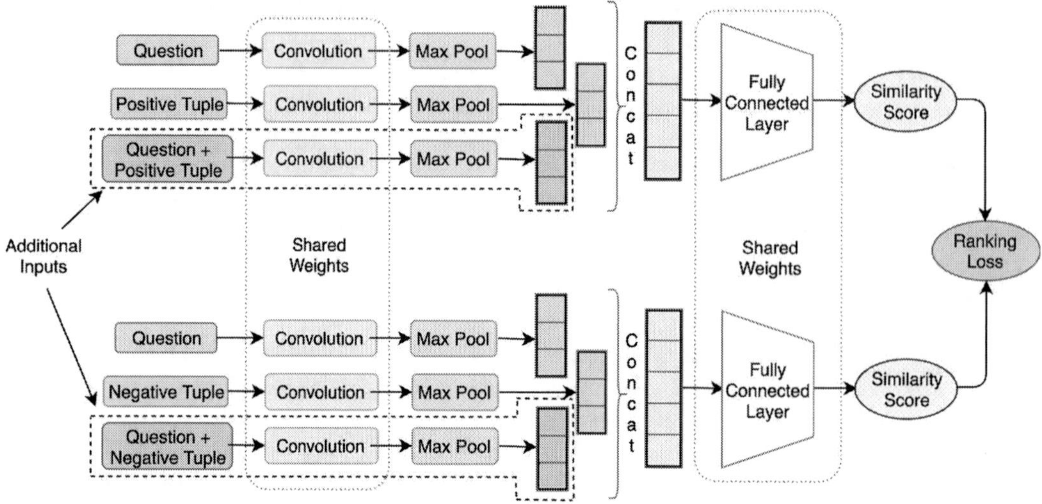

Figure 1: TSHCNN Architecture

to the matching. This is a limiting factor in candidate generation for CM questions.

4.2 Candidate Re-ranking

We use Convolutional Neural Networks (CNNs) to learn the semantic representation for input text (Kim, 2014; Hu et al., 2015; Lai et al., 2015; Cho et al., 2014; Johnson and Zhang, 2015; Zhang et al., 2015). CNNs learn globally word order invariant features and at the same time pick order in short phrases. This ability of CNNs is important since different languages[3] have different word orders.

Retrieving a semantically similar answer to a given question can be modelled as a classification problem with a large number of classes. Here, each answer is a potential class and the number of questions per class is small (Could be zero, one or more than one. Since we match only the subject and predicate, there could be multiple questions having a common subject and predicate combination). An intuitive approach to tackle this problem would be to learn a similarity metric between the question to be classified and the set of answers. We find Siamese networks have shown promising results in such distance-based learning methods (Bromley et al., 1993; Chopra et al., 2005; Das et al., 2016).

Our Candidate Re-ranking module is in-

spired by the success of neural models in various image and text tasks (Vo and Hays, 2016; Das et al., 2016). Our network is a Triplet-Siamese Hybrid Convolutional neural network (TSHCNN), see figure 1. Vo and Hays (2016) show that classification-siamese hybrid and triplet networks work well on image similarity tasks. Our hybrid model can jointly extract and exchange information from the question and tuple inputs.

All convolution layers share weights in TSHCNN. The fully connected layers are also Siamese and share weights. This weight sharing helps project both questions and tuples into a similar semantic space and reduces the required number of parameters to be learned.

Additional Input: Concatenate question + tuple Our initial network only had two inputs (question and tuple) to each corresponding branch. We further modify our network to provide a third input in the form of the concatenation of question and tuple. This additional input helps our network learn much better feature representations. We discuss this in the results section.

As shown in figure 1, questions and candidate tuples are provided to our system. Our experiments vary in the input questions (English and CM variations of questions), but the candidates (tuples or answers) are always in monolingual English. Thus our final answer is always in English.

---

[3]English is SVO whereas Hindi is free word order. SVO means Subject Verb Object.

4.2.1 K-Nearest Bilingual Embedding Transformation (KNBET)

The standard approach given bilingual (say English-French) embeddings (Plank, 2017; Da San Martino et al., 2017; Klementiev et al., 2012) has been to use the English word vector corresponding to the English word and the French word vector for the French word. Also, the network is trained only on the English corpora, i.e. trained using English word vectors only. When the input is say, a French sentence, they use French word vectors. Bilingual embeddings try and project both the English and French word vectors in the same semantic space, but these vectors are not perfectly aligned and might lead to errors in the networks' prediction.

We propose to obtain the average of the nearest k-english-word-vectors for the given french word and use it as the embedding for the French word. For k=1, this reduces to a bilingual lexical dictionary using bilingual embeddings (Vulic and Moens, 2015; Madhyastha and España-Bonet, 2017). Since the bilingual embeddings are not perfectly aligned, Smith et al. (2017) show[4] that precision@k increases as k increases (e.g. for Hindi P@1 is 0.39, P@3 is 0.58 and P@10 is 0.63), when we obtain French (or any other language) translations for an English word. Thus, we conduct experiments with varying values of k and report the best results for the optimal k. Our experiments confirm the efficacy of KNBET. Further, we believe this KNBET can be used to improve the performance of any multilingual system that uses bilingual embeddings.

4.2.2 Loss Function

We use the distance based logistic triplet loss (Vo and Hays, 2016) which gave better results than a contrastive loss (Bordes et al., 2014). This has also been reported by Vo and Hays (2016) to exhibit better performance in image similarity tasks as well. Here, S_{pos} and S_{neg} are the similarity scores obtained by the question+positive tuple and question+negative tuple respectively.

$$Loss = \log(1 + e^{(S_{neg} - S_{pos})}) \qquad (1)$$

---

[4]Results available on the GitHub repo: github.com/Babylonpartners/fastText_multilingual

5 Experiments

5.1 Dataset

We use the SimpleQuestions (Bordes et al., 2015) dataset which comprises 75.9k/10.8k/21.7k training/validation/test questions. Each question is associated with an answer, i.e. a tuple (subject, predicate, object) from a Freebase (Google, 2017) subset (FB2M or FB5M). The subject is given as a MID [5] and we obtain its corresponding entity name by processing the Freebase data dumps. We were unable to obtain entity name mappings for some MIDs, and these were removed from our final set. We also obtain Hindi translations for all questions in SimpleQuestions using Google Translate. Note, these translations are not perfect and serve as a noisy input to the network. Also, we only translate the questions, and the answers remain in English. As with previous work, we show results over the 2M-subset of Freebase (FB2M).

We use pre-trained word embeddings[6] provided by Fasttext (Bojanowski et al., 2016) and use alignment matrices[7] provided by Smith et al. (2017) to obtain English-Hindi bilingual embeddings. Smith et al. (2017) use a small set of 5000 words to obtain the alignment matrices. The provided Hindi embeddings are in Devanagari script. We use randomly initialised embeddings between [-0.25, 0.25] for words without embeddings.

We have prepared a dataset of Hindi-English CM questions for a smaller set of 250 tuples obtained from the test split of SimpleQuestions dataset. We gathered these questions from Hindi-English speakers, who were asked to form a natural language CM question, shown a tuple. Further, for every tuple we obtained CM questions from 5 different annotators and pick one at random for the final test set, to ensure multiple variations. Each CM question is in Roman script, and annotators anglicise (or transliterate) Hindi words (Devanagari script) to Roman script, to the best of their ability. This introduces variations in spellings and posses a challenge for the network and also back-transliteration.

---

[5]A unique ID referring to an entity in Freebase.
[6]https://fasttext.cc/
[7]https://goo.gl/Lwgu1D

Table 1: Network Parameters

Parameter	Value
Batch Size	100
Non-linearity	Relu
CNN Filters & Width	20 filters each of width 1, 2 and 4 resp.
Pool Type	Global Max Pooling
Stride Length	1
FC Layer 1	100 units + 0.2 Dropout
FC Layer 2	100 units + 0.2 Dropout
FC Layer 3	1 unit + No Relu
Optimizer	Adam (default params)

Table 2: End-to-End Answer Accuracy for English Questions

Model	Acc.
Bordes et al. (2015)	62.7
Golub and He (2016)	70.9
Lukovnikov et al. (2017)	71.2
Yin et al. (2016)	76.4
Yu et al. (2017)	77.0
Ture and Jojic (2017)	86.8
Ours: Candidate Generation	68.5
Ours: Candidate Re-Ranking	77.0

5.2 Generating negative samples

We generate 10 negative samples for each training sample. We follow Bordes et al. (2014) to generate 5 negative samples. These candidates are samples picked at random and then corrupted following Bordes et al. (2014). We further use 5 more negative samples obtained by querying the Solr index. This gives us negative samples which are very similar to the actual answer and further the discriminatory ability of our network. This second policy is unique, and our experiments show that it gives us better performance.

5.3 Evaluation and Baselines

We report results using the standard evaluation criteria (Bordes et al., 2015), in terms of path-level accuracy, which is the percentage of questions for which the top-ranked candidate fact is correct. A prediction is correct if the system correctly retrieved the subject and the relationship.

Since there is no earlier work on CM QA over KBs, we compare the different ways a CM question can be answered using our QA sys-

Table 3: Candidate generation results: Recall of top-k answer candidates for each question type

K	English	CM-MT	CM-LT	CM-TL
1	68.4	39.1	54.6	58.4
2	75.7	42.3	59.3	63.8
5	82.3	49.4	67.2	70.0
10	85.5	53.4	71.5	73.4
50	91.4	56.9	78.7	78.6
100	92.9	59.7	80.6	81.0
200	94.3	62.1	83.0	83.1

tem. We translate the entire CM question to English using Google translate (cm-mt). We also lexically translate the CM question to English (cm-lt). Further, since the CM question is in Roman script, we apply language identification (LI), and back-transliteration (BTL) for Hindi words using Bhat et al. (2018)[8] and obtain a CM question which has English words in Roman script and Hindi words in Devanagari (cm-tl). We report results for all these different CM question variations using our TSHCNN. We tried Raghavi et al. (2017) WebShodh[9] system, but it did not return any answers, and hence we are unable to use it for comparison.

We also report results for the English questions in SimpleQuestions on our model trained only on English. This serves as a benchmark for our model as compared to other work on SimpleQuestions (Ture and Jojic, 2017; Yu et al., 2017; Yin et al., 2016; Lukovnikov et al., 2017; Golub and He, 2016; Bordes et al., 2015).

Network parameters and decisions are presented in Table 1. We train our model until the validation loss on the validation set stops improving further for 3 epochs. We report the results on the epoch with the best validation loss. We use K = 200 for the initial candidate generation step.

6 Results

6.1 Quantitative Analysis

In Table 2, we present end-to-end results using our CMQA system. It shows competi-

---

[8] The LI system is trained on CM data and the BTL system is trained with parallel transliteration pairs.

[9] http://tts.speech.cs.cmu.edu/webshodh/cmqa.php

Table 4: End-to-End Results. We train on different inputs: only English questions, only Hindi questions and both English and Hindi questions. The answers are in English for all training scenarios. TO: Train on, E: English questions, H: Hindi questions, EH: English and Hindi questions, BE: Bilingual Embeddings, CQT: Concatenate question + tuple , KNB: KNBET (K-Nearest Bilingual Embedding Transformation), SCNS: Solr Candidates as Negative Samples, E2E Scores: Candidates obtained using the same CM question variation, cm-lt-tl: Candidates obtained using lexical translation of cm-tl questions and input question was cm-tl.

TO	BE	CQT	KNB	SCNS	Codemix Question Accuracy						
					English Candidates			E2E Scores			
					cm-mt	cm-lt	cm-tl	cm-mt	cm-lt	cm-tl	cm-lt-tl
E	no	yes	no	yes	0.39	0.58	0.37	0.31	0.51	0.32	0.33
H	no	yes	no	yes	0.08	0.07	0.17	0.07	0.06	0.16	0.15
EH	no	yes	no	yes	0.40	0.53	0.53	0.31	0.50	0.48	0.47
E	yes	yes	no	yes	0.41	0.57	0.46	0.34	0.53	0.41	0.41
H	yes	yes	no	yes	0.39	0.54	0.57	0.30	0.50	0.52	0.54
EH	yes	yes	no	yes	**0.46**	**0.59**	**0.62**	0.34	**0.55**	0.55	**0.57**
E	yes	yes	k=3	yes	0.42	0.57	0.53	0.34	0.54	0.50	0.49
H	yes	yes	k=3	yes	0.44	0.53	0.59	0.33	0.46	0.54	0.55
EH	yes	yes	k=3	yes	**0.46**	**0.59**	0.61	**0.35**	**0.55**	**0.56**	0.54
E	yes	yes	no	no	0.42	0.50	0.55	0.33	0.50	0.53	0.52
EH	yes	no	no	yes	0.29	0.44	0.40	0.21	0.37	0.37	0.38

tive results on English questions with all but one of the more recent approaches for SimpleQuestions. This shows the effectiveness of our model for English QA. Our initial candidate generation step surprisingly surpasses the original Bordes et al. (2015) paper.

In Table 3, we report candidate generation results. We obtain candidates for each CM question variation using the question itself as a query. Further, cm-tl has words in Devanagari script which do not contribute to the search similarity scores when searching over an English corpus. Thus we use the candidates obtained for the lexical translation of cm-tl questions as candidates for cm-tl. This variation with candidates of cm-lt and questions of cm-tl is termed as cm-lt-tl. Additionally, we show results using the candidates obtained for the English question as the candidates for all three CM question variations (cm-mt, cm-lt and cm-tl). This ensures a fair comparison of all three CM question variations using TSHCNN.

In Table 4, we show results on the CM questions. Our model TSHCNN, trained on both English and Hindi questions gives the best scores. It is better by 3 - 8% for various CM question variations. Although, training only on English and using bilingual embeddings should offer performance that matches training on both English and Hindi. However, this does not happen since the bilingual embeddings are not perfect (see subsection KNBET). We do an ablation study of the various components and describe them in more detail further.

Monolingual vs Bilingual Embeddings Results clearly show that improvements are obtained when we use bilingual embeddings. There is an improvement of 17% for cm-tl questions when the network is trained on English and Hindi using bilingual embeddings versus using monolingual embeddings. This is because bilingual embeddings project words with similar semantics more closely. This difference is much more pronounced when we train the network only on Hindi questions. The tuples were still in English, and the misaligned semantic space (when using monolingual embeddings) for English and Hindi made it difficult for the Siamese network to learn anything meaningful. We can also observe an improvement of 11% for cm-lt questions (when trained on English and Hindi questions and using bilingual embeddings). We attribute this to the fact that CM questions have a different word order than English questions. Moreover,

Table 5: Qualitative Analysis. CA: Correct Answer, EC: Candidates obtained for English question used as candidates for CM questions, E2E: Candidates obtained in an end-to-end manner i.e., the same question variation was used to obtain candidates, PA: Predicted Answer, EC, E2E & CM-LT-TL PA: Predicted answers grouped if same.

Examples
Example 1: CA (have wheels will travel, book written work subjects, family) English Question: what is the have wheels will travel book about? Predicted Answer: (have wheels will travel, book written work subjects, adolescence)
CM Question: have wheel will travel kitaab kis vishaya par likhi gyi hai? PA: NA
CM-MT Question: howe wheel will travel book written on? EC & E2E PA: (travel, media common literary genre books in this genre, michael palin)
CM-LT Question: have wheel will travel book what subject on wrote added is? EC & E2E PA: (have wheels will travel, book written work subjects, adolescence)
CM-TL Question: have wheel will travel किताब किस विषय पर लिखी गयी है? EC, E2E & CM-LT-TL PA: (have wheels will travel, book written work subjects, adolescence)
Example 2: CA (traditional music, music genre artists, the henrys) English Question: which quartet is known for traditional music? Predicted Answer: (traditional music, music genre albums, music and friends)
CM Question: traditional music ke liye konse artist jaane jate hain? PA: NA
CM-MT Question: which artists are known for traditional music? EC & E2E PA: (traditional music, music genre artists, sally jaye)
CM-LT Question: traditional music of for which one artist life goes are there? EC PA: (bbc music volume 19 number 6 chamber music elias string quartet, music album artist, franz schubert) E2E PA: (the way life goes, music album artist, tom keifer)
CM-TL Question: traditional music के लिए कोनसे artist जान जाते हैं? EC, E2E & CM-LT-TL PA: (traditional music, music genre artists, sally jaye)

with the use of bilingual embeddings, our network can project both Hindi and English questions into the same semantic space, which in turn helps CM questions. The effect of monolingual embeddings is visible when we train only on Hindi. We notice accuracies for all CM question variations drop significantly.

K-Nearest Bilingual Embedding Transformation (KNBET) With k = 3, the results obtained with KNBET are higher by 16% for cm-tl trained only on English compared to no KNBET. This demonstrates that our transformation increases the effectiveness of bilingual embeddings. This is attributed to the fact that our transformation reduces the errors that bilingual embeddings may otherwise possess due to imperfect alignment.

Training on Hindi Questions Training with Hindi questions helps the network learn the different word orders that are present in Hindi questions. This improves scores for cm-tl questions when trained only on Hindi. Further, joint training on both English and Hindi questions gives us the best results.

SCNS: Using Solr Candidates as Negative Samples We ran experiments using 10 negative samples generated as per Bordes et al. (2014). However, the scores obtained when using a combination of both negative sample generation policies: corrupted tuples and Solr candidates, was 12.7% higher. This is a significant improvement in scores.

CQT: Additional Input, Concatenate question + tuple [10] We obtain an improve-

---

[10]We made sure that the experiments with no CQT

ment of 34% - 62% in our scores when we provide additional input in the form of concatenated question and tuple. One plausible explanation for this improvement is the 50% more features for the network. To verify this, we added more filters to our convolution layer such that total features equalled that when additional input was provided. However, the improvement in results was only marginal. Another, more likely explanation would be that the max pooling layer picks out the dominant features from this additional input, and these features increase the discriminatory ability of our network.

EC: English candidates We perform experiments wherein we use the same set of candidates obtained for English questions as the candidates for all CM question variations (cm-mt, cm-lt and cm-tl). Results show that cm-tl questions give the highest scores on a network trained on both English and Hindi questions using bilingual embeddings. This result shows that lexical translation might not be the best strategy to tackle CM questions. Further, more techniques should be devised to handle the CM question in its original form rather than translating it at the sentence or lexical level.

6.2 Qualitative Analysis

In Table 5, some examples are shown to depict how results of transliterated CM question fare better than their translated counterparts. Example 1 shows that machine translation fails to translate the CM question correctly. The predicted answer is henceforth incorrect. Example 2 highlights limitations for lexical translation. Lexically translated questions lose their intended meaning if a word has multiple possible translations and it results in an incorrect prediction.

7 Conclusion

This paper proposes techniques for Code-Mixed Question Answering over a Knowledge Base in the absence of direct supervision of CM questions for training neural models. We use only monolingual data [11] and bilingual embeddings to achieve promising results. Our TSHCNN model shows impressive results for English QA. It outperforms many other complicated architectures that use Bi-LSTMs and Attention mechanisms. We also introduce two techniques which significantly enhance results. KNBET reduces the errors that may exist in bilingual embeddings and could be used by any system working with bilingual embeddings. Additionally, negative samples obtained through Solr are useful for the network to learn to differentiate between fine-grained inputs. Despite imperfect bilingual embeddings, our model shows impressive results for CM QA. Our experiments highlight the need for CM QA system, since CM questions in their original form outperforms translated CM questions.

References

Arvind Agarwal, Hema Raghavan, Karthik Subbian, Prem Melville, Richard D. Lawrence, David Gondek, and James Z Fan. 2012. Learning to rank for robust question answering. In *CIKM*.

Kisuh Ahn, Beatrice Alex, Johan Bos, Tiphaine Dalmas, Jochen L. Leidner, and Matthew Smillie. 2004. Cross-lingual question answering using off-the-shelf machine translation. In *CLEF*.

Waleed Ammar, George Mulcaire, Yulia Tsvetkov, Guillaume Lample, Chris Dyer, and Noah A. Smith. 2016. Massively multilingual word embeddings. *CoRR*, abs/1602.01925.

Mikel Artetxe, Gorka Labaka, and Eneko Agirre. 2017. Learning bilingual word embeddings with (almost) no bilingual data. *Proceedings of the 55th Annual Meeting of the Association for Computational Linguistics (Volume 1: Long Papers)*, pages 451–462.

Somnath Banerjee, Sudip Kumar Naskar, Paolo Rosso, and Sivaji Bandyopadhyay. 2016. The first cross-script code-mixed question answering corpus. In *MultiLingMine@ECIR*.

Irshad Ahmad Bhat, Riyaz Ahmad Bhat, Manish Shrivastava, and Dipti Misra Sharma. 2018. Universal dependency parsing for hindi-english code-switching.

Riyaz Ahmad Bhat, Manish Shrivastava, Irshad Ahmad Bhat, and Dipti Misra Sharma. 2017. Joining hands: Exploiting monolingual treebanks for parsing of code-mixing data. In *Proceedings of the 15th Conference of the European Chapter of the Association for Computational Linguistics, EACL 2017, Valencia, Spain,*

---

had the same number of features as that of with CQT.

[11] The language identification system uses CM data. We could instead use a rule-based system using no CM data without much loss in performance.

April 3-7, 2017, Volume 2: Short Papers, pages 324–330.

Piotr Bojanowski, Edouard Grave, Armand Joulin, and Tomas Mikolov. 2016. Enriching word vectors with subword information. *arXiv preprint arXiv:1607.04606*.

Antoine Bordes, Nicolas Usunier, Sumit Chopra, and Jason Weston. 2015. Large-scale Simple Question Answering with Memory Networks.

Antoine Bordes, Jason Weston, and Nicolas Usunier. 2014. Open Question Answering with Weakly Supervised Embedding Models. In *Lecture Notes in Computer Science (including subseries Lecture Notes in Artificial Intelligence and Lecture Notes in Bioinformatics)*, volume 8724 LNAI, pages 165–180.

Jane Bromley, Isabelle Guyon, Yann LeCun, Eduard Säckinger, and Roopak Shah. 1993. Signature verification using a "siamese" time delay neural network. In *Proceedings of the 6th International Conference on Neural Information Processing Systems*, NIPS'93, pages 737–744, San Francisco, CA, USA. Morgan Kaufmann Publishers Inc.

Özlem Çetinoğlu, Sarah Schulz, and Ngoc Thang Vu. 2016. Challenges of computational processing of code-switching. In *Proceedings of the Second Workshop on Computational Approaches to Code Switching*, pages 1–11. Association for Computational Linguistics.

Danqi Chen, Adam Fisch, Jason Weston, and Antoine Bordes. 2017a. Reading wikipedia to answer open-domain questions. In *Proceedings of the 55th Annual Meeting of the Association for Computational Linguistics (Volume 1: Long Papers)*, pages 1870–1879. Association for Computational Linguistics.

Muhao Chen, Yingtao Tian, Mohan Yang, and Carlo Zaniolo. 2017b. Multilingual Knowledge Graph Embeddings for Cross-lingual Knowledge Alignment. In *Proceedings of the Twenty-Sixth International Joint Conference on Artificial Intelligence*, pages 1511–1517, California. International Joint Conferences on Artificial Intelligence Organization.

Kyunghyun Cho, Bart van Merrienboer, Dzmitry Bahdanau, and Yoshua Bengio. 2014. On the properties of neural machine translation: Encoder-decoder approaches. In *SSST@EMNLP*.

Sumit Chopra, Raia Hadsell, and Yann LeCun. 2005. Learning a similarity metric discriminatively, with application to face verification. In *Proceedings of the 2005 IEEE Computer Society Conference on Computer Vision and Pattern Recognition (CVPR'05) - Volume 1 - Volume 01*, CVPR '05, pages 539–546, Washington, DC, USA. IEEE Computer Society.

Alexis Conneau, Guillaume Lample, Marc'Aurelio Ranzato, Ludovic Denoyer, and Hervé Jégou. 2017. Word translation without parallel data. *CoRR*, abs/1710.04087.

Giovanni Da San Martino, Salvatore Romeo, Alberto Barroón-Cedeño, Shafiq Joty, Lluís Maàrquez, Alessandro Moschitti, and Preslav Nakov. 2017. Cross-language question re-ranking. In *Proceedings of the 40th International ACM SIGIR Conference on Research and Development in Information Retrieval*, SIGIR '17, pages 1145–1148, New York, NY, USA. ACM.

Arpita Das, Harish Yenala, Manoj Kumar Chinnakotla, and Manish Shrivastava. 2016. Together we stand: Siamese networks for similar question retrieval. In *Proceedings of the 54th Annual Meeting of the Association for Computational Linguistics, ACL 2016, August 7-12, 2016, Berlin, Germany, Volume 1: Long Papers*.

Anik Dey and Pascale Fung. 2014. A hindi-english code-switching corpus. In *LREC*.

Anthony Fader, Luke Zettlemoyer, and Oren Etzioni. 2014. Open question answering over curated and extracted knowledge bases. In *Proceedings of the 20th ACM SIGKDD International Conference on Knowledge Discovery and Data Mining*, KDD '14, pages 1156–1165, New York, NY, USA. ACM.

David Golub and Xiaodong He. 2016. Character-Level Question Answering with Attention.

Google. 2017. Freebase data dumps. `https://developers.google.com/freebase/data`.

Jeenu Grover, Prabhat Agarwal, Ashish Sharma, Mayank Sikka, Koustav Rudra, and Monojit Choudhury. 2017. I may talk in english but gaali toh hindi mein hi denge: A study of english-hindi code-switching and swearing pattern on social networks. In *Proceedings of the Social Networking Workshop, COMSNETS 2017*. IEEE.

Sherzod Hakimov, Soufian Jebbara, and Philipp Cimiano. 2017. AMUSE: Multilingual semantic parsing for question answering over linked data. *Lecture Notes in Computer Science (including subseries Lecture Notes in Artificial Intelligence and Lecture Notes in Bioinformatics)*, 10587 LNCS:329–346.

Karl Moritz Hermann, Tomáš Kočiský, Edward Grefenstette, Lasse Espeholt, Will Kay, Mustafa Suleyman, and Phil Blunsom. 2015. Teaching machines to read and comprehend. In *Proceedings of the 28th International Conference on Neural Information Processing Systems - Volume 1*, NIPS'15, pages 1693–1701, Cambridge, MA, USA. MIT Press.

Mark Hopkins, Cristian Petrescu-Prahova, Roie Levin, Ronan Le Bras, Alvaro Herrasti, and Vidur Joshi. 2017. Beyond sentential semantic parsing: Tackling the math sat with a cascade of tree transducers. In *Proceedings of the 2017 Conference on Empirical Methods in Natural Language Processing*, pages 795–804. Association for Computational Linguistics.

Baotian Hu, Zhengdong Lu, Hang Li, and Qingcai Chen. 2015. Convolutional Neural Network Architectures for Matching Natural Language Sentences. *NIPS*, page 2009.

Rie Johnson and Tong Zhang. 2015. Effective use of word order for text categorization with convolutional neural networks. In *HLT-NAACL*.

Aditya Joshi, Ameya Prabhu, Manish Shrivastava, and Vasudeva Varma. 2016. Towards subword level compositions for sentiment analysis of hindi-english code mixed text. In *COLING 2016, 26th International Conference on Computational Linguistics, Proceedings of the Conference: Technical Papers, December 11-16, 2016, Osaka, Japan*, pages 2482–2491.

Mandar Joshi, Eunsol Choi, Daniel Weld, and Luke Zettlemoyer. 2017. Triviaqa: A large scale distantly supervised challenge dataset for reading comprehension. In *Proceedings of the 55th Annual Meeting of the Association for Computational Linguistics (Volume 1: Long Papers)*, pages 1601–1611. Association for Computational Linguistics.

Yoon Kim. 2014. Convolutional Neural Networks for Sentence Classification. pages 1746–1751.

Alexandre Klementiev, Ivan Titov, and Binod Bhattarai. 2012. Inducing Crosslingual Distributed Representations of Words. *24th International Conference on Computational Linguistics - Proceedings of COLING 2012: Technical Papers (2012)*, (December):1459–1474.

Siwei Lai, Liheng Xu, Kang Liu, and Jun Zhao. 2015. Recurrent convolutional neural networks for text classification. In *AAAI*.

Chuan-Jie Lin and Yu-Min Kuo. 2010. Description of the ntou complex qa system. In *NTCIR*.

Denis Lukovnikov, Asja Fischer, Jens Lehmann, and Sören Auer. 2017. Neural Network-based Question Answering over Knowledge Graphs on Word and Character Level. *Proceedings of the 26th International Conference on World Wide Web - WWW '17*, pages 1211–1220.

Thang Luong, Hieu Pham, and Christopher D. Manning. 2015. Bilingual word representations with monolingual quality in mind. In *VS@HLT-NAACL*.

Pranava Swaroop Madhyastha and Cristina España-Bonet. 2017. Learning bilingual projections of embeddings for vocabulary expansion in machine translation. In *Proceedings of the 2nd Workshop on Representation Learning for NLP*, pages 139–145. Association for Computational Linguistics.

Carol Myers-Scotton. 2002. *Contact linguistics: Bilingual encounters and grammatical outcomes*. Oxford University Press on Demand.

Sarath Chandar A P, Stanislas Lauly, Hugo Larochelle, Mitesh M. Khapra, Balaraman Ravindran, Vikas Raykar, and Amrita Saha. 2014. An Autoencoder Approach to Learning Bilingual Word Representations.

Barbara Plank. 2017. All-in-1 at ijcnlp-2017 task 4: Short text classification with one model for all languages.

Amir Pouran Ben Veyseh. 2016. Cross-Lingual Question Answering Using Common Semantic Space. *Workshop on Graph-based Methods for Natural Language Processing, NAACL-HLT 2016 ,*, pages 15–19.

Khyathi Chandu Raghavi, Manoj Kumar Chinnakotla, Alan W. Black, and Manish Shrivastava. 2017. Webshodh: A code mixed factoid question answering system for web. In *CLEF*.

Khyathi Chandu Raghavi, Manoj Kumar Chinnakotla, and Manish Shrivastava. 2015. "Answer ka type kya he?". In *Proceedings of the 24th International Conference on World Wide Web - WWW '15 Companion*, pages 853–858, New York, New York, USA. ACM Press.

Pranav Rajpurkar, Jian Zhang, Konstantin Lopyrev, and Percy Liang. 2016. Squad: 100,000+ questions for machine comprehension of text. In *Proceedings of the 2016 Conference on Empirical Methods in Natural Language Processing*, pages 2383–2392. Association for Computational Linguistics.

Han Ren, Dong-Hong Ji, and Jing Wan. 2010. Whu question answering system at ntcir-8 aclia task. In *NTCIR*.

Shruti Rijhwani, Royal Sequiera, Monojit Choudhury, Kalika Bali, and Chandra Sekhar Maddila. 2017. Estimating code-switching on twitter with a novel generalized word-level language detection technique. In *Proc. of ACL 2017*. ACL.

Samuel L. Smith, David H. P. Turban, Steven Hamblin, and Nils Y. Hammerla. 2017. Offline bilingual word vectors, orthogonal transformations and the inverted softmax. pages 1–10.

Ferhan Ture and Elizabeth Boschee. 2016. Learning to translate for multilingual question answering. In *EMNLP*.

Ferhan Ture and Oliver Jojic. 2017. No Need to Pay Attention: Simple Recurrent Neural Networks Work! (for Answering "Simple" Questions). *Empirical Methods in Natural Language Processing (EMNLP)*, pages 2866–2872.

Nam N. Vo and James Hays. 2016. Localizing and orienting street views using overhead imagery. *Lecture Notes in Computer Science (including subseries Lecture Notes in Artificial Intelligence and Lecture Notes in Bioinformatics)*, 9905 LNCS:494–509.

Ivan Vulic and Marie-Francine Moens. 2015. Bilingual word embeddings from non-parallel document-aligned data applied to bilingual lexicon induction. In *Proceedings of the 53rd Annual Meeting of the Association for Computational Linguistics (ACL 2015)*, pages 719–725. ACL.

Yogarshi Vyas, Spandana Gella, Jatin Sharma, Kalika Bali, and Monojit Choudhury. 2014. Pos tagging of english-hindi code-mixed social media content. In *Proceedings of the 2014 Conference on Empirical Methods in Natural Language Processing (EMNLP)*, pages 974–979. Association for Computational Linguistics.

Jieyu Wang and Anita Komlodi. 2016. Understanding users' language selection: Code-switching in online searches. In *Proceedings of the 2016 ACM on Conference on Human Information Interaction and Retrieval*, CHIIR '16, pages 377–379, New York, NY, USA. ACM.

Wenpeng Yin, Mo Yu, Bing Xiang, Bowen Zhou, and Hinrich Schütze. 2016. Simple question answering by attentive convolutional neural network. In *Proceedings of COLING 2016, the 26th International Conference on Computational Linguistics: Technical Papers*, pages 1746–1756. The COLING 2016 Organizing Committee.

Mo Yu, Wenpeng Yin, Kazi Saidul Hasan, Cicero dos Santos, Bing Xiang, and Bowen Zhou. 2017. Improved Neural Relation Detection for Knowledge Base Question Answering. In *Proceedings of the 55th Annual Meeting of the Association for Computational Linguistics (Volume 1: Long Papers)*, pages 571–581, Stroudsburg, PA, USA. Association for Computational Linguistics.

Meng Zhang, Yang Liu, Huanbo Luan, and Maosong Sun. 2017. Adversarial training for unsupervised bilingual lexicon induction. In *ACL*.

Xiang Zhang, Junbo Jake Zhao, and Yann LeCun. 2015. Character-level convolutional networks for text classification. In *NIPS*.

Language Identification and Analysis of Code-Switched
Social Media Text

Deepthi Mave, Suraj Maharjan and Thamar Solorio
Department of Computer Science
University of Houston
{dmave, smaharjan2}@uh.edu, solorio@cs.uh.edu

Abstract

In this paper, we detail our work on comparing different word-level language identification systems for code-switched Hindi-English data and a standard Spanish-English dataset. In this regard, we build a new code-switched dataset for Hindi-English. To understand the code-switching patterns in these language pairs, we investigate different code-switching metrics. We find that the CRF model outperforms the neural network based models by a margin of 2-5 percentage points for Spanish-English and 3-5 percentage points for Hindi-English.

1 Introduction

Code-switching occurs when a person switches between two or more languages in a single instance of spoken or written communication (Gumperz, 1982; Myers-Scotton, 1997). Code-switching instances are prevalent in modern informal communications between multilingual individuals specially, in social media platforms such as Facebook and Twitter. Given this prevalence of code-switching, there is value in automatic processing and understanding of such data. Language identification at the word level is the first step in computational modeling of code-switched data. Language identification is important for a wide variety of end user applications such as information extraction systems, voice assistant interfaces, machine translation, as well as for tools to assist language assessment in bilingual children (Gupta et al., 2014; Chandu et al., 2017; Roy et al., 2013). Language detection, in addition, enables sociolinguistics and pragmatic studies of code-switching behavior.

Code-switching in speech is well studied in linguistics, psycholinguistic and sociolinguistics (Sankoff, 1970; Lipski, 1978; Poplack, 1980; Gumperz, 1982; Auer, 1984; Myers-Scotton, 1997, 2002). The alternation of languages across sentence boundaries is known as code-switching and the alternation within a sentence is known as code-mixing. In this paper we will refer to both instances as code-switching and differentiate between the types of code switching when necessary. Table 1 shows examples of code-switching for Hindi-English and Spanish-English.

Example 1
Good morning sir*ji*, *aaj ka* weather *kaisa hai*?
(Good morning sir, How is the weather today?)
Example 2
Styling day *trabajando con* @username
vestuario para #ElFactorX *y soy hoy chofer.*
I will get you there in pieces im a Safe Driver.
(Styling day working with @username
wardrobe for #ElFactorX and today I am a driver.
I will get you there in pieces im a Safe Driver.)

Table 1: Example 1 shows code-switching between Hindi-English and Example 2 between Spanish-English (Molina et al., 2016).

Word level language identification of code-switched text is inherently difficult. First, a single code-switched instance can have mixing at the sentence or clause level, the word level, and even at the sub-word level (e.g. sir-*ji*, *chapathi*-s). Second, the typology of the languages involved in switching and their inter-relatedness further increase the task complexity. For example, a shared Latin influence on Spanish and English results in lexical relatedness (Smith, 2001; August et al., 2002), making Spanish-English language identification harder than Hindi-English. Third, in spite of the fact that Hindi has a native script (Devanagari), most of the Hindi social media text is

Proceedings of The Third Workshop on Computational Approaches to Code-Switching, pages 51–61
Melbourne, Australia, July 19, 2018. ©2018 Association for Computational Linguistics

transliterated. Transliteration is conversion of a text from one script to another. In the case of Hindi, text is converted from native, Devanagari to Roman script. Due to lack of standardization in transliteration, a single Hindi word can have multiple surface forms (e.g. *Humara, Hamara, Hamaaraa* etc.). Some Hindi words can take the same surface form as an English word. The words *'hi'* (an auxiliary verb), *'is'* (this), and *'us'* (that) are some examples. Finally, the characteristics of social media text such as non-standard spelling, contractions, and not strictly adhering to the grammar of the language adds to the list of challenges.

In this work, we make three contributions. First, we build a new code-switched dataset for Hindi-English (HIN-ENG) language pair from Facebook public pages and Twitter. Second, we investigate different code-switching metrics for Hindi-English and a standard Spanish-English (SPA-ENG) dataset. Third, we compare a traditional machine learning model - conditional random field (CRF), and two recurrent neural network (RNN) based systems, for word-level language identification of the above language pairs. In contrast to the CRF model, the RNN-based systems do not involve language specific resources or sophisticated feature engineering. We test these models, first for each of the language pairs individually, and then for a corpus with both the language pairs combined.

Among the language identification systems, the CRF model outperforms both the RNN-based systems across language pairs. When both the language pairs are combined, the result from the best performing model (CRF) is 25% points higher than the baseline system. The RNN-based models also give reasonable results.

2   Related Work

Over the last decade several researchers have explored word-level language identification for different language pairs and dialect varieties. The FIRE shared task series - (Roy et al., 2013; Choudhury et al., 2014; Sequiera et al., 2015b) focuses on language identification of code-mixed search queries in English and Indian languages for information retrieval. We use a larger set of labels compared to these tasks. The First and Second Shared Task on Language Identification in Code-Switched Data (Solorio et al., 2014; Molina et al., 2016) show the necessity for automatic process-

ing of code-switched text and report comparison of different language identification systems. The best system from the second iteration of these shared tasks uses a logistic regression model and reports a token-level F1-score of 97.3% for SPA-ENG. Our results are competitive with this score. Das and Gambäck (2014) use a dictionary based method and SVM model with various features for Hindi-English and Bengali-English. Their system achieves an F1-score of 79% for Hindi-English. Barman et al. (2014) create a new dataset and study code mixing between the three languages - English, Hindi, and Bengali using CRF and SVM models. In another work, Gella et al. (2014) build a language detection system for synthetically created code-mixed dataset for 28 languages. Similar to some of the works in the above mentioned papers, we model the language detection task as a sequence labeling problem and explore combinations of several features using the CRF model, but we use a larger set of labels. We obtain significantly higher performance for the Hindi-English language pair than Das and Gambäck (2014).

Along with the traditional machine learning approach, some researchers have also used models based on artificial neural networks. Chang and Lin (2014) use an RNN architecture with pre-trained word2vec embeddings for SPA-ENG and the Nepali-English datasets from the First Shared Task on Language Identification in Code-Switched Data. Samih et al. (2016) build an LSTM based neural network architecture for SPA-ENG and MSA-DA datasets from the Second Shared Task on Language Identification in Code-Switched Data. Their model combines word and character representations initialized with pre-trained word2vec embeddings. We replicate their model with *softmax* output layer for SPA-ENG and run similar experiments for HIN-ENG, as well as with both the corpora combined. Our result for SPA-ENG match that of Samih et al. (2016).

3   Data

We use the SPA-ENG dataset from the EMNLP Code-Switching Workshop 2016. This data is collected from Twitter, based on the geographical areas with strong presence of Spanish and English bilingual speakers - California, Texas, Miami, and New York (Solorio et al., 2014; Molina et al., 2016). The labels used are summarized in Table 2. The hashtags are treated as a word and are la-

Label	Description	HIN-ENG (%)	SPA-ENG (%)
lang1	English words only	57.764	38.258
lang2	Hindi/Spanish words only	20.418	40.579
ne	Proper names	6.582	1.935
other	Symbols, usernames, emoticons	14.807	18.952
mixed	Words partially in both the languages	0.04	0.018
ambiguous	Can't determine whether English or Hindi/Spanish	0.009	0.137
fw	Words is not English neither Hindi/Spanish	0.369	0.01
unk	Unrecognizable word	0.012	0.11

Table 2: A brief description of the labels and label distribution for HIN-ENG and SPA-ENG datasets.

beled accordingly.

Corpus Creation for Hindi-English. For the HIN-ENG corpus, we consider Facebook pages of prominent public figures from India. Hindi-English bilingual users are highly active in these pages (Bali et al., 2014). We crawl posts and their comments from the Facebook public pages of various sports-persons, political figures, and movie stars. We also crawl random tweets from geographical locations Mumbai and Delhi using the Twitter API. From the crawled posts, we remove the posts in native scripts, and remove duplicate and promotional posts. We filter the posts containing URLs and those with less than 3 words.

Language Pair Pair	Tweets (Posts)	Tokens	Unique Tokens (%)
SPA-ENG	25,130	294,261	35,153 (11.95)
HIN-ENG	7,421	146,722	23,998 (16.36)

Table 3: Corpus statistics for the language pairs. Token ratio is the percentage of the total tokens that are unique. A higher token ratio implies a richer corpus vocabulary.

We follow EMNLP 2016 shared task annotation guidelines and use a semi-automatic approach to annotate the data. The labels are reviewed and corrected with the help of in-lab annotators. The inter-annotator agreement score over approximately $4,000$ tokens is 0.935. A portion of the Facebook dataset is annotated using the English lexicon and Hindi transliterated pairs.[1,2] We use pattern matching rules to label punctuations, emoticons, and usernames. These labels are then corrected manually for *ne*, *fw*, *mixed*, *ambiguous*, and *unk* labels. We also make use of two existing datasets - Facebook dataset from ICON2016 POS tagging shared task and the dataset from (Se-

quiera et al., 2015a).[3] We manually map the labels of these data sets to labels in Table 2. We train a character n-gram based CRF model using the above mentioned three datasets (see Section 5.2) and predict the labels for all the posts crawled from Facebook and the random tweets from Twitter. From these, we identify the posts predicted as code-switched, correct the labels where necessary, and add them to the final dataset. The F1-weighted score for this model is close to 96 percent.

4 Code-Switching Analysis

In this section we provide some descriptive statistics about the corpora to understand the language distribution and language-relatedness. Table 4 shows the language distribution at post (tweet) level. The SPA-ENG dataset has a balanced distribution where as, in the HIN-ENG dataset majority of the instances are in English. The below statistics show that both the datasets have a good amount of code-switched instances to train and test the language identification systems. Ta-

Language Pairs	CS Instances	lang1	lang2	other
HIN-ENG	43.62	51.77	4.02	0.60
SPA-ENG	34.75	33.53	28.94	2.77

Table 4: Post-level language distribution in the datasets. Column 5 corresponds to the instances that do not have any words with language tags. *lang1*: ENG, *lang2*: HIN/SPA.

ble 2 presents the label-wise token distribution for the datasets. For HIN-ENG, majority of the words (58%) are in English, 20% are in Hindi, and 7% are named-entities. The SPA-ENG dataset in comparison has a balanced distribution of the two languages with 38% of the words in English, 41% in

---

[1] http://wortschatz.uni-leipzig.de/en/download

[2] http://cse.iitkgp.ac.in/resgrp/cnerg/qa/fire13translit/

[3] http://amitavadas.com/Code-Mixing.html

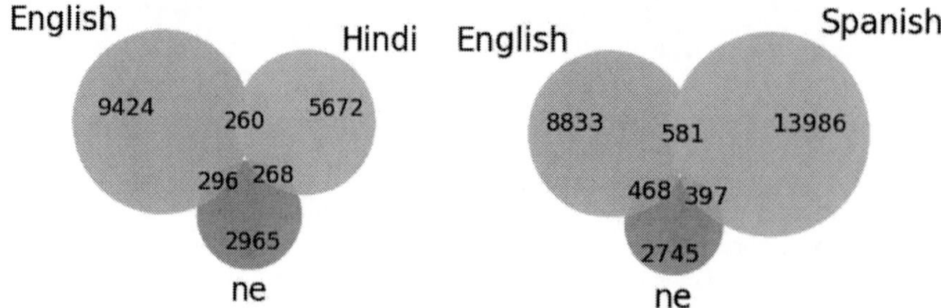

Figure 1: Vocabulary overlap for labels *lang1*, *lang2*, and *ne* for HIN-ENG and SPAN-ENG.

Spanish, and 2% are named-entities. The higher instances of the named-entities in the HIN-ENG dataset is a result of the way the data is sourced.

Figure 1 shows the overlap between the tokens belonging to *lang1*, *lang2*, and *ne*. These overlaps introduce ambiguity for the automatic labeling task. Around 2.5% of the Hindi words in HIN-ENG share the same spelling as some English words because of transliteration of Hindi text to Roman script. In comparison, there is a 6% overlap between Spanish and English words in the SPA-ENG dataset (e.g. *no, a, final*). This indicates higher degree of lexical relatedness between Spanish and English as compared to Hindi and English. The overlap between language words and named-entities is due to words such as *university* and *united*. These words can be part of names of organizations, movie titles or song titles and can also be used as language constructs in either of the languages.

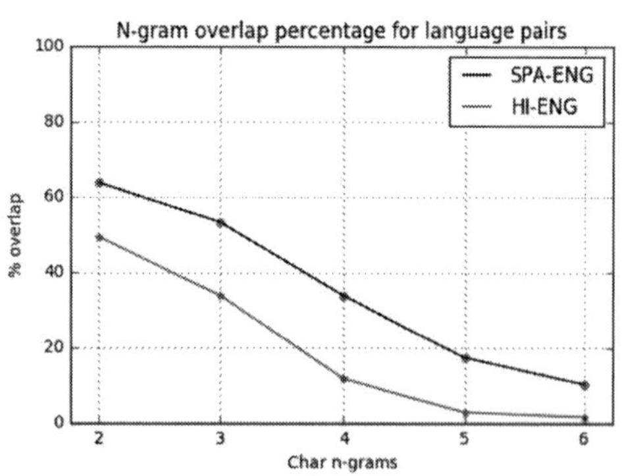

Figure 2: Plot of character n-grams overlap between the languages in the datasets, for $n = 2, 3, 4, 5$ and 6.

In another analysis, we explore the similarity in character n-gram profiles of the languages involved (Maharjan et al., 2015). A higher simi-

larity in the character n-grams increases the difficulty of the task. We generate character n-grams of length 2 to 6 from the language vocabularies of each corpora. We show the plot of the character n-gram overlaps for HIN-ENG and SPA-ENG in Figure 2. As expected, the overlap decreases rapidly with increase in n-gram length. The SPA-ENG n-gram overlap is higher than that of HIN-ENG for all n-gram lengths. This trend is consistent with the results in Figure 1. To further understand the complexity involved, for an n-gram occurring in both the languages, we calculate the probability of that n-gram being a part of an English word in the corpus. A probability closer to 50% indicates higher ambiguity in classifying that n-gram. We find that a significant fraction (25%) of these shared n-grams, averaged over all n-gram lengths, appear in the range 40%-60%.

5 Code-Switching Metrics

The code-switching behavior can be different depending on the medium of communication, context of language use, topic, authors (or speakers), and the languages being mixed among other factors. We compute 3 different metrics to understand code-switching patterns in our datasets, as well as to rationalize the performance of the language identification models.

M-Index: Multilingual index is a word-count-based measure that quantifies the inequality of the language tags distribution in a corpus of at least two languages (Barnett et al., 2000). Equation (1) defines the *M-Index* as:

$$M - Index = \frac{1 - \sum p_j^2}{(k - 1) \sum p_j^2} \quad (1)$$

where k is the total number of languages and p_j is the total number of words in the language j over the total number of words in the corpus. The value ranges between 0 and 1 where, a value of 0 corresponds to a monolingual corpus and 1 corresponds to a corpus with equal number of tokens from each language.

Integration Index: Integration Index is the approximate probability that any given token in the corpus is a switch point (Guzman et al., 2016; Guzmán et al., 2017). Given a corpus composed of tokens tagged by language $\{l_j\}$ where i ranges from 1 to $n-1$, the size of the corpus. The *I-index* is computed as follows:

$$I - Index = \frac{1}{n-1} \sum_{1 \le i=j-1 \le n-1} S(l_i, l_j) \quad (2)$$

where $S(l_i, l_j) = 1$ if $l_i \ne l_j$ and 0 otherwise. For a corpus with n tokens, there are $n-1$ possible switch points. It quantifies the frequency of code-switching in a corpus.

Code-Mixing Index: At the utterance level, this is computed by finding the most frequent language in the utterance and then counting the frequency of the words belonging to all other languages present (Gambäck and Das, 2014). It is calculated using:

$$CMI = \frac{\sum_{i=1}^{n}(w_i) - \max(w_i)}{n - u} \quad (3)$$

where $\sum_{i=1}^{n}(w_i)$ is the sum over number of words for all N languages in the utterance, $\max(w_i)$ is the highest number of words present from any language, n is the total number of tokens, and u is the number of language independent tokens. Here, we consider the labels *lang1, lang2*, and *fw* as language words and the rest as *other*. The range of CMI value is $[0, 100)$. If an utterance has language independent tokens or only monolingual tokens, then the corresponding CMI value is 0. A higher value of CMI indicates higher level of mixing between the languages. *CMI-all* is an average over all utterances in the corpus and *CMI-mixed* is an average over only code-switched instances.

Language Pairs	M-Index	CMI-all	CMI-Mixed	I-Index
HIN-ENG	0.582	8.564	22.229	0.070
SPA-ENG	0.998	7.685	22.114	0.058

Table 5: CS Metrics for the datasets.

SPA-ENG has higher *M-Index* (Table 5) value indicating a balanced ratio of words from the two languages. This is consistent with the distribution of language words in the datasets (Table 2). The differences in *CMI-all* between

HIN-ENG and SPA-ENG is about 0.9 percentage points and 0.1 percentage points for *CMI-mixed*. The higher difference for *CMI-all* could be because of the higher percentage of code-switched instances (9%) in HIN-ENG as compared to SPA-ENG (Table 4). Considering *CMI-mixed* and *I-Index* metrics together, it is evident that HIN-ENG has more language mixing and higher number of code-switching points than SPA-ENG. This is because HIN-ENG has more instances that have multiple word insertions. In SPA-ENG, instances with word insertion at more than one place in an utterance are less frequent. We also observe that a larger majority of code-switching happens between language words in HIN-ENG (76%) than in SPA-ENG (69%). For example, a number of Hindi word insertions are due to the use of the honorary article *ji* with an address form (Sir/Madam). In general, observing more code-switching in HIN-ENG is due to the fact that code-switching between Hindi and English is very widespread in India (Parshad et al., 2016; Bali et al., 2014).

6 Language Identification Models

We provide below a brief description of each of the models used.

CRF: Language identification is a sequence labeling task where the label of a token in a sequence is correlated with the labels of its neighboring tokens. So we use CRF - a sequence labeling model to capture the structure in the data. We explore different language independent features such as character n-grams, word unigram, morphological features, affixes, and contextual information for the language pairs. For each word, we generate character n-grams of length 1 to 5 and filter them based on a minimum threshold frequency of 5. To capture the morphological information of the tokens, we use binary features - is digit, is special character, is all capital, is title case, begins with @ character, has accent character (for SPA-ENG only) and has apostrophe.

We also use language dependent resources like lexicons and monolingual parts-of-speech (POS) taggers. For HIN-ENG, we use three different lexicons - Leipzig corpus for English, FIRE 2013 transliterated Hindi word pairs, and lexically normalized dictionary from Han et al. (2012) and the output of Twitter POS tagger and CRF++

based Hindi POS tagger.[4,5] For SPA-ENG, we use Leipzig corpus Spanish along with the other two lexicons mentioned above and the output from monolingual TreeTaggers for Spanish and English.[6]

Bidirectional LSTM: Long Short Term Memory networks (LSTMs) (Hochreiter and Schmidhuber, 1997) are a variation of recurrent neural networks (RNNs), that address the vanishing gradient issue (Hochreiter, 1998) by extending RNNs with memory cells. A shortcoming of LSTM is that only the

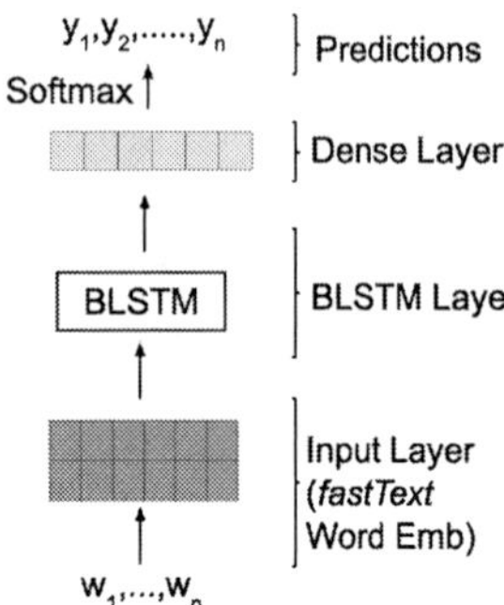

Figure 3: Bidirectional LSTM Model.

previous history in a sequence can be utilized. In a sequence labeling task like language identification, it is helpful to use the future context given in the sequence. Bidirectional LSTM (BLSTM) networks can access both the preceding and succeeding contexts by involving two separate hidden layers. These networks can capture the long distance relations in the sequence efficiently, in both directions. We build an end-to-end sequence model with a single BLSTM layer layer (Figure 3).

Word-Character LSTM: This model is a replication of the model proposed by Samih et al. (2016) (Figure 4). The input layer in this model has word and character embeddings. The latter are used to capture morphological features of a word. We use two LSTMs to learn fixed-dimensional representations from the embedding layers. At the output layer, we apply a *softmax* over the concatenated word and character vectors to obtain the token label. Unlike the BLSTM model, here current token and the neighboring tokens are considered to predict the label for the current token. We replace the emoticons in the dataset with a place-

holder character to reduce the vocabulary size and as a result reduce the dimension of character embeddings. This decreases the number of trainable model parameters and thereby mitigates overfitting to some extent.

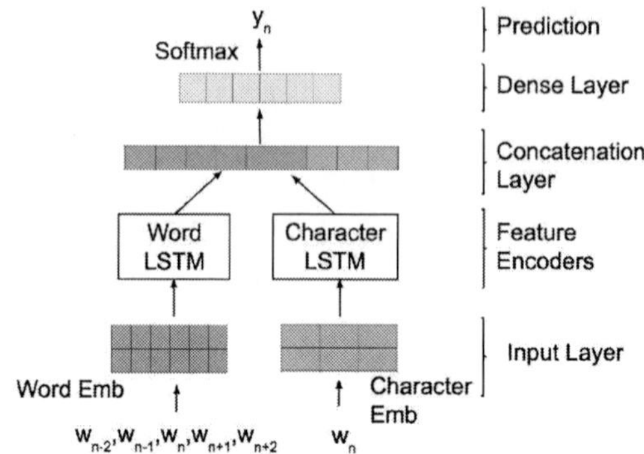

Figure 4: Word-Character LSTM Model. The input layer of word-char LSTM is initialized with *fastText* word embeddings.

7 Experiments and Results

For CRF, we run experiments with different combinations of hand-crafted features discussed in the previous section. We run three different sets of experiments- with no contextual information, and with surrounding words of context window sizes 1 and 2. Table 6 and Table 7 shows results from these experiments.

For the RNN-based systems, we use pre-trained *fastText* word embeddings.[7] We learn the embeddings using a large monolingual corpus for each of the languages and a smaller code-switched corpus for the language pairs. The rationale for using a large monolingual data is that it is readily available and that it can account for the different contexts in which words appear in different languages - thus providing an accurate separation between the languages. We train three separate sets of embeddings each for SPA-ENG, HIN-ENG, and SPA-ENG + HIN-ENG. The embeddings for SPA-ENG are trained by combining a portion of English Gigaword corpus (Graff et al., 2003) and Spanish Gigaword corpus (Graff, 2006), and a subset of tweets from Samih et al. (2016). For HIN-ENG, we combine a portion of English Gigaword corpus, transliterated Hindi monolingual corpus, and Facebook posts that contain code-switching. All

---

[4]http://www.cs.cmu.edu/ ark/TweetNLP/

[5]http://nltr.org/snltr-software/

[6]http://www.cis.uni-muenchen.de/ schmid/tools/TreeTagger/

[7]https://fasttext.cc/

Experiments	Context-0	Context-1	Context-2
Baseline	85.02	-	-
Word + 1 to 5 char n-grams (1)	96.89	96.79	96.77
(1) + word form (2)	96.95	96.77	96.78
(2) + affixes (3)	96.96	96.84	96.84
(3) + lexicons (4)	97.07	97.03	97.12
(4) + POS tags	97.05	**97.16**	97.11
(4) + Univ POS tags	97.1	97.15	97.12

Table 6: Token-level F1-weighted score of the CRF model for different feature combinations for HIN-ENG.

Experiments	Context-0	Context-1	Context-2
Baseline	83.17	-	-
Word + 1 to 5 char n-grams (1)	97.02	96.81	96.82
(1) + word form (2)	97.21	97.09	97.01
(2) + affixes (3)	97.17	97.07	97.06
(3) + lexicons (4)	97.31	97.19	97.16
(4) + POS tags	97.24	97.19	97.17
(4) + Univ POS tags	**97.25**	97.19	97.21

Table 7: Token-level F1-weighted score of the CRF model for different feature combinations for SPA-ENG.

these corpora are used to train the embeddings for SPA-ENG + HIN-ENG. This helps to capture the word usage in the context of each language and eliminates the ambiguity for the words that have same surface form in multiple languages. We train 300-dimension embedding vectors using *fastText* skip-gram model for 250 epochs with a learning rate of 0.001 and a minimum word count threshold of 5.

For BLSTM model, we initialize the embedding layer with the pre-trained *fastText* word embeddings and feed the output sequence from this layer to the BLSTM layer. At the output layer a *softmax* activation function is applied over the hidden representation learned in the BLSTM layer. For word-char model, we initialize the word embedding matrix with *fastText* embeddings and use random initialization for character embedding matrix. We train both the RNN-based models by optimizing the cross entropy objective function with *Adam* (Kingma and Ba, 2014) optimizer. We use dropout masks after BLSTM layer in BLSTM model, LSTM layers in word-char model, and embedding layer in each model to mitigate overfitting. The reported BLSTM model and word-char models have hidden units of size 80 and 100 respectively in the LSTM layers. For word-char model, for each token we try a neighboring token window size of 1, 2, and 3. The context window size of 2 gives better results and is reported here.

System	SPA-ENG	HIN-ENG	SPA-ENG + HIN-ENG
Baseline	83.17	85.02	71.49
CRF (Context-2)	**97.06**	**96.84**	**96.37**
BLSTM	92.22	93.9	88.7
Word-char LSTM	95.46	92.19	90.1

Table 8: Token-level F1-weighted score for language identification systems.

Multiple Language Pair Experiment. We use the models described in Section 6 in an experiment to identify the labels for a dataset with multiple language pairs. This dataset has both Spanish-English and Hindi-English language pairs (SPA-ENG + HIN-ENG). To account for the third language, we use an additional label - *lang3* (HIN). Except for the pre-trained word embeddings, the models do not involve any language dependent feature engineering, and are easy to scale for multiple language pairs. As the word embeddings are

HIN-ENG		SPA-ENG	
Transitions	**Weights**	**Transitions**	**Weights**
unk → unk	9.511	*fw → fw*	4.731
fw → fw	5.800	*ne → ne*	2.798
ambiguous → ambiguous	4.630	*lang2 → lang2*	1.464
lang2 → lang2	2.872	*lang2 → ne*	1.005
ne → ne	2.824	*lang1 → ne*	0.915
other → other	1.905	*lang2 → mixed*	0.833
lang1 → lang1	1.535	*lang1 → lang1*	0.707
other → lang1	0.801	*lang2 → ambiguous*	0.625
lang1 → other	0.573	*other → other*	0.483
lang1 → mixed	0.353	*other → mixed*	0.427

Table 9: The top 10 most likely transitions learned by the best CRF model for HIN-ENG and SPA-ENG datasets.

trained mostly on monolingual data, this dependency does not constrain the systems.

7.1 Results and Evaluation

We use a simple lexicon-based model as baseline for our language identification systems. We use F1-weighted scores for model evaluations to account for the imbalance in label distributions (Table 2). All the models improve the performance over the respective baseline models by 7 to 25 percentage points. For CRF, which is the best performing model across language pairs, the current word and its character n-grams are the most important features. Adding POS tags does not improve these results by much. This could be because the POS taggers are optimized for monolingual data and their output for the code-switched data contains noise. Using contextual information improves the results for HIN-ENG, but not for SPA-ENG. In Table 8 we compare the RNN-

Language Pair	System	lang1	lang2	ne
HIN-ENG	BLSTM	0.96	0.94	0.77
	Word-char LSTM	0.95	0.85	0.76
	CRF (Context-2)	**0.98**	**0.96**	**0.85**
SPA-ENG	BLSTM	0.89	0.95	0.32
	Word-char LSTM	0.89	0.97	0.40
	CRF (Context-2)	**0.94**	**0.98**	**0.57**

Table 10: Token-level F1-score of majority labels - *lang1*, *lang2* and *ne* for the models.

based models and the CRF model. We consider the performance of the CRF model using only the language independent features with a context size of 2 for a fair comparison. Among the RNN-based systems, while the results are competitive overall, there is no single system that performs the best across language pairs. The BLSTM system performs better for HIN-ENG, while word-char system performs better for SPA-ENG. The BLSTM model captures long distance dependencies in a sequence and this is in line with the observation made above with the CRF model- more context helps for HIN-ENG. It is also consistent with the code-switching patterns discussed in Section 5. A majority of code-switched tweets in SPA-ENG have a single instance of word insertion and these are being miss-labeled by the models. The overall better results for SPA-ENG are because of a larger training data used.[8] The baseline results for SPA-ENG + HIN-ENG is relatively low as compared to the individual language pairs. This shows that simultaneously identifying language for multiple language pair is harder. We obtain reasonable results for these initial experiments with all the models.

To understand these results better, we look at the label-wise F1-score for *lang1, lang2* and *ne* (Table 10). The F1-scores for CRF is better across the labels and the difference is significantly high for *ne*. The F1-score *ne* is relatively high for HIN-ENG, which can be attributed to the fact that around 58% of the named-entities in the test set appear in the training set. This overlap is only 17% for SPA-ENG. So, infrequent named-entities seems to be hardest to accurately label. In addition, the RNN-based models are more sensitive to amount of training samples.

Further, we examine the transitions learned by

---

[8]The F1-score drops by 10 percentage points for the reported experiments with the training dataset that is half in size, while maintaining the post-level language distribution.

our best CRF model for each of the language pairs (Table 9). For both language pairs, the transitions between the same languages are more likely than switching. But we also observe that the transitions from *lang1* to *lang2* and vice-versa rank higher for HIN-ENG than SPA-ENG. This is because there are fewer code-switching points in SPA-ENG as compared to HIN-ENG in these datasets.

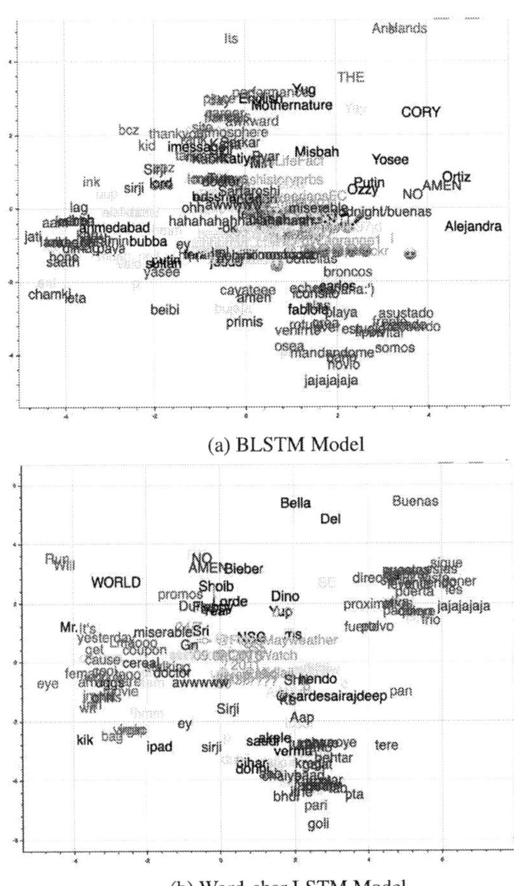

(a) BLSTM Model

(b) Word-char LSTM Model

Figure 5: Projection of word representations learned by the neural networks model for HIN-ENG + SPA-ENG. We reduce the word vector dimensions using PCA. The mapping of labels to colors: *lang1* - red, *lang2* - green, *lang3* - blue, *ne* - black, *other* - orange, *ambiguous* - purple, *mixed* - purple, *fw* - yellow, *unk* - yellow.

We also visualize the feature representations learned by the RNN-based models by projecting the word embeddings for a randomly selected subset of words from the development datasets for SPA-ENG + HIN-ENG (Figure 5). The word-char model gives a clearer separation between the three languages, the words belonging to the labels *other* and *ne*. While the BLSTM model also provides clear separation between the language words, there is an overlap with the tokens from *other*. These results show that these models can be scaled to detect code-switching in multiple language pairs without any additional feature engineering.

8 Conclusions

The complexity of language identification of code-switched data depends on the data source, code-switching behavior, and the typology and relation between the languages involved. We find that the code-switching metrics complement each other in explaining the code-switching patterns across language pairs. The analysis of code-switching metrics shows that in our datasets Hindi-English speakers tend to switch languages more often than Spanish-English speakers. In future, it would be interesting to explore and compare the code-switching behavior of data from different sources such as movie scripts, song lyrics, and chat conversations across different language pairs.

We successfully use two different deep learning architectures without involving sophisticated feature engineering for the task and obtain competitive results. However a traditional CRF model performs better than the deep learning models for the language pairs considered. This is probably due to the amount of training data we have. The results show that word embeddings are able to capture the language separation well. Scaling these systems to identify languages in datasets with many language pairs and datasets with switching between more than two languages is a potential future direction to explore.

Acknowledgments

We would like to thank the National Science Foundation for partially supporting this work under award number 1462143 as well as the U.S. Department of Defense for the support received under grant W911NF-16-1-0422.

References

Peter Auer. 1984. *Bilingual conversation*. John Benjamins Publishing.

Diane August, Margarita Calderón, and María Carlo. 2002. Transfer of skills from Spanish to English: A study of young learners. *Washington, DC: Center for Applied Linguistics*, 24:148–158.

Kalika Bali, Jatin Sharma, Monojit Choudhury, and Yogarshi Vyas. 2014. "I am borrowing ya mixing ?" An Analysis of English-Hindi Code Mixing in Facebook. In *Proceedings of the First Workshop on Computational Approaches to Code Switching*, pages 116–126, Doha, Qatar. Association for Computational Linguistics.

Utsab Barman, Amitava Das, Joachim Wagner, and Jennifer Foster. 2014. Code mixing: A challenge for language identification in the language of social media. In *Proceedings of the First Workshop on Computational Approaches to Code Switching*, pages 13–23, Doha, Qatar. Association for Computational Linguistics.

Ruthanna Barnett, Eva Codó, Eva Eppler, Montse Forcadell, Penelope Gardner-Chloros, Roeland van Hout, Melissa Moyer, Maria Carme Torras, Maria Teresa Turell, and Mark Sebba. 2000. The LIDES Coding Manual: A document for preparing and analyzing language interaction data Version 1.1July, 1999. *International Journal of Bilingualism*, 4(2):131–271.

Khyathi Raghavi Chandu, Sai Krishna Rallabandi, Sunayana Sitaram, and Alan W Black. 2017. Speech Synthesis for Mixed-Language Navigation Instructions. In *Interspeech 2017, 18th Annual Conference of the International Speech Communication Association, Stockholm, Sweden, August 20-24, 2017*, pages 57–61.

Joseph Chee Chang and Chu-Cheng Lin. 2014. Recurrent-neural-network for language detection on Twitter code-switching corpus. *arXiv preprint arXiv:1412.4314*.

Monojit Choudhury, Gokul Chittaranjan, Parth Gupta, and Amitava Das. 2014. Overview of FIRE 2014 track on transliterated search. *Proceedings of FIRE*, pages 68–89.

Amitava Das and Björn Gambäck. 2014. Identifying languages at the word level in code-mixed indian social media text. In *Proceedings of the 11th International Conference on Natural Language Processing*, pages 378–387, Goa, India. NLP Association of India.

Björn Gambäck and Amitava Das. 2014. On measuring the complexity of code-mixing. In *Proceedings of the 11th International Conference on Natural Language Processing, Goa, India*, pages 1–7.

Spandana Gella, Kalika Bali, and Monojit Choudhury. 2014. ye word kis lang ka hai bhai? testing the limits of word level language identification. In *Proceedings of the 11th International Conference on Natural Language Processing*, pages 368–377.

Dave Graff. 2006. LDC2006T12: Spanish Gigaword. *Linguistic Data Consortium, Philadelphia*.

David Graff, Junbo Kong, Ke Chen, and Kazuaki Maeda. 2003. LDC2003T05:English Gigaword.

John J Gumperz. 1982. *Discourse strategies*, volume 1. Cambridge University Press.

Parth Gupta, Kalika Bali, Rafael E. Banchs, Monojit Choudhury, and Paolo Rosso. 2014. Query expansion for mixed-script information retrieval. In *Proceedings of the 37th International ACM SIGIR Conference on Research & Development in Information Retrieval*, SIGIR '14, pages 677–686, New York, NY, USA. ACM.

Gualberto Guzmán, Joseph Ricard, Jacqueline Serigos, Barbara E Bullock, and Almeida Jacqueline Toribio. 2017. Metrics for modeling code-switching across corpora. *Proc. Interspeech 2017*, pages 67–71.

Gualberto A Guzman, Jacqueline Serigos, Barbara E Bullock, and Almeida Jacqueline Toribio. 2016. Simple tools for exploring variation in code-switching for linguists. In *Proceedings of the Second Workshop on Computational Approaches to Code Switching*, pages 12–20.

Bo Han, Paul Cook, and Timothy Baldwin. 2012. Automatically constructing a normalisation dictionary for microblogs. In *Proceedings of the 2012 Joint Conference on Empirical Methods in Natural Language Processing and Computational Natural Language Learning*, pages 421–432, Jeju Island, Korea. Association for Computational Linguistics.

Sepp Hochreiter. 1998. The vanishing gradient problem during learning recurrent neural nets and problem solutions. *International Journal of Uncertainty, Fuzziness and Knowledge-Based Systems*, 6(2):107–116.

Sepp Hochreiter and Jürgen Schmidhuber. 1997. Long short-term memory. *Neural computation*, 9(8):1735–1780.

Diederik P Kingma and Jimmy Ba. 2014. Adam: A method for stochastic optimization. *arXiv preprint arXiv:1412.6980*.

John Lipski. 1978. Code-switching and the problem of bilingual competence. *Aspects of bilingualism*, pages 250–264.

Suraj Maharjan, Elizabeth Blair, Steven Bethard, and Thamar Solorio. 2015. Developing language-tagged corpora for code-switching tweets. In *Proceedings of The 9th Linguistic Annotation Workshop*, pages 72–84, Denver, Colorado, USA. Association for Computational Linguistics.

Giovanni Molina, Fahad AlGhamdi, Mahmoud Ghoneim, Abdelati Hawwari, Nicolas Rey-Villamizar, Mona Diab, and Thamar Solorio. 2016. Overview for the second shared task on language identification in code-switched data. In *Proceedings of the Second Workshop on Computational Approaches to Code Switching*, pages 40–49, Austin, Texas. Association for Computational Linguistics.

Carol Myers-Scotton. 1997. *Duelling languages: Grammatical structure in codeswitching*. Oxford University Press.

Carol Myers-Scotton. 2002. *Contact linguistics: Bilingual encounters and grammatical outcomes*. Oxford University Press on Demand.

Rana D Parshad, Suman Bhowmick, Vineeta Chand, Nitu Kumari, and Neha Sinha. 2016. What is India speaking? Exploring the Hinglish invasion. *Physica A: Statistical Mechanics and its Applications*, 449:375–389.

Shana Poplack. 1980. Sometimes ill start a sentence in Spanish y termino en espaol: toward a typology of code-switching. *Linguistics*, 18(7-8):581–618.

Rishiraj Saha Roy, Monojit Choudhury, Prasenjit Majumder, and Komal Agarwal. 2013. Overview of the FIRE 2013 track on transliterated search. In *Post-Proceedings of the 4th and 5th Workshops of the Forum for Information Retrieval Evaluation*, page 4. ACM.

Younes Samih, Suraj Maharjan, Mohammed Attia, Laura Kallmeyer, and Thamar Solorio. 2016. Multilingual code-switching identification via lstm recurrent neural networks. In *Proceedings of the Second Workshop on Computational Approaches to Code Switching*, pages 50–59. Association for Computational Linguistics.

Gillian Sankoff. 1970. Social aspects of multilingualism in New Guinea. *Ph.D. thesis, McGill University*.

Royal Sequiera, Monojit Choudhury, and Kalika Bali. 2015a. POS Tagging of Hindi-English Code Mixed Text from Social Media: Some Machine Learning Experiments. In *Proceedings of the 12th International Conference on Natural Language Processing*, pages 237–246.

Royal Sequiera, Monojit Choudhury, Parth Gupta, Paolo Rosso, Shubham Kumar, Somnath Banerjee, Sudip Kumar Naskar, Sivaji Bandyopadhyay, Das Amitava Chittaranjan, Gokul, and Kunal Chakma. 2015b. Overview of fire-2015 shared task on mixed script information retrieval. In *FIRE Workshops*, volume 1587, pages 19–25.

Bernard Smith. 2001. *Learner English: A teacher's guide to interference and other problems*. Ernst Klett Sprachen.

Thamar Solorio, Elizabeth Blair, Suraj Maharjan, Steven Bethard, Mona Diab, Mahmoud Ghoneim, Abdelati Hawwari, Fahad AlGhamdi, Julia Hirschberg, Alison Chang, and Pascale Fung. 2014. Overview for the first shared task on language identification in code-switched data. In *Proceedings of the First Workshop on Computational Approaches to Code Switching*, pages 62–72, Doha, Qatar. Association for Computational Linguistics.

Code-Switching Language Modeling using Syntax-Aware Multi-Task Learning

Genta Indra Winata, Andrea Madotto, Chien-Sheng Wu, Pascale Fung
Center for Artificial Intelligence Research (CAiRE)
Department of Electronic and Computer Engineering
Hong Kong University of Science and Technology, Clear Water Bay, Hong Kong
{giwinata, eeandreamad, cwuak}@ust.hk, pascale@ece.ust.hk

Abstract

Lack of text data has been the major issue on code-switching language modeling. In this paper, we introduce multitask learning based language model which shares syntax representation of languages to leverage linguistic information and tackle the low resource data issue. Our model jointly learns both language modeling and Part-of-Speech tagging on code-switched utterances. In this way, the model is able to identify the location of code-switching points and improves the prediction of next word. Our approach outperforms standard LSTM based language model, with an improvement of 9.7% and 7.4% in perplexity on SEAME Phase I and Phase II dataset respectively.

1 Introduction

Code-switching has received a lot of attention from speech and computational linguistic communities especially on how to automatically recognize text from speech and understand the structure within it. This phenomenon is very common in bilingual and multilingual communities. For decades, linguists studied this phenomenon and found that speakers switch at certain points, not randomly and obeys several constraints which point to the code-switched position in an utterance (Poplack, 1980; Belazi et al., 1994; Myers-Scotton, 1997; Muysken, 2000; Auer and Wei, 2007). These hypotheses have been empirically proven by observing that bilinguals tend to code-switch intra-sententially at certain (morpho)-syntactic boundaries (Poplack, 2015). Belazi et al. (1994) defined the well-known theory that constraints the code-switch between a functional head and its complement is given the strong relationship between the two constituents, which corresponds to a hierarchical structure in terms of Part-of-Speech (POS) tags. Muysken (2000) introduced Matrix-Language Model Framework for an intra-sentential case where the primary language is called Matrix Language and the second one called Embedded Language (Myers-Scotton, 1997). A language island was then introduced which is a constituent composed entirely of the language morphemes. From the Matrix-Language Frame Model, both matrix language (ML) island and embedded language (EL) islands are well-formed in their grammars and the EL islands are constrained under ML grammar (Namba, 2004). (Fairchild and Van Hell, 2017) studied determiner–noun switches in Spanish–English bilinguals .

Code-switching can be classified into two categories: intra-sentential and inter-sentential switches (Poplack, 1980). Intra-sentential switch defines a shift from one language to another language within an utterance. Inter-sentential switch refers to the change between two languages in a single discourse, where the switching occurs after a sentence in the first language has been completed and the next sentence starts with a new language. The example of the intra-sentential switch is shown in (1), and the inter-sentential switch is shown in (2).

(1) 我 要 去 check.

   (I want to go) check.

(2) 我 不 懂 要 怎么 讲 一 个 小时 seriously I
   didn't have so much things to say

   (I don't understand how to speak for an hour) seriously I didn't have so much things to say

Proceedings of The Third Workshop on Computational Approaches to Code-Switching, pages 62–67
Melbourne, Australia, July 19, 2018. ©2018 Association for Computational Linguistics

Language modeling using only word lexicons is not adequate to learn the complexity of code-switching patterns, especially in a low resource setting. Learning at the same time syntactic features such as POS tag and language identifier allows to have a shared grammatical information that constraint the next word prediction. Due to this reason, we propose a multi-task learning framework for code-switching language modeling task which is able to leverage syntactic features such as language and POS tag.

The main contribution of this paper is two-fold. First, multi-task learning model is proposed to jointly learn language modeling task and POS sequence tagging task on code-switched utterances. Second, we incorporate language information into POS tags to create bilingual tags - it distinguishes tags between Chinese and English. The POS tag features are shared towards the language model and enrich the features to better learn where to switch. From our experiments result, we found that our method improves the perplexity on SEAME Phase I and Phase II dataset (Nanyang Technological University, 2015).

2   Related Work

The earliest language modeling research on code-switching data was applying linguistic theories on computational modelings such as Inversion Constraints and Functional Head Constraints on Chinese-English code-switching data (Li and Fung, 2012; Ying and Fung, 2014). Vu et al. (2012) built a bilingual language model which is trained by interpolating two monolingual language models with statistical machine translation (SMT) based text generation to generate artificial code-switching text. Adel et al. (2013a,b) introduced a class-based method using RNNLM for computing the posterior probability and added POS tags in the input. Adel et al. (2015) explored the combination of brown word clusters, open class words, and clusters of open class word embeddings as hand-crafted features for improving the factored language model. In addition, Dyer et al. (2016) proposed a generative language modeling with explicit phrase structure. A method of tying input and output embedding helped to reduce the number of parameters in language model and improved the perplexity (Press and Wolf, 2017).

Learning multiple NLP tasks using multi-task learning have been recently used in many do-mains (Collobert et al., 2011; Luong et al., 2016; Hashimoto et al., 2016). They presented a joint many-task model to handle multiple NLP tasks and share parameters with growing depth in a single end-to-end model. A work by Aguilar et al. (2017) showed the potential of combining POS tagging with Named-Entity Recognition task.

3   Methodology

This section shows how to build the features and how to train our multi-task learning language model. Multi-task learning consists of two NLP tasks: Language modeling and POS sequence tagging.

3.1   Feature Representation

In the model, word lexicons and syntactic features are used as input.

Word Lexicons: Sentences are encoded as 1-hot vectors and our vocabulary is built from training data.

Syntactic Features: For each *language island*, phrase within the same language, we extract POS Tags iteratively using Chinese and English Penn Tree Bank Parser (Tseng et al., 2005; Toutanova et al., 2003). There are 31 English POS Tags and 34 Chinese POS Tags. Chinese words are distinguishable from English words since they have different encoding. We add language information in the POS tag label to discriminate POS tag between two languages.

3.2   Model Description

Figure 1 illustrates our multi-task learning extension to recurrent language model. In this multi-task learning setting, the tasks are language modeling and POS tagging. The POS tagging task shares the POS tag vector and the hidden states to LM task, but it does not receive any information from the other loss. Let w_t be the word lexicon in the document and p_t be the POS tag of the corresponding w_t at index t. They are mapped into embedding matrices to get their d-dimensional vector representations x_t^w and x_t^p. The input embedding weights are tied with the output weights. We concatenate x_t^w and x_t^p as the input of LSTM_{lm}. The information from the POS tag sequence is shared to the language model through this step.

$$u_t = \text{LSTM}_{lm}(x_t^w \oplus x_t^p, u_{t-1})$$

$$v_t = \text{LSTM}_{pt}(x_t^p, v_{t-1})$$

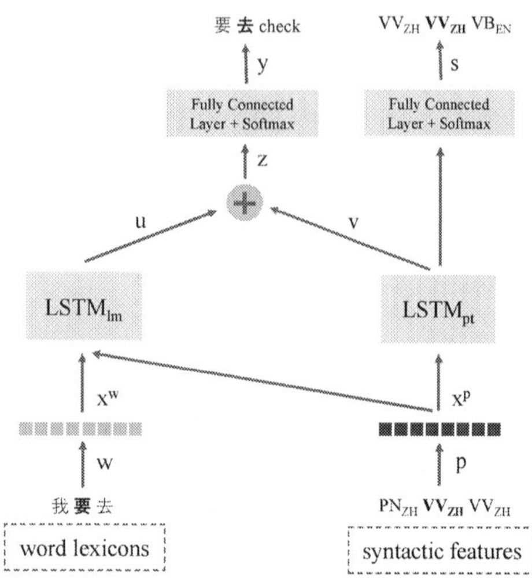

Figure 1: Multi-Task Learning Framework

where $\oplus$ denotes the concatenation operator, u_t and v_t are the final hidden states of LSTM$_{lm}$ and LSTM$_{pt}$ respectively. u_t and v_t, the hidden states from both LSTMs are summed before predicting the next word.

$$z_t = u_t + v_t$$

$$y_t = \frac{e^{z_t}}{\sum_{j=1}^{T} e^{z_j}}, \text{ where } j = 1, .., T$$

The word distribution of the next word y_t is normalized using softmax function. The model uses cross-entropy losses as error functions $\mathcal{L}_{lm}$ and $\mathcal{L}_{pt}$ for language modeling task and POS tagging task respectively. We optimize the multi-objective losses using the Back Propagation algorithm and we perform a weighted linear sum of the losses for each individual task.

$$\mathcal{L}_{total} = p\mathcal{L}_{lm} + (1-p)\mathcal{L}_{pt}$$

where p is the weight of the loss in the training.

3.3 Experimental Setup

In this section, we present the experimental setting for this task

Corpus: SEAME (South East Asia Mandarin-English), a conversational Mandarin-English code-switching speech corpus consists of spontaneously spoken interviews and conversations (Nanyang Technological University, 2015). Our dataset (LDC2015S04) is the most updated version of the Linguistic Data Consortium (LDC)

database. However, the statistics are not identical to Lyu et al. (2010). The corpus consists of two phases. In Phase I, only selected audio segments were transcribed. In Phase II, most of the audio segments were transcribed. According to the authors, it was not possible to restore the original dataset. The authors only used Phase I corpus. Few speaker ids are not in the speaker list provided by the authors Lyu et al. (2010). Therefore as a workaround, we added these ids to the train set. As our future reference, the recording lists are included in the supplementary material.

Table 1: Data Statistics in SEAME Phase I

	Train set	Dev set	Test set
# Speakers	139	8	8
# Utterances	45,916	1,938	1,228
# Tokens	762K	31K	17K
Avg. segments length	3.67	3.68	3.18
Avg. switches	3.60	3.47	3.67

Table 2: Data Statistics in SEAME Phase II

	Train set	Dev set	Test set
# Speakers	138	8	8
# Utterances	78,815	4,764	3,933
# Tokens	1.2M	65K	60K
Avg. segment length	4.21	3.59	3.99
Avg. switches	2.94	3.12	3.07

Table 3: Code-Switching Trigger Words in SEAME Phase II

POS Tag	Freq	POS Tag	Freq
VV$_{ZH}$	107,133	NN$_{EN}$	31,031
AD$_{ZH}$	97,681	RB$_{EN}$	12,498
PN$_{ZH}$	92,117	NNP$_{EN}$	11,734
NN$_{ZH}$	45,088	JJ$_{EN}$	5,040
VA$_{ZH}$	27,442	IN$_{EN}$	4,801
CD$_{ZH}$	20,158	VB$_{EN}$	4,703

Preprocessing: First, we tokenized English and Chinese word using Stanford NLP toolkit (Manning et al., 2014). Second, all hesitations and punctuations were removed except apostrophe, for examples: "let's" and "it's". Table 1 and Table 2 show the statistics of SEAME Phase I and II corpora. Table 3 shows the most common trigger POS tag for Phase II corpus.

Training: The baseline model was trained using RNNLM (Mikolov et al., 2011)[1]. Then, we trained our LSTM models with different hidden sizes [200, 500]. All LSTMs have 2 layers and unrolled for 35 steps. The embedding size is equal to the LSTM hidden size. A dropout regularization (Srivastava et al., 2014) was applied to the word embedding vector and POS tag embedding vector, and to the recurrent output (Gal and Ghahramani, 2016) with values between [0.2, 0.4]. We used a batch size of 20 in the training. EOS tag was used to separate every sentence. We chose Stochastic Gradient Descent and started with a learning rate of 20 and if there was no improvement during the evaluation, we reduced the learning rate by a factor of 0.75. The gradient was clipped to a maximum of 0.25. For the multi-task learning, we used different loss weights hyper-parameters p in the range of [0.25, 0.5, 0.75]. We tuned our model with the development set and we evaluated our best model using the test set, taking perplexity as the final evaluation metric. Where the latter was calculated by taking the exponential of the error in the negative log-form.

$$\text{PPL}(w) = e^{\mathcal{L}_{total}}$$

4 Results

Table 4 and Table 5 show the results of multi-task learning with different values of the hyper-parameter p. We observe that the multi-task model with $p = 0.25$ achieved the best performance. We compare our multi-task learning model against RNNLM and LSTM baselines. The baselines correspond to recurrent neural networks that are trained with word lexicons. Table 6 and Table 7 present the overall results from different models. The multi-task model performs better than LSTM baseline by 9.7% perplexity in Phase I and 7.4% perplexity in Phase II. The performance of our model in Phase II is also better than the RNNLM (8.9%) and far better than the one presented in Adel et al. (2013b) in Phase I.

Moreover, the results show that adding shared POS tag representation to LSTM_{lm} does not hurt the performance of the language modeling task. This implies that the syntactic information helps the model to better predict the next word in the sequence. To further verify this hypothesis, we

[1]downloaded from Mikolov's website http://www.fit.vutbr.cz/ imikolov/rnnlm/

Table 4: Multi-task results with different weighted loss hyper-parameter in Phase I

Hidden size	p	PPL Dev	PPL Test
200	**0.25**	**180.90**	**178.18**
	0.5	182.6	178.75
	0.75	**180.90**	**178.18**
500	**0.25**	**173.55**	**174.96**
	0.5	175.23	173.89
	0.75	185.83	178.49

Table 5: Multi-task results with different weighted loss hyper-parameter in Phase II

Hidden size	p	PPL Dev	PPL Test
200	**0.25**	**149.68**	**149.84**
	0.5	150.92	152.38
	0.75	150.32	151.22
500	**0.25**	**141.86**	**141.71**
	0.5	144.18	144.27
	0.75	145.08	144.85

Table 6: Results in Phase I

Model	PPL Dev	PPL Test
RNNLM (Adel et al., 2013a)	246.60	287.88
(Adel et al., 2015)	238.86	245.40
FI + OF (Adel et al., 2013a)	219.85	239.21
FLM (Adel et al., 2013b)	177.79	192.08
LSTM	190.33	185.91
+ syntactic features	178.51	176.57
Multi-task	**173.55**	**174.96**

Table 7: Results in Phase II

Model	PPL Dev	PPL Test
RNNLM	178.35	171.27
LSTM	150.65	153.06
+ syntactic features	147.44	148.38
Multi-task	**141.86**	**141.71**

conduct two analysis by visualizing our prediction examples in Figure 2:

a) Measure the improvement of the target word's log probability by multi-task model compared to standard LSTM model. This is computed by calculating the log probability difference between two models. According to Figure 2, in most of the

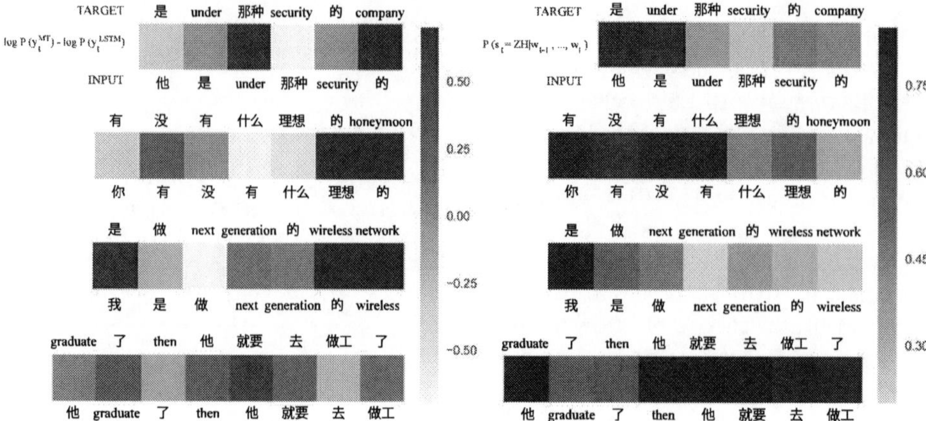

Figure 2: Prediction examples in Phase II. **Left:** Each square shows the target word's log probability improvement by multi-task model compared to LSTM model (Darker color is better). **Right:** Each square shows the probability of the next POS tag is Chinese (Darker color represents higher probability)

cases, the multi-task model improves the prediction of the monolingual segments and particularly in code-switching points such as "under", "security", "generation", "then", "graduate", "他", and "的". It also shows that the multi-task model is more precise in learning where to switch language. On the other hand, Table 3 shows the relative frequency of the trigger POS tag. The word "then" belong to RB_{EN}, which is one of the most common trigger words in the list. Furthermore, the target word prediction is significantly improved in most of the trigger words.

b) Report the probability that the next produced POS tag is Chinese. It is shown that words "then", "security", "了", "那种", "做", and "的" tend to switch the language context within the utterance. However, it is very hard to predict all the cases correctly. This is may due to the fact that without any switching, the model still creates a correct sentence.

5 Conclusion

In this paper, we propose a multi-task learning approach for code-switched language modeling. The multi-task learning models achieve the best performance and outperform LSTM baseline with 9.7% and 7.4% improvement in perplexity for Phase I and Phase II SEAME corpus respectively. This implies that by training two different NLP tasks together the model can correctly learn the correlation between them. Indeed, the syntactic information helps the model to be aware of code-switching

points and it improves the performance over the language model. Finally, we conclude that multi-task learning has good potential on code-switching language modeling research and there are still rooms for improvements, especially by adding more language pairs and corpora.

Acknowledgments

This work is partially funded by ITS/319/16FP of the Innovation Technology Commission, HKUST 16214415 & 16248016 of Hong Kong Research Grants Council, and RDC 1718050-0 of EMOS.AI.

References

Heike Adel, Ngoc Thang Vu, Katrin Kirchhoff, Dominic Telaar, and Tanja Schultz. 2015. Syntactic and semantic features for code-switching factored language models. *IEEE Transactions on Audio, Speech, and Language Processing*, 23(3):431–440.

Heike Adel, Ngoc Thang Vu, Franziska Kraus, Tim Schlippe, Haizhou Li, and Tanja Schultz. 2013a. Recurrent neural network language modeling for code switching conversational speech. In *Acoustics, Speech and Signal Processing (ICASSP), 2013 IEEE International Conference on*, pages 8411–8415. IEEE.

Heike Adel, Ngoc Thang Vu, and Tanja Schultz. 2013b. Combination of recurrent neural networks and factored language models for code-switching language modeling. In *Proceedings of the 51st Annual Meeting of the Association for Computational Linguistics (Volume 2: Short Papers)*, volume 2, pages 206–211.

Gustavo Aguilar, Suraj Maharjan, Adrian Pastor López Monroy, and Thamar Solorio. 2017. A multi-task approach for named entity recognition in social media data. In *Proceedings of the 3rd Workshop on Noisy User-generated Text*, pages 148–153.

Peter Auer and Li Wei. 2007. *Handbook of multilingualism and multilingual communication*, volume 5. Walter de Gruyter.

Hedi M Belazi, Edward J Rubin, and Almeida Jacqueline Toribio. 1994. Code switching and x-bar theory: The functional head constraint. *Linguistic inquiry*, pages 221–237.

Ronan Collobert, Jason Weston, Léon Bottou, Michael Karlen, Koray Kavukcuoglu, and Pavel Kuksa. 2011. Natural language processing (almost) from scratch. *Journal of Machine Learning Research*, 12(Aug):2493–2537.

Chris Dyer, Adhiguna Kuncoro, Miguel Ballesteros, and Noah A Smith. 2016. Recurrent neural network grammars. In *Proceedings of NAACL-HLT*, pages 199–209.

Sarah Fairchild and Janet G Van Hell. 2017. Determiner-noun code-switching in spanish heritage speakers. *Bilingualism: Language and Cognition*, 20(1):150–161.

Yarin Gal and Zoubin Ghahramani. 2016. A theoretically grounded application of dropout in recurrent neural networks. In *Advances in neural information processing systems*, pages 1019–1027.

Kazuma Hashimoto, Caiming Xiong, Yoshimasa Tsuruoka, and Richard Socher. 2016. A joint many-task model: Growing a neural network for multiple nlp tasks. *arXiv preprint arXiv:1611.01587*.

Ying Li and Pascale Fung. 2012. Code-switch language model with inversion constraints for mixed language speech recognition. *Proceedings of COLING 2012*, pages 1671–1680.

Thang Luong, Quoc V Le, Ilya Sutskever, Oriol Vinyals, and Lukasz Kaiser. 2016. Multi-task sequence to sequence learning.

Dau-Cheng Lyu, Tien-Ping Tan, Eng-Siong Chng, and Haizhou Li. 2010. An analysis of a mandarin-english code-switching speech corpus: Seame. *Age*, 21:25–8.

Christopher D. Manning, Mihai Surdeanu, John Bauer, Jenny Finkel, Steven J. Bethard, and David McClosky. 2014. The Stanford CoreNLP natural language processing toolkit. In *Association for Computational Linguistics (ACL) System Demonstrations*, pages 55–60.

Tomas Mikolov, Stefan Kombrink, Anoop Deoras, Lukar Burget, and Jan Cernocky. 2011. Rnnlm-recurrent neural network language modeling toolkit. In *Proc. of the 2011 ASRU Workshop*, pages 196–201.

Pieter Muysken. 2000. *Bilingual speech: A typology of code-mixing*, volume 11. Cambridge University Press.

Carol Myers-Scotton. 1997. *Duelling languages: Grammatical structure in codeswitching*. Oxford University Press.

Kazuhiko Namba. 2004. An overview of myers-scotton's matrix language frame model. *Senri International School (SIS) Educational Research Bulletin*, 9:1–10.

Universiti Sains Malaysia Nanyang Technological University. 2015. Mandarin-english code-switching in south-east asia ldc2015s04. web download. philadelphia: Linguistic data consortium.

Shana Poplack. 1980. Sometimes i'll start a sentence in spanish y termino en espanol: toward a typology of code-switching1. *Linguistics*, 18(7-8):581–618.

Shana Poplack. 2015. Code-switching (linguistic). *International encyclopedia of the social and behavioral sciences*, pages 918–925.

Ofir Press and Lior Wolf. 2017. Using the output embedding to improve language models. In *Proceedings of the 15th Conference of the European Chapter of the Association for Computational Linguistics: Volume 2, Short Papers*, volume 2, pages 157–163.

Nitish Srivastava, Geoffrey Hinton, Alex Krizhevsky, Ilya Sutskever, and Ruslan Salakhutdinov. 2014. Dropout: A simple way to prevent neural networks from overfitting. *The Journal of Machine Learning Research*, 15(1):1929–1958.

Kristina Toutanova, Dan Klein, Christopher D Manning, and Yoram Singer. 2003. Feature-rich part-of-speech tagging with a cyclic dependency network. In *Proceedings of the 2003 Conference of the North American Chapter of the Association for Computational Linguistics on Human Language Technology-Volume 1*, pages 173–180. Association for Computational Linguistics.

Huihsin Tseng, Daniel Jurafsky, and Christopher Manning. 2005. Morphological features help pos tagging of unknown words across language varieties. In *Proceedings of the fourth SIGHAN workshop on Chinese language processing*.

Ngoc Thang Vu, Dau-Cheng Lyu, Jochen Weiner, Dominic Telaar, Tim Schlippe, Fabian Blaicher, Eng-Siong Chng, Tanja Schultz, and Haizhou Li. 2012. A first speech recognition system for mandarin-english code-switch conversational speech. In *Acoustics, Speech and Signal Processing (ICASSP), 2012 IEEE International Conference on*, pages 4889–4892. IEEE.

LI Ying and Pascale Fung. 2014. Language modeling with functional head constraint for code switching speech recognition. In *Proceedings of the 2014 Conference on Empirical Methods in Natural Language Processing (EMNLP)*, pages 907–916.

Predicting the presence of a Matrix Language in code-switching

Barbara E. Bullock, Gualberto Guzmán, Jacqueline Serigos
Vivek Sharath, Almeida Jacqueline Toribio
{gualbertoguzman,vivek.sharath}@utexas.edu
{bbullock,toribio}@austin.utexas.edu
{jserigos}@gmu.edu

Abstract

One language is often assumed to be dominant in code-switching (C-S), but this assumption has not been empirically tested. We operationalize the matrix language (ML) at the level of the sentence, using three common definitions. We test whether these converge and then model this convergence via a set of metrics that together quantify the nature of C-S. We conduct our experiment on four different Spanish-English corpora. Our results demonstrate that our model can separate some corpora according to whether they have a dominant ML or not but that the corpora span a range of mixing types that cannot be sorted neatly into an insertional vs. alternational dichotomy.

1 Introduction

From Joshi (1982) forward, many researchers assume that one of the participating languages in code-switching (C-S) is dominant. This notion is theorized in linguistics as the Matrix Language Frame model (MLF) (Myers-Scotton, 1997). The MLF assumes an asymmetry between the languages involved in C-S, with the matrix language (ML) providing the frame into which embedded language elements (EL) from the contact language are inserted, as well as an asymmetry between system vs. content morphemes. System morphemes in the MLF comprise a subset of closed class morphemes that neither assign nor receive a thematic role (e.g., determiners, quantifiers, auxiliaries, conjunctions). Constraints on language mixing follow from the asymmetry: The ML provides the grammatical elements and framing while the EL provides merely content morphemes. Nevertheless, there are two long-standing criticisms of

the ML: (1) the criteria for the identification of the ML are not straightforward (Winford, 2003; Meakins, 2011; Bhat et al., 2016); and (2) the consistent identification of a single ML might not be possible (Auer and Muhamedova, 2005; Bhat et al., 2016; Liu, 2008; Adamou, 2016). To this we add a third concern: In ascertaining an ML, researchers often rely on selected, decontextualized example sentences. With some exceptions, most in NLP (Gambäck and Das, 2016; Bhat et al., 2016; Vyas et al., 2014), few scholars have calculated the ML for each sentence or utterance in a sizable dataset (Blokzijl et al., 2017). Thus, tests of the MLF using replicable methods are lacking, despite the fact that the determination of an ML has consequences for linguistic analyses and for accurate models of multilingual texts for language processing (Bhat et al., 2016; Solorio and Liu, 2008a,b) and for applications like TTS (Sitaram and Black, 2016; Sitaram et al., 2015) and ASR (Li et al., 2012).

In this paper, we attempt to quantify the nature of mixing using multiple measures and to operationalize the concept of the ML at the sentence level using code-switched Spanish-English corpora. We then test the concept of the ML and its applicability to different degrees of mixing as quantified by the ratio of languages represented in a sentence, by the probability of switching from one word to the next, and by the regularity vs. intermittency of switching as defined by the distribution of the interevent spans of each language. We operationalize the ML for the instances of intrasentential mixing identified in our corpora along three different parameters: numerically dominant language overall, numerically dominant language of all verbs, and numerically dominant language of a subset of system morphemes. We then predict the likelihood that these different calculations of the ML converge to the same language

Proceedings of The Third Workshop on Computational Approaches to Code-Switching, pages 68–75
Melbourne, Australia, July 19, 2018. ©2018 Association for Computational Linguistics

result (i.e., point to a unique ML) as a function of our corpus metrics. Our result is a model that classifies C-S data according to how likely it is that all three measures of the ML agree on the same language label. Our contribution is three-fold: first, we show that one can ascribe a single ML with a high degree of likelihood given a particular pattern of C-S and that a simple word-count method is sufficient to do so; secondly, we empirically demonstrate that there is a cline of C-S such that corpora cannot always be neatly separated into insertional and alternational types as is generally claimed in the sociolinguistic literature; thirdly, we find that measures designed to assess the time-course of complex systems like C-S are lacking for small datasets.

2   Related Work

2.1   Debates about the MLF Model

Studies of C-S commonly distinguish between insertional and alternational patterns (Muysken, 2000). With insertional switching, speakers are said to know which one language an utterance is "coming from" (Joshi, 1982; Romaine, 1995; Sitaram and Black, 2016). In the MLF model (Myers-Scotton, 1997), this language is formalized as the ML. Insertional C-S, which may be indistinguishable from borrowing (Poplack et al., 1988), is encountered in many sociolinguistic settings irrespective of the typologies of the language pairing studied (Poplack et al., 1988; Muysken, 2000; Li and Fung, 2013; Vyas et al., 2014; Adamou, 2016). In Sentence 1, Marathi is the ML, identified by the relative ordering of words in the clause and by the language of the system or closed-class morphemes, such as the quantifier *kahi* and the light verb *kar*; English contributes only the EL lexeme *paint*. Hindi is argued to be the ML in Sentence 2 (Bhat et al., 2016) , which presents an EL Island (ELI), an English-language embedded constituent with its own internal structure.[1]

- Sentence 1
  mula kahi khurcya **paint** kartat
  [boys some chairs paint do+TNS]

- Sentence 2
  Shanivar neeras hai **from that perspective**
  [Saturday boring is from that perspective]

The means by which the ML of a clause or extended discourse is determined remains debated. The ML has been variously associated with the numerically dominant language, (Myers-Scotton, 1997; Gambäck and Das, 2016; Sharma and Motlani, 2015), with the language of the finite verb (Klavans, 1985; Treffers-Daller, 1994; Meakins, 2011), or with the first language in a left-to-right parsing (Doron, 1983). It should be noted that the ML, as defined by Myers-Scotton, operates over a unit she calls the CP, which is co-extensive with the clause. For the purpose of this paper, we define the ML over a sentence, which may contain more than one clause. Since the majority of the corpora to be examined are from natural conversations, it is likely that most sentences consist of a single clause, as sentences are known to be shorter and syntactically less complex in spoken language.

The ML is not argued to be applicable to alternational switching, because speakers move from one grammar to another within an utterance. But it is often not clear from cited examples whether a new language span constitutes the alternation of MLs, as appears to be the case in Sentence 3 from the bilingual memoire *Killer Crònicas*, or whether the span is an ELI inserted into an ML, as is argued to be the case for Sentence 2. For instance, examining natural Japanese-English data within the MLF, Namba (2012) could not determine the ML of C-S utterances such as Sentence 4, which accounted for 42% of the clauses in the corpus.

- Sentence 3
  Anyway, just leave him plantado, al taxista este, **or throw some money at him** y salir
  [stranded that taxi-driver ... and leave]

- Sentence 4
  I want to be goorukiipaa ni nari-tai
  [goalkeeper RESULTATIVE become]

2.2   Measuring the complexity of code-switching

Importantly, bilingual speech practices are complex and it is not clear that the traditional binary typology of insertional and alternational C-S, while useful as a heuristic, is adequate to characterize

---

[1] In the NLP literature, insertionanal mixing is often referred to as *code-mixing* (CM), following Gumperz (1982) (Vyas et al., 2014; Bali et al., 2014), though some researchers employ CM as an umbrella term for both insertional and alternational mixing (Sequiera et al., 2015). Others use CM for any switching that occurs within an utterance (and C-S for switching at or above the utterance level) (Gambäck and Das, 2016).

the nature of C-S (Auer and Muhamedova, 2005). There have been recent attempts to quantify mixing complexity with the aim of arriving at empirically reliable comparisons of C-S between corpora (Gambäck and Das, 2016; Das and Gambäck, 2014; Jamatia et al., 2015; Guzman et al., 2016; Guzmán et al., 2017a). Each aims to capture the fact that C-S may vary along multiple planes. We follow Guzmán et al. (2016, 2017a) who quantify mixing in terms of several parameters calculated from language labels at the word level: (1) the ratio of languages represented; (2) the probability of switching language between any two words; (3) the burstiness of switching as characterized by the distribution of the length of spans; and (4) the sequential ordering of alternating monolingual spans.

3 Data

Bhat et al. (2016) built models for generating C-S sentences based on input sentences and the constraints of the MLF and of the Equivalence Constraint, a symmetrical model for alternating C-S (Poplack, 1980). When the sentences were submitted to human evaluation, there was significant variance in acceptability, potentially attributable to discrepancies in the register of some of the words used, as C-S tends to be informal and conversational. For our study, we avoid confounds that can be introduced by generated C-S by drawing on C-S data generated by bilingual speakers themselves. We were restricted in our choice of data by the requirement that all data bear a language label and a POS tag. As is commonly observed, POS tagged bilingual data are rare because the accuracy of monolingual taggers is reduced when the context is broken by C-S (Vyas et al., 2014).

The corpora that we use reflect degrees of mixing so that we test the viability of the MLF hypothesis across varying types of C-S. Each corpus was previously tagged for language and POS by its creators. In order to be able to compare between, the original POS tags used for each datasets were mapped to the core POS tagset from the Universal Dependencies (UD) framework (Nivre et al., 2016). The corpora to be modeled are the following.

1. *S7* was created by Thamar Solorio (2008a; 2008b). It documents a conversation among three Spanish-English bilinguals, resulting in approximately 8,000 words. It was tagged

for language and POS, using TreeTagger's English and Spanish parameters (Solorio and Liu, 2008a).

2. *Miami* consists of files from the Bangor Miami Corpus, transcripts of informal conversations between Spanish-English bilinguals in Miami. The data was automatically annotated for language and POS, using the Bangor Autoglosser (Donnelly and Deuchar, 2011).

3. *SpinTX* comprises selected transcripts of speakers from the Spanish in Texas Corpus, a set of recorded interviews between Spanish-English bilinguals residing in Texas (Bullock and Toribio, 2013; Toribio and Bullock, 2016). The corpus in its entirety was automatically tagged for POS using the English and Spanish versions of TreeTagger (Schmid, 1995) applied sequentially.[2]

4. *KC* is an excerpt of the epistolary work *Killer Crónicas: Bilingual Memoires* by Susana Chavez-Silverman. Nearly evenly balanced between English and Spanish, the POS annotated segment contains approximately 8,000 words. It was automatically tagged for language following Guzmán et al. (2016) and then manually annotated for POS using the UD tagset.

4 Procedures

In order to examine the viability and agreement of the MLF across the four corpora, we converted all POS labels to the core UD tagset. For *S7, Miami*, and *SpinTX*, we remapped the existing POS-tagset from either TreeTagger or the Bangor Autoglosser using a lookup table. In the case of *KC*, we manually tagged every token according to the UD framework since we had no previous tagging. The POS annotations were completed by a Spanish-English bilingual, professional linguist and then each annotation was checked by two others.

Each corpus was submitted to sentence tokenization, breaking on full or sentential stops. For *S7, Miami*, and *SpinTX*, we followed the existing sentence end markers, such as "SENT" and "FS", from the original POS tagging before conversion to UD. For *KC*, we performed a manual

---

[2]The Spanish in Texas Corpus is available through a creative commons license for non- commercial download in various file formats from `http://corpus.spanishintexas.org/en`.

Table 1: Anyway, **al taxista** right away **le noté un acentito**, not too specific

ML Definition	English	Spanish	ML
Word Count	6	6	Tie
Verb	0	1	Spanish
Functional words	2	3	Spanish

sentence-tagging since the UD tagset collapses all punctuation under the "." tag, which loses all sentence boundary information. There are currently no workable sentence tokenizers for C-S data.

As it is designed to permit the comparison of syntax in a language independent manner, the 17-tag core UD provides adequate POS annotations for capturing the system morphemes for Spanish-English. But the core level does not provide the level of granularity to distinguish finite verbs from non-finite ones (infinitives, participles and gerunds). Thus, we operationalized the ML for each sentence using three methods: the numerically dominant language of all tokens (TOTAL), the numerically dominant language of all verbs (VERB), and the numerically dominant language of functional elements (FUNC), i.e. DET, SCONJ, CCONJ, PRON, and AUX. Each of these three methods predicted "English", "Spanish", or "Tie" as the ML for each sentence in our datasets. We quantified agreement between these measures using the logical AND of all three. If at least one method predicted a different ML than the other two, then the agreement was 0 for DISAGREE.

As an example, consider Sentence 5 in Table 1. Since there is an equal number of tokens from English and Spanish, the word count or TOTAL method predicts a Tie. However, both VERB and FUNC predict a Spanish ML because of the higher number of Spanish verbs and functional elements. In this case, the sentence-level agreement is DIS-AGREE because the measures do not all concur.

We operationalize the nature of mixing via three metrics: M-Index, I-Index and Burstiness, each defined below.

1. The Mixing Index (M-Index), developed by the LIPPES Group (Barnett et al., 2000) from the Gini coefficient defines the ratio of languages in a text. It is bounded by 0 (a monolingual text) and 1 (a text with an even distribution of languages).

2. The Integration Index, (I-Index), created by Guzmán et al. (2016; 2017b; 2017a) describes the probability of switching. It ranges from 0 (monolingual text) to 1 (a text in which every other word is drawn from a different language).

3. Burstiness, proposed by Goh and Barabási for complex systems (2008), defines the regularity of switching. It is adapted here to apply to the interevent level of sequences of monolingual tokens, called spans, after every C-S. It is bounded within the interval of -1 (anti-bursty, periodic dispersion of switching) and 1 (predictable patterns of switching).

A fourth metric, Memory (Goh and Barabási, 2008), which models the temporal order of the spans, is desirable for examining C-S in larger corpora (Guzman et al., 2016; Guzmán et al., 2017b,a), and was calculated at the sentence level over the test corpora. We were forced to exclude it from further consideration because the sentences were short and often included spans of equal length, yielding a standard deviation of zero. Since the multiplicand and the multiplier in the divisor of the Memory function are standard deviations, our sentences yielded many divisors of 0.

We tested our ML methods only on the subsets of the datasets that contained C-S, i.e. we eliminated all monolingual sentences from our corpora. This has the consequence of removing conversational disfluencies such as restarts, which are unlikely to to demonstrate a C-S. In addition, we excluded all parts of the SpinTX and Miami corpora that did not contain a base-line amount of mixing. For Miami, we removed the herring11 and maria21 conversations. Similarly, in SpinTX we removed all conversations with an I-index of less than 0.1. The final test corpus contained 7,879 C-S sentences, each coded for the three sentence-level metrics described above, for the ML predictions from each of the three numerical methods TOTAL, VERB, and FUNC, and for whether the numerical ML predictions agreed or not.

Across all sentences, the three methods converge on an ML 58% of the time. There were notable differences in the range of convergence at the corpus-level. For *S7*, they agree 65%; for *Miami* 57%; for *SpinTX* 71%, and for *KC* only 45%.

Figure 1: Effects Plot for Corpus and I-index

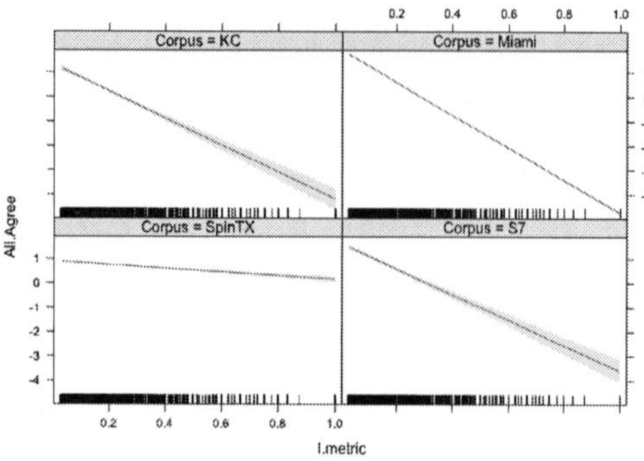

dictors for each sentence yields Figure 4, which shows the model's prediction of agreement for the data from all four corpora.

Although the model does not cleanly split all sentences of *KC* and *SpinTX* by agreement, we do see a clear preference for predicting AGREE for *SpinTX* and DISAGREE for *KC*. However, we also find that the model predicts multi-modal agreement distributions for the S7 and Miami corpora. The small peaks around 0 indicate that the model does not have sufficient information to distinguish between predicting AGREE or DIS-AGREE for a small amount of data, which we discuss below.

Figure 2: Agreement by Predictor Value

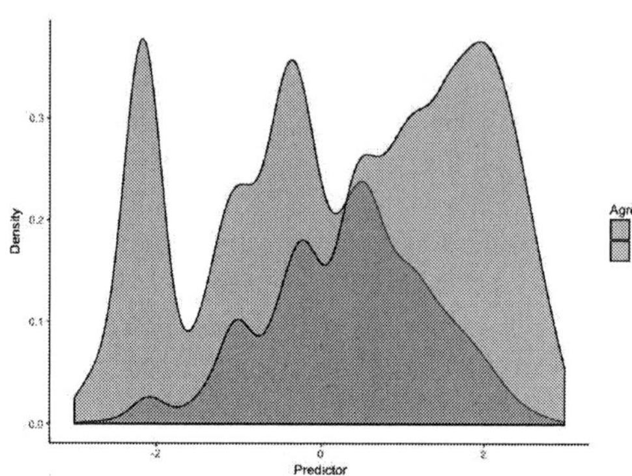

Figure 3: Odds Ratio Plot

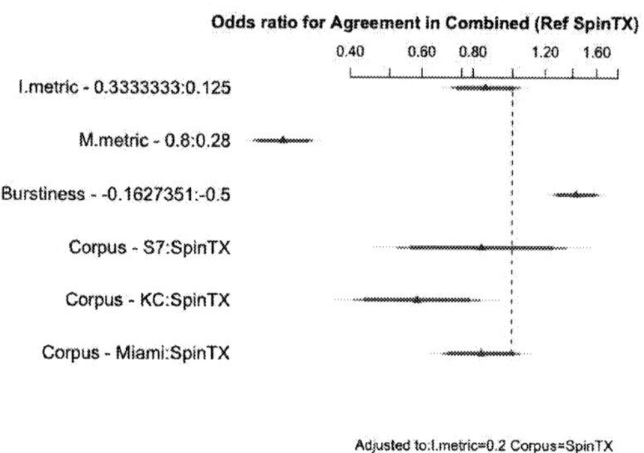

5　Methods

We fit a logistic regression to predict AGREE (i.e., there is an ML upon which all three measures agree) with three continuous predictor variables (M-Index, I-Index, Burstiness) and one categorical predictor (Corpus). An analysis of the model output revealed significant variability as to the effect of the I-index depending on the corpus, visualized in Figure 1. To capture this variability, an interaction between Corpus * I-Index was added to the model. The updated model is able to correctly predict AGREE or DISAGREE across all corpora with an F1-score of 69.3%, as shown in predictor density plot of Figure 2. All three metrics and the corpus as a categorical variable were significant in predicting agreement. The strongest predictors are the M-Index and Burstiness, with opposite effects, as seen in Figure 3. The M-Index inversely affects agreement; as the M-Index increases, the determinations of the ML are less likely to agree. Conversely, as the Burstiness increases, all three ML methods are more likely to agree. Plotting the pre-

Figure 4: Agreement Density over all Corpora

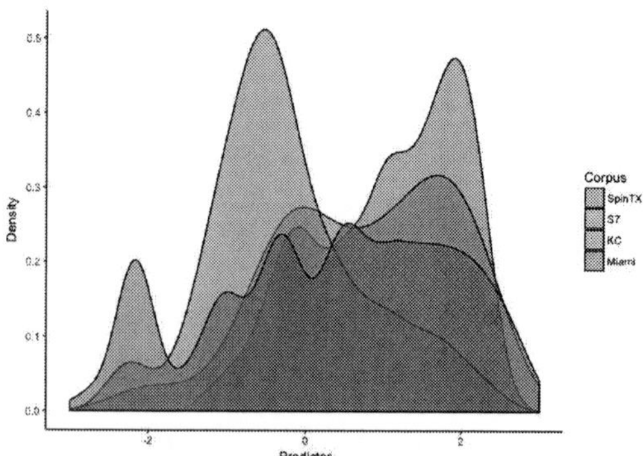

6　Discussion

In this paper we found that the three different methods for determining the ML of a sentence agreed 58% of the time across different mixing types. Further, we found a clear distinction between the rate of agreement for corpora that appear to be more insertional versus others. We also demonstrated that, collectively, these corpora span a range of types with some clearly intermediary between insertion and alternation. These intermediary patterns may correspond to instances of congruent lexicalization, a mix of insertion and alternation (Muysken, 2014).

Our model performance across all four corpora leads us to believe that language tagging is much more useful than previously thought and it may suffice in many cases for determining the ML. In fact, we can reliably predict the agreement of different ML methods with an accuracy of 69.3% using our metrics on language tags. The implication is that researchers in linguistics and in NLP could use word-count alone to determine the ML as a good first-approximation depending on the type of mixing in their data. Corpora with sporadic embeddings present an ideal case where the linguistic methods of determining ML often agree with word-count and these are likely to be prolific. In the Pangloss Collection of endangered Slavic languages in Europe, three of the six corpora contain less than 5% borrowed words (Adamou, 2016), a percentage that parallels the findings in other contact corpora of naturally produced speech (Treffers-Daller, 1994; Bullock et al., 2016; Cacoullos and Aaron, 2003; Varra, 2013). But, the performance of the model on the *S7* and *Miami* datasets indicate that our current metrics are not sufficient to predict agreement even when corpora have characteristics that indicate that they are largely insertional (low M-Index + high Burstiness). The uncertainty in the model predictions leads us to conclude that there is a continuum of mixing types within the existing typology of alternational and insertional mixing.

7 Future Research

In on-going work, we need to examine the methods of determining the ML in natural interactions in finer detail in order to determine which method is most likely to diverge from the other two. To further examine the viability of the MLF hypothesis, we are exploring other language pairings and analyzing the effectiveness of our current metrics at clustering and comparing across corpora, although we are hampered by the lack of POS-tagged bilingual data from natural speech. In addition, we are currently testing the performance of entropy-based measures (Guzmán et al., 2017a) as predictors for ML agreement. Finally, the performance of our model requires deeper syntactic analysis of the nature of mixing types and of the grammatical structures of the *S7* and *Miami* datasets in particular.

References

Evangelia Adamou. 2016. *A corpus-driven approach to language contact: Endangered languages in a comparative perspective*, volume 12. Walter de Gruyter GmbH & Co KG.

Peter Auer and Raihan Muhamedova. 2005. Embedded language'and 'matrix language'in insertional language mixing: Some problematic cases. *Rivista di linguistica*, 17(1):35–54.

Kalika Bali, Jatin Sharma, Monojit Choudhury, and Yogarshi Vyas. 2014. "i am borrowing ya mixing?" an analysis of english-hindi code mixing in facebook. In *Proceedings of the First Workshop on Computational Approaches to Code Switching*, pages 116–126.

Ruthanna Barnett, Eva Codó, Eva Eppler, Montse Forcadell, Penelope Gardner-Chloros, Roeland van Hout, Melissa Moyer, Maria Carme Torras, Maria Teresa Turell, Mark Sebba, et al. 2000. The lides coding manual: A document for preparing and analyzing language interaction data version 1.1– july 1999. *International Journal of Bilingualism*, 4(2):131–271.

Gayatri Bhat, Monojit Choudhury, and Kalika Bali. 2016. Grammatical constraints on intra-sentential code-switching: From theories to working models. *arXiv preprint arXiv:1612.04538*.

Jeffrey Blokzijl, Margaret Deuchar, and M Couto. 2017. Determiner asymmetry in mixed nominal constructions: The role of grammatical factors in data from miami and nicaragua. *Languages*, 2(4):20.

Barbara E Bullock, Jacqueline Serigos, and Almeida Jacqueline Toribio. 2016. The stratification of english-language lone-word and multi-word material in puerto rican spanish-language press outlets. *Spanish-English Codeswitching in the Caribbean and the US*, 11:171.

BE Bullock and AJ Toribio. 2013. The spanish in texas corpus project. *Center for Open Education Resources and Language Learning (COERLL)*.

Rena Torres Cacoullos and Jessi Elana Aaron. 2003. Bare english-origin nouns in spanish: Rates, constraints, and discourse functions. *Language Variation and Change*, 15(3):289–328.

Amitava Das and Björn Gambäck. 2014. Identifying languages at the word level in code-mixed indian social media text.

Kevin Donnelly and Margaret Deuchar. 2011. Using constraint grammar in the bangor autoglosser to disambiguate multilingual spoken text.

Edit Doron. 1983. On a formal model of code-switching. In *Texas Linguistic Forum Austin, Tex.*, 22, pages 35–59.

Björn Gambäck and Amitava Das. 2016. Comparing the level of code-switching in corpora. In *LREC*.

K-I Goh and A-L Barabási. 2008. Burstiness and memory in complex systems. *EPL (Europhysics Letters)*, 81(4):48002.

John J Gumperz. 1982. *Discourse strategies*, volume 1. Cambridge University Press.

Gualberto Guzmán, Joseph Ricard, Jacqueline Serigos, Barbara E Bullock, and Almeida Jacqueline Toribio. 2017a. Metrics for modeling code-switching across corpora. *Proc. Interspeech 2017*, pages 67–71.

Gualberto A Guzmán, Joseph Ricard, Jacqueline Serigos, Barbara Bullock, and Almeida Jacqueline Toribio. 2017b. Moving code-switching research toward more empirically grounded methods. In *CDH@ TLT*, pages 1–9.

Gualberto A Guzman, Jacqueline Serigos, Barbara E Bullock, and Almeida Jacqueline Toribio. 2016. Simple tools for exploring variation in code-switching for linguists. In *Proceedings of the Second Workshop on Computational Approaches to Code Switching*, pages 12–20.

Anupam Jamatia, Björn Gambäck, and Amitava Das. 2015. Part-of-speech tagging for code-mixed english-hindi twitter and facebook chat messages. In *Proceedings of the International Conference Recent Advances in Natural Language Processing*, pages 239–248.

Aravind K Joshi. 1982. Processing of sentences with intra-sentential code-switching. In *Proceedings of the 9th conference on Computational linguistics-Volume 1*, pages 145–150. Academia Praha.

Judith L Klavans. 1985. The syntax of code-switching: Spanish and english. In *Proceedings of the Linguistic Symposium on Romance Languages*, pages 213–231. Benjamins.

Ying Li and Pascale Fung. 2013. Language modeling for mixed language speech recognition using weighted phrase extraction. In *Interspeech*, pages 2599–2603.

Ying Li, Yue Yu, and Pascale Fung. 2012. A mandarin-english code-switching corpus. In *LREC*, pages 2515–2519.

Yu Liu. 2008. Evaluation of the matrix language hypothesis: Evidence from chinese-english code-switching phenomena in blogs. *Journal of Chinese Language and Computing*, 18(2):75–92.

Felicity Meakins. 2011. *Case-marking in contact: The development and function of case morphology in Gurindji Kriol*, volume 39. John Benjamins Publishing.

Pieter Muysken. 2000. *Bilingual speech: A typology of code-mixing*, volume 11. Cambridge University Press.

Pieter Muysken. 2014. Deja voodoo or new trails ahead. *Linguistic Variation: Confronting Fact and Theory*, page 242.

Carol Myers-Scotton. 1997. *Duelling languages: Grammatical structure in codeswitching*. Oxford University Press.

Kazuhiko Namba. 2012. Non-insertional code-switching in english–japanese bilingual children: alternation and congruent lexicalisation. *International Journal of Bilingual Education and Bilingualism*, 15(4):455–473.

Joakim Nivre, Marie-Catherine de Marneffe, Filip Ginter, Yoav Goldberg, Jan Hajic, Christopher D Manning, Ryan T McDonald, Slav Petrov, Sampo Pyysalo, Natalia Silveira, et al. 2016. Universal dependencies v1: A multilingual treebank collection. In *LREC*.

Shana Poplack. 1980. Sometimes i'll start a sentence in spanish y termino en espanol: toward a typology of code-switching1. *Linguistics*, 18(7-8):581–618.

Shana Poplack, David Sankoff, and Christopher Miller. 1988. The social correlates and linguistic processes of lexical borrowing and assimilation.

Suzanne Romaine. 1995. *Bilingualism*. Wiley-Blackwell.

Helmut Schmid. 1995. Treetagger— a language independent part-of-speech tagger. *Institut für Maschinelle Sprachverarbeitung, Universität Stuttgart*, 43:28.

Royal Sequiera, Monojit Choudhury, and Kalika Bali. 2015. Pos tagging of hindi-english code mixed text from social media: Some machine learning experiments. In *Proceedings of the 12th International Conference on Natural Language Processing*, pages 237–246.

Arnav Sharma and Raveesh Motlani. 2015. Pos tagging for code-mixed indian social media text: Systems from iiit-h for icon nlp tools contest.

Sunayana Sitaram and Alan W Black. 2016. Speech synthesis of code-mixed text.

Sunayana Sitaram, Sai Krishna Rallabandi, and SRAW Black. 2015. Experiments with cross-lingual systems for synthesis of code-mixed text.

Thamar Solorio and Yang Liu. 2008a. Learning to predict code-switching points. In *Proceedings of the Conference on Empirical Methods in Natural Language Processing*, pages 973–981. Association for Computational Linguistics.

Thamar Solorio and Yang Liu. 2008b. Part-of-speech tagging for english-spanish code-switched text. In *Proceedings of the Conference on Empirical Methods in Natural Language Processing*, pages 1051–1060. Association for Computational Linguistics.

Almeida J Toribio and Barbara E Bullock. 2016. A new look at heritage spanish and its speakers. *Advances in Spanish as a Heritage Language*, 49:27–50.

Jeanine Treffers-Daller. 1994. *Mixing two languages: French-Dutch contact in a comparative perspective*, volume 9. Walter de Gruyter.

Rachel Marie Varra. 2013. *The Social Correlates of Lexical Borrowing in Spanish in New York City*. ERIC.

Yogarshi Vyas, Spandana Gella, Jatin Sharma, Kalika Bali, and Monojit Choudhury. 2014. Pos tagging of english-hindi code-mixed social media content. In *Proceedings of the 2014 Conference on Empirical Methods in Natural Language Processing (EMNLP)*, pages 974–979.

Donald Winford. 2003. *An introduction to contact linguistics*. Wiley-Blackwell.

Automatic Detection of Code-switching Style from Acoustics

SaiKrishna Rallabandi*, Sunayana Sitaram, Alan W Black*
*Language Technologies Institute, Carnegie Mellon University, USA
Microsoft Research India
srallaba@cs.cmu.edu, susitara@microsoft.com, awb@cs.cmu.edu

Abstract

Multilingual speakers switch between languages displaying inter sentential, intra sentential, and congruent lexicalization based transitions. While monolingual ASR systems may be capable of recognizing a few words from a foreign language, they are usually not robust enough to handle these varied styles of code-switching. There is also a lack of large code-switched speech corpora capturing all these styles making it difficult to build code-switched speech recognition systems. We hypothesize that it may be useful for an ASR system to be able to first detect the switching style of a particular utterance from acoustics, and then use specialized language models or other adaptation techniques for decoding the speech. In this paper, we look at the first problem of detecting code-switching style from acoustics. We classify code-switched Spanish-English and Hindi-English corpora using two metrics and show that features extracted from acoustics alone can distinguish between different kinds of code-switching in these language pairs.

Index Terms: speech recognition, code-switching, language identification

1 Introduction

Code-switching refers to the phenomenon where bilingual speakers alternate between the languages while speaking. It occurs in multilingual societies around the world. As Automatic Speech Recognition (ASR) systems are now recognizing conversational speech, it becomes important that they handle code-switching. Furthermore, code-switching affects co-articulation and context dependent acoustic modeling (Elias et al., 2017). Therefore, developing systems for such speech requires careful handling of unexpected language switches that may occur in a single utterance. We hypothesize that in such scenarios it would be desirable to condition the recognition systems on the type (Muysken, 2000) or style of language mixing that might be expected in the signal. In this paper, we present approaches to detecting code-switching 'style' from acoustics. We first define style of an utterance based on two metrics that indicate the level of mixing in the utterance: CodeMixing Index(CMI) and CodeMixing Span Index. Based on these, we classify each mixed utterance into 5 style classes. We also obtain an utterance level acoustic representation for each of the utterances using a variant of SoundNet. Using this acoustic representation as features, we try to predict the style of utterance.

2 Related Work

Prior work on building Acoustic and Language Models for ASR systems for code-switched speech can be categorized into the following approaches: (1) Detecting code-switching points in an utterance, followed by the application of monolingual acoustic and language models to the individual segments (Chan et al., 2004; Lyu and Lyu, 2008; Shia et al., 2004). (2)Employing a shared phone set to build acoustic models for mixed speech with standard language models trained on code-switched text (Imseng et al., 2011; Li et al., 2011; Bhuvanagiri and Kopparapu, 2010; Yeh et al., 2010). (3) Training Acoustic or Language models on monolingual data in both languages with little or no code-switched data (Lyu et al., 2006; Vu et al., 2012; Bhuvanagirir and Kopparapu, 2012; Yeh and Lee, 2015). We attempt to approach this

Proceedings of The Third Workshop on Computational Approaches to Code-Switching, pages 76–81
Melbourne, Australia, July 19, 2018. ©2018 Association for Computational Linguistics

Class	CMI	Hi-En Utts	En-Es Utts
C1	0	6771	41624
C2	0-0.15	13986	2284
C3	0.15-0.30	492	2453
C4	0.30-0.45	8865	1025
C5	0.45-1	2496	1562

Table 1: Distribution of CMI classes for Hinglish and Spanglish

Class	Description	Hi-En	En-Es
S1	Mono En	5413	27960
S2	Mono Hi/Es	0	12749
S3	En Matrix	626	2883
S4	Hi/Es Matrix	36454	1986
S5	Others	8307	3345

Table 2: Distribution of span based classes for Hinglish and Spanglish. Note that the term 'Matrix' is used just here notionally to indicate larger word span of the language.

problem by first identifying the style of code mixing from acoustics. This is similar to the problem of language identification from acoustics, which is typically done over the span of an entire utterance.

Deep Learning based methods have recently proven very effective in speaker and language recognition tasks. Prior work in Deep Neural Networks (DNN) based language recognition can be grouped into two categories: (1) Approaches that use DNNs as feature extractors followed by separate classifiers to predict the identity of the language (Jiang et al., 2014; Matejka et al., 2014; Song et al., 2013) and (2) Approaches that employ DNNs to directly predict the language ID (Richardson et al., 2015b,a; Lopez-Moreno et al., 2014). Although DNN based systems outperform the iVector based approaches, the output decision is dependent on the outcome from every frame. This limits the real time deployment capabilities for such systems. Moreover, such systems typically use a fixed contextual window which spans hundreds of milliseconds of speech while the language effects in a code-switched scenario are suprasegmental and typically span a longer range. In addition, the accuracies of such systems, especially ones that employ some variant of iVectors drop as the duration of the utterance is reduced. We follow the approach of using DNNs as utterance level feature extractors. Our interest is in adding long term information to influence the recognition model, particularly at the level of the complete utterance, representing stylistic aspects of the degree and style of code-switching throughout the utterances.

3 Style of Mixing and Motivation

Multiple metrics have been proposed to quantify codemixing (Guzmán et al., 2017; Gambäck and Das, 2014) such as span of the participating languages, burstiness and complexity. For our current study, we categorize the utterances into dif-

ferent styles based on two metrics: (1) Code Mixing index (Gamback and Das, 2014) which attempts to quantify the codemixing based on the word counts and (2) CodeMixed Span information which attempts to quantify codemixing of an utterance based on the span of participating languages.

3.1 Categorization based on Code Mixing Index

Code Mixing Index (Gamback and Das, 2014) was introduced to quantify the level of mixing between the participating languages in a codemixed utterance. CMI can be calculated at the corpus and utterance level. We use utterance CMI, which is defined as:

$$C_u(x) = 100 \frac{w_m(N(x) - \max_{L_i \in L}\{t_{L_i}\}(x)) + w_p P(x)}{N(x)}$$

(1)

where N is the number of languages, t_{L_i} are the tokens in language L_i, P is the number of code alternation points in utterance x and w_m and w_p are weights. In our current study, we quantize the range of codemixed index (0 to 1) into 5 styles and categorize each utterance as shown in Table 1. A CMI of 0 indicates that the utterance is monolingual. We experimented with various CMI ranges and found that the chosen ranges led to a reasonable distribution within the corpus. For example, the C2 CMI class in Hindi-English code switched data has utterances such as "पंधरा पे start किये थे ग्यारा पंधरा पे यार अभी तो कुछ नही हुआ" ('started at fifteen, eleven or fifteen but buddy nothing has happened so far'). The C4 class on the other hand, has utterances such as "actual में आज यह rainy season का मौसम था ना" ('actually the weather today was like rainy season, right?'). An example of a C5 utterance is "ohh English अच्छा English कौनसा favourite singer मतलब English में?" ('Ohh English, ok who is your favorite English singer?')

3.2 Categorization based on Span of codemixing

While CMI captures the level of mixing, it does not take to account the span information (regularity) of mixing. Therefore, we use language span information (Guzmán et al., 2017) to categorize the utterances into 5 different styles as shown in Table 2. We divide each utterance based on the span of the participating languages into five classes - monolingual English, monolingual Hindi or Spanish, classes where the two languages are dominant (70% or more) and all other utterances. The classes S3 and S4 indicate that the primary language in the utterance has a span of at least 70% with respect to the length of utterance. This criterion makes these classes notionally similar to the construct of 'matrix' language. However, we do not consider any information related to the word identity in this approach. As we can see from both the CMI and span-based classes, the distributions of the two language pairs are very different. The Spanglish data contains much more monolingual data, while the Hinglish data is predominantly Hindi matrix with English embeddings. The Hinglish data set does not have monolingual Hindi utterances which is due to the way the data was selected, as explained in Section 4.1.

3.3 Style Modeling using Modified SoundNet

SoundNet (Aytar et al., 2016) is a deep convolutional network that takes raw waveforms as input and is trained to predict objects and scenes in video streams. Once the network is trained, the activations of intermediate layers can be considered as a high level representation which can be used for other tasks. However, SoundNet is a fully convolutional network, in which the frame rate decreases with each layer. Each convolutional layer doubles the number of feature maps and halves the frame rate. The network is trained to minimize the KL divergence from the ground truth distributions to the predicted distributions. The higher layers in SoundNet are subsampled too much to be used directly for feature extraction. To alleviate this, we train a fully connected variant of Soundnet (Wang and Metze, 2017): Instead of using convolutional layers all the way up, we switch to fully connected layers after the 5th layer. We have also change the input sampling rate to 16 KHz to match the rate of provided data.

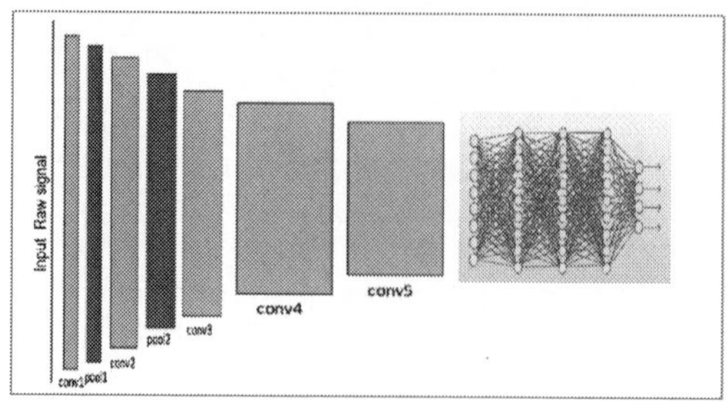

Figure 1: Architecture for style modeling using modified Soundnet

4 Experimental Setup

4.1 Data

We use code-switched Spanish English (referred to as Spanglish hereafter) released as a part of Miami Corpus (Deuchar et al., 2014) for training and testing. The corpus consists of 56 audio recordings and their corresponding transcripts of informal conversation between two or more speakers, involving a total of 84 speakers. We segment the files based on the transcriptions provided and obtain a total of 51993 utterances. For Hinglish, we use an in-house speech corpus of conversational speech. Participants were given a topic and asked to have a conversation in Hindi with another speaker. 40% of the data had at least one English word in it, which was transcribed in English, while the Hindi portion of the data was transcribed in Devanagari script. We split the data into Hindi and Hinglish by filtering for English words, hence the Hinglish data does not contain monolingual Hindi utterances. Note that this data did contain a few monolingual English sentences, but they were typically single word sentences. Such English utterances were considered to be part of the Hinglish class. The number of Hinglish utterances is 54279.

4.2 Style Identification

For style identification we perform the following procedure: We first categorize the utterances into 5 styles based on the criteria described in section 3. We pass each utterance through pretrained modified SoundNet and obtain the representations at all the layers. We use the representation from 7th (penultimate) layer as embedding for the utterance. We experimented with combining the representations at multiple layers but found that they do not outperform the representation at the 7th layer

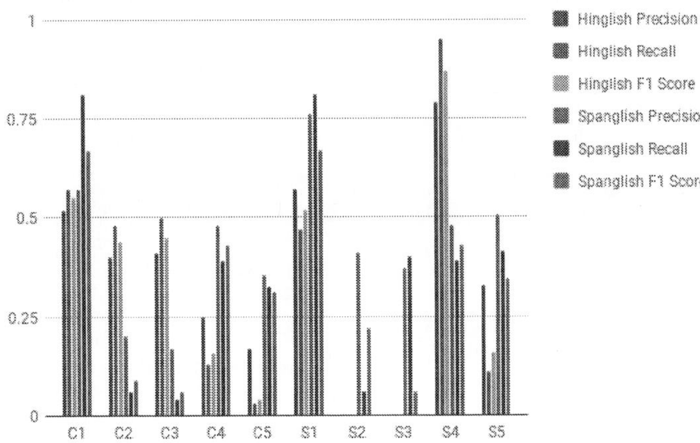

Figure 2: Precision, Recall and F1 scores for 5 way style classification of Hinglish and Spanglish

alone. Therefore for the purposes of this paper, we restrict ourselves to the representation at the penultimate layer. The embedding is obtained by performing mean pooling on the representation. Finally, we train a Random Forest classifier using the obtained embedding to predict the style of mixing.

4.3 Results and Discussion

Figure 2 shows the results for 5 class classification for Hinglish and Spanglish based on CMI (classes C1-C5) and span (classes S1-S5). Some classes (C1, C2, C3, S1, S4 for Hi-En and C1, C4, C5, S1, S4, S5 for En-Es) are easier to predict and are not always the majority classes. In our current implementation, we use a two stage approach for feature extraction and classification. We hypothesize that there might be better approaches to perform each of the components independently. It might also be possible to incorporate a style discovery module in an end to end fashion (Wang et al., 2018). As we plan to include the predicted style information in our recognition system, we also evaluate our approach using language models. For this, we build style specific language models tested on style specific test sets and include the average perplexity values for all of them in table 3. Ground Truth indicates that the model was built on the classes segregated based on approaches described in section 3. Predicted indicates that the language model was built based on the classes predicted by the model described in section 4.2. We also build a language model on utterances from the majority class for CMI and Span, as well as all the Spanglish data with no style information. As can be observed, the

perplexity has a considerable reduction when using style specific information, while the majority style does not lead to the same reduction over the model with no style information. This further validates our hypothesis that style specific models may help decrease LM perplexities and ASR error rates.

Table 3: Language Model Experiments

Language			Avg Ppl
Spanglish	CMI	GroundTruth	54.8
		Predicted	56.2
		Majority Class	81.2
	Span	GroundTruth	59.1
		Predicted	62.8
		Majority Class	80.2
No Style Info			82.1

5 Conclusion

In this paper, we present a preliminary attempt at categorizing code-switching style from acoustics, that can be used as a first pass by a speech recognition system. Language Model experiments indicate promising results with considerable reduction in perplexity for style-specific models. In future work, we plan to improve our feature extraction and classification models and test our language models on code-switched speech recognition.

References

Yusuf Aytar, Carl Vondrick, and Antonio Torralba. 2016. Soundnet: Learning sound representations from unlabeled video. In *Advances in Neural Information Processing Systems*. pages 892–900.

K Bhuvanagiri and Sunil Kopparapu. 2010. An approach to mixed language automatic speech recognition. *Oriental COCOSDA, Kathmandu, Nepal* .

Kiran Bhuvanagirir and Sunil Kumar Kopparapu. 2012. Mixed language speech recognition without explicit identification of language. *American Journal of Signal Processing* 2(5):92–97.

Joyce YC Chan, PC Ching, Tan Lee, and Helen M Meng. 2004. Detection of language boundary in code-switching utterances by bi-phone probabilities. In *Chinese Spoken Language Processing, 2004 International Symposium on*. IEEE, pages 293–296.

Margaret Deuchar, Peredur Davies, Jon Herring, M Carmen Parafita Couto, and Diana Carter. 2014. Building bilingual corpora. *Advances in the Study of Bilingualism* pages 93–111.

Vanessa Elias, Sean McKinnon, and Ángel Milla-Muñoz. 2017. The effects of code-switching and lexical stress on vowel quality and duration of heritage speakers of spanish. *Languages* 2(4):29.

B. Gamback and A Das. 2014. On measuring the complexity of code-mixing. In *Proc. of the 1st Workshop on Language Technologies for Indian Social Media (Social-India)*.

Björn Gambäck and Amitava Das. 2014. On measuring the complexity of code-mixing. In *Proceedings of the 11th International Conference on Natural Language Processing, Goa, India*. pages 1–7.

Gualberto Guzmán, Joseph Ricard, Jacqueline Serigos, Barbara E Bullock, and Almeida Jacqueline Toribio. 2017. Metrics for modeling code-switching across corpora. *Proc. Interspeech 2017* pages 67–71.

David Imseng, Hervé Bourlard, Mathew Magimai Doss, and John Dines. 2011. Language dependent universal phoneme posterior estimation for mixed language speech recognition. In *Acoustics, Speech and Signal Processing (ICASSP), 2011 IEEE International Conference on*. IEEE, pages 5012–5015.

Bing Jiang, Yan Song, Si Wei, Jun-Hua Liu, Ian Vince McLoughlin, and Li-Rong Dai. 2014. Deep bottleneck features for spoken language identification. *PloS one* 9(7):e100795.

Ying Li, Pascale Fung, Ping Xu, and Yi Liu. 2011. Asymmetric acoustic modeling of mixed language speech. In *Acoustics, Speech and Signal Processing (ICASSP), 2011 IEEE International Conference on*. IEEE, pages 5004–5007.

Ignacio Lopez-Moreno, Javier Gonzalez-Dominguez, Oldrich Plchot, David Martinez, Joaquin Gonzalez-Rodriguez, and Pedro Moreno. 2014. Automatic language identification using deep neural networks. In *Acoustics, Speech and Signal Processing (ICASSP), 2014 IEEE International Conference on*. IEEE, pages 5337–5341.

Dau-Cheng Lyu and Ren-Yuan Lyu. 2008. Language identification on code-switching utterances using multiple cues. In *Ninth Annual Conference of the International Speech Communication Association*.

Dau-Cheng Lyu, Ren-Yuan Lyu, Yuang-chin Chiang, and Chun-Nan Hsu. 2006. Speech recognition on code-switching among the chinese dialects. In *2006 IEEE International Conference on Acoustics Speech and Signal Processing Proceedings*. IEEE, volume 1, pages I–I.

Pavel Matejka, Le Zhang, Tim Ng, Harish Sri Mallidi, Ondrej Glembek, Jeff Ma, and Bing Zhang. 2014. Neural network bottleneck features for language identification. *Proceedings of IEEE Odyssey* pages 299–304.

Pieter Muysken. 2000. *Bilingual speech: A typology of code-mixing*, volume 11. Cambridge University Press.

Fred Richardson, Douglas Reynolds, and Najim Dehak. 2015a. Deep neural network approaches to speaker and language recognition. *IEEE Signal Processing Letters* 22(10):1671–1675.

Fred Richardson, Douglas Reynolds, and Najim Dehak. 2015b. A unified deep neural network for speaker and language recognition. *arXiv preprint arXiv:1504.00923* .

Chi-Jiun Shia, Yu-Hsien Chiu, Jia-Hsin Hsieh, and Chung-Hsien Wu. 2004. Language boundary detection and identification of mixed-language speech based on map estimation. In *Acoustics, Speech, and Signal Processing, 2004. Proceedings.(ICASSP '04). IEEE International Conference on*. IEEE, volume 1, pages I–381.

Yan Song, Bing Jiang, YeBo Bao, Si Wei, and Li-Rong Dai. 2013. I-vector representation based on bottleneck features for language identification. *Electronics Letters* 49(24):1569–1570.

Ngoc Thang Vu, Dau-Cheng Lyu, Jochen Weiner, Dominic Telaar, Tim Schlippe, Fabian Blaicher, Eng-Siong Chng, Tanja Schultz, and Haizhou Li. 2012. A first speech recognition system for mandarin-english code-switch conversational speech. In *2012 IEEE International Conference on Acoustics, Speech and Signal Processing (ICASSP)*. IEEE, pages 4889–4892.

Yun Wang and Florian Metze. 2017. A transfer learning based feature extractor for polyphonic sound event detection using connectionist temporal classification. *Proceedings of Interspeech, ISCA* pages 3097–3101.

Yuxuan Wang, Daisy Stanton, Yu Zhang, RJ Skerry-Ryan, Eric Battenberg, Joel Shor, Ying Xiao, Fei Ren, Ye Jia, and Rif A Saurous. 2018. Style tokens: Unsupervised style modeling, control and transfer in end-to-end speech synthesis. *arXiv preprint arXiv:1803.09017* .

Ching Feng Yeh, Chao Yu Huang, Liang Che Sun, and Lin Shan Lee. 2010. An integrated framework for transcribing mandarin-english code-mixed lectures with improved acoustic and language modeling. In *Chinese Spoken Language Processing (ISC-SLP), 2010 7th International Symposium on*. IEEE, pages 214–219.

Ching-Feng Yeh and Lin-Shan Lee. 2015. An improved framework for recognizing highly imbalanced bilingual code-switched lectures with cross-language acoustic modeling and frame-level language identification. *IEEE/ACM Transactions on Audio, Speech, and Language Processing* 23(7):1144–1159.

Accommodation of Conversational Code-Choice

Anshul Bawa   **Monojit Choudhury**   **Kalika Bali**
Microsoft Research
Bangalore, India
{t-anbaw,monojitc,kalikab}@microsoft.com

Abstract

Bilingual speakers often freely mix languages. However, in such bilingual conversations, are the language choices of the speakers coordinated? How much does one speaker's choice of language affect other speakers? In this paper, we formulate code-choice as a linguistic style, and show that speakers are indeed sensitive to and accommodating of each other's code-choice. We find that the salience or markedness of a language in context directly affects the degree of accommodation observed. More importantly, we discover that accommodation of code-choices persists over several conversational turns. We also propose an alternative interpretation of conversational accommodation as a retrieval problem, and show that the differences in accommodation characteristics of code-choices are based on their markedness in context.

1   Introduction

Code-switching (CS) refers to the fluid alteration between two or more languages within a conversation, and is a common feature of all multilingual societies. (Auer, 2013). Multilingual speakers are known to code-switch in spoken conversations for a variety of reasons, motivated by information-theoretic and cognitive principles, and also as a result of numerous social, communicative and pragmatic functions (Scotton and Ury, 1977; Söderberg Arnfast and Jørgensen, 2003; Gumperz, 1982).

Code-choice refers to a speaker's decision of which code to use in a given utterance, and in case of a CS utterance, to what extent the different codes are to be used. Depending on the sociolinguistic and conversational context, a speaker's

code-choice may be unexpected and noticed by other speakers, and is likely to affect other speakers' subsequent code-choice. In other words, speakers may *accommodate* to each other's code-choice, positively or negatively (Genesee, 1982).

In this work, we propose a set of metrics to study the social accommodation of code-choice as a sociolinguistic style marker. We build upon the existing framework on accommodation by Danescu-Niculescu-Mizil et al. (2011) and adapt that for code-choice by introducing relevant features for code-choice. We then motivate and illustrate the effect of code markedness on the degree of accommodation - the more salient code is more strongly accommodated for. We further generalize the framework to also account for *delayed* accommodation, instead of only next-turn or *immediate* accommodation.

In addition, we introduce an alternative view of accommodation as a query-response task, and employ mean reciprocal rank, a well-understood metric from the domain of Information Retrieval, as a metric for latency of accommodation. We measure how quickly a style marker (code-choice in our case) introduced by a speaker is retrieved by the other speaker during the conversation. Our approach is developed for analyzing code-choice but is applicable to other dimensions of linguistic style as well (Tausczik and Pennebaker, 2010). This presents an alternative view of conversational style accommodation and offers a simple but effective way of measuring, characterizing and even predicting elements of conversational style.

We test this formulation on two CS conversational datasets - dialog scripts of bilingual Indian movies (in English and Hindi) and a transcription of real-world conversations between Spanish-English bilinguals in Florida, US. In both the corpora, we observe strong signals of interpersonal code-choice accommodation for the salient or marked code. We also observe that on average,

82

Proceedings of The Third Workshop on Computational Approaches to Code-Switching, pages 82–91
Melbourne, Australia, July 19, 2018. ©2018 Association for Computational Linguistics

the marked code is accommodated within the first three to four conversational turns, beyond which the effect of accommodation on code-choice decays gradually. Contextually-unmarked code is less strongly accommodated for, even when it occurs relatively infrequently within a conversation.

As far as we know, this is the first computational study of code-choice accommodation, and first work that introduces and formalizes the concept of delayed accommodation, that can be applied to other style dimensions as well.

The rest of the paper is organized as follows. We describe the background and related work in Section 2, which motivates the first formulation of code-choice accommodation in Section 3. We improve this by formulation by modifying the features in Section 4. We generalize the formulation to multiple turns and introduce the analogy to retrieval in Section 5, along with the results. We wrap up with a discussion in Section 6 that we conclude in Section 7.

2 Related Work

CS is employed by speakers to signal a common multilingual identity(Auer, 2005), and can be effectively used to reduce (or increase) the perceived social distance between the speakers (Camilleri, 1996). As a marker of *informality*, it has been shown to lower interpersonal distance (Myers-Scotton, 1995; Genesee, 1982).

Common structural patterns in CS as well as the choice to switch between languages have been the focus of many linguistic studies(Poplack, 1988)(Auer, 1995). As CS is typically used as a conversation strategy by bilinguals who are proficient in both languages (Auer, 2013), it is not surprising that certain pragmatic and socio-linguistic factors, such as formality of context (Fishman, 1970), age (Ervin-Tripp and Reyes, 2005), expression of emotion (Dewaele, 2010) and sentiment (Rudra et al., 2016), are found to signal language preference in CS conversations. A Twitter study of CS patterns across several geographies (Rijhwani et al., 2017), also suggests that there might be complex sociolinguistic reasons for code-choice. Thus, CS, and the choice of language or *code* in which one communicates during a multilingual conversation, could be considered a marker of *linguistic style*.

Communication accommodation theory (Giles et al., 1973; Giles, 2007) states that speakers shift their linguistic styles towards (or away from) each other in a conversation for social effect. In the CAT framework, the interlocutors' desire for 'social approval' results in an attempt to match each other's linguistic style. Accommodation has been studied for many markers of linguistic style like tense, negations, articles, prepositions, pronouns and sentiment (Taylor and Thomas, 2008; Niederhoffer and Pennebaker, 2002).

Since it is possible to convey the same semantic content while widely varying the extent of CS, we also consider code-choice as a linguistic style dimension. Therefore, we expect to observe accommodation in terms of code-choice in similar manner to that of variables for other linguistic styles. While there have been linguistic and small-scale studies (Sachdev and Giles, 2004; Bourhis, 2008; Bissoonauth and Offord, 2001; y Bourhis et al., 2007) that argue for prevalence of code-choice accommodation, there are no large-scale quantitative or computational studies that corroborate this and shed light on the various patterns of code-choice accommodation. Further, these studies rely on simple correlation-based measures.

The first computational study of linguistic style accommodation (Danescu-Niculescu-Mizil et al., 2011) shows that it is highly prevalent in Twitter conversations. They use binary features for the presence of various psychologically meaningful word categories as described by the LIWC method(Tausczik and Pennebaker, 2010) to identify stylistic variations in tweets. They then define a probabilistic framework that mathematically models style accommodation in terms of the likelihood of an addressee to respond in the same style as the speaker.

Though CS is similar enough to other kinds of linguistic style to allow analysis using the same framework, it also differs from them in being a strong sociological indicator of identity (Auer, 2005) and in not being processed nonconsciously (Levelt and Kelter, 1982). We demonstrate that a model that does not account for these crucial differences fails to capture the accommodative patterns of code-choice. Because of being processed consciously, code-choice also exhibits accommodation over several conversational turns, an effect which is not observed as strongly for other style dimensions (Danescu-Niculescu-Mizil et al., 2011). Long-term effects in accommodation have received very little attention, and have mostly studied based on crude conversation-level correlation values (Niederhoffer and Pennebaker, 2002).

3 Accommodation of Code-Choice as Linguistic Style

As a first step, we adapt an existing framework (Danescu-Niculescu-Mizil et al., 2011) that quantifies *accommodation* of a given linguistic style. Any linguistic feature is said to exhibit accommodation if it is more likely to be expressed in response to a dialog that also expresses it, than otherwise. In other words, an accommodative feature in a dialog begets the same feature in the next dialog. We use the term 'dialog' or 'turn' to refer to a single spoken utterance or dialog within a conversation, and the term 'speaker' to refer to conversation participants. This framework thus restricts the definition of accommodation to only single-turn effects.

3.1 Measuring Accommodation

Mathematically, let F denote some binary feature over a dialog (we describe the features themselves in Section 3.2 below). F is said to exhibit accommodation if the likelihood of a user expressing F increases when F has been expressed in the previous dialog. We define the degree of accommodation as follows

$$Acm(F) = P\big(\delta_{d_i^F} \big| \delta_{d_{i-1}^F}\big) - P\big(\delta_{d_i^F}\big) \qquad (1)$$

Here, dialog d_{i-1} immediately precedes dialog d_i, and δ_{d^F} is the *event* that the dialog d exhibits F. The first term can be thought of as the *reciprocity* over F. The second term is the fraction of dialogs in the corpus for which $F = 1$, which is also the empirical probability of observing F in a dialog d.

Instead of computing these likelihoods over the entire corpus, we could also compute them individually for each speaker, and doing so yields a fairer condition for accommodation. Different speakers can have widely different base likelihoods. This metric requires an average speaker to reciprocate more than their own (individual) baseline likelihood of expressing F, rather than simply more than the population baseline. Denoting the event that a dialog d is spoken by a speaker s as $\delta_{S(d)=s}$, we redefine accommodation as follows

(E_s denotes an expectation over all speakers s)

$$
\begin{aligned}
Acm^*(F) &= E_s\big(Acm_s(F)\big) \\
&= E_s\Big(P\big(\delta_{d_i^F}\delta_{S(d)=s}\big|\delta_{d_{i-1}^F}\big) \\
&\quad - P\big(\delta_{d_i^F}\delta_{S(d)=s}\big)\Big)
\end{aligned} \qquad (2)
$$

3.2 Measuring Code-Choice

Our general hypothesis is that code-choice is reciprocated in a bilingual conversation. To measure this, we introduce simple binary features for presence of each code, along the lines of the binary features in (Danescu-Niculescu-Mizil et al., 2011), with individual language expression substituting for the style dimensions. For each language L, we define a feature F_L indicating, for a dialog d, if the dialog contains words in the language L. The event that dialog d is at least partially in L, is denoted by $\delta_{d^{F_L}}$. In other words, $\delta_d^{F_L}$ is true if the language L is expressed in dialog d, and false otherwise.

3.3 Data

We employ two datasets of bilingual conversations, each in a different conversational context and a different pair of languages, to test the occurrence of code-choice accommodation. Table 1 reports the number of dialogs and words for the two datasets, and the fraction of words that are in English.

Dataset	Dialogs	Words	%En
Movies (*En-Hi*)	20.1K	240K	24.1
Bangor (*Es-En*)	18.5K	216K	62.9

Table 1: Conversational dataset overview

Hindi Movies

The data comprises of scripts of 32 Hindi movies released between 2012 and 2017. 17 of these scripts were collected by Pratapa and Choudhury (2017) from scripts posted online[1]. We collected 15 scripts of our own from a similar online source[2] and parsed them replicating the methodology of Pratapa and Choudhury (2017).

All the scripts have word-level language tags as created by the language identification system from (Gella et al., 2013). The language labels on manual inspection were found to have significant

---

[1] https://moifightclub.com/category/scripts
[2] http://www.filmcompanion.in/category/fc-pro/scripts/

amount of noise, we corrected frequently observed errors with manual supervision.

Each dialog is assumed to be in response to the immediately preceding dialog within a scene. We restrict our analysis to dialogs that are between no more than two speakers, to avoid confounding effects of multi-party conversations on accommodation. This also filters out most dialogs in the scripts which are not conversational in nature.

Movie conversations, even though imagined, are designed to sound natural, and therefore, are suitable for studying style accommodation, as is argued in Danescu-Niculescu-Mizil and Lee (2011), and also multilingualism (Bleichenbacher, 2008) and code-choice (Vaish, 2011). It is true that movie dialogs promote stereotypes that may affect characters' expression of code-choice, however *accommodative effects* can still be expected to play out largely independent of such stereotypes. There have been several linguistic and quantitative studies on Hindi-English CS in Hindi movies (Parshad et al., 2016; Lösch, 2007; Pratapa and Choudhury, 2017).

Bangor Corpus

We use the Bangor Miami corpus[3] of word-level language labeled transcripts of spoken conversations between Spanish-English bilinguals in Florida, US. The original dataset contains 56 conversations, from which we selected 40 conversations that have non-trivial amount of English and Spanish, and sufficient dialogs from each speaker.

Figure 1 shows the fraction of Spanish used by a dyad of speakers in a sample conversation from this dataset (the complement fraction being English). Intuitively, we expect our metrics to capture how coordinated two speakers are.

3.4 Results

Table 2 shows the metrics from Section 3.1 computed over the features in Section 3.2 on the two datasets.

While these numbers do suggest that accommodative effects are present, they seem to be fairly weak. The rate of reciprocation is only slightly higher than the base rate, and in some cases the difference isn't statistically significant.

However, looking at individual differences in these values reveals an interesting observation. For each speaker s in the Movies dataset, we

---

[3]http://bangortalk.org.uk/speakers.php?c=miami

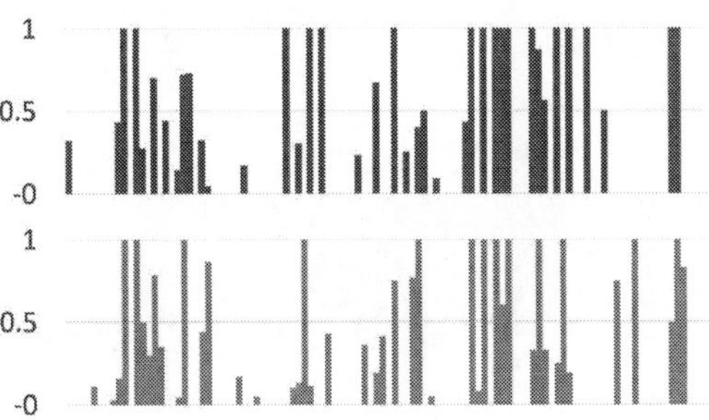

Figure 1: Fraction of Spanish over time in a conversation. The x-axis denotes consecutive dialog pairs, with dialog i above aligned with dialog $i + 1$ below, so two aligned bars denote two consecutive dialogs.

Dataset	Code (L)	$Acm(F_L)$	$Acm^*(F_L)$
Bangor	En	0.06†	0.04
	Es	0.12	0.09
Movies	En	0.10	0.06
	Hi	0.02†	-0.02†

Table 2: Accommodation values for different codes. Values with a (†) are not significant. Significance for $Acm(F)$ is computed using Fisher's exact test, and significance for $Acm^*(F)$ is computed using one-tailed paired t-test.

plot in Figure 2, the rate of accommodation by s, $Acm_s(F)$, against the respective base rate $P(d_s^F)$, for $F \in \{F_{En}, F_{Hi}\}$.

Clearly, we see that a high base rate of expression corresponds to far less accommodation. In other words, the instances of code-choice that are uncommon and therefore unexpected within the conversational context are likely to be accommodated for. In a conversation that is predominantly in Hindi, a dialog uttered in Hindi carries little salience and doesn't stand out. This code-choice is unlikely to be registered as a communicative signal or a marked expression of any linguistic style, and therefore wouldn't elicit accommodation. English and Spanish are respectively less common in Movies and Bangor, and indeed their rates of accommodation are higher than the rates for the corresponding dominant languages.

Since the metrics in Section 3.1 compute likelihoods over all instances of code-choice irrespective of salience, the observed rates of accommodation are low. We borrow the notion of *markedness* of code-choice, as described in Myers-Scotton (2005), and incorporate it into our framework, as

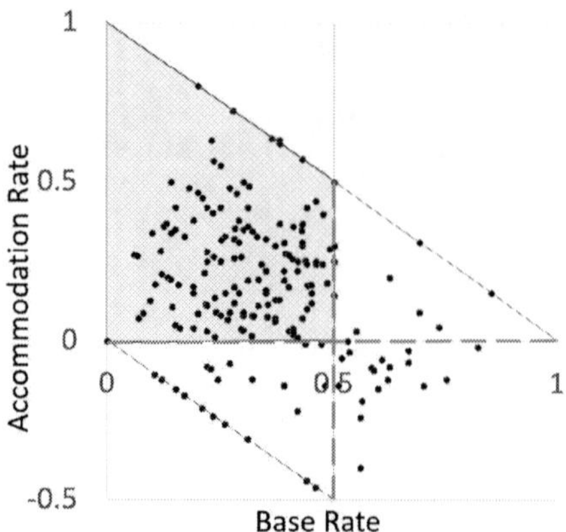

Figure 2: Variation of accommodation rate against base rate. Observed rate $(x + y)$ can vary between 0 and 1. The highlighted region denotes positive accommodation and a low base rate ($x < 0.5$ and $y > 0$). In contrast, all other regions, as demarcated by dashed lines, are sparser.

described in the next section.

4   Marked Code-Choice Features

4.1   Code Salience

As shown earlier, measuring accommodation makes sense only over marked instances of code-choice. Thus, for every conversation in our dataset, we identify the marked language, and measure accommodation only over that language. We choose a conversation as the unit for deciding if a code is marked because the set of speakers and the conversation context typically dictates code-choice in multilingual societies.

A language is considered marked if it is the non-dominant language - we keep the threshold of markedness at no more than 40% of total words in the entire conversation. We discard highly mixed conversations where none of the languages meets the threshold. This consideration also makes the calculation of accommodation more robust, as for a high fraction of incidence of a code, the effect of the previous turn would be harder to isolate.

4.2   Threshold of Occurrence

Another limitation of the formulation in Section 3 is that it doesn't incorporate the *extent* of presence of each code in a dialog. Consequently, even named entities, frequently borrowed words and frozen expressions from the marked language, would be considered as candidates for accommo-

dation. The Bangor corpus came with named-entity tags, and in the Movies corpus we removed all character names from the dialogs, but we were not aware of any NER system for Hindi-English CS data that we could have used to remove other named entities. Ideally, we would like to exclude all such words from the triggers expected to elicit accommodation, as their usage isn't stylistically marked (Auer, 1999). The word-level language tags also have some amount of noise, and it is desirable to use features that are resilient to it.

Besides, it is possible that a relatively high incidence of marked code in a dialog is perceived as a stronger style marker, and is perhaps accommodated for more strongly than a lower incidence. We introduce a simple fraction-based thresholding that allows us to test the same.

For every dialog d, we define feature $F_{L,\tau}$ such that $d^{F_{L,\tau}} = 1$ if and only if (a) d is sufficiently long and (b) fraction of words of d in the marked language L is more than τ. We consider an utterance to be sufficiently long if it contains more than 4 words, as this is expected to filter out most frozen expressions and named entities that may be borrowed from one language to another. We show results for accommodation of F_τ for $\tau \in \{0, 0.2, 0.5\}$. While F_0 would capture presence of even one word in a marked code, $F_{0.2}$ represents a non-trivial occurrence and $F_{0.5}$ represents majority occurrence of the marked code in context.

5   Beyond Immediate Accommodation

The metrics in Section 3 and those in Danescu-Niculescu-Mizil et al. (2011) only consider the immediate next turn as a candidate for reciprocation. However, it is possible for accommodative effects to span a few conversation turns. Consider the following snippet from one of the conversations in Bangor (Spanish code is in bold and its translation is in italics).

In cases like this, the content of the conversation prevents a possibility of accommodating immediately, but the speaker *Sarah* still reciprocates *Paige*'s code-choice at the first instance possible. We can test if such cases of delayed accommodation are indeed common in the data, by extending our formulation to an arbitrary number of turns. We extend Equation (2) below, and Equation (1) can be extended analogously.

Paige	i wanna see them.
Sarah	pick. pick like (name) flowers or ...
Paige	**¡ay qué lindo está ese!**
	oh, how pretty that is!
	ok, enter the date.
	it will be ...
Sarah	may.
Paige	may. ninth?
Sarah	ninth.
Paige	two thousand and eight.
	and then you put what you want.
	(name) trip?
Sarah	**no te cabe.**
	it doesn't fit you.
	just (name).

5.1 Generalization of Immediate Accommodation

The baseline rate of a speaker s using a feature F across n (consecutive) turns is the likelihood that at least one the n turns expresses F, and is given by $1 - (1 - p_s)^n$, where p_s is simply $P(d_s^F)$. For a speaker s, the rate of n-turn accommodation is the increase in likelihood of occurrence of F in either of the n dialogs $d_{s,1}$ to $d_{s,n}$, conditioned on the event that the preceding dialog d_0 expresses F.

$$Acm_{n,s}(F) = P\left(\bigvee_{i=1}^{n} \left(d_{s,i}^F\right) \middle| d_0^F \right) \tag{3}$$
$$- \left(1 - (1 - p_s)^n\right)$$

$$Acm_n^*(F) = E_s\left(Acm_{n,s}(F)\right) \tag{4}$$

When $n = 1$, this resolves to Equation (2). Note that d_1 to d_n are the first n dialogs spoken by s immediately after the dialog d_0. As before, E_s denotes expected value over all speakers.

5.2 Accommodation as Retrieval

Responding to marked code-choice with marked code-choice can be thought of or reformulated as a retrieval task. For a speaker s, each instance of a dialog addressed to s with a feature F would be a *query* posed to s. The next n dialogs spoken by s would be the top-n retrieved *responses* to the query. We are interested in the retrieval of responses that also have feature F, so we call a response with feature F to be *relevant* response and *irrelevant* otherwise, in keeping with the standard terminology in information retrieval. We consider s to have retrieved a relevant response in n-turns if at least one of the first n responses is relevant.

When formulated this way, the *recall* of s, the probability of retrieving a relevant response, is precisely equal to the first term in Equation 3, the probability using F in responding to a dialog c^F. The second term in Equation 3 is the expected value of recall under the independence assumption, i.e., if s randomly introduces marked code at every turn with probability p_s. Therefore, a speaker is accommodative if their recall is higher than that of this random baseline.

A popular metric to evaluate retrieval systems is the mean reciprocal rank (MRR). The reciprocal rank of a query response is the multiplicative inverse of the rank of the first relevant response. The MRR of a system is simply the mean of the reciprocal ranks of all its responses. Since we expect the accommodative speaker to have a higher recall than the random baseline, we also expect the accommodative speaker to have a higher MRR, with the difference from baseline MRR being proportional to its accommodativeness.

Not only does this present an alternative view of accommodation and exposes well-studied formalisms and concepts from information retrieval, but the ability to capture speakers' styles as response characteristics also facilitates predictive conversational modelling.

Mean reciprocal ranks for the random baselines can be computed analytically as follows. We first compute the expected reciprocal rank r for any given query as a function of the correctness probability p_s. For the first relevant response to be at rank i, all previous responses must be irrelevant. Since each response is relevant with a probability p_s, the probability of the i-th response being the first relevant response is given by :

$$P\left(r_{p_s} = \frac{1}{i}\right) = (1 - p_s)^{i-1} * p_s \tag{5}$$

The baseline MRR of a speaker s, denoted by $Base_s$, is then the expected value of r, also as function of p_s :

$$\begin{aligned} Base_s &= E\left(r_{p_s}\right) \\ &= \sum_{i=1}^{\infty} (1 - p_s)^{i-1} * p_s / i \\ &= -\frac{p_s}{1 - p_s} \ln p_s \end{aligned} \tag{6}$$

The overall baseline MRR, $Base$ is then simply $E_s(Base_s)$. We compare the observed MRR on the data (denoted by Obs) with the expected MRR of the random baselines ($Base$), with their difference being indicative of the degree and immediacy of accommodation.

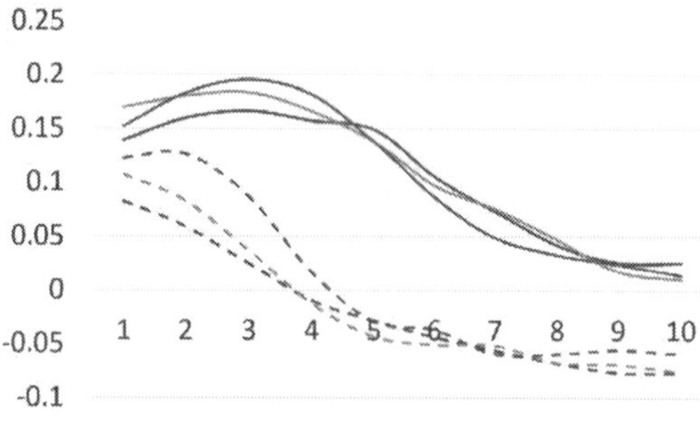

(a) Bangor; $L = Es$ for solid lines (significant for $n < 6$) and $L = En$ for dashed (significant for $n < 4$).

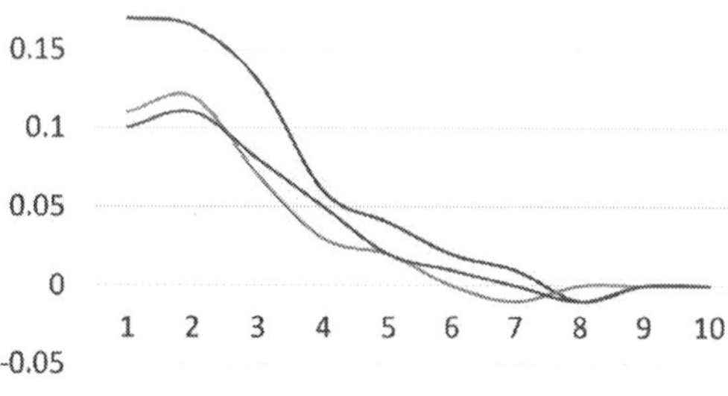

(b) Movies; $L = En$. Significant for $n < 4$.

Figure 3: Accommodation rates ($Acm_n^*(F_{L,\tau})$) versus n. Red, green and blue lines indicate $\tau = 0$, 0.2 and 0.5 respectively. Accommodation of Hindi is not significant.

5.3 Results and Observations

Figure 3 shows the trends in $Acm_n^*(F_{L,\tau})$ for different values of n, L and τ. Significance scores are computed in the same way as for Table 2.

Table 3 shows the real and baseline MRR values for each corpus over different values of τ.

It is evident that accommodation of code-choice is a prevalent and robust phenomenon. The values of accommodation are consistently positive for all the different marked-code features, languages and datasets, and for low values of n.

In Table 3, the less common codes in each dataset, Es and En respectively, have a lower baseline while having comparable or even higher observed MRRs as their more common counterpart. This reiterates that accommodation is more pronounced for more marked codes.

From Figure 3, a higher fraction of marked code ($\tau = 0.5$) does not seem to elicit stronger accommodation than $\tau = 0$. However, it is important to note that the base rate for F_0 is much higher than that of $F_{0.5}$, so in relative terms, the latter exhibits

MRR	τ	Bangor		Movies	
		Es	En	En	Hi
Obs	0	0.48	0.52	0.67	0.62
$Base$		0.18	0.34	0.32	0.40
Obs	0.2	0.46	0.54	0.57	0.45
$Base$		0.15	0.26	0.25	0.35
Obs	0.5	0.46	0.49	0.54	0.4
$Base$		0.12	0.22	0.15	0.25

Table 3: Mean Reciprocal Ranks of the observed responses (Obs) and the random baseline ($Base$) for different features F_τ and different corpora.

a stronger tendency to accommodate (since the increase over respective base rate is identical). The difference between the retrieval characteristics for the different thresholds is more salient in Table 3 - higher thresholds correspond to a smaller average likelihood, and lower baseline MRRs. The difference between observed and baseline MRR does slightly increase with τ, making higher fraction of marked code somewhat more accommodated for.

In contrast to English, the accommodation for Hindi code-choice in conversations dominated by English is not significant. This suggests that Hindi code isn't marked even when it is the minority code in a scene, an inference that aligns with the claim from Myers-Scotton (2005) that Hindi is not marked in Hindi movies, even when it is the non-dominant language in context.

Hindi in Movies and English in Bangor have a lower strength of accommodation than their respective counterparts, even when measured over conversations where they are uncommon. Not only is accommodation stronger for Spanish, it also persists for more number of turns as compared to English. This suggests that the context of markedness is larger than the immediate conversation, and the being the dominant language of the corpus as a whole reduces markedness.

In most cases, accommodation is salient and significant even after a few turns. Delayed accommodation is as prevalent as immediate accommodation. And the likelihood of a given speaker reciprocating code-choice in kind, remains significant for several turns in a conversation.

6 Discussion

Accommodation is prevalent and robust, but not universal. While it is observed across conversations spanning different media and language pairs, there is significant variation among speakers within a dataset. As many as 18% of the speakers exhibit what may be considered negative accommodation, or non-accommodation. Half of these do so with a value of $Acm_1^*(F_0)$ less than -0.10.

It is in fact known that accommodation or convergence is neither a universal nor a positive interpersonal strategy (Genesee and Bourhis, 1988; Giles et al., 1991; Burt, 1994). In-group/out-group identity as well as attitudes towards CS and the languages involved can cause negative accommodation as well as a negative perception of accommodation. Burt (1994) show that while convergence is largely viewed positively, some multilingual speakers may oppose it as either misplaced solidarity with an in-group, or a slur on the language capability of an interlocutor.

While we work under the assumption that code-choice is a style dimension, largely independent of content, it is in fact influenced by factors like topic (Sert, 2005) and sentiment (Rudra et al., 2016). These influences could either align or compete with the socially accommodative code-choice, and this explains several-turn accommodation - it is not always possible to accommodate immediately. The difference between code-choice and other linguistic style markers is also indicated by the poor results of Section 3, which naively applies the style accommodation framework to code-choice.

It is worth noting that the baselines throughout the paper assume that speakers do not adjust their overall rate of employing a particular code, in order to accommodate. This is in fact a fairly strict assumption. In fact, the same speaker typically has widely varying base rates in conversations with multiple other speakers. The extent of marked code to be used is itself often negotiated within a conversation, and adjusting one's base rate can be construed as accommodation, and harder to analyze. Nevertheless, this assumption gives us a strong and realistic baseline to judge the observations against.

One limitation of our formulation is that we do not look at individual words. Word or code saliency in context is actually more complex that just language saliency in current conversation. Some words are more marked than others, with borrowed words carrying very little salience. It would be nice to have more complex features, aware of the syntactic structure of dialogs. It would also be worthwhile to apply this formula-

tion to study conversation-wide accommodation effects and convergence of code-choice at scale.

7 Conclusion

We demonstrate that code-choice is a marker of linguistic style, and when it is marked in context, it is interpersonally accommodated for. We extend the probabilistic formulation to multiple conversation turns, and show equivalence with a retrieval task, both facilitating better conversational analysis of code-choice in particular and style interactions in general.

In the future, we would like to use richer and linguistically motivated features for code-choice, including parts-of-speech, and indicators of borrowing across languages. Another generalization would be to also study LIWC words and markers of sociolinguistic style in this framework. Finally, longer-term accommodation effects, like convergence being succeeded by divergence, or topical effects on convergence, remain to be explored using a quantitative method like ours.

References

Peter Auer. 1995. The pragmatics of code-switching: a sequential approach. In Lesley Milroy and Pieter Muysken, editors, *One speaker, two languages*, pages 115–135. Cambridge University Press.

Peter Auer. 1999. From codeswitching via language mixing to fused lects: Toward a dynamic typology of bilingual speech. *International journal of bilingualism*, 3(4):309–332.

Peter Auer. 2005. A postscript: Code-switching and social identity. *Journal of pragmatics*, 37(3):403–410.

Peter Auer. 2013. *Code-switching in conversation: Language, interaction and identity*. Routledge.

Anu Bissoonauth and Malcolm Offord. 2001. Language use of mauritian adolescents in education. *Journal of Multilingual and Multicultural Development*, 22(5):381–400.

Lukas Bleichenbacher. 2008. *Multilingualism in the movies: Hollywood characters and their language choices*, volume 135. BoD–Books on Demand.

Richard y Bourhis, Shaha El-Geledi, and Itesh Sachdev. 2007. Language, ethnicity and intergroup relations. In *Language, discourse and social psychology*, pages 15–50. Springer.

Richard Y Bourhis. 2008. The english-speaking communities of quebec: Vitality, multiple identities and linguicism. *The Vitality of the English-Speaking*

Communities of Quebec: From Community Decline to Revival, Montréal, Centre détudes ethniques des universités montréalaises, Université de Montréal.

Susan Meredith Burt. 1994. Code choice in intercultural conversation. *Pragmatics. Quarterly Publication of the International Pragmatics Association (IPrA)*, 4(4):535–559.

Antoinette Camilleri. 1996. Language values and identities: Code switching in secondary classrooms in malta. *Linguistics and education*, 8(1):85–103.

Cristian Danescu-Niculescu-Mizil, Michael Gamon, and Susan Dumais. 2011. Mark my words!: linguistic style accommodation in social media. In *Proceedings of the 20th international conference on World wide web*, pages 745–754. ACM.

Cristian Danescu-Niculescu-Mizil and Lillian Lee. 2011. Chameleons in imagined conversations: A new approach to understanding coordination of linguistic style in dialogs. In *Proceedings of the 2nd Workshop on Cognitive Modeling and Computational Linguistics*, pages 76–87. Association for Computational Linguistics.

Jean-Marc Dewaele. 2010. *Emotions in multiple languages.* Palgrave Macmillan, Basingstoke, UK.

Susan Ervin-Tripp and Iliana Reyes. 2005. Child codeswitching and adult content contrasts. *International Journal of Bilingualism*, 9(1):85–102.

J.A. Fishman. 1970. *Sociolinguistics: a brief introduction.* Newbury House language series. Newbury House.

Spandana Gella, Jatin Sharma, and Kalika Bali. 2013. Query word labeling and back transliteration for indian languages: Shared task system description. *FIRE Working Notes*, 3.

Fred Genesee. 1982. The social psychological significance of code switching in cross-cultural communication. *Journal of language and social psychology*, 1(1):1–27.

Fred Genesee and Richard Y Bourhis. 1988. Evaluative reactions to language choice strategies: The role of sociostructural factors. *Language & Communication*, 8(3-4):229–250.

Howard Giles. 2007. *Communication accommodation theory.* Wiley Online Library.

Howard Giles, Nikolas Coupland, and IUSTINE Coupland. 1991. 1. accommodation theory: Communication, context, and. *Contexts of accommodation: Developments in applied sociolinguistics*, 1.

Howard Giles, Donald M Taylor, and Richard Bourhis. 1973. Towards a theory of interpersonal accommodation through language: Some canadian data. *Language in society*, 2(2):177–192.

John J Gumperz. 1982. *Discourse strategies*, volume 1. Cambridge University Press.

Willem JM Levelt and Stephanie Kelter. 1982. Surface form and memory in question answering. *Cognitive psychology*, 14(1):78–106.

Eva Lösch. 2007. The construction of social distance through code-switching: an exemplary analysis for popular indian cinema. *Department of Linguistics, Technical University of Chemnitz.*

Carol Myers-Scotton. 1995. *Social motivations for codeswitching: Evidence from Africa.* Oxford University Press.

Carol Myers-Scotton. 2005. *Multiple voices: An introduction to bilingualism.* Wiley-Blackwell.

Kate G Niederhoffer and James W Pennebaker. 2002. Linguistic style matching in social interaction. *Journal of Language and Social Psychology*, 21(4):337–360.

Rana D. Parshad, Suman Bhowmick, Vineeta Chand, Nitu Kumari, and Neha Sinha. 2016. What is India speaking? Exploring the "Hinglish" invasion. *Physica A*, 449:375–389.

Shana Poplack. 1988. Contrasting patterns of codeswitching in two communities. *Codeswitching: Anthropological and sociolinguistic perspectives*, 215:44.

Adithya Pratapa and Monojit Choudhury. 2017. Quantitative characterization of code switching patterns in complex multi-party conversations: A case study on hindi movie scripts. In *Proceedings of the 14th International Conference on Natural Language Processing*, pages 75–84.

Shruti Rijhwani, Royal Sequiera, Monojit Choudhury, Kalika Bali, and Chandra Sekhar Maddila. 2017. Estimating code-switching on Twitter with a novel generalized word-level language identification technique. In *Proceedings of the Annual Meeting of the ACL.*

Koustav Rudra, Shruti Rijhwani, Rafiya Begum, Kalika Bali, Monojit Choudhury, and Niloy Ganguly. 2016. Understanding language preference for expression of opinion and sentiment: What do Hindi-English speakers do on Twitter? In *EMNLP*, pages 1131–1141.

Itesh Sachdev and Howard Giles. 2004. Bilingual accommodation. *The handbook of bilingualism*, pages 353–378.

Carol Myers Scotton and William Ury. 1977. Bilingual strategies: The social functions of code-switching. *International Journal of the sociology of language*, 1977(13):5–20.

Olcay Sert. 2005. The functions of code-switching in elt classrooms. *Online Submission*, 11(8).

Juni Söderberg Arnfast and J Normann Jørgensen.
2003. Code-switching as a communication, learning, and social negotiation strategy in first-year
learners of danish. *International journal of applied
linguistics*, 13(1):23–53.

Yla R Tausczik and James W Pennebaker. 2010. The
psychological meaning of words: Liwc and comput-
erized text analysis methods. *Journal of language
and social psychology*, 29(1):24–54.

Paul J Taylor and Sally Thomas. 2008. Linguistic style
matching and negotiation outcome. *Negotiation and
Conflict Management Research*, 1(3):263–281.

Viniti Vaish. 2011. Terrorism, nationalism and west-
ernization: Code switching and identity in bolly-
wood. *FM Hult, & KA King, K. A (Eds.). Educational linguistics in practice: Applying the local
globally and the global locally*, pages 27–40.

Language Informed Modeling of Code-Switched Text

Khyathi Raghavi Chandu[*]   **Thomas Manzini**[*]   **Sumeet Singh**[*]   **Alan Black**

Language Technologies Institute, Carnegie Mellon University
{kchandu,tmanzini,sumeets,awb}@cs.cmu.edu

Abstract

Code-switching (CS), the practice of alternating between two or more languages in conversations, is pervasive in most multilingual communities. CS texts have a complex interplay between languages and occur in informal contexts that make them harder to collect and construct NLP tools for. We approach this problem through Language Modeling (LM) on a new Hindi-English mixed corpus containing 59,189 unique sentences collected from blogging websites. We implement and discuss different Language Models derived from a multi-layered LSTM architecture. We hypothesize that encoding language information strengthens a language model by helping to learn code-switching points. We show that our highest performing model achieves a test perplexity of 19.52 on the CS corpus that we collected and processed. On this data we demonstrate that our performance is an improvement over AWD-LSTM LM (a recent state of the art on monolingual English).

1   Introduction

Code-switching (CS) is a widely studied linguistic phenomenon where two different languages are interleaved. This occurs within multilingual communities (Poplack, 1980; Myers-Scotton, 1997; Muysken, 2000; Bullock and Toribio, 2009). Typically one language (the *matrix language*) provides the grammatical structure for CS text and words from another language (the *embedded language*) are inserted. However, CS data is challenging to obtain because this phenomenon is usually observed in informal settings. Data obtained from online sources is often noisy because of spelling, script, morphological, and grammatical variations.

These sources of noise make it quite challenging to build robust NLP tools (Çetinoğlu et al., 2016). Our goal is to improve LM for Hindi-English code-mixed data (*Hinglish*) where similar challenges are apparent. The task of language modeling is very important to several downstream applications in NLP including speech recognition, machine translation, etc. This is particularly important in domains that lack annotated data, such as code-switching, where the need to leverage unsupervised techniques is a must. We address the task of language modeling in CS text with a dual objective: (1) predicting the next word, and (2) predicting the language of the next word.

In addition to the techniques used for monolingual language modeling, providing information about the language is a key component in CS domain. Our main goal in this paper is to examine the effect of language information in modeling CS text. We approach this systematically by experimenting with ablations of encoding and decoding language IDs along with the word itself. In this way, the model implicitly learns the switch points between the languages. We achieve the least perplexity score using a combination of a language informed encoder and a language informed decoder.

The current material begins with a review of LM techniques for CS text in section 2. Then we describe our data collection and processing steps in Section 3 and model architecture in Section 4. Section 5 contains a brief quantitative and qualitative discussion of our observations and promising directions for future work. We then conclude in section 6.

2   Related Work

The increased reach of Internet and social media has led to proliferation of noisy CS data where earlier computational frameworks for code-switching, such as Joshi (1982); Goyal et al. (2003); Sinha and Thakur (2005); Solorio and Liu (2008a,b), are not readily applicable. In recent times, the community has focused on develop-

---

[*] These authors contributed equally

Proceedings of The Third Workshop on Computational Approaches to Code-Switching, pages 92–97
Melbourne, Australia, July 19, 2018. ©2018 Association for Computational Linguistics

ing a variety of NLP tools for CS data such language models by Li and Fung (2013, 2014); Adel et al. (2015, 2013a,b); Garg et al. (2017), POS taggers by Vyas et al. (2014); Jamatia et al. (2015); Çetinoğlu and Çöltekin (2016), automatic language identification by Jurgens et al. (2017); King and Abney (2013); Rijhwani et al. (2017); Jhamtani et al. (2014), prediction of code-switch points by Das and Gambäck (2014), sentiment analysis by Rudra et al. (2016) and also certain meta level studies that include understanding metrics to characterize code-mixing Patro et al. (2017); Guzmán et al. (2017). The idea of including language identifier vectors on the input and/or output side has become fairly common for other tasks as well, e.g. in Johnson et al. (2016) for machine translation, Ammar et al. (2016) for parsing, or Östling and Tiedemann (2016) for language modeling.

2.1 Code-Switched Language Models

There has been some recent focus on adapting existing language models for CS text. Li and Fung (2013, 2014) use a translation model together with the language model of the matrix language to model the mixed language. The search space within the translation model is reduced by linguistic features in CS texts like inversion constraint and functional head constraint (Sankoff and Poplack, 1981).

In another approach Adel et al. (2015), use a Factored Language Model (FLM) that includes syntactic and semantic features found in CS text that are indicative of a switch e.g. trigger words, trigger POS tags, brown cluster of function and content words that result in significant reduction in perplexity.

Another recent method called Dual Language Model (DLM) (Garg et al., 2017), combines two monolingual language models by introducing a '*switch*' token common to both languages. Predicting this word in either languages acts a proxy to the probability of a switch and the next word is then predicted using the LM of the language that was switched to.

Among neural methods, Adel et al. (2013a) use a Recurrent Neural Network based LM to predict the language of the next word along with the actual word to model CS text. Following on these intuitions, our models are built on top of the AWD-LSTM LM (Merity et al., 2017) that was chosen due to its accessibility and high performance (recently State of the Art) on the Penn-Tree Bank and Wikitext-2 dataset (Merity et al., 2016). Extensive work has been done on this model through investigation on relative importance of hyper-parameters (Merity et al., 2018).

Criteria	Train	Dev	Test
# Sentences	35513	11839	11837
Avg Length of Sentences	18.90	17.58	18.22
Multilingual Index	0.8892	0.8905	0.8914
Language Entropy	0.6635	0.6639	0.6641
Integration Index	0.3304	0.3314	0.3312
Unique Unigrams	35,769	18,053	19,330
Unique Bigrams	276,552	125,108	130,947
Unique Trigrams	553,866	219,098	229,967

Table 1: Hinglish Data Statistics

3 Data Analysis

Curating a reasonable dataset for CS text is an important challenge for researchers in this domain. To the knowledge of the authors, there is no benchmark CS corpus for language modeling as there is for English (Merity et al., 2016; Marcus et al., 1994). The two potential source choices to gather data include social media (such as Twitter and Facebook) and blogging websites. We decided to go with the latter due to comparatively lesser noise and availability of more descriptive text. Our CS LM data was collected after having crawled eight Hinglish blogging websites[1], that were returned by popular search engines (such as Google and Bing) with simple code-switched queries in the domains of health and technology. The topics covered in these CS texts include technical reviews of electronic and general e-commerce products as well as several health related articles.

These texts were tokenized at the sentence level over which we ran a language identifier. Language detection is performed both at the word level and also at the sentence level by treating the entire sentence as a sequence labeling problem. Naive Bayes and Hidden Markov Models with Viterbi Decoding were used respectively that gave an accuracy of around 97% on a subset of our data. Moreover, all the sentences that did not have at least one word each from both languages were discarded to channel our problem towards tackling intra-sentential code-switching. This resulted in a total of 59189 unique sentences. To estimate the quality and extent of mixing and frequency of switching in our data, we measured Multilingual index (M-Index), Language Entropy and Integration index (I-index) that were introduced in the domain of CS by Guzmán et al. (2017). These metrics along with other n-gram statistics over our data are presented in Table 1. A multilingual index of 1 indicates that there is equal extent of mix-

[1]Some Hinglish websites:
www.hinglishpedia.com,
www.hindimehelp.com,
www.pakkasolutionhindi.com

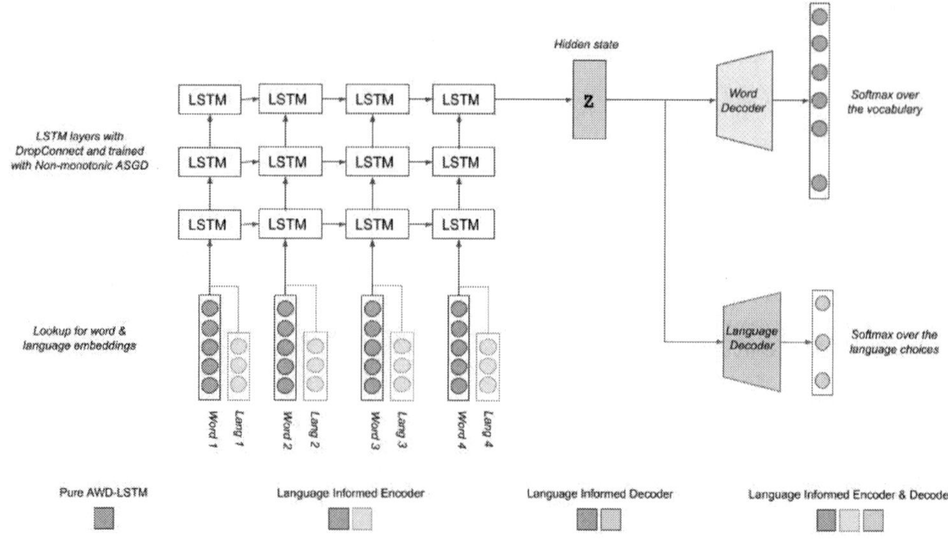

Figure 1: Various CS LM models that we explored in this work

ing from both the participating languages. As we can observe, the mixing is close to 0.8 which indicates that both Hindi and English are participating in the ratio 4:5. The metric itself does not reveal about which is the embedded language and which is the matrix language. Note that the CS metrics for each of the train, validate and test splits of the data are almost the same, indicating a similar extent of mixing in them.

4 Models and Experiments

There are a number of ways to frame the desire for humans to switch between languages (Skiba, 1997; Moreno et al., 2002), however, we view the human desire as out of scope for this work. Instead, our focus is on how we can incorporate linguistic information while training a statistical model for code-switched text. We discuss two main choices as to where we can introduce this information: either at the encoding stage or at the decoding stage of an RNN language model.

Given a CS sentence $X_{cs} = (x^1, x^2 \dots , x^n)$ which has lexical level language sequence $L_{cs} = (l^1, l^2 \dots , l^n)$, our model has to predict the word at the next time step. Note that this vector l^i is the language of the ith lexical item trained in concert with the model. This allows our model to encode the distributional properties of the language switching. We experimented with encoding and decoding the word and language embeddings for this task. θ_{E_X}, θ_{E_L}, θ_{D_X} and θ_{D_L} are the parameters for the word encoder, language encoder, word decoder and language decoder respectively.

We identify four different model architectures

(Figure 1) that could be useful in training code-switched language models. In the first model, our baseline, we have a sequence of words and we are trying to predict the following word. This model is identical to running a traditional RNN language model on CS text.

For our baseline model we adapt the state-of-the-art language model, the AWD-LSTM, for this domain. This model is a 3 layered stacked LSTM trained via Averaged SGD with tied weights between the embedding and the softmax layer. There are several other important elements of this model, all of which are detailed in (Merity et al., 2017). The next word in this model is given by:

$$z = Encoder(X_{cs}, \theta_E)$$

In our second model we extend our baseline such that we have a sequence of words and their language IDs and we try to predict the following word. In this and all the subsequent models, language ID is represented as a vector of length sixteen. This model can be seen as a factored language model operating with code-switched data. So, the next word in this model is given by:

$$Decoder(Encoder(X_{cs}, \theta_{E_X}), \theta_{D_X})$$

In our third model we take a sequence of words as an input and attempt to predict both the language and the value of the following word. The next word in this model is given by:

$$Decoder(Encoder(X_{cs}, \theta_{E_X}) \bigoplus Encoder(L_{cs}, \theta_{E_X})), \theta_{D_X})$$

94

Model/Data	Train	Dev	Test
Base AWD-LSTM Model	10.08	19.73	20.92
Language Aware Encoder AWD-LSTM	10.07	19.00	20.18
Language Aware Decoder AWD-LSTM	11.60	20.72	22.01
Language Aware Encoder & Decoder AWD-LSTM	9.47	18.51	19.52

Table 2: Perplexity scores of different models

In our fourth model we take a sequence of words and their corresponding language IDs as input and attempt to predict both the language and value of the subsequent word. In our third and fourth models we operate with two loss values being calculated for (one for the word error, and one for the language error multiplied by 0.1) and gradients for both losses are propagated through the network and are used to update the weights.

5 Results and Discussion

We trained 4 different models based on the description in Section 4. The results of these experiments are presented in Table 2. We observe that the Language Aware Encoding and Decoding with the AWD-LSTM gives the least perplexity. This aligns with our hypothesis that providing language information of the current word at encoding and enabling the model to decode the language of the next word allows the model to learn a higher level context of switch points between the languages.

5.1 Challenges and Future Work

Robustness of the language model also depends on the diversity of context in which the words co-occur. Since most of the articles belong to the topics of e-commerce, latest technology and health, this may be affected. Hence, we plan to use pre-trained word embeddings based on large monolingual corpora after aligning the embedding spaces of both the participating languages such as MUSE embeddings (Conneau et al., 2017). However, due to the non-standardized spellings in the *romanized* Hinglish text, most words that are incorrectly transliterated will not be found in the MUSE embeddings and such errors from transliteration will propagate through the subsequent parts of model. To avoid this, we plan to extend this work by using character encodings in future. Incorporating factors beyond language such as parts of speech, and sentence level features like root words or code-switching metrics could be another direction for future work. Incidentally, the hyper-parameters for our model were tuned on the Wikitext-2 dataset and it would be interesting to tune them on the Hinglish data itself. Lastly, and arguably most importantly, the accumulation and release of additional CS data would be a significant contribution to this field. Much of the work involved in this project was to properly clean, parse, and represent the CS data that was scraped from the online sources discussed above that could not be released because of copyright concerns. These sources remain limited in topic and variation and additional sources of CS data would be the best way to improve how well our model can generalize.

6 Conclusion

We hypothesize that incorporating the information of language aids in building more robust language models for code-switched text. This is substantiated by experimenting with different combinations of providing the language of the current word as input and decoding the language of the next word along with the word itself. We conclude that we are able to improve the State-of-The-Art language model for monolingual text by both explicitly providing the language information and decoding the language of the next word to perform this task for CS domain. We treat this problem as a multi-task learning problem where the same embedding and LSTM layers are shared. These two comparable tasks are predicting the next word and predicting the language of the next word. So far, our best test perplexity is 18.51 on development and 19.52 on test sets. This is in comparison to the baseline model which is 19.73 and 20.92 on development and test sets respectively.

We believe that further research can be done to not only improve perplexity, but to also improve the quality of the training and testing dataset. Language models are a core element in multiple tasks, from speech recognition to machine translation and we hope that this work will support future research into the development of such NLP tools for CS domain.

Acknowledgments

We would like to thank our reviewers for their insightful comments. We would also like to thank Graham Neubig at our institute who gave valuable feedback throughout the course of this work.

References

Heike Adel, Ngoc Thang Vu, Katrin Kirchhoff, Dominic Telaar, and Tanja Schultz. 2015. Syntactic and semantic features for code-switching factored language models. *IEEE Transactions on Audio, Speech, and Language Processing* 23(3):431–440.

Heike Adel, Ngoc Thang Vu, Franziska Kraus, Tim Schlippe, Haizhou Li, and Tanja Schultz. 2013a. Recurrent neural network language modeling for code switching conversational speech. In *Acoustics, Speech and Signal Processing (ICASSP), 2013 IEEE International Conference on*. IEEE, pages 8411–8415.

Heike Adel, Ngoc Thang Vu, and Tanja Schultz. 2013b. Combination of recurrent neural networks and factored language models for code-switching language modeling. In *Proceedings of the 51st Annual Meeting of the Association for Computational Linguistics (Volume 2: Short Papers)*. volume 2, pages 206–211.

Waleed Ammar, George Mulcaire, Miguel Ballesteros, Chris Dyer, and Noah A Smith. 2016. Many languages, one parser. *arXiv preprint arXiv:1602.01595* .

Barbara E Bullock and Almeida Jacqueline Ed Toribio. 2009. *The Cambridge handbook of linguistic code-switching.*. Cambridge University Press.

Özlem Çetinoğlu and Çağrı Çöltekin. 2016. Part of speech annotation of a turkish-german code-switching corpus. In *Proceedings of the 10th Linguistic Annotation Workshop held in conjunction with ACL 2016 (LAW-X 2016)*. pages 120–130.

Özlem Çetinoğlu, Sarah Schulz, and Ngoc Thang Vu. 2016. Challenges of computational processing of code-switching. *arXiv preprint arXiv:1610.02213* .

Alexis Conneau, Guillaume Lample, Marc'Aurelio Ranzato, Ludovic Denoyer, and Hervé Jégou. 2017. Word translation without parallel data. *arXiv preprint arXiv:1710.04087* .

Amitava Das and Björn Gambäck. 2014. Identifying languages at the word level in code-mixed indian social media text .

Saurabh Garg, Tanmay Parekh, and Preethi Jyothi. 2017. Dual language models for code mixed speech recognition. *arXiv preprint arXiv:1711.01048* .

P Goyal, Manav R Mital, A Mukerjee, Achla M Raina, D Sharma, P Shukla, and K Vikram. 2003. A bilingual parser for hindi, english and code-switching structures. In *10th Conference of The European Chapter*. page 15.

Gualberto Guzmán, Joseph Ricard, Jacqueline Serigos, Barbara E Bullock, and Almeida Jacqueline Toribio. 2017. Metrics for modeling code-switching across corpora. *Proc. Interspeech 2017* pages 67–71.

Anupam Jamatia, Björn Gambäck, and Amitava Das. 2015. Part-of-speech tagging for code-mixed english-hindi twitter and facebook chat messages. In *Proceedings of the International Conference Recent Advances in Natural Language Processing*. pages 239–248.

Harsh Jhamtani, Suleep Kumar Bhogi, and Vaskar Raychoudhury. 2014. Word-level language identification in bi-lingual code-switched texts. In *Proceedings of the 28th Pacific Asia Conference on Language, Information and Computing*.

Melvin Johnson, Mike Schuster, Quoc V Le, Maxim Krikun, Yonghui Wu, Zhifeng Chen, Nikhil Thorat, Fernanda Viégas, Martin Wattenberg, Greg Corrado, et al. 2016. Google's multilingual neural machine translation system: enabling zero-shot translation. *arXiv preprint arXiv:1611.04558* .

Aravind K Joshi. 1982. Processing of sentences with intra-sentential code-switching. In *Proceedings of the 9th conference on Computational linguistics-Volume 1*. Academia Praha, pages 145–150.

David Jurgens, Yulia Tsvetkov, and Dan Jurafsky. 2017. Incorporating dialectal variability for socially equitable language identification. In *Proceedings of the 55th Annual Meeting of the Association for Computational Linguistics (Volume 2: Short Papers)*. volume 2, pages 51–57.

Ben King and Steven Abney. 2013. Labeling the languages of words in mixed-language documents using weakly supervised methods. In *Proceedings of the 2013 Conference of the North American Chapter of the Association for Computational Linguistics: Human Language Technologies*. pages 1110–1119.

Ying Li and Pascale Fung. 2013. Improved mixed language speech recognition using asymmetric acoustic model and language model with code-switch inversion constraints. In *Acoustics, Speech and Signal Processing (ICASSP), 2013 IEEE International Conference on*. IEEE, pages 7368–7372.

Ying Li and Pascale Fung. 2014. Code switch language modeling with functional head constraint. In *Acoustics, Speech and Signal Processing (ICASSP), 2014 IEEE International Conference on*. IEEE, pages 4913–4917.

Mitchell Marcus, Grace Kim, Mary Ann Marcinkiewicz, Robert MacIntyre, Ann Bies, Mark Ferguson, Karen Katz, and Britta Schasberger. 1994. The penn treebank: Annotating predicate argument structure. In *Proceedings of the Workshop on Human Language Technology*. Association for Computational Linguistics, Stroudsburg, PA, USA, HLT '94, pages 114–119. https://doi.org/10.3115/1075812.1075835.

Stephen Merity, Nitish Shirish Keskar, and Richard Socher. 2017. Regularizing and optimizing lstm language models. *arXiv preprint arXiv:1708.02182* .

Stephen Merity, Nitish Shirish Keskar, and Richard Socher. 2018. An analysis of neural language modeling at multiple scales. *arXiv preprint arXiv:1803.08240* .

Stephen Merity, Caiming Xiong, James Bradbury, and Richard Socher. 2016. Pointer sentinel mixture models. *CoRR* abs/1609.07843. http://arxiv.org/abs/1609.07843.

Eva M Moreno, Kara D Federmeier, and Marta Kutas. 2002. Switching languages, switching palabras (words): An electrophysiological study of code switching. *Brain and language* 80(2):188–207.

Pieter Muysken. 2000. *Bilingual speech: A typology of code-mixing*, volume 11. Cambridge University Press.

Carol Myers-Scotton. 1997. *Duelling languages: Grammatical structure in codeswitching*. Oxford University Press.

Robert Östling and Jörg Tiedemann. 2016. Continuous multilinguality with language vectors. *arXiv preprint arXiv:1612.07486* .

Jasabanta Patro, Bidisha Samanta, Saurabh Singh, Abhipsa Basu, Prithwish Mukherjee, Monojit Choudhury, and Animesh Mukherjee. 2017. All that is english may be hindi: Enhancing language identification through automatic ranking of the likeliness of word borrowing in social media. In *Proceedings of the 2017 Conference on Empirical Methods in Natural Language Processing*. pages 2264–2274.

Shana Poplack. 1980. Sometimes ill start a sentence in spanish y termino en espanol: toward a typology of code-switching1. *Linguistics* 18(7-8):581–618.

Shruti Rijhwani, Royal Sequiera, Monojit Choudhury, Kalika Bali, and Chandra Shekhar Maddila. 2017. Estimating code-switching on twitter with a novel generalized word-level language detection technique. In *Proceedings of the 55th Annual Meeting of the Association for Computational Linguistics (Volume 1: Long Papers)*. volume 1, pages 1971–1982.

Koustav Rudra, Shruti Rijhwani, Rafiya Begum, Kalika Bali, Monojit Choudhury, and Niloy Ganguly. 2016. Understanding language preference for expression of opinion and sentiment: What do hindi-english speakers do on twitter? In *Proceedings of the 2016 Conference on Empirical Methods in Natural Language Processing*. pages 1131–1141.

David Sankoff and Shana Poplack. 1981. A formal grammar for code-switching. *Research on Language & Social Interaction* 14(1):3–45.

R Mahesh K Sinha and Anil Thakur. 2005. Machine translation of bi-lingual hindi-english (hinglish) text. *10th Machine Translation summit (MT Summit X), Phuket, Thailand* pages 149–156.

Richard Skiba. 1997. Code switching as a countenance of language interference. *The internet TESL journal* 3(10):1–6.

Thamar Solorio and Yang Liu. 2008a. Learning to predict code-switching points. In *Proceedings of the Conference on Empirical Methods in Natural Language Processing*. Association for Computational Linguistics, pages 973–981.

Thamar Solorio and Yang Liu. 2008b. Part-of-speech tagging for english-spanish code-switched text. In *Proceedings of the Conference on Empirical Methods in Natural Language Processing*. Association for Computational Linguistics, pages 1051–1060.

Yogarshi Vyas, Spandana Gella, Jatin Sharma, Kalika Bali, and Monojit Choudhury. 2014. Pos tagging of english-hindi code-mixed social media content. In *Proceedings of the 2014 Conference on Empirical Methods in Natural Language Processing (EMNLP)*. pages 974–979.

GHHT at CALCS 2018: Named Entity Recognition for Dialectal Arabic Using Neural Networks

Mohammed Attia
Google Inc.
New York City
NY, 10011
attia@google.com

Younes Samih
Dept. of Computational Linguistics
Heinrich Heine University,
Düsseldorf, Germany
samih@phil.hhu.de

Wolfgang Maier
Independent Researcher
Tübingen, Germany
wolfgang.maier@gmail.com

Abstract

This paper describes our system submission to the CALCS 2018 shared task on named entity recognition on code-switched data for the language variant pair of Modern Standard Arabic and Egyptian dialectal Arabic. We build a a Deep Neural Network that combines word and character-based representations in convolutional and recurrent networks with a CRF layer. The model is augmented with stacked layers of enriched information such pre-trained embeddings, Brown clusters and named entity gazetteers. Our system is ranked second among those participating in the shared task achieving an FB1 average of 70.09%.

1 Introduction

The CALCS 2018 shared task (Aguilar et al., 2018) is about performing named entity recognition (NER) on Modern Standard Arabic (MSA) - Egyptian Arabic (EGY) code-switched tweets. Unlike previous shared tasks on code-switching, the data provided contains no code-switching annotation. Only nine categories of named entities are annotated using BIO tagging. While this makes the task a "pure" NER task, the difficulty is to design a model which can cope with the noise introduced by code-switching, challenging old systems tailored around MSA.

NER is a well-studied sequence labeling problem. Earlier work has applied standard supervised learning techniques to the problem, such as Hidden Markov Models (HMM) (Bikel et al., 1999), Maximum-Entropy Model (ME) (Bender et al., 2003; Curran and Clark, 2003; Finkel et al., 2005), Support Vector Machines (SVM) (Takeuchi and Collier, 2002), and Conditional Random Fields (CRF) (McCallum and Li, 2003). Standard data sets came from the English MUC-6 (Sundheim, 1995) and the multilingual CoNLL-02 (Tjong Kim Sang, 2002) and 03 (Tjong Kim Sang and De Meulder, 2003) shared tasks.

More recent work relies on neural networks. A number of architecture variants have proven to be effective (Huang et al., 2015; Lample et al., 2016; Chiu and Nichols, 2016; Ma and Hovy, 2016; Reimers and Gurevych, 2017). What they have in common is that they use a bidirectional LSTM (bi-LSTM) over vector representations of the input words in order model their left and right contexts. On top of the bi-LSTM, they use a CRF layer to take the final tagging decisions. Other than a softmax layer which would treat tagging decisions independently, the CRF is able to model the linear dependencies between labels. This is essential for NER, where for instance, B-LOCATION cannot be followed by I-PERSON. The architectures differ in their way of obtaining a vector representation for the input words. For instance, in Lample et al. (2016), each word embedding is obtained as a concatenation of the output of a bidirectional LSTM (bi-LSTM) over its characters and a pre-trained word vector. Ma and Hovy (2016) use convolutions over character embeddings with max-pooling for obtaining morphological features from the character level, similar to Chiu and Nichols (2016).

Proceedings of The Third Workshop on Computational Approaches to Code-Switching, pages 98–102
Melbourne, Australia, July 19, 2018. ©2018 Association for Computational Linguistics

Our system also relies on the bi-LSTM-CRF architecture. As input representation, we use both word embeddings and a character-level representation based on CNNs. Our system additionally employs a Brown Cluster representation, oversampling, and NE gazetteers.

The remainder of the paper is structured as follows in the following section, we provide a short decription of the task and the data set. Sect. 3 describes our system in detail. Sect. 4 presents our experiments, and Sect. 5 concludes the paper.

2 Task and Data Description

The shared task posed the problem of performing named-entity recognition on code-switched data given nine categories, namely PERSON, LOCATION, ORGANIZATION, GROUP, TITLE, PRODUCT, EVENT, TIME, OTHER.

The training set contains 10,100 tweets and 204,286 tokens, with an average tweet length of 20.2 tokens and 91.5 characters. 11.3% of all tokens are labeled as named entities. The most frequent category is PERSON with 4.3% of all tokens, followed by LOCATION (2.2%), GROUP and ORGANIZATION (1.3% each), as well as TITLE (1%). All other categories cover less than 1% of all tokens each, the least frequent category being OTHER (0.06%).

The validation set contains 1,122 tweets and 22,742 tokens, and exhibits similar average tweets lengths, as well as a similar distribution of labels.

3 System Description

We used a DNN model which is mainly suited for sequence tagging. It is a variant of the bi-LSTM-CRF architecture proposed by Ma and Hovy (2016); Lample et al. (2016); Huang et al. (2015).[1] It combines a double representation of the input words by using word embeddings and a character-based representation (with CNNs). The input sequence is processed with bi-LSTMs, and the output layer is a linear chain CRF. The model uses the following.

Word-level embeddings allow the learning algorithms to use large unlabeled data to generalize beyond the seen training data. We explore randomly initialized embeddings based on the seen training data and pre-trained embedding.

We train our word embeddings using word2vec (Mikolov et al., 2013) on a corpus we crawled from the web with total size of 383,261,475 words, consisting of dialectal texts from Facebook posts (8,241,244), Twitter tweets (2,813,016), user comments on the news (95,241,480), and MSA texts of news articles (from Al-Jazeera and Al-Ahram) of 276,965,735 words.

Character-level CNNs have proven effective for various NLP tasks due to their ability to extract sub-word information (ex. prefixes or suffixes) and to encode character-level representations of words (Collobert et al., 2011; Chiu and Nichols, 2016; dos Santos and Guimarães, 2015).

Bi-LSTM Recurrent neural networks (RNN) are well suited for modeling sequential data, achieving ground-breaking results in many NLP tasks (e.g., machine translation).

Bi-LSTMs (Hochreiter and Schmidhuber, 1997; Schuster and Paliwal, 1997) are capable of learning long-term dependencies and maintaining contextual features from both past and future states while avoiding the vanishing/exploding gradients problem. They consist of two separate bidirectional hidden layers that feed forward to the same output layer.

CRF is used jointly with bi-LSTMs to avoid the output label independence assumptions of bi-LSTMs and to impose sequence labeling constraints as in Lample et al. (2016).

Brown clusters (BC) Brown clustering is an unsupervised learning method where words are grouped based on the contexts in which they appear (Brown et al., 1992). The assumption is that words that behave in similar ways tend to appear in similar contexts and hence belong to the same cluster. BCs can be learned from large unlabeled texts and have been shown to improve POS tagging (Owoputi et al., 2013; Stratos and Collins, 2015). We test the effectiveness of using Brown clusters in the context of named entity recognition in a DNN model. We train BCs on our crawled code-switched corpus of 380 million words (mentioned above) with 100 Brown Clusters.

Named Entity Gazetteers We use a large collec-

---

[1] Our implementation is mostly inspired by the work of Reimers and Gurevych (2017).

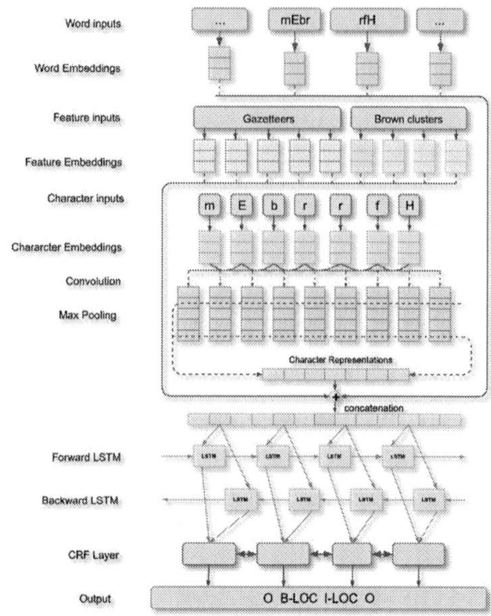

Figure 1: DNN Architecture.

tion of named entity gazetteers of 40,719 unique names from Attia et al. (2010), who collected named entities from the Arabic Wikipedia, and Benajiba et al. (2007), who annotated a corpus as part of a named entity recognition system.

The architecture of our model is shown in Figure 1. For each word in the sequence, the CNN computes the character-level representation with character embeddings as inputs. Then the character-level representation vector is concatenated with both word embeddings vector and feature embedding vectors (Brown Clusters and Gazetteers) to feed into the bi-LSTM layer. Finally, an affine transformation followed by a CRF is applied over the hidden representation of the bi-LSTM to obtain the probability distribution over all the named entity labels. Training is performed using stochastic gradient descent with momentum of 0.9 and batch size equal to 150. We employ dropout (Hinton et al., 2012) and early-stopping (Caruana et al., 2000) (with patience of 35) to mitigate overfitting. We use the hyper-parameters detailed in Table 1.

The only preprocessing operation we conducted on the data was to convert it into Buckwalter transliteration (a character-to-character mapping) in order to avoid the complexity of dealing with UTF-8 characters.

Layer	Hyper-Parameters	Value
Characters CNN	window size	4
	number of filters	40
Bi-LSTM	state size	100
Dropout	dropout rate	0.5
Word Emb.	dimension	300
Characters Emb.	dimension	100
Clustering Emb.	dimension	100
Gazetteer Emb.	dimension	2
	batch size	150

Table 1: Parameter fine-tuning

4 Experiments

We conduct five experiments with different layers stacked on top of each other, making use of word embeddings, character representation, and other features. The experiments are as follows:

Experiments	f-score	f-score macro
Baseline	95.70	66.49
Word+Chars	96.06	69.60
Word+Chars +Embed	96.92	72.38
Word+Chars +Embed+BC	96.99	72.30
Word+Chars +Embed+BC+OS	96.92	73.05
Word+Chars +Embed+BC +OS+GZ	97.33	77.97
Results on Test set	–	70.09

Table 2: DNN experiments and Results

Baseline. We use word representations only with randomly-initialized embeddings. It is to be mentioned that the shared task baseline for the test set is 62.71%.

Word+Chars. We add character representations in a one-dimensional CNN layer.

Word+Chars+Embed. We use pre-trained embeddings for words trained on a corpus of about 380 million words (described above) consisting of dialectal Egyptian and MSA data.

Word+Chars+Embed+BC. We add Brown Clusters (BC) to the network.

Word+Chars+Embed+BC+OS. We add oversampling (OS) to the network. We conduct oversampling by heuristically making 10-fold repetitions of sentences containing minority labels, in this case all classes other than the "O" label.

Word+Chars+Embed+BC+GZ. We further add a new layer for the named entity gazetteer (GZ).

Label	Total	% of data	Accuracy %
O	20031	88.08	99.20
B-PER	705	3.10	92.34
I-PER	408	1.79	89.71
B-LOC	358	1.57	88.83
I-LOC	116	0.51	79.31
B-GROUP	191	0.84	81.68
I-GROUP	112	0.49	76.79
B-ORG	149	0.66	79.19
I-ORG	114	0.50	80.70
B-TITLE	115	0.51	69.57
I-TITLE	143	0.63	81.12
B-PROD	55	0.24	76.36
I-PROD	26	0.11	61.54
B-EVENT	69	0.30	43.48
I-EVENT	52	0.23	51.92
B-TIME	61	0.27	85.25
I-TIME	18	0.08	38.89
B-OTHER	17	0.07	82.35
I-OTHER	2	0.01	50.00

Table 3: Results breakdown on the validation set

The results in Table 2 are reported on the validation set (except for the last row), and they show that the DNN model is incrementally improving by adding more features and external resources. The best result is obtained with the aggregation of all features.

Table 3 shows a breakdown of our system performance (in terms of accuracy) on the validation set. It also shows the number of instances and the ratio percentage for each label. As the table shows, the category "other" accounts for 88% of the entire data, while all other tags combined make up the remaining 12% which shows an imbalance in the representation of the other categories. Our system performs best with 'B-PER', 'I-PER', 'B-LOC' and 'B-TIME'.

Our system is ranked second among those par-ticipating in the shared task achieving an FB1 average of 70.09% with the first scoring 71.62%, which is a difference of about 1.5% absolute.

5 Conclusion

We have presented a description of our system participating in the Shared Task on "Named Entity Recognition on Code-switched Data". We build a deep neural network with multiple layers for accommodating various features, such as pre-trained word embeddings, Brown Clustering and named entity gazetteers. We have not relied on any linguistic rules, morphological analyzers or PoS taggers. We also make the different layers as optional plug-ins, which makes our system more adaptable and scalable for languages that do not have similar external resources.

References

Gustavo Aguilar, Fahad AlGhamdi, Victor Soto, Diab Mona, Julia Hirschberg, and Thamar Solorio. 2018. Overview of the CALCS 2018 Shared Task: Named Entity Recognition on Code-switched Data. In *Proceedings of the Third Workshop on Computational Approaches to Linguistic Code-Switching*, Melbourne, Australia. Association for Computational Linguistics.

Mohammed Attia, Antonio Toral, Lamia Tounsi, Monica Monachini, and Josef van Genabith. 2010. An automatically built named entity lexicon for arabic. In *European Language Resources Association*, pages 3614–3621, Valletta, Malta.

Yassine Benajiba, Paolo Rosso, and José Miguel Benedíruiz. 2007. Anersys: An arabic named entity recognition system based on maximum entropy. In *International Conference on Intelligent Text Processing and Computational Linguistics*, pages 143–153. Springer.

Oliver Bender, Franz Josef Och, and Hermann Ney. 2003. Maximum entropy models for named entity recognition. In *Proceedings of the Seventh Conference on Natural Language Learning at HLT-NAACL 2003*, pages 148–151.

Daniel M. Bikel, Richard Schwartz, and Ralph M. Weischedel. 1999. An algorithm that learns what's in a name. *Mach. Learn.*, 34(1-3):211–231.

Peter F Brown, Peter V Desouza, Robert L Mercer, Vincent J Della Pietra, and Jenifer C Lai. 1992. Class-based n-gram models of natural language. *Computational linguistics*, 18(4):467–479.

Rich Caruana, Steve Lawrence, and Lee Giles. 2000. Overfitting in neural nets: Backpropagation, conjugate gradient, and early stopping. In *NIPS*, pages 402–408.

Jason Chiu and Eric Nichols. 2016. Named entity recognition with bidirectional lstm-cnns. *Transactions of the Association for Computational Linguistics*, 4:357–370.

R. Collobert, J. Weston, L. Bottou, M. Karlen, K. Kavukcuoglu, and P. Kuksa. 2011. Natural language processing (almost) from scratch. *Journal of Machine Learning Research*, 12:2493–2537.

James Curran and Stephen Clark. 2003. Language independent ner using a maximum entropy tagger. In *Proceedings of the Seventh Conference on Natural Language Learning at HLT-NAACL 2003*.

Jenny Rose Finkel, Trond Grenager, and Christopher Manning. 2005. Incorporating non-local information into information extraction systems by gibbs sampling. In *Proceedings of the 43rd Annual Meeting on Association for Computational Linguistics*, ACL '05, pages 363–370, Stroudsburg, PA, USA. Association for Computational Linguistics.

Geoffrey E Hinton, Nitish Srivastava, Alex Krizhevsky, Ilya Sutskever, and Ruslan R Salakhutdinov. 2012. Improving neural networks by preventing co-adaptation of feature detectors. *arXiv preprint arXiv:1207.0580*.

Sepp Hochreiter and Jürgen Schmidhuber. 1997. Long short-term memory. *Neural computation*, 9(8):1735–1780.

Zhiheng Huang, Wei Xu, and Kai Yu. 2015. Bidirectional LSTM-CRF models for sequence tagging. *CoRR*, abs/1508.01991.

Guillaume Lample, Miguel Ballesteros, Sandeep Subramanian, Kazuya Kawakami, and Chris Dyer. 2016. Neural architectures for named entity recognition. In *Proceedings of the 2016 Conference of the North American Chapter of the Association for Computational Linguistics: Human Language Technologies*, pages 260–270, San Diego, California. Association for Computational Linguistics.

Xuezhe Ma and Eduard Hovy. 2016. End-to-end sequence labeling via bi-directional lstm-cnns-crf. In *Proceedings of the 54th Annual Meeting of the Association for Computational Linguistics (Volume 1: Long Papers)*, pages 1064–1074, Berlin, Germany. Association for Computational Linguistics.

Andrew McCallum and Wei Li. 2003. Early results for named entity recognition with conditional random fields, feature induction and web-enhanced lexicons. In *Proceedings of the Seventh Conference on Natural Language Learning at HLT-NAACL 2003*, pages 188–191.

Tomas Mikolov, Kai Chen, Greg Corrado, and Jeffrey Dean. 2013. Efficient estimation of word representations in vector space. *CoRR*, abs/1301.3781.

Olutobi Owoputi, Brendan O'Connor, Chris Dyer, Kevin Gimpel, Nathan Schneider, and Noah A Smith. 2013. Improved part-of-speech tagging for online conversational text with word clusters. In *Proceedings of NAACL-HLT 2013*, pages 380–390. Association for Computational Linguistics.

Nils Reimers and Iryna Gurevych. 2017. Reporting score distributions makes a difference: Performance study of lstm-networks for sequence tagging. In *Proceedings of the 2017 Conference on Empirical Methods in Natural Language Processing (EMNLP)*, pages 338–348, Copenhagen, Denmark.

Cicero dos Santos and Victor Guimarães. 2015. Boosting named entity recognition with neural character embeddings. In *Proceedings of the Fifth Named Entity Workshop*, pages 25–33, Beijing, China. Association for Computational Linguistics.

Mike Schuster and Kuldip K Paliwal. 1997. Bidirectional recurrent neural networks. *IEEE Transactions on Signal Processing*, 45(11):2673–2681.

Karl Stratos and Michael Collins. 2015. Simple semi-supervised pos tagging. In *VS@ HLT-NAACL*, pages 79–87.

Beth M. Sundheim. 1995. Overview of results of the muc-6 evaluation. In *Proceedings of the 6th Conference on Message Understanding*, MUC6 '95, pages 13–31, Stroudsburg, PA, USA. Association for Computational Linguistics.

Koichi Takeuchi and Nigel Collier. 2002. Use of support vector machines in extended named entity recognition. In *Proceedings of the 6th Conference on Natural Language Learning - Volume 20*, COLING-02, pages 1–7, Stroudsburg, PA, USA. Association for Computational Linguistics.

Erik F. Tjong Kim Sang. 2002. Introduction to the conll-2002 shared task: Language-independent named entity recognition. In *Proceedings of the 6th Conference on Natural Language Learning - Volume 20*, COLING-02, pages 1–4, Stroudsburg, PA, USA. Association for Computational Linguistics.

Erik F. Tjong Kim Sang and Fien De Meulder. 2003. Introduction to the conll-2003 shared task: Language-independent named entity recognition. In *Proceedings of the Seventh Conference on Natural Language Learning at HLT-NAACL 2003*, pages 142–147.

Simple Features for Strong Performance on Named Entity Recognition in Code-Switched Twitter Data

Devanshu Jain   Maria Kustikova   Mayank Darbari
Rishabh Gupta   Stephen Mayhew
University of Pennsylvania
{devjain, mkust, mdarbari, rgupt, mayhew}@seas.upenn.edu

Abstract

In this work, we address the problem of Named Entity Recognition (NER) in code-switched tweets as a part of the Workshop on Computational Approaches to Linguistic Code-switching (CALCS) at ACL'18 (Aguilar et al., 2018). Code-switching is the phenomenon where a speaker switches between two languages or variants of the same language within or across utterances, known as intra-sentential or inter-sentential code-switching, respectively. Processing such data is challenging using state of the art methods since such technology is generally geared towards processing monolingual text. In this paper we explored ways to use language identification and translation to recognize named entities in such data, however, utilizing simple features (sans multi-lingual features) with Conditional Random Field (CRF) classifier achieved the best results. Our experiments were mainly aimed at the (ENG-SPA) English-Spanish dataset but we submitted a language-independent version of our system to the (MSA-EGY) Arabic-Egyptian dataset as well and achieved good results.

1 Introduction

Recently, social media texts such as tweets and Facebook posts have attracted attention from the Natural Language Processing (NLP) research community. This content has many applications as it provides clues to analyze sentiments of the masses towards areas ranging from basic electronic products to mental health issues to even national political candidates. These applications have motivated the NLP community to rethink strategies for common tools, such as tokenizers, named entity taggers, POS taggers, dependency parsers, in the context of informal and noisy text.

As access to the internet becomes more and more universal, a linguistically diverse population has come online. Hong et al. (2011) showed that in a collection of 62 million tweets, only a little over 50% of them were in English. This multilingualism has given rise to such interesting patterns as transliteration and code-switching. The multilingual behavior combined with the informal nature of the content makes the task of building NLP tools even harder.

In this paper, we solve the problem of Named Entity Recognition (NER) for code-switched twitter data as a part of the ACL'18 Computational Approaches to Linguistic Code-switching (CALCS) Shared Task (Aguilar et al., 2018). Code-switching is a phenomenon that occurs when multilingual speakers alternate between two or more languages or dialects. This phenomenon can be observed across different sentences, within the same sentence or even in the same word. This shared task is similar to other social media tasks, except that the data is explicitly chosen to contain code-switching. The entities for the task are: Event, Group, Location, Organization, Other, Person, Product, Time, and Title. Below is an example of some code-switched data, switching between English and Spanish:

My   [Facebook]$_{Prod}$,   [Ig]$_{Prod}$ &
[Twitter]$_{Prod}$ is hellaa dead yall Jk soy
yo que has no life!

In this example, there is a combination of English and Spanish words and slang words within a tweet, with 3 entities: Facebook, Instagram (commonly referred to as 'Ig') and Twitter.

Proceedings of The Third Workshop on Computational Approaches to Code-Switching, pages 103–109
Melbourne, Australia, July 19, 2018. ©2018 Association for Computational Linguistics

Value / Data	Train	Development	Test
Total number of tweets	50,757	832	15,634
Total number of tokens	616,069	9,583	183,011
Average number of tokens per tweet	12.14	11.52	15.9
Standard deviation of the number of tokens per tweet	7.6	7.12	7.11

Table 1: (ENG-SPA) English-Spanish number of tweets and tokens for train, development, and test data

Value / Data	Train	Development	Test
Total number of tweets	10,103	1,122	1,110
Total number of tokens	204,323	22,742	21,414
Average number of tokens per tweet	20.22	20.27	21.91
Standard deviation of the number of tokens per tweet	6.63	6.76	6.18

Table 2: (MSA-EGY) Modern Standard Arabic-Egyptian number of tweets and tokens for train, development, and test data

2 Related Work

NER is a fundamental part of the Information Extraction pipeline. Most of the available off-the-shelf systems are trained on formal content, and consequently do not generalize well when evaluated on twitter data (Ritter et al., 2011). This can be explained by the fact that such systems rely on hand-crafted standard local features and some background knowledge, which is not reliable in data as noisy as tweets. With only a limited number of characters, people use a variety of creative ways to express their thoughts, including emoticons and novel abbreviations.

There have been few recent workshops and shared-tasks on analysis of such noisy social media data, such as Workshop on Noisy User-Generated Text (WNUT) at EMNLP (2014, 2016, 2017), Workshop on Approaches to Subjectivity, Sentiment and Social Media (WASSA) at NAACL (2016), and Forum for Information Retrieval Evaluation (FIRE: 2015, 2016, 2017).

3 Experimental Setup

Here we describe the data, evaluation, and the model we used.

3.1 Data

In our experiments, we focus primarily on the English-Spanish (ENG-SPA) dataset. However, we submitted our basic system results for Arabic-Egyptian (MSA-EGY) dataset as well.

The organizers provided annotated train and development sets for each language. They also provided an unannotated set of test data, which we annotated with our system, and submitted for evaluation. We never had access to the gold annotated test set, before or after the evaluation.

Tables 1 and 2 provide information about the data in terms of number of tweets and tokens for the (EN-SPA) English-Spanish and (MSA-EGY) Modern Standard Arabic-Egyptian language pairs. Tables 3 and 4 provide statistics of the named entities for both (EN-SPA) English-Spanish and (MSA-EGY) Modern Standard Arabic-Egyptian language pairs, where each cell can be interpreted as *Number (Percentage)* and entity 'O' represents all non-NE tokens. Please note that the data has been tagged using the IOB scheme and data in Tables 3 and 4 is the result of grouping named entities according to the IOB scheme.

3.2 Evaluation

We used the standard harmonic mean F1 score to evaluate the system performance. Additionally, we used surface form F1 score as described in Derczynski et al. (2017). Both of these metrics were a part of the evaluation in the CALCS shared task.

3.3 Method

We used the sklearn implementation of Conditional Random Field (CRF)[1] (McCallum and Li, 2003) as the base model in our NER system.

---

[1] https://sklearn-crfsuite.readthedocs.io/

Entity	Train Count	Development Count
O	597,526 (97%)	9,361 (97.68%)
Event	232 (0.04%)	4 (0.04%)
Group	718 (0.12%)	4 (0.04%)
Location	2,810 (0.46%)	10 (0.1%)
Organization	811 (0.13%)	9 (0.09%)
Other	324 (0.05%)	6 (0.06%)
Person	4,701 (0.76%)	75 (0.78%)
Product	1,369 (0.22%)	16 (0.17%)
Time	577 (0.09%)	6 (0.06%)
Title	824 (0.13%)	22 (0.23%)

Table 3: (ENG-SPA) English-Spanish named entities counts for train and development data

Entity	Train Count	Development Count
O	181,230 (88.7%)	20,031 (88.08%)
Event	535 (0.26%)	69 (0.3%)
Group	1,799 (0.88%)	191 (0.84%)
Location	3,275 (1.6%)	358 (1.57%)
Organization	1504 (0.74%)	149 (0.66%)
Other	116 (0.06%)	17 (0.07%)
Person	5705 (2.79%)	698 (3.07%)
Product	538 (0.26%)	55 (0.24%)
Time	466 (0.23%)	61 (0.27%)
Title	896 (0.44%)	115 (0.51%)

Table 4: (MSA-EGY) Modern Standard Arabic-Egyptian entities counts for train and development data

System	ENG-SPA	MSA-EGY
Org. Baseline	53.28	62.70
Experiment 1	62.13	67.44
Top System	63.76	71.61

Table 5: (ENG-SPA) and (MSA-EGY) Our best F1 scores on the test datasets compared with the organizer's baseline and the top performing system in the Shared Task.

4 Experiments

This section gives an overview of our experiments. First, we identify various local and global features using a variety of monolingual tweets and Gazetteers and train a CRF-based classifier on the data. Second, we try to improve system recall using a 2-step NER process. Third, we convert the convert the code-mixed data to monolingual data using language identification (using a character-based language model) and translation.

Of the three experiments that we tried, the first method gave the best results. We compare against the best performing system in the shared task as well as the organizer's baseline in Table 5. The baseline was provided by the organizers and used Bi-directional LSTMs followed by softmax layer (trained for 5 epochs) to infer the output labels.

The shared task used Surface Form F1 scores as well, but we omit them from our results as they were the same as harmonic mean F1 in all cases. All scores are reported in Table 6. Detailed scores are available in the appendix.

4.1 Experiment 1

Our first experiment used a standard set of features, augmented with some task-specific ideas, and defined as follows. Given a sequence of words in a sentence: ..., w_{i-2} , w_{i-1} , w_i , w_{i+1} , w_{i+2} , ... and the current word in consideration is w_i , we used the following features:

- If w_i is in the beginning of sentence

		Development Data			Test Data		
		Precision	Recall	F1	Precision	Recall	F1
ENG-SPA	Exp. 1	69.44	32.89	44.64	**72.75**	54.22	**62.13**
	Exp. 2	**71.29**	**47.37**	**56.92**	46.22	**64.66**	53.91
	Exp. 3	66.27	36.18	46.81	71.88	54.00	61.67
MSA-EGY	Exp. 1 (no Gaz)	83.29	73.91	78.32	74.43	61.65	67.44

Table 6: Results on all submissions. Bold indicates best performance for that language.

- If w_i is in the end of sentence
- Lower-case version of w_i
- If w_i is title-cased
- Prefixes and Suffixes of length 4 of w_i
- Brown Clusters[2] (Cluster Size - 40) of w_i
- Word2Vec Clusters: We trained a Word2Vec (Řehůřek and Sojka, 2010) model on the combined tweets dataset (dimension: 100 ; window: 7). Then, we clustered these embeddings into 40 clusters and used cluster IDs as features.
- Gazetteer: We used the Gazetteer (extracted from Wikidata by Mishra and Diesner (2016)) labels as features.
- For each word w_k in a context window of ± 2:
  - The word w_k itself
  - If w_k is upper case
  - Shape and Short shape (where same consecutive characters in the shape are compressed to a single character) of w_k
  - If w_k contains any special symbol like: ,#,$,-,,,etc. or an emoji.
  - If w_k is alphabetic or alphanumeric
  - Emoji Description: We identified the 40 most common emojis present in our dataset and manually labelled them with representative words, such as smile, kiss, sad, etc. These emoji description (sense) of every context word were used as another feature.

We also ran the experiment on the MSA-EGY dataset (without the Gazetteer features).

4.2 Experiment 2

Following the first experiment, our main observation was that the recall was quite low. One reason for this could be the presence of a large amount of tokens tagged as 'O' ($\sim$97%). In contrast, the standard CONLL 2002 Spanish training NER corpus (Tjong Kim Sang, 2002) had $\sim$87% of the tokens tagged as 'O'.

To solve this issue, we experimented with a 2-step NER process (similar to (Eiselt and Figueroa, 2013)):

1. Train a CRF model to identify whether a token is 'O' or not
2. Train a CRF model to identify the type of named-entity (if identified as non-'O')

As expected, we saw major improvements in recall, but these were offset by a substantial drop in precision. Overall, this led to a lower F1 score than before. In light of these results, we did not use the 2-step approach for any other experiments.

4.3 Experiment 3

In this experiment, we tried to eliminate the code-switching by converting the data to a monolingual form. Our method is to identify the language of each token in the dataset and translate into a common language.

We collected training data for language identification using the Twitter API. We downloaded tweets for English and Spanish and assumed that each word in those tweets belonged to that particular language. The statistics for the downloaded data is shown below:

1. 3000 Spanish tweets (7700 tokens $\sim$56%)
2. 1900 English tweets (6100 tokens $\sim$44%)

Then, we trained a character-level RNN-based language model on this data to do language identification. In order to validate, we split our data and used 80% for training and rest for validating, achieving an accuracy of 79% on this validation data. We used this model to identify the language of all the tokens in dataset, then used Google Translate API to translate English tokens to Spanish.

---

[2] `https://github.com/percyliang/brown-cluster`

Finally, we used the language identification and the translation as features in our CRF model, in addition to all the features used in experiment 1.

As compared to the results from experiment 1, this improved the recall on both development and test sets, but again, the loss in precision caused a slight overall drop in performance.

5 Conclusion

Our submissions earned 4th place out of 8 submissions in the ENG-SPA task, and 3rd place out of 6 submissions in the MSA-EGY task.

Surprisingly, our simplest NER model, trained without using any language identification or translations, worked best. The other more sophisticated experiments showed promise in improving the recall, but damaged the precision too much to improve the F1 score.

One of the challenges we faced was dissimilarity between development and test dataset. Although some of the techniques that we tried on the development dataset improved the system performance, the same effect was not seen in the test dataset. For example, see the change in performance between Table 7 and Table 8. The F1 score on the development set jumped 12 points, but the score on the test set dropped 9 points. This could be explained by the very small size of the development dataset, where a few errors or successes could change the score dramatically. Without access to the test data, we could not do any qualitative error analysis.

Finally, since the 2-Step NER achieved such a high recall, we believe that creating an ensemble of 1-Step and 2-Step systems could achieve a better overall F1 score.

References

Gustavo Aguilar, Fahad AlGhamdi, Victor Soto, Mona Diab, Julia Hirschberg, and Thamar Solorio. 2018. Overview of the CALCS 2018 Shared Task: Named Entity Recognition on Code-switched Data. In *Proceedings of the Third Workshop on Computational Approaches to Linguistic Code-Switching*, Melbourne, Australia. Association for Computational Linguistics.

Leon Derczynski, Eric Nichols, Marieke van Erp, and Nut Limsopatham. 2017. Results of the wnut2017 shared task on novel and emerging entity recognition. In *Proceedings of the 3rd Workshop on Noisy User-generated Text*, pages 140–147. Association for Computational Linguistics.

Andreas Eiselt and Alejandro Figueroa. 2013. A two-step named entity recognizer for open-domain search queries. In *Sixth International Joint Conference on Natural Language Processing, IJCNLP 2013, Nagoya, Japan, October 14-18, 2013*, pages 829–833. Asian Federation of Natural Language Processing / ACL.

Lichan Hong, Gregorio Convertino, and Ed H. Chi. 2011. Language matters in twitter: A large scale study. In *Proceedings of the Fifth International AAAI Conference on Weblogs and Social Media*, pages 519–521.

Andrew McCallum and Wei Li. 2003. Early results for named entity recognition with conditional random fields, feature induction and web-enhanced lexicons. In *Proceedings of the Seventh Conference on Natural Language Learning at HLT-NAACL 2003*, pages 188–191. Association for Computational Linguistics.

Shubhanshu Mishra and Jana Diesner. 2016. Semi-supervised named entity recognition in noisy-text. In *Proceedings of the 2nd Workshop on Noisy User-generated Text*, pages 203–212. The COLING 2016 Organizing Committee.

Radim Řehůřek and Petr Sojka. 2010. Software Framework for Topic Modelling with Large Corpora. In *Proceedings of the LREC 2010 Workshop on New Challenges for NLP Frameworks*, pages 45–50, Valletta, Malta. ELRA.

Alan Ritter, Sam Clark, Mausam, and Oren Etzioni. 2011. Named entity recognition in tweets: An experimental study. In *Proceedings of the 2011 Conference on Empirical Methods in Natural Language Processing, EMNLP 2011, 27-31 July 2011, John McIntyre Conference Centre, Edinburgh, UK, A meeting of SIGDAT, a Special Interest Group of the ACL*, pages 1524–1534. ACL.

Erik F. Tjong Kim Sang. 2002. Introduction to the conll-2002 shared task: Language-independent named entity recognition. In *Proceedings of the 6th Conference on Natural Language Learning - Volume 20*, COLING-02, pages 1–4, Stroudsburg, PA, USA. Association for Computational Linguistics.

Appendices

A ENG-SPA detailed results

We show detailed results for ENG-SPA experiments in the following tables.

	Development Data			Test Data		
	Precision	Recall	F1	Precision	Recall	F1
Event	0.00	0.00	0.00	41.67	11.11	17.54
Group	100.00	25.00	40.00	68.89	31.96	43.66
Location	66.67	40.00	50.00	72.16	68.16	70.1
Organization	100.00	11.11	20.00	51.11	22.77	31.51
Person	73.33	44.00	55.00	83.33	69.5	75.79
Product	58.33	43.75	50.00	66.41	45.19	53.79
Time	50.00	50.00	50.00	18.10	12.58	14.84
Title	100.00	4.55	8.70	47.57	22.17	30.25
Other	0.00	0.00	0.00	0.00	0.00	0.00
Overall	69.44	32.89	44.64	72.75	54.22	62.13

Table 7: (ENG-SPA) Results for Experiment 1: simple features and gazetteers

	Development Data			Test Data		
	Precision	Recall	F1	Precision	Recall	F1
Event	50.00	25.00	33.00	18.60	17.78	18.18
Group	100.00	25.00	40.00	25.34	38.14	30.45
Location	50.00	50.00	50.00	57.16	71.38	63.48
Organization	50.00	11.11	18.18	36.31	30.20	32.97
Person	74.58	58.67	65.67	60.19	80.70	68.95
Product	62.50	62.50	62.50	50.64	51.17	50.90
Time	100.00	100.00	100.00	13.19	64.90	21.92
Title	66.67	9.09	16.00	28.23	31.67	29.85
Other	100.00	33.33	50.00	5.56	5.17	5.36
Overall	71.29	47.37	56.92	46.22	64.66	53.91

Table 8: (ENG-SPA) Results for Experiment 2: 2-step NER

	Development Data			Test Data		
	Precision	Recall	F1	Precision	Recall	F1
Event	0.00	0.00	0.00	45.45	11.11	17.86
Group	100.00	25.00	40.00	68.18	30.93	42.55
Location	55.56	50	52.63	70.97	67.80	69.35
Organization	50	11.11	18.18	48.78	19.80	28.17
Person	74.51	50.67	60.32	83.19	69.43	75.69
Product	53.85	43.75	48.28	65.54	45.45	53.68
Time	50.00	50.00	50.00	18.10	13.91	15.73
Title	0.00	0.00	0.00	45.37	22.17	29.79
Other	0.00	0.00	0.00	0.00	0.00	0.00
Overall	66.27	36.18	46.81	71.88	54.00	61.67

Table 9: (ENG-SPA) Results for Experiment 3: Language Identification + Translation

We show detailed results for the one MSA-EGY experiment in the following table.

	Development Data			Test Data		
	Precision	Recall	F1	Precision	Recall	F1
Event	66.67	43.48	52.63	67.57	35.71	46.73
Group	86.63	78.01	82.09	69.92	73.50	71.67
Location	87.14	75.70	81.02	76.64	57.95	66.00
Organization	74.24	65.77	69.75	68.75	61.60	64.98
Person	85.28	79.66	82.37	79.34	64.70	71.27
Product	79.17	69.09	73.79	66.67	54.55	60.00
Time	74.60	77.05	75.81	68.00	68.00	68.00
Title	77.11	55.65	64.65	26.32	50.00	34.48
Other	92.86	76.47	83.87	100.00	50.00	66.67
Overall	83.29	73.91	78.32	74.43	61.65	67.44

Table 10: (MSA-EGY) Results for Experiment 1 (without Gazetteer features)

Bilingual Character Representation for Efficiently Addressing Out-of-Vocabulary Words in Code-Switching Named Entity Recognition

Genta Indra Winata, Chien-Sheng Wu, Andrea Madotto, Pascale Fung

Center for Artificial Intelligence Research (CAiRE)

Department of Electronic and Computer Engineering

Hong Kong University of Science and Technology, Clear Water Bay, Hong Kong

`{giwinata, cwuak, eeandreamad}@ust.hk, pascale@ece.ust.hk`

Abstract

We propose an LSTM-based model with hierarchical architecture on named entity recognition from code-switching Twitter data. Our model uses bilingual character representation and transfer learning to address out-of-vocabulary words. In order to mitigate data noise, we propose to use token replacement and normalization. In the 3rd Workshop on Computational Approaches to Linguistic Code-Switching Shared Task, we achieved second place with 62.76% harmonic mean F1-score for English-Spanish language pair without using any gazetteer and knowledge-based information.

1 Introduction

Named Entity Recognition (NER) predicts which word tokens refer to location, people, organization, time, and other entities from a word sequence. Deep neural network models have successfully achieved the state-of-the-art performance in NER tasks (Cohen; Chiu and Nichols, 2016; Lample et al., 2016; Shen et al., 2017) using monolingual corpus. However, learning from code-switching tweets data is very challenging due to several reasons: (1) words may have different semantics in different context and language, for instance, the word "cola" can be associated with product or "queue" in Spanish (2) data from social media are noisy, with many inconsistencies such as spelling mistakes, repetitions, and informalities which eventually points to Out-of-Vocabulary (OOV) words issue (3) entities may appear in different language other than the matrix language. For example "todos los Domingos en Westland Mall" where "Westland Mall" is an English named entity.

Our contributions are two-fold: (1) bilingual character bidirectional RNN is used to capture character-level information and tackle OOV words issue (2) we apply transfer learning from monolingual pre-trained word vectors to adapt the model with different domains in a bilingual setting. In our model, we use LSTM to capture long-range dependencies of the word sequence and character sequence in bilingual character RNN. In our experiments, we show the efficiency of our model in handling OOV words and bilingual word context.

2 Related Work

Convolutional Neural Network (CNN) was used in NER task as word decoder by Collobert et al. (2011) and a few years later, Huang et al. (2015) introduced Bidirectional Long-Short Term Memory (BiLSTM) (Sundermeyer et al., 2012). Character-level features were explored by using neural architecture and replaced hand-crafted features (Dyer et al., 2015; Lample et al., 2016; Chiu and Nichols, 2016; Limsopatham and Collier, 2016). Lample et al. (2016) also showed Conditional Random Field (CRF) (Lafferty et al., 2001) decoders to improve the results and used Stack memory-based LSTMs for their work in sequence chunking. Aguilar et al. (2017) proposed multi-task learning by combining Part-of-Speech tagging task with NER and using gazetteers to provide language-specific knowledge. Character-level embeddings were used to handle the OOV words problem in NLP tasks such as NER (Lample et al., 2016), POS tagging, and language modeling (Ling et al., 2015).

3 Methodology

3.1 Dataset

For our experiment, we use English-Spanish (ENG-SPA) Tweets data from Twitter provided by

110

Proceedings of The Third Workshop on Computational Approaches to Code-Switching, pages 110–114

Melbourne, Australia, July 19, 2018. ©2018 Association for Computational Linguistics

Table 1: OOV words rates on ENG-SPA dataset before and after preprocessing

	Train		Dev		Test
	All	**Entity**	**All**	**Entity**	**All**
Corpus	-	-	18.91%	31.84%	49.39%
FastText (eng) (Mikolov et al., 2018)	62.62%	16.76%	19.12%	3.91%	54.59%
+ FastText (spa) (Grave et al., 2018)	49.76%	12.38%	11.98%	3.91%	39.45%
+ token replacement	12.43%	12.35%	7.18%	3.91%	9.60%
+ token normalization	**7.94%**	**8.38%**	**5.01%**	**1.67%**	**6.08%**

Aguilar et al. (2018). There are nine different named-entity labels. The labels use IOB format (Inside, Outside, Beginning) where every token is labeled as `B-label` in the beginning and follows with `I-label` if it is inside a named entity, or `O` otherwise. For example "Kendrick Lamar" is represented as `B-PER I-PER`. Table 2 and Table 3 show the statistics of the dataset.

Table 2: Data Statistics for ENG-SPA Tweets

	Train	Dev	Test
# Words	616,069	9,583	183,011

Table 3: Entity Statistics for ENG-SPA Tweets

Entities	Train	Dev
# Person	4701	75
# Location	2810	10
# Product	1369	16
# Title	824	22
# Organization	811	9
# Group	718	4
# Time	577	6
# Event	232	4
# Other	324	6

"Person", "Location", and "Product" are the most frequent entities in the dataset, and the least common ones are "Time", "Event", and "Other" categories. 'Other' category is the least trivial among all because it is not well clustered like others.

3.2 Feature Representation

In this section, we describe word-level and character-level features used in our model.

Word Representation: Words are encoded into continuous representation. The vocabulary is built from training data. The Twitter data are very noisy, there are many spelling mistakes, irregular ways to use a word and repeating characters.

We apply several strategies to overcome the issue. We use 300-dimensional English (Mikolov et al., 2018) and Spanish (Grave et al., 2018) FastText pre-trained word vectors which comprise two million words vocabulary each and they are trained using Common Crawl and Wikipedia. To create the shared vocabulary, we concatenate English and Spanish word vectors.

For preprocessing, we propose the following steps:

1. **Token replacement:** Replace user hashtags (#user) and mentions (@user) with "USR", and URL (https://domain.com) with "URL".

2. **Token normalization:** Concatenate Spanish and English FastText word vector vocabulary. Normalize OOV words by using one out of these heuristics and check if the word exists in the vocabulary sequentially

   (a) Capitalize the first character
   (b) Lowercase the word
   (c) Step (b) and remove repeating characters, such as *"hellooooo"* into *"hello"* or *"lolololol"* into *"lol"*
   (d) Step (a) and (c) altogether

Then, the effectiveness of the preprocessing and transfer learning in handling OOV words are analyzed. The statistics is showed in Table 1. It is clear that using FastText word vectors reduce the OOV words rate especially when we concatenate the vocabulary of both languages. Furthermore, the preprocessing strategies dramatically decrease the number of unknown words.

Character Representation: We concatenate all possible characters for English and Spanish, including numbers and special characters. English and Spanish have most of the characters in common, but, with some additional unique Spanish characters. All cases are kept as they are.

3.3 Model Description

In this section, we describe our model architecture and hyper-parameters setting.

Bilingual Char-RNN: This is one of the approaches to learn character-level embeddings without needing of any lexical hand-crafted features. We use an RNN for representing the word with character-level information (Lample et al., 2016). Figure 1 shows the model architecture. The inputs are characters extracted from a word and every character is embedded with d dimension vector. Then, we use it as the input for a Bidirectional LSTM as character encoder, wherein every time step, a character is input to the network. Consider a_t as the hidden states for word t.

$$a_t = (a_1^1, a_t^2, ..., a_t^V)$$

where V is the character length. The representation of the word is obtained by taking a_t^V which is the last hidden state.

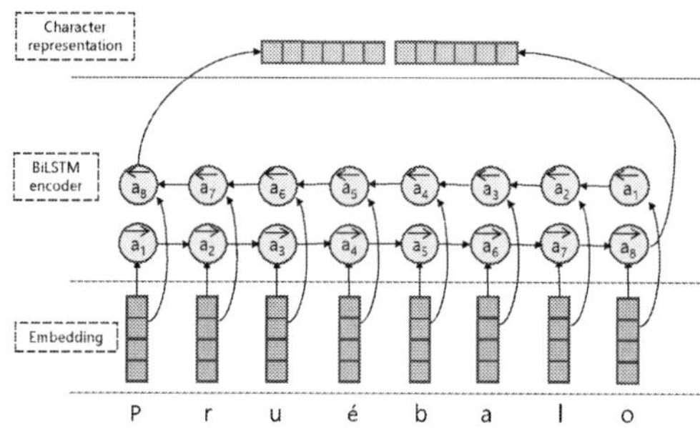

Figure 1: Bilingual Char-RNN architecture

Main Architecture: Figure 2 presents the overall architecture of the system. The input layers receive word and character-level representations from English and Spanish pre-trained Fast-Text word vectors and Bilingual Char-RNN. Consider **X** as the input sequence:

$$\mathbf{X} = (x_1, x_2, ..., x_N)$$

where N is the length of the sequence. We fix the word embedding parameters. Then, we concatenate both vectors to get a richer word representation u_t. Afterwards, we pass the vectors to bidirectional LSTM.

$$u_t = x_t \oplus a_t$$

$$\overrightarrow{h_t} = \overrightarrow{\text{LSTM}}(u_t, \overrightarrow{h_{t-1}}), \overleftarrow{h_t} = \overleftarrow{\text{LSTM}}(u_t, \overleftarrow{h_{t-1}})$$

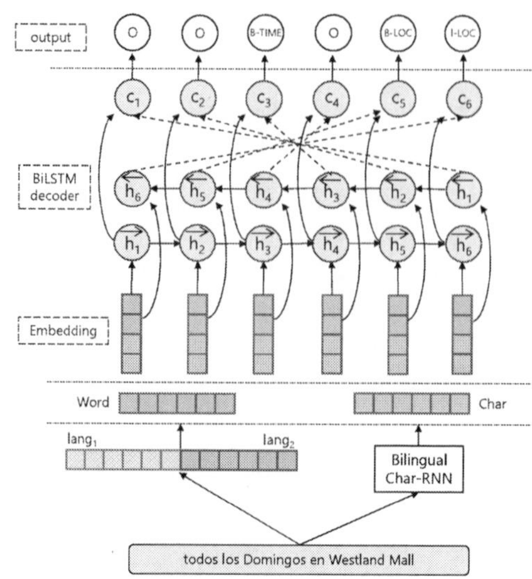

Figure 2: Main architecture

$$c_t = \overrightarrow{h_t} \oplus \overleftarrow{h_t}$$

where $\oplus$ denotes the concatenation operator. Dropout is applied to the recurrent layer. At each time step we make a prediction for the entity of the current token. A softmax function is used to calculate the probability distribution of all possible named-entity tags.

$$y_t = \frac{e^{c_t}}{\sum_{j=1}^{T} e^{c_j}}, \text{ where } j = 1, .., T$$

where y_t is the probability distribution of tags at word t and T is the maximum time step. Since there is a variable number of sequence length, we padded the sequence and applied mask when calculating cross-entropy loss function. Our model does not use any gazetteer and knowledge-based information, and it can be easily adapted to another language pair.

3.4 Post-processing

We found an issue during the prediction where some words are labeled with `O`, in between `B-label` and `I-label` tags. Our solution is to insert `I-label` tag if the tag is surrounded by `B-label` and `I-label` tags with the same entity category. Another problem we found that many `I-label` tags are paired with `B-label` in different categories. So, we replace `B-label` category tag with corresponding `I-label` category tag. This step improves the result of the pre-

Table 4: Results on ENG-SPA Dataset (‡ result(s) from the shared task organizer (Aguilar et al., 2018) † without token normalization)

Model	Features	F1 Dev	F1 Test
Baseline‡	Word	-	53.2802%
BiLSTM†	Word + Char-RNN	46.9643%	53.4759%
BiLSTM	FastText (eng)	57.7174%	59.9098%
BiLSTM	FastText (eng-spa)	57.4177%	60.2426%
BiLSTM	+ Char-RNN	65.2217%	61.9621%
+ post		**65.3865%**	**62.7608%**
Competitors‡			
IIT BHU (1st place)	-	-	63.7628% (+1.0020%)
FAIR (3rd place)	-	-	62.6671% (- 0.0937%)

diction on the development set. Figure 3 shows the examples.

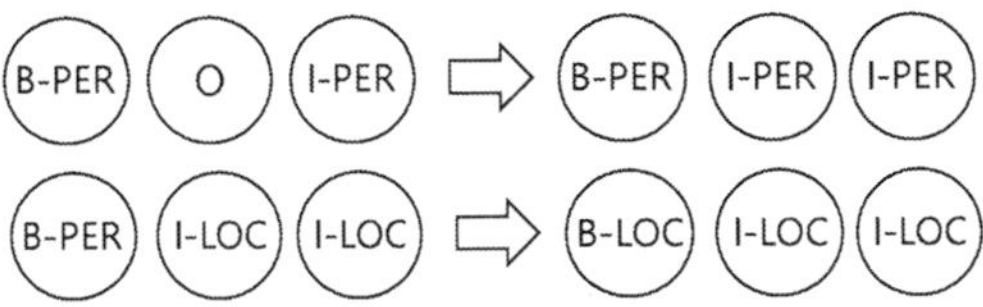

Figure 3: Post-processing examples

3.5 Experimental Setup

We trained our LSTM models with a hidden size of 200. We used batch size equals to 64. The sentences were sorted by length in descending order. Our embedding size is 300 for word and 150 for characters. Dropout (Srivastava et al., 2014) of 0.4 was applied to all LSTMs. Adam Optimizer was chosen with an initial learning rate of 0.01. We applied time-based decay of $\sqrt{2}$ decay rate and stop after two consecutive epochs without improvement. We tuned our model with the development set and evaluated our best model with the test set using harmonic mean F1-score metric with the script provided by Aguilar et al. (2018).

4   Results

Table 4 shows the results for ENG-SPA tweets. Adding pre-trained word vectors and character-level features improved the performance. Interestingly, our initial attempts at adding character-level features did not improve the overall performance, until we apply dropout to the Char-RNN. The performance of the model improves significantly after transfer learning with FastText word vectors while it also reduces the number of OOV words in the development and test set. The margin between ours and first place model is small, approximately 1%.

We try to use sub-words representation from Spanish FastText (Grave et al., 2018), however, it does not improve the result since the OOV words consist of many special characters, for example, *"/IAtrevido/Provocativo"*, *"Twets/wek"*, and possibly create noisy vectors and most of them are not entity words.

5   Conclusion

This paper presents a bidirectional LSTM-based model with hierarchical architecture using bilingual character RNN to address the OOV words issue. Moreover, token replacement, token normalization, and transfer learning reduce OOV words rate even further and significantly improves the performance. The model achieved 62.76% F1-score for English-Spanish language pair without using any gazetteer and knowledge-based information.

Acknowledgments

This work is partially funded by ITS/319/16FP of the Innovation Technology Commission, HKUST 16214415 & 16248016 of Hong Kong Research Grants Council, and RDC 1718050-0 of EMOS.AI.

References

Gustavo Aguilar, Fahad AlGhamdi, Victor Soto, Mona Diab, Julia Hirschberg, and Thamar Solorio. 2018. Overview of the CALCS 2018 Shared Task: Named

Entity Recognition on Code-switched Data. In *Proceedings of the Third Workshop on Computational Approaches to Linguistic Code-Switching*, Melbourne, Australia. Association for Computational Linguistics.

Gustavo Aguilar, Suraj Maharjan, Adrian Pastor López Monroy, and Thamar Solorio. 2017. A multi-task approach for named entity recognition in social media data. In *Proceedings of the 3rd Workshop on Noisy User-generated Text*, pages 148–153.

Jason PC Chiu and Eric Nichols. 2016. Named entity recognition with bidirectional lstm-cnns. *Transactions of the Association for Computational Linguistics*, 4:357–370.

Zhilin Yang Ruslan Salakhutdinov William Cohen. Multi-task cross-lingual sequence tagging from scratch.

Ronan Collobert, Jason Weston, Léon Bottou, Michael Karlen, Koray Kavukcuoglu, and Pavel Kuksa. 2011. Natural language processing (almost) from scratch. *Journal of Machine Learning Research*, 12(Aug):2493–2537.

Chris Dyer, Miguel Ballesteros, Wang Ling, Austin Matthews, and Noah A Smith. 2015. Transition-based dependency parsing with stack long short-term memory. In *Proceedings of the 53rd Annual Meeting of the Association for Computational Linguistics and the 7th International Joint Conference on Natural Language Processing (Volume 1: Long Papers)*, volume 1, pages 334–343.

Edouard Grave, Piotr Bojanowski, Prakhar Gupta, Armand Joulin, and Tomas Mikolov. 2018. Learning word vectors for 157 languages. In *Proceedings of the International Conference on Language Resources and Evaluation (LREC 2018)*.

Zhiheng Huang, Wei Xu, and Kai Yu. 2015. Bidirectional lstm-crf models for sequence tagging. *arXiv preprint arXiv:1508.01991*.

John Lafferty, Andrew McCallum, and Fernando CN Pereira. 2001. Conditional random fields: Probabilistic models for segmenting and labeling sequence data.

Guillaume Lample, Miguel Ballesteros, Sandeep Subramanian, Kazuya Kawakami, and Chris Dyer. 2016. Neural architectures for named entity recognition. In *Proceedings of NAACL-HLT*, pages 260–270.

Nut Limsopatham and Nigel Henry Collier. 2016. Bidirectional lstm for named entity recognition in twitter messages.

Wang Ling, Chris Dyer, Alan W Black, Isabel Trancoso, Ramon Fermandez, Silvio Amir, Luis Marujo, and Tiago Luis. 2015. Finding function in form: Compositional character models for open vocabulary word representation. In *Proceedings of the 2015 Conference on Empirical Methods in Natural Language Processing*, pages 1520–1530.

Tomas Mikolov, Edouard Grave, Piotr Bojanowski, Christian Puhrsch, and Armand Joulin. 2018. Advances in pre-training distributed word representations. In *Proceedings of the International Conference on Language Resources and Evaluation (LREC 2018)*.

Yanyao Shen, Hyokun Yun, Zachary Lipton, Yakov Kronrod, and Animashree Anandkumar. 2017. Deep active learning for named entity recognition. In *Proceedings of the 2nd Workshop on Representation Learning for NLP*, pages 252–256.

Nitish Srivastava, Geoffrey Hinton, Alex Krizhevsky, Ilya Sutskever, and Ruslan Salakhutdinov. 2014. Dropout: A simple way to prevent neural networks from overfitting. *The Journal of Machine Learning Research*, 15(1):1929–1958.

Martin Sundermeyer, Ralf Schlüter, and Hermann Ney. 2012. Lstm neural networks for language modeling. In *Thirteenth Annual Conference of the International Speech Communication Association*.

Named Entity Recognition on Code-Switched Data Using Conditional Random Fields

Utpal Kumar Sikdar[1], Biswanath Barik[2] and **Björn Gambäck[2]**

[1]Flytxt, Thiruvananthapuram, India

`utpal.sikdar@gmail.com`

[2]Dpt. of Computer Science, Norwegian University of Science and Technology

`{biswanath.barik,gamback}@ntnu.no`

Abstract

Named Entity Recognition is an important information extraction task that identifies proper names in unstructured texts and classifies them into some pre-defined categories. Identification of named entities in code-mixed social media texts is a more difficult and challenging task as the contexts are short, ambiguous and often noisy. This work proposes a Conditional Random Fields based named entity recognition system to identify proper names in code-switched data and classify them into nine categories. The system ranked fifth among nine participant systems and achieved a 59.25% F1-score.

1 Introduction

With the increasing usage of social media, micro blogs and chats in various socio-economical classes, ethnicities and genres in the global society, a new category of informal short texts has evolved in recent years. One of the important phenomena that can appear in such texts is code-mixing or *code-switching* (CS), where bi-lingual users often switch back and forth between their common languages during interactions. Processing of such texts by automatic means encounters several challenges due to the usage of mixed vocabulary, misspellings, abbreviations, transliterations, emojis, and many more. Furthermore, it is in many cases difficult to interpret the texts because of the short contexts.

The Natural Language Processing and text mining communities have taken necessary initiatives to encourage researchers through organizing various workshops and shared-tasks, and by opening mainstream research tracks to develop resources and novel approaches to processing code-mixed texts efficiently and for extracting valuable information from such messy contents. In this direction, the CALCS 2018 Shared Task (Aguilar et al., 2018) focused on identifying a predefined set of nine Named Entity (NE) types: `Person`, `Location`, `Organization`, `Group`, `Title`, `Product`, `Event`, `Time`, and `Other`. The NE identification task addressed code-mixed texts of Spanish-English (SPA-ENG) and Modern Standard Arabic-Egyptian (MSA-EGY); here we will look at the first pair (SPA-ENG) only.

Previously, several machine learning techniques have been applied to the NE recognition problem such as Hidden Markov Models (HMM) (Bikel et al., 1997), Maximum Entropy models (Borthwick, 1999), Conditional Random Fields (CRF) (Lafferty et al., 2001), and Support Vector Machines (SVM) (Isozaki and Kazawa, 2002), as well as deep neural network-based Long Short-Term Memories (LSTM) (Limsopatham and Collier, 2016), Convolutional Neural Networks (CNN) (Santos and Guimaraes, 2015), or hybrid combinations (Chiu and Nichols, 2016).

In this work, the named entity recognition task is considered as a sequence labeling problem, for which CRF is a natural choice to identify entity mentions from code-switched data and classify them to one of the nine aforementioned NE categories. With initial named entity token and language identification, a wide range of features (described in Section 3) are explored for this purpose. As per the overall ranking of the submitted systems under the shared task, our approach is reasonably effective.

The paper is organized as follows: The shared task datasets are presented in Section 2. The named entity recognition system is described in Section 3. Results are presented in Section 4, with error analysis reported in Section 5. Section 6 addresses future work and concludes.

Proceedings of The Third Workshop on Computational Approaches to Code-Switching, pages 115–119

Melbourne, Australia, July 19, 2018. ©2018 Association for Computational Linguistics

Dataset	#Tweets	#Named Entities
Training	50,238	12,365
Development	828	151
Test	15,634	-

Table 1: Code-switched dataset statistics

2 Datasets

The shared task organizers provided three different datasets: training, development and test sets. The statistics of the datasets are reported in Table 1, with the total number of tweets and total number of named entities. No gold standard annotation of the test data was made available.

3 Named Entity Recognition

To identify and classify each token from the code-switched data into nine categories (Person, Location, Organization, Group, Title, Product, Event, Time and Other), a supervised CRF-based (Lafferty et al., 2001) approach was used. Different features were extracted from external sources and applied to recognize the target entities.

In a first step, each token was identified as either being a named entity (called a mention) or not. All the beginning and intermediate parts of named entities (for all nine entity categories) were converted into 'B-mention' and 'I-mention', respectively, and a CRF-based model was applied to identify the mentions.

In the next step, the identified mentions ('B-mention' and 'I-mention') were used as features along with other features described in subsections 3.1 and 3.2 to classify each token into one of the nine categories. The 'BIO'[1] notation was used to represent the named entities.

The CRF-based mention and named entity identification models were implemented using CRFsuite (python-crfsuite),[2] which allows for fast training by utilizing L-BFGS (Liu and Nocedal, 1989), a limited memory quasi-Newton algorithm for large scale numerical optimization. The classifier was trained both on features retrieved from external resources and on features directly extracted from the training data, as detailed in the following two subsections.

3.1 Features from external sources

The following features were extracted from other external resources:

3.1.1 Language identification

The language identification data from the previous code-switching workshop (Diab et al., 2016) was collected and converted into 'lang1', 'lang2' and 'other' (with 'other' grouping the labels 'mixed', 'ne', 'fw' and 'unknown'). If any token of the 'other' categories was followed by 'lang1', it was assigned to 'lang1'. If the token was followed by 'lang2', it was assigned to 'lang2'. A model described by Sikdar and Gambäck (2016) was built using the converted language identification data and applied to the current shared task's (Aguilar et al., 2018) training and development sets to get language information ('lang1', 'lang2' and 'other') for each token. This language information was then used as a feature for named entity identification in the current shared task.

3.1.2 Named entity token identification

Only the tweets containing named entities were extracted from the data from the previous code-switched workshop, and a CRF based model was built using these tweets with different features (local context, suffix, prefix, all-upper-case, starts-with-upper-case, and hash symbol) and applied to the current shared task's training, development and test data to get named entity information for each token.

3.1.3 Part-of-speech information

The Stanford tagger[3] was used to extract part-of-speech (POS) information for training, development and test data. First, the English version of the Stanford tagger was applied to get English POS tags, and then the Spanish version of the tagger was applied. For tokens belonging to 'lang1' or 'other', the English POS tag was considered. For tokens belonging to 'lang2', the Spanish POS was picked. The POS information for a word together with its two preceding and two following tokens' part-of-speech tags (i.e., a -2 to +2 window) were used as features.

In addition, the first two characters of the current word's POS tag and those of the previous and next two words' POS tags (-2 to +2 tokens) were used as features.

---

[1] Here 'B' represents the beginning of, 'I' inside, and 'O' outside of a named entity.

[2] www.chokkan.org/software/crfsuite/

[3] https://nlp.stanford.edu/software/tagger.shtml

3.1.4 Stem

The stem of each token was identified using the Stanford parser.[4]

3.1.5 Noisy data named entity recognizer

The named entities of the current workshop's datasets were identified using the model for named entity recognition in noisy user generated texts described by Sikdar and Gambäck (2017).

3.2 Features from training data

The following features were extracted from the training data.

- word itself: the current word.
- word in lower case: all alphabetic characters in the word converted to lower-case.
- local context of word in lower-case (with a -2 to +2 window, i.e., from two preceding to two following tokens).
- all-upper-case: binary feature checking whether the current token only has upper-case letters or not.
- starts-with-upper-case: binary feature checking whether the current token starts with a capital letter or not.
- word-length: binary feature set if the length of a word is greater than a threshold (> 5).
- suffix: n-grams of the last 1, 2 or 3 characters.
- prefix characters: n-grams of the first 1, 2 or 3 characters.
- is-digit: binary feature checking whether the current word contains any digit or not.
- two-digit: binary feature set if the current word contains two digits.
- is-alphanumeric: current word contains both digits and letters.
- is-special-characters: binary feature set if the current word contains either '#' or '@'.
- is-stop-word: the current word is on NLTK's[5] stop word list.
- most-frequent-word: after removing all stop words, a list was prepared based on high frequency of words (1000 words from the training data). The feature is set if the current word belongs to this high frequency word list.
- word-normalization: the current word with all lower-case letters replaced with 'a', all upper-case letters replaced with 'A', all digits replaced with '0', and all other characters left unaltered.
- Pair-wise-mutual-information-score: PMI calculated based on the number of times the current word belongs to each NE category divided by the word's total number of occurrences in training data.
- beginning-of-the-word: binary feature checking whether the current token belongs to beginning of the sentence or not.
- ending-of-the-word: binary feature checking whether the current token belongs to end of the sentence or not.

To identify the mentions, the above features were used together. To identify named entities, the predicted mentions along with contexts consisting of the previous two and the next two tokens were used as features, in addition to the other features described in subsections 3.1 and 3.2.

Data	Precision	Recall	F-score
5-fold	80.64	71.82	75.95
Dev_Data	81.10	50.20	62.00

Table 2: Mention identification results (%)

Data	F-score
5-fold	59.19
Dev_Data	41.70
Test	59.25

Table 3: Named entity recognition results (%)

Team	F-score
IIT BHU	63.76
CAiRE++	62.76
FAIR	62.66
Linguists	62.13
Flytxt	**59.25**
semantic	56.72
WallyGuzman	54.16
Fraunhofer FKIE	53.65
Baseline	53.28

Table 4: Comparison with other systems (%)

[4]https://nlp.stanford.edu/
IR-book/html/htmledition/
stemming-and-lemmatization-1.html
[5]https://www.nltk.org/

	EVENT	GROUP	LOC	ORG	OTHER	PER	PROD	TIME	TITLE	O
EVENT	1	0	0	0	0	3	0	0	0	2
GROUP	0	2	1	0	0	0	0	0	0	2
LOC	2	0	7	0	0	1	0	0	0	6
ORG	0	0	0	0	0	4	5	0	0	1
OTHER	0	0	0	0	1	0	0	0	0	6
PER	0	0	1	0	0	52	0	0	0	42
PROD	0	0	0	0	0	2	11	0	0	8
TIME	0	0	0	0	0	0	0	6	0	3
TITLE	0	0	2	0	0	6	0	0	2	40
O	0	0	6	2	1	4	1	2	0	9348

Table 5: Confusion matrix for NER on the development data

4 Results

The supervised learning approach was applied to identify mentions. Identified mentions were taken as features along with the other features mentioned in Section 3 to recognize named entities. The classifiers were learned from the training data and tested on the development data. 5-fold cross-validation (CV) was applied to the training data.

The mention identification results are shown in Table 2. The average precision, recall and F1-score values of 5-fold CV on the training data were 80.64%, 71.82% and 75.95%, respectively. The F1-score on the development data was 62.00% due to a significant drop in recall.

The system was applied to named entity recognition and results are shown in Table 3. The average F1-score of 5-fold cross-validation was 59.19%. When tested on the development data, the system achieved an F-score of 41.70%.

The system was then applied to the unseen test data and achieved an F1-score of 59.25%, which is similar to the 5-fold CV F1-score.

Comparing our system ('Flytxt') to the other systems participating in the shared task, Table 4 reports the results and shows that the system secured fifth position and achieved clearly better scores than the baseline system ('Baseline').

5 Error Analysis

When analyzing the output on the development data for named entity recognition, it is clear that many of the named entities are not identified at all by the system. This might be due to the word itself and/or some the contexts word not occurring in the training data.

Furthermore, some named entities are misclas-sified into other categories, plausibly since those words occur in both named entity categories.

The confusion matrix for named entity recognition is reported in Table 5, for each of the nine classes ('EVENT', 'GROUP','LOC', 'ORG', 'OTHER', 'PER', 'PROD', 'TIME', 'TITLE'). The matrix was built using relaxed match, with the 'B-' and 'I-' distinctions ignored for each named entity class.

6 Conclusion

This paper proposed a Conditional Random Field based approach to identifying and classifying named entities. Compared to the baseline, the proposed system achieved better results.

To investigate the effectiveness of the external features, a feature ablation study should be the next step. Most of the features have been extracted directly from training data, but the features could have been further optimized using grid search and evolutionary approaches.

As an alternative to the feature-based classifier, deep learning-based approaches such as LSTM (Long Short-Term Memory), stack-based LSTM and CNN (Convolution Neural Network) can be explored to classify the proper names into the nine categories.

Acknowledgements

Thanks to the organizers of the 2016 and 2018 code-switching workshops for providing and annotating the training and test data. Thanks also to the three anonymous reviewers for comments that helped improve the paper and for suggestions that can be useful in the future.

References

Gustavo Aguilar, Fahad AlGhamdi, Victor Soto, Mona Diab, Julia Hirschberg, and Thamar Solorio. 2018. Overview of the CALCS 2018 shared task: Named entity recognition on code-switched data. In *Proceedings of the 3rd Workshop on Computational Approaches to Linguistic Code-Switching*, Melbourne, Australia. ACL.

Daniel M. Bikel, Scott Miller, Richard Schwartz, and Ralph Weischedel. 1997. Nymble: a high-performance learning name-finder. In *Proceedings of the 5th Conference on Applied Natural Language Processing*, pages 194–201, Washington, DC, USA. ACL.

Andrew Borthwick. 1999. *A Maximum Entropy Approach to Named Entity Recognition*. Ph.D. thesis, Computer Science Department, New York University, New York, NY, USA.

Jason P.C. Chiu and Eric Nichols. 2016. Named entity recognition with bidirectional LSTM-CNNs. *Transactions of the Association for Computational Linguistics*, 4:357–370.

Mona Diab, Pascale Fung, Mahmoud Ghoneim, Julia Hirschberg, and Thamar Solorio, editors. 2016. *Proceedings of the 2nd Workshop on Computational Approaches to Code Switching@EMNLP 2016*. ACL, Austin, Texas, USA.

Hideki Isozaki and Hideto Kazawa. 2002. Efficient support vector classifiers for named entity recognition. In *Proceedings of the 19th International Conference on Computational Linguistics*, volume 1, pages 1–7, Taipei, Taiwan. ACL.

John Lafferty, Andrew McCallum, and Fernando C.N. Pereira. 2001. Conditional Random Fields: Probabilistic models for segmenting and labeling sequence data. In *Proceedings of the 18th International Conference on Machine Learning*, pages 282–289, Williamstown, MA, USA. IMIS.

Nut Limsopatham and Nigel Henry Collier. 2016. Bidirectional LSTM for named entity recognition in Twitter messages. In *Proceedings of the 2nd Workshop on Noisy User-generated Text, WNUT@COLING2016*, pages 145–152, Osaka, Japan. ACL.

Dong C. Liu and Jorge Nocedal. 1989. On the limited memory BFGS method for large scale optimization. *Mathematical Programming*, 45(1):503–528.

Cicero Nogueira dos Santos and Victor Guimaraes. 2015. Boosting named entity recognition with neural character embeddings. In *Proceedings of the 5th Named Entity Workshop (NEWS 2015)*, Beijing, China. ACL.

Utpal Kumar Sikdar and Björn Gambäck. 2016. Language identification in code-switched text using Conditional Random Fields and Babelnet. In *Proceedings of the 2nd Workshop on Computational Approaches to Code Switching@EMNLP 2016*, pages 127–131, Austin, Texas, USA. ACL.

Utpal Kumar Sikdar and Björn Gambäck. 2017. A feature-based ensemble approach to recognition of emerging and rare named entities. In *Proceedings of the 3rd Workshop on Noisy User-generated Text, NUT@EMNLP*, pages 177–181, Copenhagen, Denmark. ACL.

The University of Texas System Submission for the Code-Switching Workshop Shared Task 2018

Florian Janke, Tongrui Li, Gualberto Guzmán,
Eric Rincón, Barbara Bullock, Almeida Jacqueline Toribio
Bilingual Annotation Task (BATs) Research Group
University of Texas at Austin
{florian,tli1998,eric.rincon,gualbertoguzman}@utexas.edu
{bbullock,toribio}@austin.utexas.edu

Abstract

This paper describes the system for the Named Entity Recognition Shared Task of the Third Workshop on Computational Approaches to Linguistic Code-Switching (CALCS) submitted by the Bilingual Annotations Tasks (BATs) research group of the University of Texas. Our system uses several features to train a Conditional Random Field (CRF) model for classifying input words as Named Entities (NEs) using the Inside-Outside-Beginning (IOB) tagging scheme. We participated in the Modern Standard Arabic-Egyptian Arabic (MSA-EGY) and English-Spanish (ENG-SPA) tasks, achieving weighted average F-scores of 65.62 and 54.16 respectively. We also describe the performance of a deep neural network (NN) trained on a subset of the CRF features, which did not surpass CRF performance.

1 Introduction & Prior Approaches

Named entity recognition (NER) and classification are essential tasks in information extraction (Nadeau and Sekine, 2007). However, NER in texts in which multiple languages are represented is not straightforward because NEs can be language-specific (e.g., *Estados Unidos* in Spanish vs. *United States*) or language-neutral but regionally specific (e.g., *Los Angeles*) or even mixed (e.g., *Nueva York* in Spanish) (Çetinoglu, 2016; Guzman et al., 2016). The task is further complicated by the fact that names of companies, institutions and brands in one language can be common nouns in another (e.g, *Toro* is a brand name for a U.S. company but *toro* in Spanish means bull'). These challenges confound the already difficult task of working with multilingual texts,

which can be considered resource scarce' with respect to the availability of NLP tools (Riaz, 2010; Zirikly and Diab, 2015; Sitaram and Black, 2016; Guzmán et al., 2017). But NER in multilingual communication is essential given that multilingualism is common throughout the world, and, for many speakers, language mixing is a shared practice and one that can be prevalent in social media like Twitter (Jurgens et al., 2014; Jamatia et al., 2015, 2016; Vilares et al., 2015).

2 Data Description

Over 62k Tweets were collected and manually annotated for NEs to be used in this shared task (Aguilar et al., 2018). The annotators labeled each NE using one of ten tags: PERSON, LOCATION, ORGANIZATION, PRODUCT, GROUP, EVENT, TIME, TITLE, OTHER, or NOT-NE. All tokens are tagged using the IOB scheme while ignoring hashtags and @-mentions, i.e. *Louis Vuitton* is tagged with B-ORG and I-ORG but *@RideAlong* is tagged as O. NEs can occur in all languages and, since this is Twitter data, can frequently be misspelled or missing orthographic features that would ease identification. The Tweets were divided into training, development, and test sets and released to the participants of the shared task along with tools for preprocessing of the Tweets.

3 Approach & Methodology

3.1 Conditional Random Field

One approach we used to perform NE recognition in this shared task was the usage of conditional random fields (Lafferty et al., 2001), a technique used for sequence labeling. More specifically, *python-crfsuite* (Peng and Korobov, 2014) was used, a Python wrapper around *CRFsuite* (Okazaki, 2007), an implementation of CRFs in C/C++. CRFs work by looking at several words

Proceedings of The Third Workshop on Computational Approaches to Code-Switching, pages 120–125
Melbourne, Australia, July 19, 2018. ©2018 Association for Computational Linguistics

and their features and expected classification (in this case the NE classification) as examples and using the information gained to predict classifications on future data that has not been seen before. For our use of *CRFsuite*, the values of 1.0 for L1 and 0.001 for L2 regularization (from the NER example provided by the package) were used with a total of 150 training iterations. All other parameters were left at their default values.

3.1.1 Features Used

Several different features of the tweets as whole and individual tokens were used as input, some of which rely on external resources to generate. Initially we developed our features on the ENG-SPA dataset. Interestingly many of the features used for ENG-SPA performed well on the MSA-EGY data. Inspiration for the features used was drawn from various papers from the *First Workshop on CALCS* (Chittaranjan et al., 2014; Lin et al., 2014). The features used can be grouped into five categories:

1. Word features: lowercase copy of the word, its two last characters, length, whether it is the first word or not, whether this word is all alphanumeric characters (only for the MSA-EGY dataset), if this word is made up of digits or not, and if the word contains emoji.

2. Capitalization: is the word all uppercase or title case?

3. Language tags: off-the-shelf taggers from the *Natural Language Toolkit* (NLTK) (Bird and Loper, 2004) were used to perform NE and part of speech (POS) tagging on one tweet at a time and the tags were applied to individual tokens.

4. Language detection: in the ENG-SPA dataset only, language detection on entire tweets was done using langdetect, a Python port (Danilák, 2017) of language-detection (Nakatani, 2010) originally written in Java. Probabilities of the tweet being English or Spanish rounded to 2 digits after the decimal point were used. If the tweet was classified as neither English or Spanish, the probability was set to be 0. For example, "Quiero un roadtrip asap" was falsely classified as Romanian.

5. Twitter functionality: does the overall tweet contain an @mention or #hashtag? Is this word itself one of the two? Is this a URL?

A subset of the features mentioned above were applied to the next and previous words and used as features to classify the current word: the word in lowercase form, its last two characters, if it is the first word, title case, uppercase, a URL, @-mention, or #hashtag, if it contains an emoji, its NE and POS tag classification by NTLK.

Additional features have been experimented with and their results are included in section 4. These features include the last three characters of the word, whether it contains a digit (not if it is a digit itself), or if it is made up of exclusively ASCII characters.

3.2 Deep / Wide Model

The deep and wide architectures have had recent success for the use of recommendation engines (Cheng et al., 2016), but here we adapt it for the use of NER. Deep and wide architectures have the benefit of embedding categorical variables in a vector space allowing for unseen feature combinations and the use of cross-product feature transformations for effective and interpretable features. This combination of cross-product feature combinations and dense embeddings allows for deep and wide models to memorize and generalize to the input data while reducing feature engineering efforts.

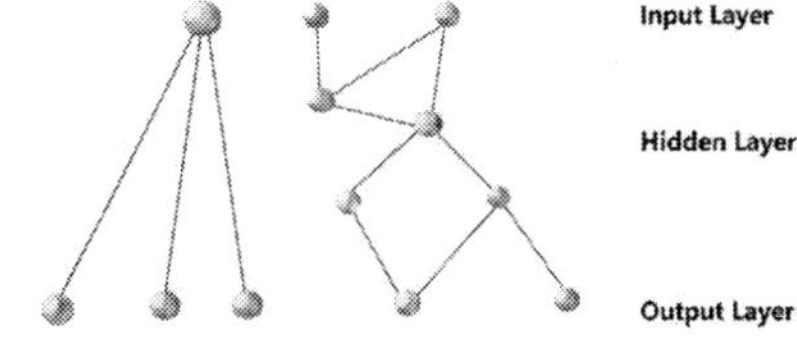

Figure 1: layers in wide (left) and deep (right) models

3.2.1 Training process

The model was trained using Tensorflow, an open-source machine learning framework designed by Google (Abadi et al., 2016). The classifier provides a general purpose wide and deep learning model for users to train. The wide model is a pre-built linear classifier which attempts to classify each word in a particular tweet based on values from their linear combinations.

The deep model used a pre-built neural network to classify the data by letting its features propagate through the network. Using Python, Tweets from the tsv file were first parsed into a internal data model where the features are computed as properties of the individual words. The model outputs a csv file with each feature listed as a column that can be conveniently passed to the `DNNLinearCombinedClassifier`. We used a subset of the CRF features including the word itself, capitalization of the word, word type, and the adjacent words.

The wide portion of the model enables NER tagging through linear properties. Features were inputted as the base column to provide information to the activation layer of the neural network. Some features such as the word, word's capitalization, word's type were cross validated as a set and hence would make the model recognize that these grouped features would have dependencies among themselves. Implementing a neural network, the deep model greatly increased the training time with a ratio of roughly 1:20 per iteration. The models did not perform well against the CRF possibly due to a lack of features, hence the CRF was used in the final submission of the project.

4   Results & Analysis

4.1   CRF Performance

Our submission for the shared task was evaluated using both the harmonic mean F1 and the surface forms F1 metrics (Derczynski et al., 2017) on each dataset. In line with the baseline performance, our system performs better on the MSA-EGY data than the ENG-SPA data despite the difference in data size. The scores on the two challenges were 65.62 for MSA-EGY and 54.16 for ENG-SPA. After the shared task submission closed, we continued experimenting with different features. The F1-scores (computed using scikit-learn (Pedregosa et al., 2011)) of the CRF trained on the training data set and evaluated on the testing set using various configurations of features are shown in table 2. These results are different from those submitted to the competition as they were evaluated on a different data set.

Inclusion or omission of certain features affected the two sets of data differently: for example including the ASCII feature improves scores for ENG-SPA but decreases that for MSA-EGY. The last row (special) shows an attempt to maximize the score by combining successful individual features and while scores do increase, this attempt does not perform as well as expected. For ENG-SPA the submitted configuration excluding POS and NE seems to work best while the submitted configuration with a combination of changes (shown in table 1) works best for MSA-EGY going by F1-score.

Table 1 shows the features that were modified for use. An asterisk (*) indicates that this is a change compared to the submitted configuration *a*. Rows not included are features that remained unchanged throughout.

4.2   NN Performance

As shown in table 3, the F1-score was suboptimal due to a low recall score. Two different models, one implementing only the wide portion and the other implementing the deep and wide models were trained with features extracted from the data set. Three different variants of the features and the results are displayed in table 2. Surprisingly, the wide model showed an overall better performance than the wide and deep model. This may be due to a lack of the features extracted from the dataset for the deep learning to build on. The lack of recall may occur due to the same reason, which eventually leads to the rejection of this model.

5   Conclusion

In this paper, we described the University of Texas BATs research group's submission for the CALCS 2018 Shared Task for NER. We found that some features improved results of the CRF model on one language combination, but not on the other. In both cases, our CRF model outperformed the baseline NER performance. However, training an NN using the same features as the CRF did not significantly improve F1-scores, but further feature engineering on or combination of both models could improve the performance.

Features	ENG-SPA								MSA-EGY							
	a	b	c	d	e	f	g	h	a	b	c	d	e	f	g	h
en prob	✓	✓	*	✓	✓	✓	✓									
es prob	✓	✓	*	✓	✓	✓	✓									
ar prob											✓*					✓*
last 3 chars		✓*						✓*		✓*						✓*
has emoji	✓	✓	✓	✓	*	✓	✓	*	✓	✓	✓	✓	*	✓	✓	*
ascii				✓*				✓*				✓*				
NE	✓	✓	✓	✓	✓	*	✓	*	✓	✓	✓	✓	✓	*	✓	*
POS	✓	✓	✓	✓	✓	*	✓	*	✓	✓	✓	✓	✓	*	✓	*
two words							✓*		✓	✓	✓	✓	✓	✓	*	✓

Table 1: Feature configurations

Configuration	ENG-SPA			MSA-EGY		
	precision	recall	F1-score	precision	recall	F1-score
a (submission)	0.69	0.25	0.32	0.86	0.68	0.76
b (include last 3 characters)	0.67	0.26	0.33	0.84	0.7	0.76
c (toggle language probabilities)	0.49	0.24	0.31	0.86	0.68	0.76
d (check for ascii)	0.73	0.25	0.34	0.86	0.67	0.75
e (no emoji)	0.71	0.25	0.33	0.87	0.68	0.76
f (exclude POS and NE tags)	0.69	0.27	0.34	0.86	0.68	0.76
g (toggle surrounding two words)	0.50	0.23	0.30	0.84	0.65	0.73
h (special)	0.63	0.27	0.33	0.84	0.71	0.77

Table 2: Performance of CRF on various configurations

Configuration	ENG-SPA (Wide model only)			ENG-SPA (Deep + Wide model)		
	precision	recall	F1-score	precision	recall	F1-score
original	0.23	0.03	0.05	0.22	0.0373	0.06
excluding next word	0.28	0.04	0.07	0.13	0.02	0.03
excluding next word and length	0.31	0.04	0.07	0.13	0.03	0.05

Table 3: Performance of NN on various configurations

References

Martín Abadi, Paul Barham, Jianmin Chen, Zhifeng Chen, Andy Davis, Jeffrey Dean, Matthieu Devin, Sanjay Ghemawat, Geoffrey Irving, Michael Isard, et al. 2016. Tensorflow: A system for large-scale machine learning. In *OSDI*, volume 16, pages 265–283.

Gustavo Aguilar, Fahad AlGhamdi, Victor Soto, Mona Diab, Julia Hirschberg, and Thamar Solorio. 2018. Overview of the CALCS 2018 Shared Task: Named Entity Recognition on Code-switched Data. In *Proceedings of the Third Workshop on Computational Approaches to Linguistic Code-Switching*, Melbourne, Australia. Association for Computational Linguistics.

Steven Bird and Edward Loper. 2004. Nltk: the natural language toolkit. In *Proceedings of the ACL 2004 on Interactive poster and demonstration sessions*, page 31. Association for Computational Linguistics.

Özlem Çetinoglu. 2016. A turkish-german code-switching corpus. In *LREC*.

Heng-Tze Cheng, Levent Koc, Jeremiah Harmsen, Tal Shaked, Tushar Chandra, Hrishi Aradhye, Glen Anderson, Greg Corrado, Wei Chai, Mustafa Ispir, Rohan Anil, Zakaria Haque, Lichan Hong, Vihan Jain, Xiaobing Liu, and Hemal Shah. 2016. Wide & deep learning for recommender systems. In *Proceedings of the 1st Workshop on Deep Learning for Recommender Systems*, DLRS 2016, pages 7–10, New York, NY, USA. ACM.

Gokul Chittaranjan, Yogarshi Vyas, Kalika Bali, and Monojit Choudhury. 2014. Word-level language identification using crf: Code-switching shared task report of msr india system. In *Proceedings of The First Workshop on Computational Approaches to Code Switching*, pages 73–79.

Michal Danilák. 2017. Python port of google language detection library.

Leon Derczynski, Eric Nichols, Marieke van Erp, and Nut Limsopatham. 2017. Results of the wnut2017 shared task on novel and emerging entity recognition. In *Proceedings of the 3rd Workshop on Noisy User-generated Text*, pages 140–147. Association for Computational Linguistics.

Gualberto Guzmán, Joseph Ricard, Jacqueline Serigos, Barbara E Bullock, and Almeida Jacqueline Toribio. 2017. Metrics for modeling code-switching across corpora. *Proc. Interspeech 2017*, pages 67–71.

Gualberto A Guzman, Jacqueline Serigos, Barbara E Bullock, and Almeida Jacqueline Toribio. 2016. Simple tools for exploring variation in code-switching for linguists. In *Proceedings of the Second Workshop on Computational Approaches to Code Switching*, pages 12–20.

Anupam Jamatia, Björn Gambäck, and Amitava Das. 2015. Part-of-speech tagging for code-mixed english-hindi twitter and facebook chat messages. In *Proceedings of the International Conference Recent Advances in Natural Language Processing*, pages 239–248.

Anupam Jamatia, Björn Gambäck, and Amitava Das. 2016. Collecting and annotating indian social media code-mixed corpora. In *the 17th International Conference on Intelligent Text Processing and Computational Linguistics*, pages 3–9.

David Jurgens, Stefan Dimitrov, and Derek Ruths. 2014. Twitter users# codeswitch hashtags!# moltoimportante# wow. In *Proceedings of the First Workshop on Computational Approaches to Code Switching*, pages 51–61.

John Lafferty, Andrew McCallum, and Fernando CN Pereira. 2001. Conditional random fields: Probabilistic models for segmenting and labeling sequence data.

Chu-Cheng Lin, Waleed Ammar, Lori Levin, and Chris Dyer. 2014. The cmu submission for the shared task on language identification in code-switched data. In *Proceedings of the First Workshop on Computational Approaches to Code Switching*, pages 80–86.

David Nadeau and Satoshi Sekine. 2007. A survey of named entity recognition and classification. *Lingvisticae Investigationes*, 30(1):3–26.

Shuyo Nakatani. 2010. Language detection library for java.

Naoaki Okazaki. 2007. Crfsuite: a fast implementation of conditional random fields (crfs).

F. Pedregosa, G. Varoquaux, A. Gramfort, V. Michel, B. Thirion, O. Grisel, M. Blondel, P. Prettenhofer, R. Weiss, V. Dubourg, J. Vanderplas, A. Passos, D. Cournapeau, M. Brucher, M. Perrot, and E. Duchesnay. 2011. Scikit-learn: Machine learning in Python. *Journal of Machine Learning Research*, 12:2825–2830.

Terry Peng and Mikhail Korobov. 2014. python-crfsuite. https://python-crfsuite.readthedocs.org/.

Kashif Riaz. 2010. Rule-based named entity recognition in urdu. In *Proceedings of the 2010 named entities workshop*, pages 126–135. Association for Computational Linguistics.

Sunayana Sitaram and Alan W Black. 2016. Speech synthesis of code-mixed text. In *LREC*.

David Vilares, Miguel A Alonso, and Carlos Gómez-Rodríguez. 2015. Sentiment analysis on monolingual, multilingual and code-switching twitter corpora. In *Proceedings of the 6th Workshop on Computational Approaches to Subjectivity, Sentiment and Social Media Analysis*, pages 2–8.

Ayah Zirikly and Mona Diab. 2015. Named entity recognition for arabic social media. In *Proceedings of the 1st Workshop on Vector Space Modeling for Natural Language Processing*, pages 176–185.

Tackling Code-Switched NER: Participation of CMU

[*,0]Parvathy Geetha   [+,0]Khyathi Raghavi Chandu   [+]Alan W Black

[*]Electrical and Computer Engineering, [+]Language Technologies Institute
Carnegie Mellon University
{pgeetha, kchandu, awb}@andrew.cmu.edu

Abstract

Named Entity Recognition plays a major role in several downstream applications in NLP. Though this task has been heavily studied in formal monolingual texts and also noisy texts like Twitter data, it is still an emerging task in code-switched (CS) content on social media. This paper describes our participation in the shared task of *NER on code-switched data* for Spanglish (Spanish + English) and Arabish (Arabic + English). In this paper we describe models that intuitively developed from the data for the shared task *Named Entity Recognition on Code-switched Data*. Owing to the sparse and non-linear relationships between words in Twitter data, we explored neural architectures that are capable of non-linearities fairly well. In specific, we trained character level models and word level models based on Bidirectional LSTMs (Bi-LSTMs) to perform sequential tagging. We trained multiple models to identify nominal mentions and subsequently used this information to predict the labels of named entity in a sequence. Our best model is a character level model along with word level pre-trained multilingual embeddings that gave an F-score of 56.72 in Spanglish and a word level model that gave an F-score of 65.02 in Arabish on the test data.

1 Introduction

Named Entity Recognition (NER) is a challenging and one of the most fundamental tasks in NLP. NER not only has stand alone applications including search and retrieval but also aids as a prior step for downstream NLP applications like question answering and dialog state tracking. It has been fairly researched in the community using both supervised (Azpeitia et al., 2014) and semi-supervised (Nadeau, 2007), (Nadeau, 2007) techniques. Moreover, this has also been studied on multiple languages including English (Lample et al., 2016), Spanish (Zea et al., 2016) and Arabic (Shaalan, 2014). The task is projected into an even complex space when there are words from multiple languages interleaved within and between sentences. This phenomenon is commonly known as code switching (CS).

CS is typically used in informal or semi-formal communication and social media stages an accessible platform to interact in this manner. This also comes with additional nuances observed in social media text that can be broadly characterized as noisy text with spelling errors and ungrammatical constructions. Often, the shorthand representations observed in this data are non-standardized and are one to many functions of standard spelling to a non-standard spelling. This makes this task significantly different from NER on formal monolingual texts and the techniques are not directly transferable to the domain of CS text. Supervised techniques to address the task in the domain of noisy texts such as Twitter have been explored (Ritter et al., 2011), (Tran et al., 2017). We leverage these techniques in order to deal with the sparse distribution of entities.

In this paper, we discuss the techniques used from the participation of our team in the shared task of *Named Entity Recognition of Code-switched Data* (Aguilar et al., 2018). We model the problem at both word and character levels along with attempting attention mechanism. We discuss the intuitions from the data that motivate the models. We have also explored ensembling multiple models that cater to identification of the named entity and labeling it with a tag. Our best performing system is the combination of character and word level representations (using pre-trained

---

[0]Denotes equal contribution

Proceedings of The Third Workshop on Computational Approaches to Code-Switching, pages 126–131
Melbourne, Australia, July 19, 2018. ©2018 Association for Computational Linguistics

Criteria	Spanglish			Arabish		
	Train	Dev	Test	Train	Dev	Test
# Tweets	41,024	832	15,634	10,091	1,121	1,110
# Unique Words	57,892	2,559	27,756	44,024	9,800	9,316
# Unique NEs	4,788	156	-	4,435	1,107	-
OOV with Train (%)	0	18.67	52.16	0	30.76	40.79
OOV of NEs with Train (%)	0	62.82	-	0	25.92	-
OOV with MUSE (%)	64.43	20.94	57.23	99.74	99.82	97.44
OOV of NEs with MUSE (%)	17.41	5.76	-	97.74	99.90	-

Table 1: Data Analysis

multilingual embeddings) in a Bi-LSTM that resulted in an F1 score of 56.72 in Spanglish and a word level Bi-LSTM that gave an F1 of 65.02 in Arabish.

2 Related Work

NER is a fairly well researched topic and a lot of literature (Nadeau and Sekine, 2007) is available with regard to this. In this section we focus and present a comprehensive overview of the techniques that lay motivations to our models and experiments.

While traditionally hand crafted features are reliably used (Carreras et al., 2002), neural models have recently been emerging as effective techniques to perform the task. This is owed to the substantial reduction of manual expense in building hand-crafted features for each language. Qi et al. (2009) leverages unannotated sentences to improve supervised classification tasks using Word-Class Distribution Learning. Passos et al. (2014) were among the first to use a neural network to learn word embeddings that leverage information from related lexicon to perform NER. Collobert et al. (2011) used convolution for embeddings with a CRF layer to attain alongside benchmarking several NLP tasks including NER. Lample et al. (2016) achieves the state-of-the-art performance on 4 languages by training models based on BiLSTM and CRF by using word representations from unannotated text and character representations from annotated text. This work has been extended to transfer settings by Bharadwaj et al. (2016) to multiple languages by representing word sequences in IPA. Huang et al. (2015) use a BiLSTM with a CRF layer in addition to making use of explicit spelling and context features along with word embeddings.

Aguilar et al. (2017) use a character level CNN followed by a word level Bi-LSTM in a multi-task learning setting and also emphasize the importance of gazetteer lists for the task. Multilingual NER on informal text in Twitter was also studied by Etter et al. (2013). Zirikly and Diab (2015)

explore the impact of embeddings and representations of words without gazetteer features on NER for social media text in Arabic. Luo et al. (2017) have also shown that attention based Bi-LSTM with additional architecture achieves higher performance than other state-of-the-art techniques to recognize chemical named entities which lean to low resource settings. We hypothesize that CS also belongs to low resource settings and explore the impact of attention. The task of NER becomes harder especially in low resource settings (Tsai et al., 2017), which is similar to CS setting.

3 Data Analysis

Code-switching is more prominently observed in informal communication which is observed in social media platforms. Hence the organizers of the shared task (Aguilar et al., 2018) have provided us with English-Spanish (ENG-SPA) and Arabic-English (MSA-EGY) tweets. In this section, we present an overlap analysis of the tweets from the train and the development set that lead to intuitions of model performance.

An important characteristic of the nature of social media data is that the named entities are very sparse. While table 1 shows that the training data is comprised of 8.27% of unique named entities, we observe that 2.93% of overall surface form distribution belong to named entities. This number is significantly smaller than the number of named entities found in formal texts traditionally used for training this task. For instance, a widely standardized and accepted dataset that is proposed by Tjong Kim Sang and De Meulder (2003) for monolingual English contains 15.04% tagged named entities. This makes the task harder in social media settings.

In order to analyze the distribution of named entities across the different splits in the data, we look at the out of vocabulary (OOV) percentages with respect to different sources. This is performed to estimate the significance of that particular source with respect to the task at hand. There is quite a high OOV percentage of named entities from the training data.

In Section 4 we elaborate on leveraging pre-trained multilingual embeddings MUSE (Multi-lingual Unsupervised or Supervised word Embeddings) (Conneau et al., 2017) which contain multilingual embeddings based on Fast Text (Bojanowski et al., 2016). Table 1 presents these statistics which helps provide intuitions on the approach that needs to be taken for this data. For Spanglish data, there are 62.82% of named entities that are not present in training data and 5.76% that are not present in the development data.

4 Models and Intuitions

Based on the three main observations in Section 3, we frame the following intuitions to build our model architectures.

- *Sparsity of named entities:* Training a model that classifies nominal entities from their counterparts and using this information to tag them.
- *High OOV with training data:*
  - Character level models that are capable of capturing sequential sub-word level information
  - External knowledge sources like gazetteer lists and/or pre-trained word embeddings such as MUSE.

4.1 Model Architecture

The first architecture is a simple bidirectional LSTM (Bi-LSTM) at word level that captures sequential context information. In addition to this, the second model also needs to learn sub-word level information that is based on characters of words. Soft combinations of character sequences act as a proxy to the valid sequences of phonemes allowed by a sentence. We have not used phonetic features directly as performed by Bharadwaj et al. (2016) due to the noisy nature of the text with multiple instances of shorthand notations. However, we believe that this is an interesting direction and plan to explore this beyond the scope of this paper.

Recurrent Neural Networks (RNNs) model sequential data and are capable of transforming the current sequence into latent space. In our case, the former is a sequence of words and the latter is a sequence of Named Entity tags. While in theory, RNNs are capable of learning dependencies ranging over long distances, in practice this is hindered due to vanishing or exploding gradients. Alternatively, a variant of this model, LSTM (Gers et al., 1999) is used to model the influence of the longer range dependencies since it maintains a memory

cell. At this point, we have a couple of options to feed into this network. The first is to directly feed the words into a Bi-LSTM and the second is to include character level information as well.

In each word, each of the characters has a 50 dimensional embedding (let it be e). We pass it through an LSTM to get the latent representation z of the word, over which a $tanh$ non-linearity is applied. This character level modeling of the word is concatenated with the 200 dimensional word lookup embeddings to form the final word level representation. These final modified word embeddings are fed into a Bi-LSTM which computes a hidden left context representation $\overrightarrow{h_t}$ and hidden right context representation $\overleftarrow{h_t}$ which are concatenated. Finally, this is fed into a fully connected layer with a cross entropy loss function to predict the sequence of tags. All the weights in the model are initialized with Xavier distribution. The model is trained with an Adam optimizer for minimum validation loss for 10 epochs.

We then extended the model to explore the effect of attention over the Bi-LSTM model but it did not show any improvements over the base model.

Classifying Nominalization:

To deal with the problem of sparse distribution of named entities, we model the problem in 2 phases. The first phase is a binary classification of named entities in a sequence of words. The second phase is to add additional features based on the prediction of the first network to the embeddings in the second network to label the tags. We intentionally used the same network architecture excepting for the final transformation layer to predict the tags. This is because we intend to pose this as a Multi Task Learning (MTL) problem (Collobert and Weston, 2008), where we can share the bottom layers so the network can generalize better with sparse distribution of tags. This idea is similar to the work by Aguilar et al. (2017) but we restrict to predicting the named entities since we do not have POS information of the words. We present the results of hierarchical phase formulation of this method in Table 2 and leave the end to end MTL training (where the first task is predicting whether it is an NE and the second task is predicting the tag of NE which are jointly trained) for future work.

Pre-trained multilingual Embeddings: Since the data is too sparse, we leveraged pre-trained multilingual word embeddings that are trained based on fastText embeddings (Conneau et al., 2017) and are aligned across multiple languages.

Models/Metrics		Spanglish		Arabish
	Entity	Surface Form	Entity	Surface Form
Word Bi-LSTM	52.34	51.34	**73.05**	**60.80**
Char Bi-LSTM + Word Bi-LSTM	50.22	50.95	73.95	61.38
Pre-trained MUSE + Char Bi-LSTM + Word Bi-LSTM	**54.47**	**53.27**	64.38	47.23
Attention + Word Bi-LSTM	36.50	35.19	68.11	53.86
NE v non-NE + Char Bi-LSTM + Word Bi-LSTM	49.48	49.61	70.70	10.87

Table 2: F scores of different models motivated by intuitions from the data

This boosted the F score by 2 points which is comparatively better performing model in our space of models.

5 Results and Discussion

We have tried different models based on the intuitions from this domain of data that are explained in Section 4. The F1 scores of these different architectures are presented in table 2 for both Spanglish and Arabish. As it is observed from the data, the model that performed best is the character level model with pre-trained MUSE embeddings (Conneau et al., 2017) and a word level Bi-LSTM for Spanglish data. However, this is not the case with Arabish data where a simple word level Bi-LSTM performed better. This can be explained from Table 1 as there are 99.82% of vocabulary that is not present in the MUSE embeddings.

Based on automatic as well as a brief manual analysis of the entity wise scores on the development set, we identify that our models do not perform very well on TITLE entities. One interesting challenge for this category is that the word level composition of the entities comprise of several common terms. Examples of this include *'High School Musical'*, *'Oh My God'* etc., which are very hard to be identified as named entities. This category can co-occur in similar contexts of other named entities. For example *'Keep calm and enjoy your GYPSY SUMMER'*, where *'GYPSY SUMMER'* is a named entity (which could have easily been *'drink'*).

We annotated the development data to understand and motivate the need to build an NER for CS contexts as opposed to using monolingual NERs. The annotation is done in the perspective of whether the words belong to one of the following 4 categories: *English*, *Spanish*, *Mixed* and *Ambiguous*, which are 156, 54, 4 and 5 respectively. This might give a naive impression that an NER trained on English is sufficient to perform reasonably well for this data as well. This in in contrary to the results that Stanford NER (Finkel et al., 2005) performed on this data by giving an Entity F1 of 10.89 and Surface F1 of 11.96. Hence we need to train the models explicitly for the switched language by treating it as a new language or by transferring learning from both the individual languages.

As described in Section 4, we experimented with combining multiple neural models performing different tasks (predicting a binary named entity or not, and labeling the sequence). This model did not improve the performance on development set. The binary model predicts 42 named entities correctly that the best model is unable to capture in comparison to 16 by the character model. However, the binary model gets a lot of false positives in the sense that 39 tokens are predicted as named entities incorrectly while this number for the embedding model is 7. The possible solution to leverage this model more accurately is either thresholding the softmax scores of the binary model to only get the predictions of named entities with high confidence or perform MTL where weights are updated by the loss from both the tasks.

The huge gap between entity and surface form for the Arabish data that is observed by the character model along with the binary features (based on the predictions of whether it is an NE or not), is due to a large number of invalid sequences.

Among the true named entities that are wrongly predicted in Spanglish data, 154 of them are occurring in training data. This implies that the context information can be leveraged better to improve the models since the contexts in which these entities are embedded are very broad.

6 Conclusion and Future Work

Developing intuitions from the data to build models is necessary for domains that do not have other NLP tools such POS taggers, parsers etc,. Based on these intuitions, a character level model along with pre-trained multilingual word embeddings from MUSE with a Bi-LSTM has given an F score of 56.72 on Spanglish and word level Bi-LSTM that gave an F score of 65.02 on Arabish. We believe that there is a lot of potential in exploring the attention model in synergy with predicting whether a term is named entity or not as a Multi Task Learning problem.

Language/Metrics		Event	Group	Location	Org	Other	Person	Product	Time	Title
Spanglish	Entity	0.00	33.33	57.14	30.77	0.00	69.57	60.00	28.57	0.00
	Surface Form	0.00	33.33	57.14	36.36	0.00	68.29	55.56	33.33	0.00
Arabish	Entity	51.85	71.73	74.97	57.61	68.75	81.89	64.22	66.67	56.74
	Surface Form	42.11	58.43	57.71	48.73	42.86	71.55	53.57	59.70	52.76

Table 3: F scores of best models for Spanglish and Arabish

References

Gustavo Aguilar, Fahad AlGhamdi, Victor Soto, Mona Diab, Julia Hirschberg, and Thamar Solorio. 2018. Overview of the CALCS 2018 Shared Task: Named Entity Recognition on Code-switched Data. In *Proceedings of the Third Workshop on Computational Approaches to Linguistic Code-Switching*, Melbourne, Australia. Association for Computational Linguistics.

Gustavo Aguilar, Suraj Maharjan, Adrian Pastor López Monroy, and Thamar Solorio. 2017. A multi-task approach for named entity recognition in social media data. In *Proceedings of the 3rd Workshop on Noisy User-generated Text*, pages 148–153.

Andoni Azpeitia, Montse Cuadros, Seán Gaines, and German Rigau. 2014. Nerc-fr: supervised named entity recognition for french. In *International Conference on Text, Speech, and Dialogue*, pages 158–165. Springer.

Akash Bharadwaj, David Mortensen, Chris Dyer, and Jaime Carbonell. 2016. Phonologically aware neural model for named entity recognition in low resource transfer settings. In *Proceedings of the 2016 Conference on Empirical Methods in Natural Language Processing*, pages 1462–1472.

Piotr Bojanowski, Edouard Grave, Armand Joulin, and Tomas Mikolov. 2016. Enriching word vectors with subword information. *arXiv preprint arXiv:1607.04606*.

Xavier Carreras, Lluis Marquez, and Lluís Padró. 2002. Named entity extraction using adaboost. In *proceedings of the 6th conference on Natural language learning-Volume 20*, pages 1–4. Association for Computational Linguistics.

Ronan Collobert and Jason Weston. 2008. A unified architecture for natural language processing: Deep neural networks with multitask learning. In *Proceedings of the 25th international conference on Machine learning*, pages 160–167. ACM.

Ronan Collobert, Jason Weston, Léon Bottou, Michael Karlen, Koray Kavukcuoglu, and Pavel Kuksa. 2011. Natural language processing (almost) from scratch. *Journal of Machine Learning Research*, 12(Aug):2493–2537.

Alexis Conneau, Guillaume Lample, Marc'Aurelio Ranzato, Ludovic Denoyer, and Hervé Jégou. 2017. Word translation without parallel data. *arXiv preprint arXiv:1710.04087*.

David Etter, Francis Ferraro, Ryan Cotterell, Olivia Buzek, and Benjamin Van Durme. 2013. Nerit: Named entity recognition for informal text. *The Johns Hopkins University, the Human Language Technology Center of Excellence, HLTCOE 810Wyman Park Drive Baltimore, Maryland 21211, Tech. Rep.*

Jenny Rose Finkel, Trond Grenager, and Christopher Manning. 2005. Incorporating non-local information into information extraction systems by gibbs sampling. In *Proceedings of the 43rd annual meeting on association for computational linguistics*, pages 363–370. Association for Computational Linguistics.

Felix A Gers, Jürgen Schmidhuber, and Fred Cummins. 1999. Learning to forget: Continual prediction with lstm.

Zhiheng Huang, Wei Xu, and Kai Yu. 2015. Bidirectional lstm-crf models for sequence tagging. *arXiv preprint arXiv:1508.01991*.

Guillaume Lample, Miguel Ballesteros, Sandeep Subramanian, Kazuya Kawakami, and Chris Dyer. 2016. Neural architectures for named entity recognition. *arXiv preprint arXiv:1603.01360*.

L Luo, Z Yang, P Yang, Y Zhang, L Wang, H Lin, and J Wang. 2017. An attention-based bilstm-crf approach to document-level chemical named entity recognition. *Bioinformatics (Oxford, England)*.

David Nadeau. 2007. *Semi-supervised named entity recognition: learning to recognize 100 entity types with little supervision*. Ph.D. thesis, University of Ottawa.

David Nadeau and Satoshi Sekine. 2007. A survey of named entity recognition and classification. *Lingvisticae Investigationes*, 30(1):3–26.

Alexandre Passos, Vineet Kumar, and Andrew McCallum. 2014. Lexicon infused phrase embeddings for named entity resolution. *arXiv preprint arXiv:1404.5367*.

Yanjun Qi, Ronan Collobert, Pavel Kuksa, Koray Kavukcuoglu, and Jason Weston. 2009. Combining labeled and unlabeled data with word-class distribution learning. In *Proceedings of the 18th ACM conference on Information and knowledge management*, pages 1737–1740. ACM.

Alan Ritter, Sam Clark, Oren Etzioni, et al. 2011. Named entity recognition in tweets: an experimental study. In *Proceedings of the conference on empirical methods in natural language processing*, pages 1524–1534. Association for Computational Linguistics.

Khaled Shaalan. 2014. A survey of arabic named entity recognition and classification. *Computational Linguistics*, 40(2):469–510.

Erik F Tjong Kim Sang and Fien De Meulder. 2003. Introduction to the conll-2003 shared task: Language-independent named entity recognition. In *Proceedings of the seventh conference on Natural language learning at HLT-NAACL 2003-Volume 4*, pages 142–147. Association for Computational Linguistics.

Van Cuong Tran, Ngoc Thanh Nguyen, Hamido Fujita, Dinh Tuyen Hoang, and Dosam Hwang. 2017. A combination of active learning and self-learning for named entity recognition on twitter using conditional random fields. *Knowledge-Based Systems*, 132:179–187.

Chen-Tse Tsai, Stephen Mayhew, Yangqiu Song, Mark Sammons, and Dan Roth. 2017. Illinois ccg lorehlt 2016 nmed entity recognition nd sitution frme systems. *Machine Translation*, pages 1–13.

Jenny Linet Copara Zea, Jose Eduardo Ochoa Luna, Camilo Thorne, and Goran Glavaš. 2016. Spanish ner with word representations and conditional random fields. In *Proceedings of the Sixth Named Entity Workshop*, pages 34–40.

Ayah Zirikly and Mona Diab. 2015. Named entity recognition for arabic social media. In *Proceedings of the 1st Workshop on Vector Space Modeling for Natural Language Processing*, pages 176–185.

7 Supplementary Information

The Table 3 shows category wise F scores for the experiments that gave the best results for Spanglish (the model is trained using pre-trained MUSE embeddings with a character level Bi-LSTM and a word level Bi-LSTM) and Arabish (a simple word level Bi-LSTM), which are discussed in detail in the paper.

Multilingual Named Entity Recognition on Spanish-English Code-switched Tweets using Support Vector Machines

Daniel Claeser
Fraunhofer FKIE
Fraunhoferstraße 20
53343 Wachtberg
daniel.claeser@
fkie.fraunhofer.de

Samantha Kent
Fraunhofer FKIE
Fraunhoferstraße 20
53343 Wachtberg
samantha.kent@
fkie.fraunhofer.de

Dennis Felske
Fraunhofer FKIE
Fraunhoferstraße 20
53343 Wachtberg
dennis.felske@
fkie.fraunhofer.de

Abstract

This paper describes our system submission for the ACL 2018 shared task on named entity recognition (NER) in code-switched Twitter data. Our best result (F1 = 53.65) was obtained using a Support Vector Machine (SVM) with 14 features combined with rule-based post-processing.

1 Introduction

Named Entity Recognition (NER) is a part of information extraction and refers to the automatic identification of named entities in text. The ACL 2018 shared task invited participants to extract and classify the following named entities in code-switched data obtained from Twitter: person, location, organization, group, title, product, event, time, and other (Aguilar et al., 2018). The Tweets are either Spanish-English or Modern Standard Arabic-Egyptian, and participants were free to participate in either language pair. This paper describes our system for the Spanish-English NER task.

This particular NER task is challenging for two reasons. Firstly, NER has proved to be more difficult for Tweets than for longer text, as accuracy in NER ranges from 85-90% on longer texts compared to 30-50% on Tweets (Derczynski et al., 2015). One of the reasons for this difference is that Tweets contain non-standard spelling, unusual punctuation, and unreliable capitalization. Fromheide et al. (2014) also point out that another difficulty stems from the rapidly changing topics and linguistic conventions on Twitter. The 2015 and 2016 shared tasks for NER on Noisy User-generated Text (W-NUT) reported F1 scores between 16.47 and 52.41 for identifying 10 different NE categories (Baldwin et al., 2015; Strauss et al.,

2016). NER methods range from bidirectional long short-term memory (LSTM) (Limsopatham and Collier, 2016) and Conditional Random Fields (CRF) (Toh et al., 2015), to Named Entity Linking (Yamada et al., 2015). The second added challenge for the data in this task is that the Tweets contain English and Spanish named entities. Both languages need to be taken into account in order to accurately identify the NEs in this data.

2 Data sets

The organizers provided three different English-Spanish data sets: a training set, a development set, and a test set. The data consists of multilingual Spanish-English Tweets and contains NEs in both languages. Table 1 provides an overview of the data and the total number of NEs available in each of the sets (Aguilar et al., 2018). The gold standard for the test set was not distributed and we are therefore not aware of the distribution of NEs in the test set.

Data set	#Tweets	#Tokens	#NEs
Train	50,757	616,069	12,366
Development	832	9583	152
Test	15,634	183,011	-

Table 1: Number of Tweets, tokens and Named Entities in the Spanish-English data sets.

3 System description

We used scikit-learn 0.19 (Pedregosa et al., 2011) to train and test five different types of classifiers using eight-fold cross validation:

- Support Vector Machine (SVM) (Chang and Lin, 2011)
- Decision Trees (DT)

Proceedings of The Third Workshop on Computational Approaches to Code-Switching, pages 132–137
Melbourne, Australia, July 19, 2018. ©2018 Association for Computational Linguistics

- K-nearest Neighbors (KNN)

- AdaBoost (Ada) (Freund and Schapire, 1995)

- Random Forest (RF) (Breiman, 2001)

We trained the classifiers with different training corpus sizes of 80.000, 120.000, 200.000, 300.000 and 550.000 tokens, and we reserved 10% of each size for testing to avoid overfitting on the training data. The best classifier is the Support Vector Machine using the default scikit-learn parameters and a Radial Basis Function (RBF) Kernel, which is defined as

$$K(x, x') = exp(-\frac{\|x - x'\|^2}{2\sigma^2}) \qquad (1)$$

The results are obtained using the pre- and post-processing steps that are described in further detail in sections 3.1 and 3.3.

3.1 Pre-processing

Early experiments showed that reducing the original tag set from two tags per category to one tag per category improved overall classification. 'B-LOC' refers to either the first word in a multi-word NE or a single word NE, and 'I-LOC' refers to any tokens in a multi-word NE that follows the initial 'B-' token. The information specific to the location of the NE within an NE sequence was removed and both tags are reduced to 'X-'. This improved classification performance as it reduced the number of different possible tags from 19 to 10 (one per NE category plus the "O" tag) and was easily reverted in the post-processing stage.

3.2 Feature selection

After testing numerous different features, and discarding ones such as 'proceeded by preposition or possessive pronoun' and 'difference in rank in the frequency dictionaries', we found that the features described below achieved the best result. There are three different types of features: token-centered features (1-5), context related features (6-9), and rank dictionary lookup features (10-14). To reduce dimensionality and computational workload, we condensed several mutually exclusive boolean features into common functions returning different integer values according to their outcome. For example, for the capitalization feature, rather than returning a boolean outcome for each of the four possible capitalization options (all lowercase, all uppercase length greater than 3, all

uppercase length less than 3, first letter capitalized), they are combined into one feature that returns [0,1,2,3].

All rank features are obtained by sorting the corresponding list in order of frequency, with the most frequent occurrence in rank one. We normalized the ranks so that the value stays between 0 and 1, where 0 denotes the absence in the ranked lists and the closer the figure is to 1, the more highly ranked the token is.

For each feature, the possible outcomes that are inserted into the vector are provided in square brackets, where 'int' denotes the absolute rank, pairs of [0-1] boolean outcomes, and lists of numbers correspond to the exclusive outcomes of the function.

1. *Capitalization* – Check if the token is: all lowercase, all uppercase with length greater than 3, all uppercase with length less or equal to 3, or first letter only uppercase [0,1,2,3]

2. *Token length* - Returns the token-length [int]

3. *Contains non-ASCII* - Does the token contain non-ASCII characters? [0,1]

4. *Token first or last in Tweet* - Check if token is: first token, last token, or other [0,1,2]

5. *Token in majority language* - Check if the token language is the majority language of the tweet. Determined with a lexical lookup in frequency-ranked word lists for English and Spanish extracted from Wikipedia [0,1] (Claeser et al., 2018)

6. *Code-switch* - Returns true if the token's language is different from that of the token before [0,1] (Claeser et al., 2018)

7. *Previously tagged as, single-word* - The most common tag associated with the token in the training set. The outcome is either one of the nine NE categories or the token is not present in the training data [0-9]

8. *Previously tagged as, multi-word* - Same as above but for multi-word expressions [0-9]

9. *Is multi-word time* - Regular expressions to capture multi-word time expressions such as '23 de mayo' and 'april 29th' [0,1]

10. *Rank in family names* - Rank in list of last names extracted from the Wikipedia page

'Living people' [int]

11. *Rank in first names* - Rank in list of first names extracted from the Wikipedia page 'Living people' [int]

12. *Rank in cities list* - Rank in list of all United States census designated places (2016) ordered descending by population [int]

13. *Rank in Spanish Dictionary* - Rank in word list from Spanish Wikipedia [int]

14. *Rank in English Dictionary* - Rank in word list from English Wikipedia [int]

3.3 Post-processing

The first step in post-processing was to restore all the named entity categories that were simplified during the training of the SVM. All categories were reduced, for example, from 'B-PER' and 'I-PER' to X-PER in a pre-processing step, and were changed back to the original annotation.

The second step in post-processing was to address the misclassified multi-word tokens. For example, in a sequence of 'B-TITLE', 'I-TITLE', 'I-TITLE', if the middle token is misclassified as not being an NE, the tags shift to 'B-TITLE', 'O', 'B-TITLE' and the entire multi-word NE would therefore be misclassified.

To solve this issue, we used a dictionary lookup approach and compared possible multi-word NE sequences to lists of multi-word tokens based on the types of tokens present in the training data. The '-GROUP', '-PERSON' and '-OTHER' lists stems from Wikipedia, and the '-TITLE' list contains titles of video games available from Steam. We found post-processing to be most effective when the multi-word NE consisted of at least two tokens and was no longer than five tokens. We started by checking the longest NEs first, so that, for example, 'Tomb Raider' would not split the longer NE 'Rise of the Tomb Raider'. If a match was found in any of the lists, the tags gained from post-processing replaced those tagged by the SVM.

The final step addresses specific tokens that are very frequent in many of the categories and are therefore not learned correctly by the classifiers. The Spanish particle 'de', was often classified as an NE, but should have been classified as 'O'. So, if 'de' was tagged as an NE, but not proceeded by a

Classifier	Macro F1	FB1
Support Vector Machine	0.49	0.48
Decision Tree	0.61	0.43
KNN	0.50	0.44
Random Forest	0.59	0.45
AdaBoost	0.41	0.39

Table 2: Results for the train/test set without post-processing (Macro F1) and the held-out test set (FB1).

token with a 'B-', the NE tag was removed. A similar rule applies to the article 'the', which was frequently tagged as 'O', and caused issues for multi-word NEs starting with 'the'. If 'the' is followed by a NE, the tag is switched to match the rest of the tokens in the multi-word sequence.

4 Results

Table 2 shows the best result obtained with a training size of 550.000 tokens for each of the five classifiers using 8-fold cross validation and the results of those five classifiers when applied to the held-out test data. Note that all figures are without post-processing. We only performed post-processing on the SVM to achieve the final result of 53.56. Table 2 shows that the Macro F1, which is the performance of the classifiers when splitting the training data into 90% train and 10% test, is higher for the Decision Tree, KNN and Random Forest classifiers. However, when applying the classifiers on the held-out test set, the FB1 is highest for the SVM. It is also clear that while a certain degree of overfitting is to be expected, it is much higher for the Decision Tree based classifiers than for the SVM. For the SVM, the Macro F1 and the FB1 is very similar, in contrast to the Decision Tree classifier where the difference is much larger.

Size	SVM	DT	KNN	RF	Ada
30k	0.25	0.33	0.34	0.40	0.23
80k	0.38	0.39	0.39	0.43	0.27
120k	0.43	0.45	0.44	0.48	0.28
200k	0.40	0.48	0.45	0.48	0.28
300k	0.43	0.56	0.49	0.58	0.33

Table 3: Performance of the classifiers with the different training sizes.

We also tested the classifiers with different sizes of training data. Table 3 provides the Macro

Category	Precision	Recall	FB1
EVENT	31.25%	11.11 %	16.39
GROUP	58.82 %	20.62 %	30.53
LOC	58.88 %	58.14 %	58.51
ORG	32.99 %	15.84 %	21.40
OTHER	100.00 %	3.45 %	6.67
PER	75.32 %	58.91 %	66.11
PROD	71.19 %	43.64 %	54.11
TIME	57.14 %	2.65 %	5.06
TITLE	22.45 %	14.93 %	17.93

Table 4: Results of best performing SVM per category including post-processing.

F1 from our train/test split data for the training sizes 30.000, 80.000, 120.000, 200.000, 300.000 and 550.000 tokens. The performance of all five classifiers improves significantly with increased amounts of training data.

The evaluation of the results per named entity category using the best performing SVM show that some of the categories were classified more accurately than others. The best results were obtained for person (66.11), location (58.51) and product (54.11). The most challenging categories were time (5.06) and other (6.67).

5 Discussion

The large variation in F1 per category, for example in '-TIME', is partly due to the inconsistent annotation of tokens. Table 5 below shows the days of the week present in the training data in both Spanish and English and all the tags associated with these tokens. It shows that all of these tokens are inconsistently annotated in that they are sometimes annotated as '-TIME' and sometimes annotated as 'O'. For example in Tweets (1) and (2) below, 'Happy Friday' is used in the same context, but is only tagged as 'B-TIME' in the first Tweet.

(1) Happy Friday Familia!!! #ElvacilonDe-LaGatita #battingcage #HappyHour 17 ave NW 7 Calle http://t.co/fbPk0sER05

(2) RT @isazapata : Challenge yourself and move away from your comfort zone! Happy Friday!! http://t.co/OK320hNQ

Some variation in the annotation of tokens such as 'Friday' is to be expected, as the token may not always refer to a day of the week but a title or another type of named entity, but the SVM will discard the information from the feature vector if 'Friday' is 'tagged as 'O' more often than '-TIME'.

TOKEN	-TIME	O
lunes	21	74
monday	7	11
martes	23	51
tuesday	2	3
miercoles	7	20
wednesday	1	4
jueves	18	68
thursday	5	10
viernes	48	87
friday	13	35
sabado	6	21
saturday	6	9
domingo	34	63
sunday	16	18

Table 5: Number of times the tag '-TIME' occurs for the days of the week in the training Tweets.

Whilst training the classifiers, we noticed a large amount of variation in the results for the train/test data. To find out exactly how much the results fluctuate, we used the random split function in scikit-learn and split the training data into two chunks: 90% training and 10% testing and re-trained the classifier with the new version of the training data. Consequently, the intermediate results for each of the classifiers was always on a different 10% test set. The difference between the best and the worst result can be up to an increase in macro F1 of 0.12 with the same classifier and the same size training set. The results also showed that by increasing the number of tokens in the training data, the performance of the classifiers improved.

To illustrate why this may be the case, table 6 below contains the number of overlapping NEs for three different splits for each training size. It shows the large amount of variance in the results depending on how the random split occurred. We counted all types that were tagged as an NE in the training data in total, compared to how many of those NEs were in the train and test sets. For example, for the first random 30.000 tokens split, there were 456 NEs in the training data, and 65 NEs in the training test set. A total of 17 NEs in the training test set were also present in the training data, meaning that the SVM had already encountered these tokens. Depending on how the data was split, the overlap already encountered in the training data varies from 0.19 to 0.26 for 30.000 tokens. This difference is not as large for 550.000 tokens, where it varies between 0.6 and 0.63.

Size	Total	Train	Test	Overlap
30k	504	456	65	0.26
30k	504	464	51	0.22
30k	504	454	62	0.19
80k	1096	1003	142	0.35
80k	1096	1007	147	0.39
80k	1096	996	169	0.41
120k	1561	1443	215	0.45
120k	1561	1439	227	0.46
120k	1561	1440	223	0.46
200k	2262	2085	362	0.51
200k	2262	2066	408	0.52
200k	2262	2092	365	0.53
300k	3074	2818	545	0.53
300k	3074	2824	550	0.55
300k	3074	2822	557	0.55
550k	4705	4369	854	0.61
550k	4705	4390	857	0.63
550k	4705	4331	927	0.60

Table 6: Distribution of NEs in the training data. The overlap refers to the percentage of types that was present in both the training set and the test set extracted from the training.

Table 6 also illustrates that the number of overlapping tokens increases immensely when the number of tokens in the training data increases. It ranges from .19 to .63, which means that the higher the number of tokens in the training set, the likelihood that NEs in the test set are also present in the training data increases. Therefore, the classifier does not need to classify as many unseen tokens and overall performance increases.

6   Conclusion and Future Work

We presented a named entity recognition system for Spanish-English code-switched Tweets based on a combination of classical machine learning algorithms and post-processing. The best performing classifier was a Support Vector Machine with an RBF kernel, allowing it to be flexible and less prone to overfitting compared to other classifiers on the held-out test data. We used a small set of features which were selected based on frequency observations in the training data. This provides a classifier with low computational costs and could allow for easy adaptation for other language pairs. Overall, the task of recognizing named entities in multilingual Twitter data proved to be quite challenging. We managed to achieve an overall F1 of 53.65 and thus modestly outperformed the baseline provided by Aguilar et al. (2018). The results show that there is a large amount of variation in classifier performance depending on the specific NEs present in the training and test sets. The classifiers could be improved by incorporating gazetteer resources more specific to Spanish-speaking countries, for example for geographical entities similar to that of the United States census list. Currently, the focus lies on English NEs as there are more resources available. Furthermore, the current approach relies heavily on gazetteering, and the wider context of a token could be taken into account by, for example, determining correlations of certain types of NEs with related verbs in the same Tweet.

References

Gustavo Aguilar, Fahad AlGhamdi, Victor Soto, Mona Diab, Julia Hirschberg, and Thamar Solorio. 2018. Overview of the CALCS 2018 Shared Task: Named Entity Recognition on Code-switched Data. In *Proceedings of the Third Workshop on Computational Approaches to Linguistic Code-Switching*, Melbourne, Australia. Association for Computational Linguistics.

Timothy Baldwin, Marie Catherine de Marneffe, Bo Han, Young-Bum Kim, Alan Ritter, and Wei Xu. 2015. Shared tasks of the 2015 workshop on noisy user-generated text: Twitter lexical normalization and named entity recognition. ACL Association for Computational Linguistics.

Leo Breiman. 2001. Random forests. *Machine Learning*, 45(1):5–32.

Chih-Chung Chang and Chih-Jen Lin. 2011. Libsvm: a library for support vector machines. *ACM transactions on intelligent systems and technology (TIST)*, 2(3):27.

Daniel Claeser, Dennis Felske, and Samantha Kent. 2018. Token level code-switching detection using wikipedia as a lexical resource. In *Language Technologies for the Challenges of the Digital Age*, pages 192–198, Cham. Springer International Publishing.

Leon Derczynski, Diana Maynard, Giuseppe Rizzo, Marieke van Erp, Genevieve Gorrell, Raphal Troncy, Johann Petrak, and Kalina Bontcheva. 2015. Analysis of named entity recognition and linking for tweets. *Information Processing & Management*, 51(2):32 – 49.

Yoav Freund and Robert E. Schapire. 1995. A desicion-theoretic generalization of on-line learning and an application to boosting. In *Computational Learning Theory*, pages 23–37, Berlin, Heidelberg. Springer Berlin Heidelberg.

Hege Fromreide, Dirk Hovy, and Anders Søgaard. 2014. Crowdsourcing and annotating ner for twitter #drift. In *Proceedings of the Ninth International Conference on Language Resources and Evaluation (LREC-2014)*. European Language Resources Association (ELRA).

Nut Limsopatham and Nigel Collier. 2016. Bidirectional lstm for named entity recognition in twitter messages. In *Proceedings of the 2nd Workshop on Noisy User-generated Text (WNUT)*, pages 145–152. The COLING 2016 Organizing Committee.

F. Pedregosa, G. Varoquaux, A. Gramfort, V. Michel, B. Thirion, O. Grisel, M. Blondel, P. Prettenhofer, R. Weiss, V. Dubourg, J. Vanderplas, A. Passos, D. Cournapeau, M. Brucher, M. Perrot, and E. Duchesnay. 2011. Scikit-learn: Machine learning in Python. *Journal of Machine Learning Research*, 12:2825–2830.

Benjamin Strauss, Bethany Toma, Alan Ritter, Marie-Catherine de Marneffe, and Wei Xu. 2016. Results of the wnut16 named entity recognition shared task. In *Proceedings of the 2nd Workshop on Noisy User-generated Text (WNUT)*, pages 138–144. The COLING 2016 Organizing Committee.

Zhiqiang Toh, Bin Chen, and Jian Su. 2015. Improving twitter named entity recognition using word representations. In *Proceedings of the Workshop on Noisy User-generated Text*, pages 141–145. Association for Computational Linguistics.

Ikuya Yamada, Hideaki Takeda, and Yoshiyasu Takefuji. 2015. Enhancing named entity recognition in twitter messages using entity linking. In *Proceedings of the Workshop on Noisy User-generated Text*, pages 136–140. Association for Computational Linguistics.

Named Entity Recognition on Code-Switched Data:
Overview of the CALCS 2018 Shared Task

Gustavo Aguilar [‡], **Fahad AlGhamdi, Victor Soto** [†],
Mona Diab, Julia Hirschberg, [†] and **Thamar Solorio**[‡]
Department of Computer Science, The George Washington University
{fghamdi, mtdiab}@gwu.edu
[‡]Department of Computer Science, University of Houston
[‡]{gaguilaralas, tsolorio}@uh.edu
[†]Department of Computer Science, Columbia University
[†]{vs2411, julia}@cs.columbia.edu

Abstract

In the third shared task of the Computational Approaches to Linguistic Code-Switching (CALCS) workshop, we focus on Named Entity Recognition (NER) on code-switched social-media data. We divide the shared task into two competitions based on the English-Spanish (ENG-SPA) and Modern Standard Arabic-Egyptian (MSA-EGY) language pairs. We use Twitter data and 9 entity types to establish a new dataset for code-switched NER benchmarks. In addition to the CS phenomenon, the diversity of the entities and the social media challenges make the task considerably hard to process. As a result, the best scores of the competitions are 63.76% and 71.61% for ENG-SPA and MSA-EGY, respectively. We present the scores of 9 participants and discuss the most common challenges among submissions.

1 Introduction

Code-switching (CS) is a linguistic behavior that occurs on spoken and written language. CS happens when multilingual speakers move back and forth from one language to another in the same discourse. The growing incidence of social media in the way we communicate has also increased the occurrences of code-switching on informal written language. As a result, there is a prevalent demand for more tools and resources that can help to process such phenomenon.

In the previous versions of the Computational Approaches to Linguistic Code-Switching (CALCS) workshop, we focused on providing an annotated corpora for language identification (Solorio et al., 2014; Molina et al., 2016). In this occasion, we extend the annotations to the Named Entity Recognition (NER) level. The goal of this shared task is to provide a code-switched NER dataset that can help to benchmark NER state-of-the-art approaches. This will directly impact the performance of higher-level NLP applications where the code-switching behavior is commonly found.

ENG-SPA Tweet
Original: @_xoxoBecky lmao ni ganas tengo de llorar 😭, the last movie that made me cry was [*Pineapple Express*]TITLE 😂 me dejo llorando de risa 😂😂😂
English: @_xoxoBecky lmao I don't even want to cry 😭, the last movie that made me cry was [*Pineapple Express*]TITLE 😂 it left me crying with laughter 😂😂

MSA-EGY Tweet
Buckwalter Encoding: wAy mErkp Dd [*AldAxlyp*]ORG [*wAmn Aldwlp*]ORG hbqY sEydp byhA
Arabic: وأي معركة ضد الداخلية وأمن الدولة هبقى سعيدة بيها
English: Any controversy against the Interior Ministry and State Security Service will make me feel happy

Figure 1: Examples of the CALCS 2018 dataset. In the English-Spanish data, the highlighted words represent a movie, tagged as TITLE. While in the MSA-EGY data, the bolded words represent government agencies, tagged as ORGANIZATION

We had a total of 9 participants from which we received 8 submissions on English-Spanish and 5 submissions on Modern Standard Arabic-Egyptian. The best F1-score reported for ENG-SPA[1] was **63.76%** by the **IIT BHU** team (Trivedi et al., 2018) whereas in MSA-EGY[2] was **71.61%**

---

[1]ENG-SPA competition https://competitions.codalab.org/competitions/18725

[2]MSA-EGY competition https://competitions.codalab.org/competitions/18724

Proceedings of The Third Workshop on Computational Approaches to Code-Switching, pages 138–147
Melbourne, Australia, July 19, 2018. ©2018 Association for Computational Linguistics

by the **FAIR** team (Wang et al., 2018).

2 Task definition

The task consists of recognizing entities in a relatively short code-switched context. The entity types for this task are *person, organization, location, group, title, product, event, time,* and *other*. We describe each entity type on Section 3.1. Since NER is a sequential tagging task, we use the IOB scheme to identify multiple words as a single named entity. The addition of this scheme duplicates the number of entities in the task yielding a B(eginning) and I(nside) variations of each of them. This leaves us with 19 possible labels for the classification task.

The evaluation of the task uses two versions of the F1-score. The first is the standard F1, and the second is the Surface Form F1-score introduced by Derczynski et al. (2014). The Surface Form F1-score captures the rare and emerging aspects of the entities. We average both metrics to determine the positions in the leaderboard. Additionally, the shared task was conducted on the CodaLab platform[3], where participants are able to directly evaluate their approaches against the gold data.

3 Datasets

In this section we provide the definition of our labels, describe the annotation process and show the distribution of the ENG-SPA and MSA-EGY datasets.

3.1 Entity instructions

The named entities have been annotated using the instructions below. Note that the definitions of the entity types apply to both language pairs.

- **Person**: This entity type includes proper names and nicknames that can identify a person uniquely. We ignore cases where a person is referred by nouns with adjectives that are not necessarily a nickname. Single artists and famous people are treated as *person*.

- **Organization**: This entity type includes names of companies, institutions and corporations, i.e. every entity that has employees and takes actions as a whole. If the NE can potentially be any other type, the context should be sufficient to support whether it is *organization* or not (e.g., Facebook as organization vs. Facebook as the website application).

- **Location**: This NE refers to physical places that people can visit. It includes cities, countries, addresses, facilities, touristic places, etc. This entity type is not to be confused with *organization*. For instance, when people use organization names to refer to places that can be visited (e.g., restaurants), those entities must be tagged as *location*.

- **Group**: This NE includes sports teams, music bands, duets, etc. *Group* and *organization* are not to be confused. For example, the Houston Astros as a team (i.e., *group*) is different from the Houston Astros institution.

- **Product**: This NE refers to articles that have been manufactured or refined for sale, like devices, medicine, food produced by a company, any well-defined service, website accounts, etc.

- **Title**: This type includes titles of movies, books, TV shows, songs, etc. Very often, titles can be sentences (e.g., the movie *We're the Millers*). *Titles* usually refer to media and must not be confused with the *product* type.

- **Event**: This type refers to situations or scenarios that gather people for a specific purpose such as concerts, competitions, conferences, award events, etc. *Events* do not consider holidays.

- **Time**: This NE includes months, days of the week, seasons, holidays and dates that happen periodically, which are not *events* (e.g., Christmas). It excludes hours, minutes, and seconds. 'Yesterday', 'tomorrow', 'week' and 'year' are not tagged as *time*.

- **Other**: This type includes any other named entity that does not fit in the previous categories. This may include nationalities, languages, music genres, etc.

The motivation behind these entity types partly lies on the contextual difference in which they appear. For instance, when an *organization* can be lexically confused with a *product*, the context should break down the ambiguity. Additionally,

---

[3]The competitions will be permanently open for future benchmarks

Classes	ENG-SPA			MSA-EGY		
	Train	Dev	Test	Train	Dev	Test
Person	6,226	95	1,888	8,897	1,113	777
Location	4,323	16	803	4,500	474	332
Organization	1,381	10	307	2,596	263	179
Group	1,024	5	153	2,646	303	139
Title	1,980	50	542	2,057	258	18
Product	1,885	21	481	795	81	54
Event	557	6	99	902	121	81
Time	786	9	197	578	79	28
Other	382	7	62	122	19	2
NE Tokens	18,544	219	4,532	23,093	2,711	1,610
O Tokens	614,013	9,364	178,479	181,229	20,031	19,804
Tweets	50,757	832	15,634	10,102	1,122	1,110

Table 1: The named entity distribution of the training, development and testing sets for both language pairs. Note that the *NE tokens* row contains the B(eginning) and I(nside) tokens of the datasets following the IOB scheme. The *O Tokens* row refers to the non-entity tokens.

we tried to include entity types that have an impact on higher-level NLP applications under similar social media scenarios.

3.2 ENG-SPA

Data annotation: We use the English-Spanish language identification dataset introduced in the first CALCS shared task (Solorio et al., 2014). We build upon this dataset to generate the entity labels. To annotate the data, we designed a Crowd-Flower[4] job from scratch[5]. The interface of the job is described in Figure 2. The job allows annotators to select one or many words for a single NE. When the annotators select a word the tool suggests to incorporate words surrounding the current selection. When the selection of a whole entity is done, the annotators can add the entity to the second step where the type is determined. The annotators repeat this process until no more named entities can be identified in the tweet. The output of our customized job contains the entity type of one or multiple words that identify an NE according to the criteria of the annotators. The annotators are required to know both English and Spanish, and the job is constrained to reach an accuracy of at least 80%. We also required 3 annotators per tweet. Additionally, the job was launched in geographic locations were both English and Spanish are reasonably common. Some of these places were USA, Mexico, Central America, Puerto Rico, Colombia, Venezuela, Chile, Uruguay, Paraguay and Spain. After getting the output data from CrowdFlower, we reviewed the results to correct any possible mistakes.

Data distribution: The entity types along with their distribution are listed in Table 1. We provide training, development and testing[6] sets containing 50,757, 832 and 15,634 tweets, respectively. The development and testing splits are inherited from previous CALCS Shared Tasks, whereas training uses the original split with the addition of 40,000 tweets. We added more tweets to the original training set to increase the number of samples per entity type since the NER datasets are naturally skewed. From Table 1, it is worth noting that the total number of NE training tokens is 18,544 whereas the non-entity tokens add up to 614,013. This means that only 3% of the tokens of the training set are NE-related. Likewise, the ratio of tokens for the development and testing sets are 2.3% and 2.5%, respectively. This skewed distribution poses a great challenge considering that the datasets are further separated by 18 fine-grained entity types (i.e., each entity type has a *beginning* and *inside* variations from the IOB scheme). However, we think that the skewness can be reasonably handled with the provided data. Moreover, the training, development and testing sets draw a

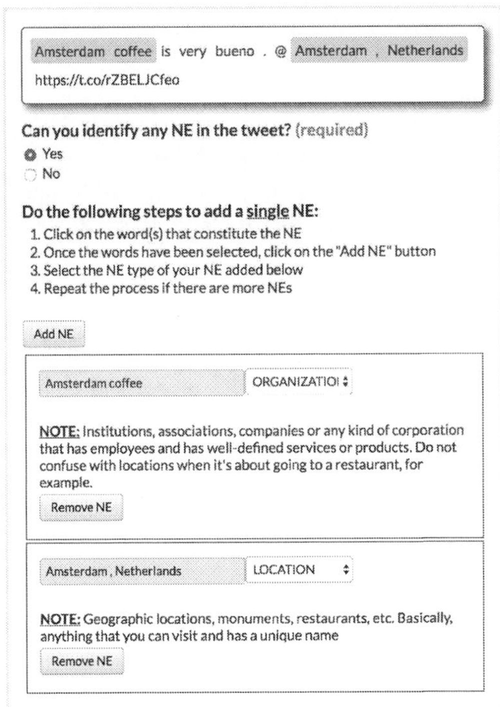

Figure 2: The CrowdFlower interface that we developed to annotate the ENG-SPA dataset. The green-highlighted words are the entities selected by the annotator. The words in the same green area describe a single entity. Once the NE selection has been added, the annotators have to select the type of the entities.

very similar data distribution, which can also help to adapt the learning from training to testing.

3.3 MSA-EGY

Validating old tweets: For the Modern Standard Arabic-Egyptian Arabic Dialect (MSA-EGY) language pair, we combined the training, development, and test sets that we used in the EMNLP 2016 CS Shared Task (Molina et al., 2016) to create the new training corpora for the NER Shared Task. The data was harvested from Twitter. We apply a number of quality and validation checks to insure the quality of the old data. Therefore, we retrieved all old tweets using the the new version of the Arabic Tweets Token Assigner which is made available through the Shared Task website [7]. One of the main reasons for the re-crawling step is

to eliminate the tweets that have been deleted, or the tweets that belong to the users whose accounts are suspended by Twitter. The other reason is that some tweets may cause encoding issues when they are retrieved using the crawler script. Thus, all these tweets were removed and eliminated. After performing the validation checks, we accepted and published 11,224 tweets (10,102 tweets for the training set, and 1,122 tweets for the development set).

Data creation and annotation: Since we combined the test set used in the EMNLP-2016 CS Shared Task (Molina et al., 2016) with the dataset used in the EMNLP-2014 CS Shared Task (Solorio et al., 2014) to form the new training and development sets, we needed to crawl and annotate a new test set for our new Shared Task. We resorted to using the Tweepy library to harvest the timeline of 12 Egyptian public figures. We applied the same filtration criteria when crawling and building the test set used in the 2016 CS shared task (Molina et al., 2016). We divided the old combined tweets into training and development sets as follows: 80% train set and 10% development set. Thus, we needed $\sim 1,110$ tweets, which represents the 10% of the new test set. As we did in the previous Shared Task, we wanted to consider choosing tweets from public figures whose tweets contain more code-switching points. Therefore, we resorted to using the Automatic Identification of Dialectal Arabic (AIDA2) tool (Al-Badrashiny et al., 2015) to perform token-level language identification for the MSA and EGY tokens in context. Public figures with more than 35% of code-switching points in their tweets were considered. The annotation work of the MSA-EGY dataset was done in-lab by two trained Egyptian native speakers. Our annotation team followed the Named Entity Annotation Guidelines for MSA-EGY, which is made available through the Shared Task website [8]. In the two previous editions of the CS Shared Task (Solorio et al., 2014; Molina et al., 2016), we used a Named Entity ("ne") tag. The "ne" tag was defined as a word or multi-word that represents names of a unique entity such as people's names, countries and places, organizations, companies, websites, etc. The AIDA2 tool (Al-Badrashiny et al., 2015) was used to assign initial automatic tags for highly confident data categories

---

[7] https://code-switching.github.io/2018/

[8] https://codeswitching.github.io/2018/

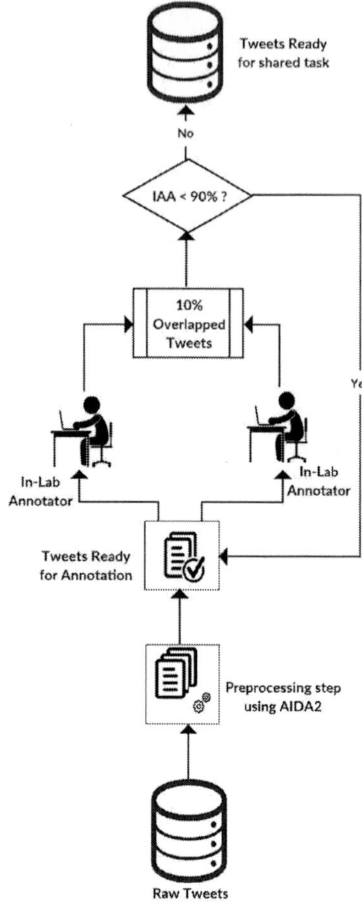

Figure 3: MSA-EGY Data Annotation

(i.e., URL, Punctuation, Number, etc) in addition to named entities. Then, we extracted and prepared all the tweets that contained "ne" for annotation. As we mentioned earlier, the IOB scheme is used as an annotation scheme to identify multiple words as a single named entity. All the URLs, Punctuation and Numbers tags are deterministically converted to "O" tag, while the tweets that include "ne" tags were given to our in-lab annotators for validation and re-annotation if needed.

Quality checks and data distribution: We computed the Inter-Annotator Agreement (IAA) on 10% of the dataset to validate the performance and agreement among annotators. One of our annotators is a specialist linguist who carried out adjudication and revisions of accuracy measurements. We approached a stable Inter Annotator Agreement (IAA) of over 92% pairwise agreement. The workflow of the annotation process for MSA-EGY

is shown in Figure-3.

The total number of tweets in MSA-EGY dataset is 12,334 tweets. It is divided into three sets train, development, and test sets (10,102, 1,122, 1,110 tweets, respectively). Table 1 shows that the total number of NE training tokens is 23,093. It means that NE tokens represent 11.3% of the total number of tokens. Similarly, the percentages of NE tokens in the development and test sets are 7.5%, 11.9%, respectively. As we mentioned earlier, the MSA-EGY tweets were harvested from the timeline of 12 Egyptian politicians public figures. Generally, politicians tend to use NEs more often when they write their tweets. This explains why the percentage of the NE tokens in MSA-EGY dataset is higher than the percentage of the NE tokens in ESP-ENG dataset.

4   Approaches

In this section, we briefly describe the systems of the participants and discuss their results as well as the final scores.

- **IIT BHU** (Trivedi et al., 2018). They proposed a "new architecture based on gating of character- and word-based representation of a token". They captured the character and the word representations using a CNN and a bidirectional LSTM, respectively. They also used the Multi-Task Learning on the output layer and transfer the learning to a CRF classifier following Aguilar et al. (2017). Moreover, they fed a gazetteers representation to their model.

- **CAiRE++** (Winata et al., 2018). They used a bidirectional LSTM model for characters and words. They primarily focused on OOV using the FastText library (Bojanowski et al., 2016).

- **FAIR** (Wang et al., 2018). They proposed a joint bidirectional LSTM-CRF network that uses attention at the embedding layer. They also preprocessed the data before feeding the network.

- **Linguists** (Jain et al., 2018). They used a Conditional Random Fields with many hand-crafted features. Their focus was primarily on English-Spanish data.

- **Flytxt** (Sikdar et al., 2018). This team also employed a Conditional Random Fields.

142

Team	Preproc	Ext Res	Hand Feats	CNN	B-LSTM	CRF	Other
IIT BHU		✓		✓	✓	✓	MTL
CAiRE++					✓		FastText
FAIR	✓				✓	✓	Attention
Linguists		✓	✓			✓	
Flytxt		✓				✓	
semantic					✓	✓	
BATs		✓	✓			✓	
Fraunhofer FKIE		✓	✓				SVM
GHHT		✓			✓	✓	

Table 2: The table shows the main component and strategies used by the participants. Ext Res means external resources such as pre-trained word embeddings, gazetteers, etc. Hand Feats means handcrafted features such as capitalization.

They fed the CRF with features from both external and internal resources. Additionally, they incorporated the language identification labels of the datasets from the previous versions of this workshop.

- **semantic** (Geetha et al., 2018). They jointly trained a Bidirectional LSTM with a Conditional Random Fields on the output layer.

- **BATs** (Janke et al., 2018). They used a Conditional Random Fields with multiple features. Some of those features were also used for neural network, but they got better results with the CRF approach.

- **Fraunhofer FKIE** (Claeser et al., 2018). They used a Support Vector Machine (SVM) classifier with a Radial Basis kernel. They handcrafted a lot of features and also included gazetteers.

- **GHHT** (Attia and Samih, 2018). They trained a BLSTM-CRF network using pre-trained word embeddings, brown clusters and gazetteers.

- **Baseline**. We used a simple Bidirectional LSTM network with randomly initialized embedding vectors of 200 dimensions. We also used dropout operations on each direction of the BLSTM component.

5 Evaluation and results

5.1 Evaluation

The evaluation of the shared task was conducted through CodaLab, where the participants were able to obtain immediate feedback of their submissions. The metrics used for the evaluation phase were the standard harmonic mean F1-score and the Surface Form F1 variation proposed by Derczynski et al. (2014). Additionally, to have a single leaderboard per language pair, we unified both metrics by averaging them. The average values are the ones described in Table 3.

As stated by (Derczynski et al., 2014), the idea of the Surface Form F1-score is to capture the *novel* and *emerging* aspects that are usually encountered in social media data. Those aspects describe a fast-moving language that constantly produces new entities challenging more the recall capabilities of state-of-the-art models than the precision side.

5.2 Results and Error analysis

Although all the scores reported by the participants outperformed the baselines in both ENG-SPA and MSA-EGY language pairs, the results are arguably low considering that the current state-of-the-art systems achieve around 91.2% of F1-score on well-formatted text (Lample et al., 2016; Ma and Hovy, 2016; Liu et al., 2017). As mentioned before, the best performing systems reached 63.76% (Trivedi et al., 2018) and 71.61% (Wang et al., 2018) for ENG-SPA and MSA-EGY, respectively. These low outcomes are aligned with the challenges that come along with social media data and the addition of more heterogeneous entity types (Ritter et al., 2011; Augenstein et al., 2017; Derczynski et al., 2014; Aguilar et al., 2018).

Most of the MSA-EGY tweets are related to politics because they were harvested from the

Team	ENG-SPA
IIT BHU	**63.7628**
CAiRE++	62.7608
FAIR	62.6671
Linguists	62.1307
Flytxt	59.2501
semantic	56.7205
BATs	54.1612
Fraunhofer FKIE	53.6514
Baseline	53.2802
	MSA-EGY
FAIR	**71.6154**
GHHT	70.0938
Linguists	67.4419
BATs	65.6207
semantic	65.0276
Baseline	62.7084

Table 3: The results of the participants in both ENG-SPA and MSA-EGY language pairs. The scores are based on the average of the standard and the Surface form F1 metrics. The highlighted teams are the best scores of the shared task.

timeline of number of Egyptian politician public figures. Generally, these kinds of tweets encompass more NEs in comparison with other kinds of tweets. This explains why the percentage of the NE tokens in MSA-EGY dataset is high compared to the NEs' percentage in ESP-ENG data set. This high percentage of NE tokens helps the submitted systems to see and learn more examples and patterns. Thus, systems can generalize more effectively.

According to the results of the participants in the ENG-SPA shared task, the top three most challenging entity types were *event*, *title*, and *time*. It is worth noting that these three classes are more or less the least frequent types in the dataset (see Table 1), which suggests that having more data samples would produce better results. However, in the case of *title*, there are 1,980 samples against 1,381 samples of *organization*, and the performance is significantly better for the latter one (19% vs. 35% of F1-scores). Additionally, looking at Table 4, the entity *Orange is the New Black* was not recognized by participants as a *title*. This is an example of what we refer to heterogeneous entity type, mean-

N	ENG-SPA Samples
1	Retiro totalmente lo dicho sobre **Orange is the New Black**. Temporada terminada y holly sh*t. HOLLY SH*T.
2	**Love Man** by **Otis Redding**, found with @Shazam. Listen now: como me hubiese gustado ver a mis padres bailando esto ...
3	**Michael Jackson** revivió en los **Billboard 2014**
4	@fairy0821 en el **show de shamu** !!!

Table 4: Challenging samples from the test set. The bold words are the ground truth samples and the underscored words are the predictions of the best performing systems.

ing that the entity instances are flexible in format that can even describe independent sentences (i.e., a homogeneous type is *person*). The entities *Love Man* (title), *Billboard 2014* (event), and *show de shamu* (event) also describe the same pattern and they were hardly identified by participants.

Unlike English and Spanish language pair which can be considered as two distinct languages, Modern Standard Arabic and Egyptian are more closely related which makes the task of identifying NE tokens more challenging. This is mainly due to the fact that Modern Standard Arabic and Egyptian are close variants of one another and hence they share considerable amount of lexical items. Some of the challenges faced by the participants include words that still have punctuation attached to them (e.g. (مصر , (mSr, (Egypt) . In order to mitigate these issues, some participants preprocessed these cases by, for example, removing any leading and trailing punctuation from those tokens. Other participants normalized these cases by unifying all the attached punctuations, while the remaining participants decided to keep them and let their model learn them. Table 5 and the following examples show some challenges faced by the submitted systems:

- Clitic attachment can obscure tokens, e.g. والله wAllh "and-God" or "swear".

- Clitic attachment can obscure tokens, e.g. ومنى wmnY "and-Mona" or "swear".

N	MSA-EGY Samples
1	**Buckwalter Encoding:**[*wAllh*]PER OnA HAss bqhr In [*ElA' Ebd AlftAH*]PER [*wmnY*]PER [*syf*]PER bytHAkmwA wfy AlqfS **Arabic:** والله أنا حاسس بقهر إن علاء عبد الفتاح ومنى سيف بيتحاكموا وفي القفص **English:** I swear I feel angry knowing that Ala Abdulfatah and-Mona are tried and jailed
2	**Buckwalter Encoding:** kl wAHd ysOl Al—n :[(*mSr*]LOC rAyHp Ely fyn ?) **Arabic:** كل واحد يسأل الآن : (مصر رايحة علي فين ؟) **English:** Everyone asks himself where is Egypt going to go?

Table 5: Challenging samples from the MSA-EGY test set. The bold words are the ground truth samples.

6 Related work

Before the CALCS workshop series, the code-switching behavior was studied from different perspectives and for many languages (Toribio, 2001; Solorio and Liu, 2008a,b; Piergallini et al., 2016; AlGhamdi et al., 2016). Most of them focused on either exploring this phenomenon or solving core code-switching tasks from the NLP pipeline. More recently, researchers have been considering the sentiment analysis task on code-switching settings (Lee and Wang, 2015; Vilares et al., 2015). However, the lack of resources at the core level of the NLP pipeline greatly reduces the chances of improving higher-level applications. In this line, we aim at providing two datasets for named entity recognition benchmarks on the English-Spanish and Modern Standard Arabic-Egyptian language pairs.

It worth noting that there are some contributions of CS corpora, such as a collection of Turkish-German CS tweets (Calzolari et al., 2016), a large collection of Modern Standrd Arabic and Egyptian Dialectal Arabic CS data (Diab et al., 2016) and a collection of sentiment annotated Spanish-English tweets (Vilares et al., 2016). Named entity recognition has been vastly studied along the years (Sang and Meulder, 2003). More recently, however, the focus has drastically moved to social media data due to the great incidence that social networks have in our daily communication (Ritter et al., 2011; Augenstein et al., 2017). The workshop on Noisy User-generated Text (W-NUT) has been a great effort towards the study of named entity recognition on noisy data. In 2016, the organizers focused on named entities from different topics to evaluate the adaptation of models from one topic to another (Strauss et al., 2016). In 2017, the organizers introduced the Surface Form F1-score metric and collected data from multiple social media platforms (Derczynski et al., 2014). The challenge not only lies on the entity types and the social media noisy but also in the distribution of the datasets and their different data domain patterns.

7 Conclusion

We presented the setup and results of the 3rd shared task of the Computational Approaches to Linguistic Code-Switching workshop. We introduced a named entity recognition dataset focused on code-switched social media text for two language pairs: English-Spanish and Modern Standard Arabic-Egyptian. We received submissions from nine teams, eight of them submitted to ENG-SPA and six to MSA-EGY. Similar to the previous sequence tagging tasks of our workshop, the predominant aspect among the approaches was the Conditional Random Fields. Additionally, the combination of the CRF with a bidirectional LSTM (with some variations) yielded the best results among participants. The best F1-score for ENG-SPA was 63.7628% and for MSA-EGY was 71.6154%. Compared to monolingual formal text (i.e., newswire), the reported scores are significantly lower due to the code-switching phenomenon as well as the noise of SM environment. This serves as strong evidence that we need more robust approaches that can detect and process named entities in such challenging conditions.

Acknowledgments

We would like to thank the National Science Foundation for partially supporting this work under award number 1462142.

References

Gustavo Aguilar, Adrian Pastor Lopez Monroy, Fabio Gonzalez, and Thamar Solorio. 2018. Modeling noisiness to recognize named entities using multi-task neural networks on social media. In *Proceedings of the 2018 Conference of the North American Chapter of the Association for Computational Linguistics: Human Language Technologies, Volume 1 (Long Papers)*, pages 1401–1412, New Orleans, Louisiana. Association for Computational Linguistics.

Gustavo Aguilar, Suraj Maharjan, Adrian Pastor López Monroy, and Thamar Solorio. 2017. A multi-task approach for named entity recognition in social media data. In *Proceedings of the 3rd Workshop on Noisy User-generated Text*, pages 148–153, Copenhagen, Denmark. Association for Computational Linguistics.

Mohamed Al-Badrashiny, Heba Elfardy, and Mona T. Diab. 2015. Aida2: A hybrid approach for token and sentence level dialect identification in arabic. In *Proceedings of the 19th Conference on Computational Natural Language Learning, CoNLL 2015, Beijing, China, July 30-31, 2015*, pages 42–51. ACL.

Fahad AlGhamdi, Giovanni Molina, Mona T. Diab, Thamar Solorio, Abdelati Hawwari, Victor Soto, and Julia Hirschberg. 2016. Part of speech tagging for code switched data. In *Proceedings of the Second Workshop on Computational Approaches to Code Switching@EMNLP 2016, Austin, Texas, USA, November 1, 2016*, pages 98–107.

Mohammed Attia and Younes Samih. 2018. GHHT at CALCS 2018: Named Entity Recognition for Dialectal Arabic Using Neural Networks. In *Proceedings of the Third Workshop on Computational Approaches to Linguistic Code-Switching*, Melbourne, Australia. Association for Computational Linguistics.

Isabelle Augenstein, Leon Derczynski, and Kalina Bontcheva. 2017. Generalisation in named entity recognition: A quantitative analysis. *CoRR*, abs/1701.02877.

Piotr Bojanowski, Edouard Grave, Armand Joulin, and Tomas Mikolov. 2016. Enriching word vectors with subword information. *arXiv preprint arXiv:1607.04606*.

Nicoletta Calzolari, Khalid Choukri, Thierry Declerck, Sara Goggi, Marko Grobelnik, Bente Maegaard, Joseph Mariani, Hélène Mazo, Asunción Moreno, Jan Odijk, and Stelios Piperidis, editors. 2016. *Proceedings of the Tenth International Conference on Language Resources and Evaluation LREC 2016, Portorož, Slovenia, May 23-28, 2016*. European Language Resources Association (ELRA).

Daniel Claeser, Samantha Kent, and Dennis Felske. 2018. System Description for the Shared Task: Named Entity Recognition on Code-switched Data. In *Proceedings of the Third Workshop on Computational Approaches to Linguistic Code-Switching*, Melbourne, Australia. Association for Computational Linguistics.

Leon Derczynski, Diana Maynard, Giuseppe Rizzo, Marieke van Erp, Genevieve Gorrell, Raphaël Troncy, Johann Petrak, and Kalina Bontcheva. 2014. Analysis of named entity recognition and linking for tweets. *CoRR*, abs/1410.7182.

Mona T. Diab, Mahmoud Ghoneim, Abdelati Hawwari, Fahad AlGhamdi, Nada AlMarwani, and Mohamed Al-Badrashiny. 2016. Creating a large multi-layered representational repository of linguistic code switched arabic data. In (Calzolari et al., 2016).

Parvathy Geetha, Khyathi Chandu, and Alan W Black. 2018. Tackling Code-Switched NER: Participation of 'semantic'. In *Proceedings of the Third Workshop on Computational Approaches to Linguistic Code-Switching*, Melbourne, Australia. Association for Computational Linguistics.

Devanshu Jain, Maria Kustikova, Mayank Darbari, Rishabh Gupta, and Stephen Mayhew. 2018. Simple Features for Strong Performance on Named Entity Recognition in Code-Switched Twitter Data. In *Proceedings of the Third Workshop on Computational Approaches to Linguistic Code-Switching*, Melbourne, Australia. Association for Computational Linguistics.

Florian Janke, Tongrui Li, Eric Rincón, Gualberto Guzmán, Barbara Bullock, and Almeida Jacqueline Toribio. 2018. Submission for the Code-Switching Workshop Shared Task 2018 . In *Proceedings of the Third Workshop on Computational Approaches to Linguistic Code-Switching*, Melbourne, Australia. Association for Computational Linguistics.

Guillaume Lample, Miguel Ballesteros, Sandeep Subramanian, Kazuya Kawakami, and Chris Dyer. 2016. Neural architectures for named entity recognition. *CoRR*, abs/1603.01360.

Sophia Lee and Zhongqing Wang. 2015. Emotion in code-switching texts: Corpus construction and analysis. In *Proceedings of the Eighth SIGHAN Workshop on Chinese Language Processing*, pages 91–99, Beijing, China. Association for Computational Linguistics.

Liyuan Liu, Jingbo Shang, Frank F. Xu, Xiang Ren, Huan Gui, Jian Peng, and Jiawei Han. 2017. Empower sequence labeling with task-aware neural language model. *CoRR*, abs/1709.04109.

Xuezhe Ma and Eduard Hovy. 2016. End-to-end sequence labeling via bi-directional lstm-cnns-crf. In *Proceedings of the 54th Annual Meeting of the Association for Computational Linguistics (Volume 1: Long Papers)*, pages 1064–1074, Berlin, Germany. Association for Computational Linguistics.

Giovanni Molina, Fahad AlGhamdi, Mahmoud Ghoneim, Abdelati Hawwari, Nicolas Rey-Villamizar, Mona Diab, and Thamar Solorio. 2016. Overview for the second shared task on language identification in code-switched data. In *Proceedings of the Second Workshop on Computational Approaches to Code Switching*, pages 40–49, Austin, Texas. Association for Computational Linguistics.

Mario Piergallini, Rouzbeh Shirvani, Gauri S. Gautam, and Mohamed Chouikha. 2016. Word-level language identification and predicting codeswitching points in swahili-english language data. In *Proceedings of the Second Workshop on Computational Approaches to Code Switching*, pages 21–29, Austin, Texas. Association for Computational Linguistics.

Alan Ritter, Sam Clark, Mausam, and Oren Etzioni. 2011. Named entity recognition in tweets: An experimental study. In *Proceedings of the Conference on Empirical Methods in Natural Language Processing*, EMNLP '11, pages 1524–1534, Stroudsburg, PA, USA. Association for Computational Linguistics.

Erik F. Tjong Kim Sang and Fien De Meulder. 2003. Introduction to the conll-2003 shared task: Language-independent named entity recognition. In *Proceedings of the Seventh Conference on Natural Language Learning, CoNLL 2003, Held in cooperation with HLT-NAACL 2003, Edmonton, Canada, May 31 - June 1, 2003*, pages 142–147.

Utpal Kumar Sikdar, Biswanath Barik, and Björn Gambäck. 2018. Named Entity Recognition on Code-Switched Data using Conditional Random Fields. In *Proceedings of the Third Workshop on Computational Approaches to Linguistic Code-Switching*, Melbourne, Australia. Association for Computational Linguistics.

Thamar Solorio, Elizabeth Blair, Suraj Maharjan, Steven Bethard, Mona Diab, Mahmoud Ghoneim, Abdelati Hawwari, Fahad AlGhamdi, Julia Hirschberg, Alison Chang, and Pascale Fung. 2014. Overview for the first shared task on language identification in code-switched data. In *Proceedings of the First Workshop on Computational Approaches to Code Switching*, pages 62–72, Doha, Qatar. Association for Computational Linguistics.

Thamar Solorio and Yang Liu. 2008a. Learning to predict code-switching points. In *Proceedings of the 2008 Conference on Empirical Methods in Natural Language Processing*, pages 973–981, Honolulu, Hawaii. Association for Computational Linguistics.

Thamar Solorio and Yang Liu. 2008b. Part-of-speech tagging for english-spanish code-switched text. In *Proceedings of the Conference on Empirical Methods in Natural Language Processing*, EMNLP '08, pages 1051–1060, Stroudsburg, PA, USA. Association for Computational Linguistics.

Benjamin Strauss, Bethany Toma, Alan Ritter, Marie-Catherine de Marneffe, and Wei Xu. 2016. Results of the wnut16 named entity recognition shared task. In *Proceedings of the 2nd Workshop on Noisy User-generated Text (WNUT)*, pages 138–144, Osaka, Japan. The COLING 2016 Organizing Committee.

Almeida Jacqueline Toribio. 2001. Accessing bilingual code-switching competence. *International Journal of Bilingualism*, 5(4):403–436.

Shashwat Trivedi, Harsh Rangwani, and Anil Kumar Singh. 2018. IIT (BHU) Submission for the ACL Shared Task on Named Entity Recognition on Code-switched Data. In *Proceedings of the Third Workshop on Computational Approaches to Linguistic Code-Switching*, Melbourne, Australia. Association for Computational Linguistics.

David Vilares, Miguel A. Alonso, and Carlos Gómez-Rodríguez. 2015. Sentiment analysis on monolingual, multilingual and code-switching twitter corpora. In *Proceedings of the 6th Workshop on Computational Approaches to Subjectivity, Sentiment and Social Media Analysis*, pages 2–8. Association for Computational Linguistics.

David Vilares, Miguel A. Alonso, and Carlos Gómez-Rodríguez. 2016. En-es-cs: An english-spanish code-switching twitter corpus for multilingual sentiment analysis. In *Proceedings of the Tenth International Conference on Language Resources and Evaluation (LREC 2016)*, Paris, France. European Language Resources Association (ELRA).

Changhan Wang, Kyunghyun Cho, and Douwe Kiela. 2018. Code-Switched Named Entity Recognition with Embedding Attention. In *Proceedings of the Third Workshop on Computational Approaches to Linguistic Code-Switching*, Melbourne, Australia. Association for Computational Linguistics.

Genta Indra Winata, Chien-Sheng Wu, Andrea Madotto, and Pascale Fung. 2018. Bilingual Character Representation for Efficiently Addressing Out-of-Vocabulary in Code-Switching Named Entity Recognition. In *Proceedings of the Third Workshop on Computational Approaches to Linguistic Code-Switching*, Melbourne, Australia. Association for Computational Linguistics.

IIT (BHU) Submission for the ACL Shared Task on Named Entity Recognition on Code-switched Data

Shashwat Trivedi*, Harsh Rangwani*and Anil Kumar Singh

Indian Institute of Technology (Banaras Hindu University), Varanasi, India
{shashwat.trivedi.cse15, harsh.rangwani.cse15, aksingh.cse}@iitbhu.ac.in

Abstract

This paper describes the best performing system for the shared task on Named Entity Recognition (NER) on code-switched data for the language pair Spanish-English (ENG-SPA). We introduce a gated neural architecture for the NER task. Our final model achieves an F1 score of 63.76%, outperforming the baseline by 10%.

1 Introduction

Named Entity Recognition (NER) is an important Natural Language Processing task, which involves extracting named entities (i.e., Names of Persons, Entities, Organizations etc.) from the provided text, and the classification of entities into a certain number of predefined categories. The extracted entities provide us with the important information about the content of the text (Nadeau and Sekine, 2007). For example, "New Delhi is famous for its historical past.". The extracted entity (*New Delhi*) gives us an idea that the text is associated with the *location* called *New Delhi*. The ability of NER to extract this useful information makes it an essential part of the Information Extraction pipeline.

The social media platforms like Twitter, Reddit etc. have become a massive source of information due to their growth in the recent past. Performing NER on social texts can be challenging due to the unstructured and colloquial nature of social texts. Various attempts have been made in the past to solve the problem of NER on social texts (Derczynski et al., 2017; Strauss et al., 2016). However, most of the previous systems were developed to work with monolingual texts (Ritter et al., 2011; Lin et al., 2017), ignoring the phenomena of code-switching (i.e., switching between different lan-

guages within a sentence), which is quite prevalent in social media texts.

This paper describes our system for Named Entity Recognition Shared Task on English-Spanish Code-switched tweets held at the ACL 2018 Workshop on Computational Approaches to Linguistic Code-switching. The task involves categorizing a token into 19 different categories. More details about the task can be found in the task description paper (Aguilar et al., 2018).

We use a novel architecture based on **gating** of character-based representations and word-based representations of a token (Yang et al., 2016). The character-based representation is generated using a 'Char CNN' (Zhang et al., 2015) and the word-based representation is generated using an LSTM (Hochreiter and Schmidhuber, 1997). Furthermore, the activations from the last but one layer of the neural networks, trained with different hyperparameters, are ensembled and then are passed as features to a Conditional Random Field (CRF) classifier for final predictions. We make use of English Twitter embeddings (Godin et al., 2015), aligned with the Spanish embeddings (Bojanowski et al., 2016) as described in Section 2.1.

Our final submitted system achieves the best result on the shared task with 63.76% F1-score.

2 Proposed Approach

This section describes feature representations, model description and the ensembling technique in detail.

2.1 Feature Representation

The following representations are used to capture overall information for each token: Word, Character and Lexical representations.

Word Representation: Word representations are created using concatenation of two separate representations, one based on the pre-trained word vec-

---

* These authors have equal contribution to the paper

Proceedings of The Third Workshop on Computational Approaches to Code-Switching, pages 148–153
Melbourne, Australia, July 19, 2018. ©2018 Association for Computational Linguistics

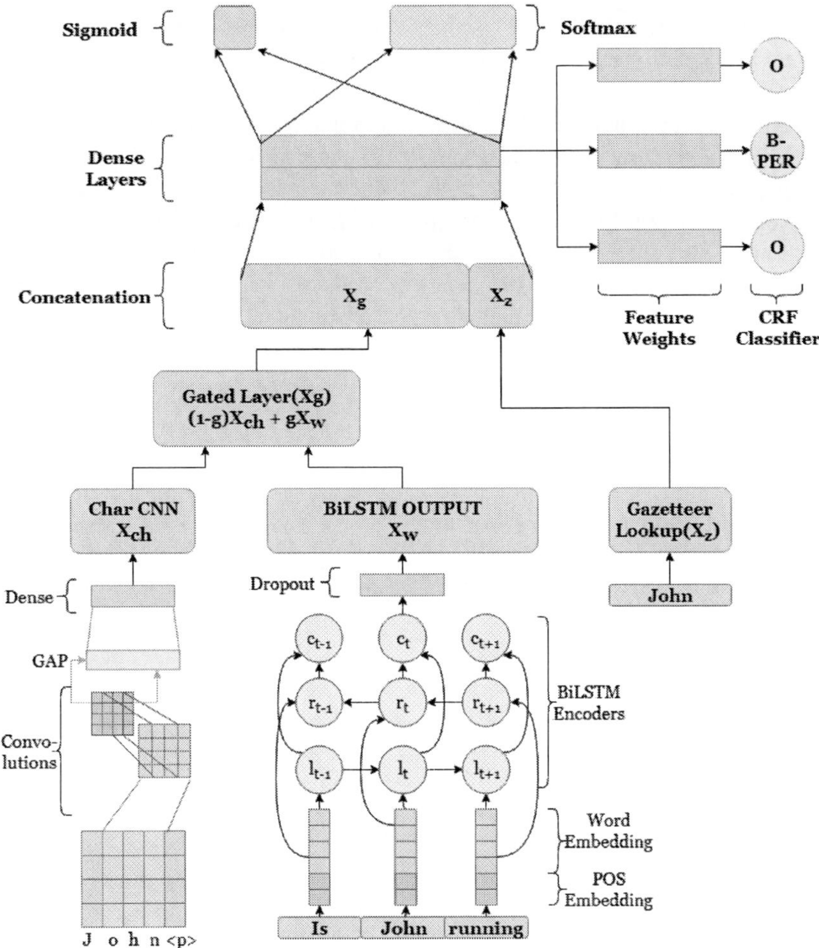

Figure 1: Final Architecture Of The System

tors and the other based on Part-of-Speech (POS) tag embeddings.

For the word vector representation, we use Spanish FastText word vectors (Bojanowski et al., 2016) of 300-dimensions, trained on Wikipedia and pre-trained word embeddings (Godin et al., 2015) of 400-dimensions, trained on 400 million tweets. We use a Principal Component Analysis (PCA) based algorithm suggested by Raunak (2017) to reduce the dimensions of the Twitter word vectors. Since these word vectors are in different vector spaces, we use Singular Value Decomposition (SVD) (Smith et al., 2017) for aligning these two embeddings to represent them in a single vector space.

For POS tagging, we use the CMU Part-of-Speech tagger (Owoputi et al., 2013). Each POS tag is represented as a vector of dimension *dim*. The vectors corresponding to the POS tags are initialized randomly with uniform distribution range $\left[\sqrt{3/dim}, \sqrt{3/dim}\right]$ as suggested by He et al. (2015). The word vector corresponding to the token is concatenated with the vector corresponding to the POS tag of the token to obtain the final vector representation.

For obtaining the label for each token, we provide a composite vector as an input to the model. The composite vector is generated by concatenation of word representations of adjacent tokens (one on each side) with its own, same as a trigram. **Character Representation**: At the character level, we represent each token as a sequence of character embeddings. These embeddings are initialized randomly with uniform distribution range, similar to POS tag embeddings. In the model, they are kept *trainable* to learn the representation cor-

149

responding to each character. Each token is either truncated or post-padded to generate a token of 20 characters.

Lexical Representation: We use the gazetteer provided by Mishra and Diesner (2016) and some Spanish gazetteers of our own to provide world knowledge to our model. Top 1000 celebrity Twitter handles from this list[1] are also added. We represent gazetteer input for a token as a 19 dimensional vector, one binary value corresponding to each class. The binary bit represents the presence (1) or absence (0) of the token in the gazetteer (i.e. word list) of the respective class.

2.2 Model Description

BiLSTM for Word Representation: We use Bidirectional LSTM (Dyer et al., 2015) in the model to learn the contextual relationship between the words. Word representations described earlier are used as input to this layer. The BiLSTM layer consists of two LSTM layers having 3 units each. With one layer connected in the forward direction and the other layer connected in the backward direction, this captures the information from the past and the future (Ma and Hovy, 2016). The outputs of both forward and backward LSTM are then concatenated to produce a final single embedding for the input token. We vary recurrent dropouts (Gal and Ghahramani, 2016), input dropouts and output dropouts as shown in the Table 1, across three different models. The gate layer is fed with the output of this layer (X_w).

Convolution Network for Character Representation: We use a CNN-architecture to learn the character based representation of a word. The character embeddings of a token, denoted as $\mathbb{R}^{d \times l}$, where d is the dimension of a single character's embedding and l is the max length of the token, is fed to a 2-stacked convolutional layer, both activated using ReLU function. Its results are then pushed into a pooling layer. We applied two different pooling techniques, specified in the Table 1, across different models. The output of the pooling layer serves as an input to a dense layer, whose activation function (*Char dense layer activation*) is varied as shown in Table 1. Finally, we use the output of the dense layer (X_{ch}) as an input to the gate layer.

Gate Layer: The concatenation of word representations and POS tag embeddings is used as input to a *sigmoid* dense layer. The value of the sigmoid output controls the relative contribution of the character and word representation in the final representation of the token. Following the work of Miyamoto and Cho (2016), the output of this layer g is used to take the weighted average of Bi-LSTM network output (X_g) and the convolutional network output (X_{ch}):

$$g = \sigma(v_g^T X_g + b_g)$$

$$X = (1 - g)X_{ch} + gX_g$$

where v_g is the trainable weight vector, b_g is the bias and $\sigma(\cdot)$ is the sigmoid function. The result of this layer X is then concatenated with the gazetteer embeddings of the token.

Fully Connected Network: We use two fully connected networks after the concatenation of the gate network output and gazetteer embeddings. The number of dense units is kept fixed to 100 each. The activation function is varied according to Table 1 for producing different models.

Multitask Learning: Multitask learning has been shown as a good way to regularize models (Baxter, 2000; Collobert and Weston, 2008). Following the work of Aguilar et al. (2017), we split the task into Named Entity (NE) categorization (classifying a token into one of the NE classes) and NE segmentation (classifying token as NE or Not-NE). We passed the dense layer's output as input to these final classification layers. A softmax layer with 19 classes is used for the categorization task and a single sigmoid neuron is used for the segmentation task as depicted in Figure 1. The cross-entropy losses for these tasks are added to yield total loss for the model.

2.3 Conditional Random Fields and Ensembling

Linear-chain CRF classifier takes advantage of the sequence information to tag a token with the most probable label (Lafferty et al., 2001). Following Aguilar et al. (2017), we use the activations of second common dense layer as input feature vector for the CRF classifier. The CRF classifier produces better results than the normal softmax classification and also reduces the number of invalid predictions (i.e., I-PER tag without a B-PER tag). For preparing the model ensemble, we make use of

---

[1]https://gist.github.com/mbejda/
9c3353780270e7298763

Table 1: Hyper-parameters for the Models and Ensemble Results

Hyper-Parameters	Model-1	Model-2	Model-3
POS and character embeddings dropout	0.500	0.500	0.247
POS embeddings dimension	50	128	128
Character embeddings dimension	100	128	128
Pooling layer	*GAP	GAP	+GMP
Char dense layer activation	ReLU	ReLU	tanh
Recurrent dropouts	0.500	0.500	0.823
BiLSTM input dropout	-	-	0.0654
BiLSTM output dropout	0.500	0.500	0.018
Dense layer activation	ReLU	ReLU	tanh
Preprocessing of Test-data	X	Y	Y
Optimiser	#nadam	nadam	rmsprop
Results (F1 score)	**61.18%**	**61.89%**	**60.23%**
Overall Ensemble of Model1 + Model2 + Model3 (F1 Score)		**63.76%**	

*GAP:Global Average Pooling +GMP:Global Max Pooling
#nadam is adam rmsprop with nesterov momentum (Dozat, 2016)

unweighted averaging of the activations generated by the networks described in Table 1.

2.4 Experimental Settings

2.4.1 Pre-processing

The data is pre-processed by doing the following replacements: All URLs are replaced with $\langle url \rangle$. All hashtags are replaced with $\langle hashtag \rangle$. Digits are replaced with the $\langle number \rangle$ token. Apostrophes are removed. Finally, emoticons are replaced with their respective meaning, for example, ':-)' with $\langle smile \rangle$.

2.4.2 Hyper-parameters

Different hyper-parameters are used to produce different models for ensembling. We set the following parameters as the same across all the models: 64 filters, kernel size of 3 and ReLU activation in convolutional network (Section 2.2), along with 50 hidden units in the BiLSTM network (Section 2.2).

Other hyperparameters are set according to the Table 1 for the respective models. All models are trained for 15 epochs with a batch size of 512. The CRF classifier is used with the following parameters: L1 penalty: 1.0, L2 penalty: 1e-3 for 80 epochs.

Hyper-parameters for Model-3 are obtained by a random search using hyperas[2]. Hyper-parameters for the other two models are set based on our own experimental observations. All our models are implemented using the Deep Learning library Keras[3].

3 Results and Discussion

We compare our final results with the RNN baseline, which is the official baseline of the task (Aguilar et al., 2018). The major highlights of our results are described below.

Table 2: Results in Different Categories

Models Used	Precision	Recall	F1
Event	37.50%	13.33%	19.67%
Group	38.36%	28.87%	32.94%
Location	70.31%	72.45%	71.37%
Organization	58.14%	24.75%	34.72%
Other	11.11%	1.72%	2.99%
Person	79.26%	77.87%	78.56%
Product	63.43%	44.16%	52.07%
Time	30.67%	30.46%	30.56%
Title	31.85%	19.46%	24.16%
Overall	**68.73%**	**59.47%**	**63.76%**
Baseline	**-**	**-**	**53.28%**

- Our model achieves an F1-score of 63.76%, which beats the baseline by around 10% on the test set. Our results depict the effectiveness of the use of gated neural architecture for Named Entity Recognition. Our system ranked first among the 8 systems submitted for the task.

[2] https://github.com/hyperopt/hyperopt

[3] https://github.com/keras-team/keras

- The system performance on the various class of entities is displayed in Table 2. Our model shows poor performance in Title, Other and Event categories. This may be attributed to both the diverse set of patterns present, and the unavailability of a large number of samples of these categories.

4 Conclusion

In this paper, we describe a gated neural network for performing NER on code-switched social media text. Our model involves the usage of SVD to align word representations of English and Spanish words. Furthermore, we also describe a novel way of ensembling activations of the last but one layer for achieving better results. Our model is described in full detail in this paper to ensure the replication of results. The final system performs the best among all the participating systems.
In future, we would like to experiment with various other ways of combining character and word representations (e.g. Fine Grained Gating (Zhang et al., 2015), Highway Networks (Liang et al., 2017) etc.) for the NER task.

References

Gustavo Aguilar, Fahad AlGhamdi, Victor Soto, Mona Diab, Julia Hirschberg, and Thamar Solorio. 2018. Overview of the CALCS 2018 Shared Task: Named Entity Recognition on Code-switched Data. In *Proceedings of the Third Workshop on Computational Approaches to Linguistic Code-Switching*. Association for Computational Linguistics, Melbourne, Australia.

Gustavo Aguilar, Suraj Maharjan, Adrian Pastor López Monroy, and Thamar Solorio. 2017. A multi-task approach for named entity recognition in social media data. In *Proceedings of the 3rd Workshop on Noisy User-generated Text*. pages 148–153.

Jonathan Baxter. 2000. A model of inductive bias learning. *J. Artif. Int. Res.* 12(1):149–198. http://dl.acm.org/citation.cfm?id=1622248.1622254.

Piotr Bojanowski, Edouard Grave, Armand Joulin, and Tomas Mikolov. 2016. Enriching word vectors with subword information. *arXiv preprint arXiv:1607.04606* .

Ronan Collobert and Jason Weston. 2008. A unified architecture for natural language processing: Deep neural networks with multitask learning. In *Proceedings of the 25th international conference on Machine learning*. ACM, pages 160–167.

Leon Derczynski, Eric Nichols, Marieke van Erp, and Nut Limsopatham. 2017. Results of the wnut2017 shared task on novel and emerging entity recognition. In *Proceedings of the 3rd Workshop on Noisy User-generated Text*. pages 140–147.

Timothy Dozat. 2016. Incorporating nesterov momentum into adam. In *Proceedings of ICLR 2016 Workshop*.

Chris Dyer, Miguel Ballesteros, Wang Ling, Austin Matthews, and Noah A Smith. 2015. Transition-based dependency parsing with stack long short-term memory. *arXiv preprint arXiv:1505.08075* .

Yarin Gal and Zoubin Ghahramani. 2016. A theoretically grounded application of dropout in recurrent neural networks. In *Advances in neural information processing systems*. pages 1019–1027.

Fréderic Godin, Baptist Vandersmissen, Wesley De Neve, and Rik Van de Walle. 2015. Multimedia lab @ acl wnut ner shared task: Named entity recognition for twitter microposts using distributed word representations. In *Proceedings of the Workshop on Noisy User-generated Text*. pages 146–153.

Kaiming He, Xiangyu Zhang, Shaoqing Ren, and Jian Sun. 2015. Delving deep into rectifiers: Surpassing human-level performance on imagenet classification. In *Proceedings of the IEEE international conference on computer vision*. pages 1026–1034.

Sepp Hochreiter and Jürgen Schmidhuber. 1997. Long short-term memory. *Neural computation* 9(8):1735–1780.

John Lafferty, Andrew McCallum, and Fernando CN Pereira. 2001. Conditional random fields: Probabilistic models for segmenting and labeling sequence data .

Dongyun Liang, Weiran Xu, and Yinge Zhao. 2017. Combining word-level and character-level representations for relation classification of informal text. In *Proceedings of the 2nd Workshop on Representation Learning for NLP*. pages 43–47.

Bill Y Lin, Frank Xu, Zhiyi Luo, and Kenny Zhu. 2017. Multi-channel bilstm-crf model for emerging named entity recognition in social media. In *Proceedings of the 3rd Workshop on Noisy User-generated Text*. pages 160–165.

Xuezhe Ma and Eduard H. Hovy. 2016. End-to-end sequence labeling via bi-directional lstm-cnns-crf. *CoRR* abs/1603.01354. http://arxiv.org/abs/1603.01354.

Shubhanshu Mishra and Jana Diesner. 2016. Semi-supervised named entity recognition in noisy-text. In *Proceedings of the 2nd Workshop on Noisy User-generated Text (WNUT)*. The COLING 2016 Organizing Committee, pages 203–212. http://aclweb.org/anthology/W16-3927.

Yasumasa Miyamoto and Kyunghyun Cho. 2016. Gated word-character recurrent language model. *CoRR* abs/1606.01700. http://arxiv.org/abs/1606.01700.

David Nadeau and Satoshi Sekine. 2007. A survey of named entity recognition and classification. *Lingvisticae Investigationes* 30(1):3–26.

Olutobi Owoputi, Brendan O'Connor, Chris Dyer, Kevin Gimpel, Nathan Schneider, and Noah A Smith. 2013. Improved part-of-speech tagging for online conversational text with word clusters. Association for Computational Linguistics.

Vikas Raunak. 2017. Effective dimensionality reduction for word embeddings. *CoRR* abs/1708.03629. http://arxiv.org/abs/1708.03629.

Alan Ritter, Sam Clark, Oren Etzioni, et al. 2011. Named entity recognition in tweets: an experimental study. In *Proceedings of the conference on empirical methods in natural language processing*. Association for Computational Linguistics, pages 1524–1534.

Samuel L. Smith, David H. P. Turban, Steven Hamblin, and Nils Y. Hammerla. 2017. Offline bilingual word vectors, orthogonal transformations and the inverted softmax. *CoRR* abs/1702.03859. http://arxiv.org/abs/1702.03859.

Benjamin Strauss, Bethany Toma, Alan Ritter, Marie-Catherine de Marneffe, and Wei Xu. 2016. Results of the wnut16 named entity recognition shared task. In *Proceedings of the 2nd Workshop on Noisy User-generated Text (WNUT)*. pages 138–144.

Z. Yang, B. Dhingra, Y. Yuan, J. Hu, W. W. Cohen, and R. Salakhutdinov. 2016. Words or characters? fine-grained gating for reading comprehension. *ArXiv e-prints* http://adsabs.harvard.edu/abs/2016arXiv161101724Y.

Xiang Zhang, Junbo Jake Zhao, and Yann LeCun. 2015. Character-level convolutional networks for text classification. *CoRR* abs/1509.01626. http://arxiv.org/abs/1509.01626.

Code-Switched Named Entity Recognition with Embedding Attention

Changhan Wang[†], Kyunghyun Cho[†‡] and Douwe Kiela[†]
[†] Facebook AI Research; [‡] New York University
{changhan, kyunghyuncho, dkiela}@fb.com

Abstract

We describe our work for the CALCS 2018 shared task on named entity recognition on code-switched data. Our system ranked first place for MS Arabic-Egyptian named entity recognition and third place for English-Spanish.

1 Introduction

The tendency for multilingual speakers to engage in code-switching—i.e, alternating between multiple languages or language varieties—poses important problems for NLP systems: traditional monolingual techniques quickly break down with input from mixed languages. Even for problems such as POS-tagging and language identification, which the community often considers "solved", performance deteriorates proportional to the degree of code-switching in the data. The shared task for the third workshop on Computational Approaches on Linguistic Code-Switching concerned named entity recognition (NER) for two code-switched language pairs (Aguilar et al., 2018): Modern Standard Arabic and Egyptian (MSA-EGY); and English-Spanish (ENG-SPA). Here, we describe our work on the shared task.

Traditional NER systems used to rely heavily on hand-crafted features and gazetteers, but have since been replaced by neural architectures that combine bidirectional LSTMs and CRFs (Lample et al., 2016). Equipped with supervised character-level representations and pre-trained unsupervised word embeddings, such neural architectures have not only come to dominate named entity recognition, but have also successfully been applied to code-switched language identification (Samih et al., 2016), which makes them highly suitable for the current task as well.

In this paper, we exploit recent advances in neural NLP systems, tailored to code-switching. We use high-quality FastText embeddings trained on Common Crawl (Grave et al., 2018; Mikolov et al., 2018) and employ shortcut-stacked sentence encoders (Nie and Bansal, 2017) to obtain deep token-level representations to feed into the CRF. In addition, we make use of an embedding-level attention mechanism that learns task-specific attention weights for multilingual and character-level representations, inspired by context-attentive embeddings (Kiela et al., 2018). In what follows, we describe our system in detail.

2 Approach

The input data consists of noisy user-generated social media text collected from Twitter. Code-switching can occur between different tweets in the training data, with many tweets being monolingual, but can also occur within tweets (e.g. *"[USER]: en los finales be like [URL]"*) or even morphologically within words (e.g. *"pero esta twitteando y pitchandome los textos"*). The goal is to predict the correct IOB entity type for the following categories:

- [BI]-PER: Person
- [BI]-LOC: Location
- [BI]-ORG: Organization
- [BI]-GROUP: Group
- [BI]-TITLE: Title
- [BI]-PROD: Product
- [BI]-EVENT: Event
- [BI]-TIME: Time
- [BI]-OTHER: Other
- O: Any other token that is not an NE

Proceedings of The Third Workshop on Computational Approaches to Code-Switching, pages 154–158
Melbourne, Australia, July 19, 2018. ©2018 Association for Computational Linguistics

The train/valid/test split for MSA-EGY was 10102/1122/1110. The train/valid/test split for ENG-SPA was 50757/832/15634.

The first work to combine CRFs with modern neural representation learning for NER is, to our knowledge, by Collobert et al. (2011). Our architecture is similar to more recent neural architectures for NER, e.g. Huang et al. (2015); Lample et al. (2016); Ma and Hovy (2016). Instead of using a straightforward bidirectional LSTM (BiLSTM), we use several layers and add shortcut connections. Instead of simply feeding in word (and/or character) embeddings, we add a self-attention mechanism.

2.1 Embedding Attention

We represent the input tweets on the word level and character level. For all available words in the data, we obtained FastText embeddings trained on Common Crawl and Wikipedia[1] for each language. For every word, we try to find an exact match in the FastText embeddings, or if that is not available we check if it is present in lower case. When a word embedding is available in one language but not in the other, it is initialized as a zero-vector in the second language. Totally unseen words are initialized uniformly at random in the range $[-0.1, 0.1]$. Thus, for every language pair, we obtain word embeddings $\mathbf{w}_L$.

On the character level, we encode every word using a BiLSTM, to which we apply max-pooling to obtain the token-level representation. That is, for a sequence of T characters, $\{c^t\}_{t=1,\dots,T}$ a standard BiLSTM computes two sets of T hidden states, one for each direction. The hidden states are subsequently concatenated for each timestep to obtain the final hidden states, after which a max-pooling operation is applied over their components:

$$\overrightarrow{\mathbf{h}_t^{\tilde{c}}} = \overrightarrow{\mathrm{LSTM}}_t(\mathbf{c}^1, \dots, \mathbf{c}^t)$$
$$\overleftarrow{\mathbf{h}_t^{c}} = \overleftarrow{\mathrm{LSTM}}_t(\mathbf{c}^t, \dots, \mathbf{c}^T)$$
$$\mathbf{w}_{char} = \max(\{[\overrightarrow{\mathbf{h}_t^{\tilde{c}}}, \overleftarrow{\mathbf{h}_t^{c}}]\}_{t=1,\dots,T})$$

We take inspiration from context-attentive embeddings (Kiela et al., 2018), in that we learn weights over the embeddings, but do not include the contextual dependency for reasons of efficiency given the shared task's tight deadline. That

is, we combine the language-specific word embeddings $\mathbf{w}_{L_1}$ and $\mathbf{w}_{L_2}$ with the character-level word representation via a simple self-attention mechanism:

$$\alpha_i = \mathrm{softmax}(U \ \tanh(V \ [\mathbf{w}_{L_1}, \mathbf{w}_{L_2}, \mathbf{w}_{char}])),$$
$$\mathbf{w}_{word+char} = [\alpha_1 \mathbf{w}_{L_1}, \alpha_2 \mathbf{w}_{L_2}, \alpha_3 \mathbf{w}_{char}]$$

2.2 Capitalization

Additionally, we concatenate an embedding to indicate the capitalization of the word, which be either no-capitals, starting-with-capitals or all-capitals:

$$\mathbf{w} = [\mathbf{w}_{word+char}, \mathbf{w}_{cap}]$$

This is already captured by the character-level encoder, but made more explicit using this method.

2.3 Shortcut-Stacked Sentence Encoders

The final word representations $\mathbf{w}$ are fed into a stacked BiLSTM with residual connections (i.e., "shortcuts"). This type of architecture has been found to work well for text classification, in conjunction with a final max-pooling operation (Nie and Bansal, 2017). Denoting the input and hidden state of the i-th stacked BiLSTM layer at timestep t as $\mathbf{x}_t^i$ and $\mathbf{h}_t^i$ respectively, we have:

$$\mathbf{x}_t^i = \begin{cases} \mathbf{w}_t & i = 1 \\ [\mathbf{w}_t, \mathbf{h}_t^1, \dots, \mathbf{h}_t^{i-1}] & i > 1 \end{cases}$$

2.4 CRFs for NER

The hidden states of the last stacked BiLSTM layer are fed into a CRF (Lafferty et al., 2001). CRFs are used to estimate probabilities for entire sequences of tags $\mathbf{s}$ corresponding to sequences of tokens $\mathbf{x}$:

$$\begin{aligned} p(\mathbf{s}|\mathbf{x}; \mathbf{w}) &= \frac{\exp(\mathbf{w} \cdot \Phi(\mathbf{x}, \mathbf{s}))}{\sum_{\mathbf{s}'} \exp(\mathbf{w} \cdot \Phi(\mathbf{x}, \mathbf{s}'))} \\ &= \frac{\exp(\sum_j \mathbf{w} \cdot \phi_j(\mathbf{x}, j, s_{j-1}, s_j))}{\sum_{\mathbf{s}'} \exp(\sum_j \mathbf{w} \cdot \phi_j(\mathbf{x}, j, s'_{j-1}, s'_j))} \\ &= \frac{\prod_j \exp(\psi_j(\mathbf{w}, \mathbf{x}, j, s_{j-1}, s_j))}{\sum_{\mathbf{s}'} \prod_j \exp(\psi_j(\mathbf{w}, \mathbf{x}, j, s'_{j-1}, s'_j))}. \end{aligned}$$

To make the CRF tractable, the potentials must look only at local features. We experiment with two different score functions ψ_j. One that uses bigrams:

---

[1] Available at `https://fasttext.cc/docs/en/crawl-vectors.html`.

$$\psi_j(\mathbf{w}, \mathbf{x}, j, p, q) = \mathbf{W}^\mathsf{T}_{[p,q,:]}\mathbf{x}_j + \mathbf{B}_{[p,q]},$$

where $\mathbf{W} \in \mathbb{R}^{|S| \times |S| \times H}$ is $\mathbf{w}$ but unflattened, $|S|$ is the number of possible tags, H is the dimensionality of the encoder's features $\mathbf{x}$ and $\mathbf{B} \in \mathbb{R}^{|S| \times |S|}$ is a bias matrix; and a smaller score function with unigrams:

$$\psi_j(\mathbf{w}, \mathbf{x}, j, p, q) = \mathbf{W}^\mathsf{T}_{[q,:]}\mathbf{x}_j + \mathbf{B}_{[p,q]}.$$

where instead $\mathbf{W} \in \mathbb{R}^{|S| \times H}$. The terms in the score function can be thought of as the emission and transition potentials, respectively.

3 Implementational Details

3.1 Preprocessing

The noisy nature of the data makes it necessary to apply appropriate preprocessing steps. We apply the following steps to the Twitter data:

- Replaced URLs with [url]

- Replaced users (starting with @) with [user]

- Replaced hashtags (starting with # but not followed by a number) with [hash_tag]

- Replaced punctuation tokens with [punct]

- Replaced integer and real numbers by [num]

- Replaced [num]:[num] with [time]

- Replaced [num]-[num] with [date]

- Replaced emojis[2] by [emoji]

In addition, we found that the Arabic tokenizer may have been imperfect: some words still had punctuation attached to them. In order to mitigate this, we removed any leading and trailing punctuation from tokens for MSA-EGY.

3.2 Training

The LSTMs are initialized orthogonally (Saxe et al., 2013), and the attention mechanism is initialized with Xavier (Glorot and Bengio, 2010). Word embeddings are kept fixed during training, but character embeddings and capitalization embeddings are updated. We set dropout to 0.5 and optimize using Adam (Kingma and Ba, 2014) with a learning rate of $4e^{-4}$ and batch size of

---

Model	Dev F1	Test F1
Baseline	68.17	60.28
Ours	67.74	62.39

Table 1: Results for ENG-SPA.

Model	Dev F1	Test F1
Baseline	79.55	70.08
Ours	81.41	71.62

Table 2: Results for MSA-EGY.

64. We shrink the learning rate with a factor or 0.2 every time there has been no improvement for one epoch, until a minimum learning rate of $1e^{-5}$. We early stop on the validation set, optimizing for F1. We sweep over the two CRF types and BiLSTM hidden dimensions via grid search, trying $[128, 128]$, $[128, 128, 128]$, $[64, 128]$, $[64, 128, 128]$, $[64, 64, 128, 128]$ and $[64, 128, 128, 128]$.

4 Results & Discussion

For both tasks, we compare the proposed model to a simpler baseline where we simply concatenate the FastText embeddings as input to the network.

Table 1 shows the results for ENG-SPA. We observe that our system outperforms the baseline on the test set. The dev set for this task was very small (832, versus a test set of 15.6k), which explains the discrepancy between dev set and test set performance—this discrepancy also made it difficult to tune hyperparameters properly for this task. We also tried a very simple ensembling strategy, where we took our top three models and randomly sampled a response, which only marginally improved test score performance to 62.67. We did not pursue proper ensembling due to time constraints. The best performing model had hidden dimensions $[128, 128, 128]$ and used the bigram CRF.

The results for the MSA-EGY task are reported in Table 2. While English and Spanish are two distinct languages, Modern Standard Arabic and Egyptian are more closely related, leading to interesting challenges. We observe a similar improvement in this task. As noted in the previous section, we did find that this task required slightly different preprocessing. We did not try any ensembling strategies on this task. The best performing model

---

[2]We used the emojis in https://pypi.org/project/emoji/.

	Precision	Recall	Entity F1
EVENT	56.25	20.00	29.51
GROUP	69.77	30.93	42.86
LOC	70.75	69.23	69.98
ORG	62.50	27.23	37.93
OTHER	14.29	1.71	3.08
PER	76.52	68.15	72.09
PROD	63.76	47.53	54.46
TIME	51.58	37.09	43.24
TITLE	49.14	25.79	33.83
Overall	70.62	55.88	62.39

Table 3: ENG-SPA test performance breakdown.

	Precision	Recall	Entity F1
EVENT	78.18	61.43	68.80
GROUP	69.77	76.92	73.17
LOC	76.19	67.84	71.78
ORG	66.14	67.20	66.67
OTHER	100.00	100.00	100.00
PER	77.29	69.53	73.21
PROD	76.47	78.79	77.61
TIME	64.29	72.00	67.92
TITLE	31.58	60.00	41.38
Overall	73.95	69.42	71.62

Table 4: MSA-EGY test performance breakdown.

had hidden dimensions $[64, 64, 128, 128]$ and used the unigram CRF.

While developing our system, we made some interesting observations. For instance, we noticed that performance on the Event and Time categories was greatly improved through preprocessing the numbers and splitting out patterns into date and time categories. Adding explicit capitalization features improved performance on the Person, Location and Organization categories. Tables 3 and 4 show a breakdown of the performance per task by category on the respective test sets. It is interesting to observe that the Title category is consistently hard for both tasks. The Other category was perfectly handled for MSA-EGY, while this was very bad for ENG-SPA — this could however also be an artifact, since that category was quite small.

We felt that we could have benefited from having a strong gazetteer, but also believe that this would kind of defeat the purpose of our general neural network architecture, which should not have to rely on those kinds of features.

5 Conclusion

Dealing with code-switching is a prominent problem in handling noisy user-generated social media data. The tendency for speakers to code-switch poses difficulties for standard NLP pipelines. Here, we described our work on the shared task: we introduced a system that performs self-attention over pre-trained or character-encoded word embeddings together with a shortcut-stacked sentence encoder. The system performed impressively on the task. In the future, we would like to analyze the system to see whether it has indeed learned to "code-switch" via embedding attention.

References

Gustavo Aguilar, Fahad AlGhamdi, Victor Soto, Mona Diab, Julia Hirschberg, and Thamar Solorio. 2018. Overview of the CALCS 2018 Shared Task: Named Entity Recognition on Code-switched Data. In *Proceedings of the Third Workshop on Computational Approaches to Linguistic Code-Switching*, Melbourne, Australia. Association for Computational Linguistics.

Ronan Collobert, Jason Weston, Léon Bottou, Michael Karlen, Koray Kavukcuoglu, and Pavel Kuksa. 2011. Natural language processing (almost) from scratch. *Journal of Machine Learning Research*, 12(Aug):2493–2537.

Xavier Glorot and Yoshua Bengio. 2010. Understanding the difficulty of training deep feedforward neural networks. In *Proceedings of the thirteenth international conference on artificial intelligence and statistics*, pages 249–256.

Edouard Grave, Piotr Bojanowski, Prakhar Gupta, Armand Joulin, and Tomas Mikolov. 2018. Learning word vectors for 157 languages. In *Proceedings of LREC*.

Zhiheng Huang, Wei Xu, and Kai Yu. 2015. Bidirectional lstm-crf models for sequence tagging. *arXiv preprint arXiv:1508.01991*.

Douwe Kiela, Changhan Wang, and Kyunghyun Cho. 2018. Context-attentive embeddings for improved sentence representations. *arxiv preprint arXiv:1804.07983*.

Diederik P Kingma and Jimmy Ba. 2014. Adam: A method for stochastic optimization. *arXiv preprint arXiv:1412.6980*.

John Lafferty, Andrew McCallum, and Fernando CN Pereira. 2001. Conditional random fields: Probabilistic models for segmenting and labeling sequence data.

Guillaume Lample, Miguel Ballesteros, Sandeep Subramanian, Kazuya Kawakami, and Chris Dyer. 2016. Neural architectures for named entity recognition. In *Proceedings of NAACL*.

Xuezhe Ma and Eduard H. Hovy. 2016. End-to-end sequence labeling via bi-directional lstm-cnns-crf. pages 1064—1074.

Tomas Mikolov, Edouard Grave, Piotr Bojanowski, Christian Puhrsch, and Armand Joulin. 2018. Learning word vectors for 157 languages. In *Proceedings of LREC*.

Yixin Nie and Mohit Bansal. 2017. Shortcut-stacked sentence encoders for multi-domain inference. *arXiv preprint arXiv:1708.02312*.

Younes Samih, Suraj Maharjan, Mohammed Attia, Laura Kallmeyer, and Thamar Solorio. 2016. Multilingual code-switching identification via lstm recurrent neural networks. In *Proceedings of the Second Workshop on Computational Approaches to Code Switching*, pages 50–59.

Andrew M Saxe, James L McClelland, and Surya Ganguli. 2013. Exact solutions to the nonlinear dynamics of learning in deep linear neural networks. *arXiv preprint arXiv:1312.6120*.

Author Index

Adouane, Wafia, 20
Aguilar, Gustavo, 138
AlGhamdi, Fahad, 138
Attia, Mohammed, 98

Bali, Kalika, 11, 82
Barik, Biswanath, 115
Bawa, Anshul, 82
Bernardy, Jean-Philippe, 20
Black, Alan W., 29, 76, 92, 126
Bullock, Barbara, 68, 120

Chandu, Khyathi, 29, 92, 126
Chinnakotla, Manoj, 29, 39
Cho, Kyunghyun, 154
Choudhury, Monojit, 11, 82
Claeser, Daniel, 132

Darbari, Mayank, 103
Diab, Mona, 138
Dobnik, Simon, 20

Felske, Dennis, 132
Fung, Pascale, 62, 110

Gambäck, Björn, 115
Geetha, Parvathy, 126
Genabith, Josef van, 29
Gupta, Rishabh, 103
Gupta, Vishal, 29, 39
Guzmán, Gualberto, 120
Guzman, Wally, 68

Hirschberg, Julia, 1, 138

Jain, Devanshu, 103
Janke, Florian, 120

Kent, Samantha, 132
Kiela, Douwe, 154
Kumar Singh, Anil, 148
Kustikova, Maria, 103

Li, Tongrui, 120
Loginova, Ekaterina, 29

Madotto, Andrea, 62, 110

Maharjan, Suraj, 51
Maier, Wolfgang, 98
Manzini, Thomas, 92
Mave, Deepthi, 51
Mayhew, Stephen, 103

Neuman, Günter, 29
Nyberg, Eric, 29

Rallabandi, SaiKrishna, 76
Rangwani, Harsh, 148
Rincón, Eric, 120

Samih, Younes, 98
Serigos, Jacqueline, 68
Sharath, Vivek, 68
Shrivastava, Manish, 39
Sikdar, Utpal Kumar, 115
Singh, Sumeet, 92
Sitaram, Sunayana, 11, 76
Sivasankaran, Sunit, 11
Solorio, Thamar, 51, 138
Soto, Victor, 1, 138
Srivastava, Brij Mohan Lal, 11

Toribio, Almeida Jacqueline, 68, 120
Trivedi, Shashwat, 148

Wang, Changhan, 154
Winata, Genta Indra, 62, 110
Wu, Chien-Sheng, 62, 110